Trains, Culture, and Mobility

Trains, Culture, and Mobility

Riding the Rails

Benjamin Fraser
Steven Spalding

LEXINGTON BOOKS
Lanham • Boulder • New York • Toronto • Plymouth, UK

Published by Lexington Books
A wholly owned subsidiary of The Rowman & Littlefield Publishing Group, Inc.
4501 Forbes Boulevard, Suite 200, Lanham, Maryland 20706
www.lexingtonbooks.com

Estover Road, Plymouth PL6 7PY, United Kingdom

British Library Cataloguing in Publication Information Available

Library of Congress Cataloging-in-Publication Data

Fraser, Benjamin.
  Trains, culture, and mobility : riding the rails / Benjamin Fraser and Steven D.
Spalding.
    p. cm.
  Includes bibliographical references and index.
  ISBN 978-0-7391-6749-6 (cloth : alk. paper) — ISBN 978-0-7391-6750-2 (electronic)
  1. Railroads—Social aspects. 2. Railroad travel—Social aspects. I. Spalding, Steven
D., 1971- II. Title.
  HE1031.F73 2012
  306.4'819--dc23   2011044695

Printed in the United States of America

Contents

Acknowledgments

The editors would like to thank the College of Charleston for covering the publication costs of this volume: Mark Del Mastro (Chair of Hispanic Studies) and Dean David Cohen were instrumental in securing support for this project. Thanks also to the copyright holders of images included in this volume: in particular, the National Railway Museum/Science and Society Picture Library (and Ed Bartholomew) for the images in chapters 1 and 3; Agatha Morka for the pictures in chapter 7; and César Mohedas García and Miguel A. Sandoval for photos included in chapter 8.

Benjamin Fraser would particularly like to thank Megan and Doug for the gift of the train graffiti zines (mentioned briefly in chapter 2 of this volume), Steven for the lively conversations on trains and mobility, and Abby for fond memories of the journey to Whistler.

Steven D. Spalding would to thank like the former students from Oberlin College and Connecticut College who undertook early forays with him into the themes that brought him to this book project with indulgence, intelligence, generosity of spirit, and enthusiasm. Many thanks are owed Ben for his endless patience and wisdom, and Karine and Eva for lighting up the days.

Introduction

Riding the Rails

Cultures of Trains

Benjamin Fraser and Steven D. Spalding

> More than any other technical design or social institution, the railway stands for modernity.
>
> —Tony Judt, "The Glory of the Rails," *NYRB* (Dec. 23, 2010), 60.

This collection of essays—building on its companion volume: *Trains, Literature and Culture: Reading/Writing the Rails*—goes beyond textual representations of rail travel to engage an impressive range of political, sociological, and urban theory. Taken together, the ten contributions collected here highlight the complexity of the modern experience of train mobility, as well as its salient relation to a number of cultural discourses. Incorporating traditionally marginal areas of cultural production such as graffiti, museums, and architecture, or even plunging into the social experience of travel inside the train car itself, each chapter constitutes an attempt to work from the act of riding the train toward questions of much larger significance. Crisscrossing cultures from the New World and Old, from East and West, these essays share a common preoccupation with the way in which trains and railway networks have mapped and remapped the contours of both cities and states in the modern period. Bringing together individual and large-scale social practices, this volume traces out the cultural implications of "Riding the Rails."

Readers may be relatively familiar with the fact that "[t]he creation of the modern railway occurred almost simultaneously in the U.S.A. and Great Britain" (Thorne 11) around 1830; but here we go beyond the Anglophone world, making multiple stops not only in Britain (chapters 1 and 3) but also in France (chapters 2, 5, and 7), Japan (chapters 9 and 10) and Spain (chapters 2 and 8), and travel also to Australia (chapter 4) and South Korea (chapter 6). The contribution of each chapter becomes more clear when properly contextualized within a growing discourse that remains captivated by the cultural and social import of train transportation. Throughout much of the twentieth century—traditionally, and generally speaking—books on trains have prioritized a structural or technological vision, yielding historical accounts that are important contributions, but that are not sufficiently conceived to account for the more-than-material discourses surrounding the "iron horse." Even in a publication from 2005, for example, H. Roger Grant, titles his work *The Railroad: The Life Story of a Technology* and arranges his chapters in a historical progression. In the preface to the book, Grant takes care to document such material concerns as the shift from wood to iron to steel as employed in the construction of the railways themselves (xi), emphasizing the necessary complexity of railway infrastructures: "The railroad is many things. It is track, motive power, rolling stock, signals, structures and much more" (xii).

There currently exists, of course, an ample bibliography regarding the historical significance and technological development of the railway (e.g., Bobrick). Itself a product of the industrial revolution, the train was undeniably also a catalyst further stimulating the development of trade. Scholars have certainly been able to effectively link the train with broader social shifts. The best and most comprehensive (theoretical and practical/historical) example of this trend is *The Railway Journey: The Industrialization of Time and Space in the 19th Century* by Wolfgang Schivelbusch (cited in many of the contributions to this two-volume project), where the author highlights the train's "importance in the making of industrial capitalism" (xiii–xiv). But there have been other worthwhile texts as well. In her recent work *Reforming Urban Labor: Routes to the City, Roots in the Country* (2010), for example, Janet L. Polasky traces how the train provided a way of mitigating the perceived social ills accompanying the industrial revolution's precipitation of a concentrated urban labor force, thus fostering the middle-class commute (see also John R. Stilgoe's *Train Time: Railroads and the Imminent Reshaping of the United States*, 2007). Maury Klein points to what have been quite common metaphorical invocations of the train as contradictory signifier: either as a "benign symbol" of "freedom, adventure and new possibilities" or the "darker view" of the train as "a metaphor for the price of industrial progress" (20–21). Nonetheless, while the train is admittedly a powerful and multivalent signifier—pointing at once toward progress and its price—it is also more than that.

As the essays in *Trains, Culture and Mobility: Riding the Rails* point out, the train is not merely an indicator of industrial progress or a metaphor/symbol for the contradictions of modernity but also a subject worthy of cultural analysis of all types. The essays in the first section, titled *Speed and Vision* approach the mobile and insterstitial places associated with train travel by employing an equally mobile method. In chapter 1, Colin Divall and Hiroki Shin venture outside of the train car in order to explore the "cultural construction of speed" in their analysis of Britain's railway publicity. At the center of their analysis is an engagement with a "conservative modernism," theorized as a way of reconciling urban and rural realities in a rapidly changing modern world. In the contribution by Benjamin Fraser and Steven D. Spalding (chapter 2), train graffiti problematizes the question of identity, offering countercultural alternatives to prevailing images of train mobility and raising the question of authority over such images within the context of an inherently mobile urban reality.

The next section, titled *On Passengers*, centers on the practice of train travel at the individual scale. As Thorne notes, the passenger's experience inside the railcar soon experienced a drastic evolution: "As the nineteenth century progressed, so did rail travel. The second half of the [nineteenth] century was a period of improvement in matters of safety, speed, and comfort. Sleeping cars, dining cars, air brakes, electric foot warmers, and other inventions became parts of train sets" (Thorne 12). As Alexander Medcalf explores in chapter 3, in interwar England, railway marketing photography sought innovative visual means of increasing passenger traffic, and shifted from landscape imagery to pictures of passengers reconceived as consumers. Rowan Wilken's innovative chapter 4 blends observational analysis on trains in Melbourne, Australia with Henri Lefebvre's notion of the method of rhythmanalysis in order to paint a complex picture of experiences inside the train carriage. Ultimately is it necessary to see the act of riding the rails as an active negotiation of "intricate mediated engagements" involving both individual and social factors.

City Networks moves from the mobile character of train travel to the new contours of relatively static networked urban areas. Reviewing the debates over the implementation of mass transit systems in *fin-de-siècle* Paris, Peter Soppelsa (chapter 5) sorts out the aesthetic and technological issues informing the cultural politics behind Paris' emergence as a modern capital cityscape. Samuel Gerald Collins (chapter 6) scrutinizes the recent implementations of technology in the transportation system in Seoul, Korea, as part of a network of new forms of social interaction and urban cultural life.

The next two chapters venture *Inside the Station*. Martha Thorne's illuminating look at the "Renaissance of the Train Station" notes that the first railway station was built in Liverpool (11), and that "the most significant numbers of grand stations were built during the final decades of the nineteenth century and the first ones of the twentieth" (13). In her contribution to this volume, Agata Morka (chapter 7) reads train stations as spaces of "ever-faster movement" through Marc Augé's notion of "supermodernity," looking at stations in Lille, Lyon Saint-Exupery, Liége, Southern Cross, Florence, and Naples through the trope of "unleashed mobility." In her reading of the recently opened Metro station turned museum in Madrid, "Anden 0 [Platform 0]" (chapter 8), Araceli Masterson-Algar parses out the complex set of cultural discourses informing the museum's recuperation of the subway as a metonymy for the city and its relation to its past. The various narratives at play in *Anden 0* appear aimed at displacing the historical processes behind the Madrilenian Metro in favor of nostalgia, commercialism and the burnishing of an icon of the modern urban metropolis.

The final contributions to this second volume—under the subheading *Shifting States*—capture the intersection of modern train travel with nationalist ideologies. Tristan Grunow's essay (chapter 9) traces the process of ideological unification in Japan through the contribution of railways and train stations to the production of a modern built environment. Hiraku Shimoda's reading of episodes from a popular technology-oriented television series (chapter 10) brings a critical lens to the railway's place in discourses of nationalist nostalgia. In contemporary Japan, recent television programming has reasserted the role of its railway system within the powerful mythology of Japan's postwar economic and cultural resurgence. Ultimately the essays published here serve as complements to the more literary focus of its companion volume (*Trains, Literature and Culture*).

All aboard!

BIBLIOGRAPHY

Bobrick, Benson. *Labyrinths of Iron: A History of the World's Subways*. New York: Newsweek Books, 1982.

Grant, H. Roger. *The Railroad: The Life Story of a Technology*. Westport, CT: Greenwood Press, 2005.

Klein, Maury. *Unfinished Business: The Railroad in American Life*. Hanover and London: University Press of New England, 1994.

Polasky, Janet L. *Reforming Urban Labor: Routes to the City, Roots in the Country*. Ithaca and London: Cornell University Press, 2010.

Schivelbusch, Wolfgang. *The Railway Journey: The Industrialization of Time and Space in the 19th Century*. Berkeley: U California Press, 1986.

Stilgoe, John R. *Train Time: Railroads and the Imminent Reshaping of the United States Landscape*. Charlottesville: U Virginia P, 2007.

Thorne, Martha (Ed.). "Renaissance of the Train Station." *Modern Trains and Splendid Stations: Architecture, Design and Rail Travel for the Twenty-First Century*. Chicago: Merrell/The Art Institute of Chicago, 2001. 11–23.

Part I

Speed and Vision

Chapter 1

Cultures of Speed and Conservative Modernity

Representations of Speed in Britain's Railway Marketing

Colin Divall and Hiroki Shin

"To observe the passage of Inter-City 125, British Rail's new thorough-bred, is to savour fresh dimensions in high-speed and muffled sound. To travel in its armchair air-conditioned comfort is to experience an exciting new chapter in rail travel. Very soon these thoroughbreds of tomorrow, ranking with the swiftest and most comfortable trains in the world, will bridge astonishing new frontiers in rail travel between London, Yorkshire, the North-east and Scotland . . . Previous limits in the realms of speed will become dim memories as Inter-City 125 flashes into this last quarter of the Twentieth Century."

—British Rail, *Quest for Speed*

From its early years as a means of transporting people, the railway has been linked with speed. Cultural commentary on this aspect of the railway abounds, from Turner, Carlyle, and Dickens to Betjeman. In the late twentieth century, with the immensely increased possibilities and developments of air and space travel, the train disappeared from its position at the forefront of high-speed technology. However, as the above quote suggests, speed remained firmly within the cultural and, just as important, the commercial vocabulary of the railways. In the twenty-first century, the association of railways with speed is being reinvigorated worldwide: in the UK, both the mass and specialist media hotly debate the politics of developing the existing high-speed link with continental Europe into a national network.

Such considerations bear directly upon the postmodern or late-modern debate over the changes wrought to human experience by the "compression" of time and space as technological advances enabled one to travel ever longer distances in ever shorter periods of time (Giddens; Harvey). Historians have long argued for the railways' pioneering role in shaping this modernity. Writing in the late 1970s, Wolfgang Schivelbusch arguably pioneered the idea that the industrialized "machine ensemble" of the Victorian railway re-framed travel experience through novel notions of time and space—spatialities and temporalities that we call railscapes (Schivelbusch; Mom, Divall & Lyth, 30–33). More recently, Ian Carter, working more in the tradition pioneered by Leo Marx which takes technological culture as a metaphor for the wider society, has explored how in the nineteenth and early twentieth centuries Britain's railways epitomized a modernity embodying progress, power, speed, and so on (Carter). Staying with Britain, Matthew Beaumont and Michael Freeman's edited collection of 2007 melds the two approaches, endorsing the railways' dominant influence on Victorian society and imagination as well as the railscapes of rail travel (Beaumont & Freeman).

Even in a post-industrial phase in which the immediacy and co-presence afforded by information technology makes distance seem almost insignificant, speed has not lost its importance. Paul Virilio's call for the need to expose the hidden logic of speed in various aspects of late-modern life is attracting an increasing number of followers (Virilio). As one such, John Tomlinson, argues, despite its overwhelming impact on the modern imagination, speed was not on the classical sociologist's agenda (Tomlinson). While Marx, Engels, and others had by the mid-19th century observed the "annihilation" of space by time, this view was taken almost literally, leading to the undervaluation of the experience of space and speed.[1] Exception can only be found in the "Impressionism" of those such as Simmel, whose work, including *Philosophy of Money* (1907), pointed to the significance of the changes in the tempo and rhythm of life wrought by capitalism (Simmel).[2] Even within the historical study of the technologies of corporeal speed—air, road, sea, and rail transport—speed tended, and still tends, to be treated as a numerical description; witness, for example, the recent revival of interest among econometricians for calculating the value of the time savings brought about by the railways (Leunig).

There is no doubt that as a category of lived experience "speed" is elusive: how can one possibly know and describe the personal reality of speed apart from one's "impression" of it? Schivelbusch tried to resolve this conundrum by looking at railway speed as a psychosocial experience. Despite its value, this kind of analysis has its limitation, as it tends to exaggerate heightened emotions—shock, fear, pleasure—that are not necessarily the major components of the experience of speed, especially when people become accustomed to a certain level of velocity. Yet speed remains a promising field of research with historical and geographical diversities that are worth exploring (Duffy). More particularly, by revisiting the history of railway speed this chapter warns against some of the generalized assumptions of the wider literature on speed.

The most important point to keep in mind is the complex, hybrid nature of the railway "machine ensemble." Familiar from Actant Network Theory, hybridity dissolves the sharp distinction between human agents and objects, replacing it by networks within which non-human "agency" may be incorporated (Latour).[3] On this view, technologically enabled speed's absolute, mechanized or objective nature cannot be radically separated from its imagined, represented and experienced forms. This techno-social hybridity was arguably implicit in Schivelbusch, although his conceptualization of the machine ensemble tended more to a tightly bound system of *physical* technologies—infrastructure, locomotives, vehicles, and so on (Revill). For our purposes, what has not been sufficiently addressed is the hybridity of railway business, railscapes, and the wider cultures and experiences of mobility inherent in "modernity," all mediated through the technologies of rail-objects—the physical hardware along with the "firmware" of social-institutional entities such as operating rules, regulatory regimes, and management structures. Once this hybridity is admitted, it becomes easier to see the diversity of ways in which the railways' commercial activities, and more particularly their discourses on and practices of speed, shaped—and were shaped by—wider notions and enactments of a thoroughly mobile "modernity."

The recent historiography of consumption strongly supports this move. Neoclassical assumptions of the profit-maximizing firm serving rational customers have given way—at least in some quarters—to models in which businesses and consumers mutually construct norms, values, and attitudes that in turn inform the purchase, use, and production of material and nonmaterial commodities. Inherent in such perspectives is the possibility of alternative pathways of consumption; for example, Jackson et al. state that "economics and culture are reflexively inter-related in ways which are neither predetermined nor mono-causal" (Jackson et al. 12). This view of commercial cultures should be taken seriously when discussing railway speed, since, at least in the British context, increases in maximum and average train speeds and their allocation to particular services—and hence markets and social groups—were usually heavily driven by business considerations (Simmons, *Express Train*, 30). The argument can be taken further: while business decisions about speed were shaped proximately by consumers' desires and needs (or more accurately by the companies' understanding of such factors), these in turn were bound up with wider evaluations of particular kinds of rail-based mobility in British society. And the converse might well be true; the business allocation of speed at one point can subsequently affect the wider mobility cultures.

When dealing with such wide and historically changing phenomena, traditional terms to describe the world of rail-based mobility such as "train travel" are perhaps too tainted by older forms of analysis. Hence, taking inspiration from other commodified means of mobility, particularly motoring, we adopt the neologism of *railing*, a term intended to capture the idea that moving by train has nearly always been imbued with socially inscribed meanings that extend beyond the merely functional capacity to shift from A to B (Mom, Divall & Lyth, 28–29). Here it is sufficient to understand the term as an expression of the hybrid nature of the railways just described.

As it is impossible to cover all the diverse aspects of railway speed and its long history in a limited space, this essay concentrates mainly on its commercial component in some specific periods from the 1840s to the 1970s. More particularly, we do so in relation to so-called "conservative modernity," a concept that scholars have long employed to capture a distinctive aspect of the British cultural accommodation to industrial capitalism. As to some extent the scholarly debate over the distinctiveness of "modernity" and "postmodernity" settled down, the homogeneity of the former concept came to be questioned. Did modernity really become enacted in a uniform manner across different cultural and geographical locations? As Rieger and Daunton argue:

> The rhetoric of the "modern" . . . provided a language to appropriate certain aspects of the age while selectively rejecting others. These ambivalences not only illustrate how difficult contemporaries found it to navigate an age that they repeatedly called "modern"; they also render it impossible in retrospect to pin down neatly one authoritative meaning of modernity. (Daunton & Rieger, 8)

This implies not merely a search for alternative modernities but also a recognition that these might have been geographically dispersed beyond the industrialized urban locations that scholars once saw as the sole progenitors of "modernity" (Featherstone, 170–176; Gaonkar). "Conservative modernity" neatly fits this way of thinking. As Alison Light argues, for example, British authors of the interwar period developed a rather inward-looking, domestic, and private type of perspective which "could simultaneously look backwards and forwards; it could accommodate the past in the new forms of the present"—an outlook exploited to great party-political effect by Stanley Baldwin as prime minister (Light, 10; Williamson). Moreover, as Jeremy Burchardt has recently reminded us, urban varieties of "modernity" did not simply overwhelm traditional rural forms of life and imagery; rather, at least in the English (not British) context, the rural was discursively remade and re-appropriated partly as a balm for the unease engendered by a "much wider array of cultural fears about the rise of mechanisation, the subjugation of nature and the direction and ultimate destiny of the modernisation project," fears which dated back at least as far as the last third of the nineteenth century (Burchardt, 148–149; Trentmann). This process of accommodation included the spatial and temporary manipulation of images and notions, including those of speed (Jeremiah).

UNEVEN SPEED

Railway speed spread through British society rather gradually and unevenly. The world's first significant interurban passenger line, between Liverpool and Manchester, opened in 1830, providing some people with the experience of machine speed and its dangers. The accident which eventually killed the former president of the Board of Trade, William Huskisson, was caused by his misgauging the speed of an approaching train; he thought it was slower than it was and failed to respond in time (Garfield). This Janus-faced rail speed—full of both possibilities and dangers—was to form the key note in the railway culture of speed.

The development of the British railway network was essentially regional, at least before the emergence of an inchoate national network around 1850. The allocation of railway speed was therefore geographically uneven in the early nineteenth century, and to some extent remained so thereafter since some remote parts of the country were never connected, while others only enjoyed links that were engineered for low speeds (Casson; Simmons, *Railway in England and Wales*). There was also a social unevenness in the allocation of speed. In its early days, railing was limited to the relatively wealthy. This started to change around 1840 as the construction of what was to become the national network opened up opportunities for excursions. Thomas Cook's famous abstinence excursion had a number of predecessors from the late 1830s (Brendon; Kusamitsu). The popularity of the excursion first culminated in 1851, when a significant proportion of the Great Exhibition's 6 million visitors traveled by rail. Yet it needs to be kept in mind that railing was far from a regular, let alone everyday, experience (Barton; Thrift, *Spatial Formations*, ch. 7).

Another challenge to the uneven allocation of speed was the provision of the so-called "parliamentary trains." From 1844 (a date generally assumed to lie at the heart of the period of laissez-faire), the state required, with certain exceptions, the privately owned railway companies to run at least one passenger service a day each way at one penny a mile (Lee, 17–18).[4] The basic rationale for this provision was to supply a cheap means of mobility to the "poorer class of travellers," as well as to equip the service with minimum levels of safety and comfort. Although a minimum stop-to-start speed of

12 mph was stipulated in the act, the allocation of high speed was not the main concern of the legislation: the parliamentary train was to stop at *every* station between termini, which slowed the journey considerably (Lee, 18; Hermes, 1). Higher speeds by express trains existed well before 1844, but these early expresses operated on a different notion from that of today. They saved time chiefly by stopping only at main stations; high speed, even by comparison with that of the horse, was not necessarily the main concern (Simmons, *Express Train*, 23). The first express service that was closer to our notion of high maximum speed was introduced by the Great Western Railway (GWR) in 1845 on its Exeter trains, which ran at an average of 41.6 mph but which probably exceeded 60 mph in order to do so (Simmons, *Express Train*, 24). In both senses of the term, express trains were for richer travelers, not for the masses. And nor were parliamentary trains the social panacea that some historians think: quite apart from the inconveniences and discomforts of the typical "parliamentary," the statutory fare was pitched at a level that made feasible occasional migration for employment but that did not permit the everyday use of the train by the working classes.

In any case, most railway companies were not enthusiastic about providing cheap passenger services; they could not readily envision a mass travel market that contradicted their belief in the market's rigidity with respect to both structure and size. Parliamentary trains were not particularly profitable; the companies were more motivated by the state mandate and the remission of the 5% passenger tax payable on all other journeys. Yet the companies' belief was undermined by the massive growth in third-class passenger travel in the second half of the century. By the last third of the century, intensifying intercompany competition made it almost impossible to be content with the previous practice of barring third-class passengers from express trains. These factors formed the backdrop for Midland Railway's drastic decision in 1872 to start the third-class express service at a penny a mile (Lee, 61). This was partly an attempt to exploit the fiscal provisions for parliamentary trains, as the Midland demanded the remission of the passenger tax, despite the fact that its expresses did not stop at every station. After some political wrangling with the Inland Revenue, the Midland eventually had its way and some companies—quite often reluctantly—followed into the "cheap" express business. The general manager of the rival London & North Western Railway, George Findlay, was not alone in thinking that cheaper express service would encroach upon the value-added business of the higher classes (Findlay, 125). To their competitors' disgust, Midland Railway went on to abolish the second class in 1875. Moreover, the express trains of the 1840s had required supplementary fares that could be more than 40% of the normal price (Simmons, *Express Train*, 28). The abolition of such a practice, though it remained in some parts of the south, started in the late 1850s; the Midland was, again, the pioneer in this respect.

In sum, these developments should not be taken as being indicative of the universal speeding up of railing. Absolute, objective speeds undoubtedly increased in Britain, particularly from the 1860s, although the express train's temporal economy was still achieved as much by skipping stations as by increasing the maximum speed. But some routes, particularly those affected by intercompany competition, were more favored than others. And the socially uneven allocation of speed remained considerable, despite the "democratization of rail travel" supposedly wrought by first the parliamentary train and then widespread adoption of the Midland's business model (Freeman, "Introduction," 47). To be sure, third-class railing mushroomed from the 1880s; but some of this was because consumers "traded down" to the cheaper accommodation, while even the considerable volume of new business was probably due in no small measure to middle- and upper-class passengers traveling more often. Working-class people could now incorporate the train into their lives on something more than the basis of an occasional excursion, but we should not assume that they experienced railway speed on anything like a daily (or even a weekly or monthly) experience. The clear exception to this was in London and a few other large cities, where the availability of genuinely cheap "working-men's fares" from mid-century (and more particularly from the 1880s) encouraged the rise of daily working-class commuting: these were not fast trains, however.

ACCELERATION

The development of the railway passenger service described above had a significant impact on British society. With his wholehearted praise of Britain's express trains, Ernest Foxwell represented the optimistic side of contemporary opinion in the last two decades of the nineteenth century. In a sense, Foxwell's article, featured in *Macmillan's Magazine*, can be seen as a precursor of theories of rail travel, such as Schivelbusch's, in its depiction of the beneficial influence of railing on individuals as well as society. According to Foxwell, the express trains—the "modern gift of speed"—had energized the nation through constant motion (Foxwell, *English Express Trains*). The speed at which intention became deed—if you wanted to go somewhere, you could reach there in less time on the express—significantly increased human potentiality, and the joint experience of travel nurtured national feeling as it eroded the old antithesis of town and country (8, 14). The constant contact with distant people made them tolerant and kind (22). Once people were freed from their subjugation to distance, society became more democratic, since the communication and circulation of ideas was encouraged, and the authority of the metropolis weakened. This democratizing effect of express trains was also applicable to women (35). Foxwell asked: "imagine railways suddenly destroyed and the art forgotten: where would be any of the specially[sic] modern features of this nineteenth century?" and then went on to state that "'Nineteenth Century' only means what has happened in the decades coeval with railways" (27). Foxwell was at the forefront of late nineteenth-century speed enthusiasm (Kern, 128).

Yet enthusiasm for speed was never unalloyed. According to Samuel Smiles, even George Stephenson (who died in 1848) had believed that train speeds should be limited to 40 mph, and that anything more would be "unnecessary" and dangerously high (Smiles, 385). That probably tells us as much about Smiles as Stephenson, although there is plenty of evidence elsewhere to sustain the general point (Simmons, *Express Train*, 32). In the 1830s, for instance, *John Bull* had been known as an "anti-railway magazine" critical of railway speed (*John Bull*, 8 Oct. 1842, 487). As early as 1835 it had asked:

> Does anyone mean to say that decent people, passengers who would use their own carriages, and are accustomed to their own comforts, would consent to be hurried along thought the air upon a railroad . . . or is it to be imagined that women, who may like the fun of being whirled away on a party of pleasure for an hour to see a sight, would endure the fatigue, and misery, and danger, not only to themselves, but their children and families, of being dragged through the air at the rate of twenty miles an hour . . . ? (*John Bull*, 16 Nov. 1835, 356)

Nor were such sentiments limited to the pioneering phase of railway speed. By the 1880s, by which time speeds had increased substantially, a group of medical professionals started to express concerns about the increasing pace of life resulting from new technologies, and more specifically the railway. A new diagnosis, "railway spine," was identified as a nervous condition said to be caused by the shocks inherent in travel at heightened speeds, while James Crichton-Brown's diagnosis of the death statistics in England concluded that the increased velocity of modern mobility was a major cause of the rise in heart and other diseases (Kern, 125; Schivelbusch, ch. 7).

These critics of railway speed did not deter railway companies from accelerating trains in the late 1880s and 1890s when they saw commercial advantage. In 1888, the famous "races to the North" started between the rival routes of the West Coast, run by the London & North Western Railway and Caledonian Railway, and the East Coast whose service was provided by the Great Northern, North Eastern, and North British companies. The previous nine-hour journey between London and Edinburgh was suddenly reduced by one-and-a-half hours (Nock). The races were then repeated after completion of the Forth Bridge. This time, the 1895 race was on a longer journey between London and Aberdeen, in which the competing trains ran, on average, more than 60 mph for over 540 miles (McKean). People like Foxwell were fascinated; others were alarmed (Foxwell, *Express Trains*, 17–26).[5] Here speed was inextricably linked with a wider competition for customers. In 1888, for instance, the East Coast companies felt forced to retain second-class accommodation on the route because the West Coast companies were doing so.[6]

Apart from the increasing speed typical of this period, the commercial element became a recognizable force in the railway's corporate structure. Up to the 1890s, railway advertising—it would be too generous to yet describe it as marketing—had been largely subordinate to the operational side of the organization. This is evidenced by the fact that, for instance, up to then the Midland Railway's advertising clerk was under the direction of the time-table clerk; between the 1890s and early 1900s, with the introduction of its own head clerk, the advertising section achieved independence.[7] Practically speaking, this reflected the growing significance of marketing in the railway business. It can also be seen as a reflection of the increasing importance of the marketing of a culture of speed—one freed from the constraints of the objective time of the timetable. However, this did not signify the complete separation of the two. Disciplined speed, in contrast to unruly speed, gener-ally characterized the railway. Indeed the term velocity, which in its scientific sense includes the idea of movement in a *specified* direction, better captures the way in which the railways' peculiar techno-social character—including but by no means reducible to the timetabled passage of trains along fixed tracks—produced motion that was comparatively safe and reliable as well as speedy. As several scholars have pointed out, this timetabled velocity had a significant impact on the wider temporalities and social life in the nineteenth century; arriving at the destination earlier than scheduled was by no means a virtue (Esbester; Freeman, "Time and Space"; Thrift, "Transport and Com-munication"). Not surprisingly, railway advertising reflected this emphasis on disciplined speed or velocity. Nevertheless in the commercial culture of the railways around 1900, speed became increasingly marketed through the use of verbal and visual imagery that afforded it a degree of independence from the numerical exactitude of the timetable.

A similarly changing relationship between time/space and commercial culture can be seen in the geographical imagination. From the 1890s, for example, the early *mimetic* or *topographical* railway maps were gradually taken over by more abstract route diagrams. These, at least in the early twen-tieth century, were quite likely designed by the advertising section of the railway companies.[8] By employing a certain degree of literary license, route maps were used to bolster companies' claims to offer the "most direct"—that is, quickest—journey. Lines on posters and in tourist brochures were straightened out, suggesting a smooth and efficient trip.[9]

The most direct expression of speed came with the catchphrase in railway advertising. The Great Central Railway's (GCR) slogan, "Rapid Travel in Luxury," is said to have originated with the general manager, Sam Fay; and, according to W. J. Stuart, the company's Advertising Manager, "[T]he phrase has been very much appreciated by the public, who see the point it makes instantly" ("The Art of Advertising a Railway," 768). The vocabulary was not exclusive to the GCR; the Lancashire & Yorkshire Railway issued a poster in 1914 to attract "those who desire comfort with speed" to their line (also see "Shortest/Direct route (speed) and "Lavatory Carriage . . . heated by Steam (comfort)" in Fig. 1.1). But highlighting speed did not mean that visual images of express *trains* were much used when promoting railing. As Thomas Russell, an authority on commercial advertising in the interwar years, observed in 1924:

> The illustration of advertisements has undergone great developments in a couple of generations. Our grandfathers, when they wanted to advertise railway-travel, used the picture of a locomotive. This, to modern eyes, does not seem a very effective way to arouse in the bosom of an observer the desire to be conveyed to a far country. Perhaps, our grandfathers inherited the idea from theirs, when the railway was a new thing . . . an object of curiosity . . . In other words, the real subject of every advertisement is not the product but the service that it gives. (Russell, 550)

We cannot ignore this near-contemporary marketing discourse in our evaluation of railway advertising before World War I, though some scholars, by relying on a simplified notion of marketing in their analysis, have failed to grasp it (cf. Watts, 45–47). The disappearance of trains from representations of the railway landscape, analyzed in Matt Thompson's chapter, is consistent with the concept of conservative modernity outlined previously; it was partly a response to the need to alleviate the residual anxieties engendered by mechanized mobility.

A similar account applies to photography. Its promotional use had started in the late 1880s, although the images used were almost exclusively landscapes such as Payne Jennings' series for the Great Eastern Railway (Damant, 161). This was not because no alternative was available. Although hampered by the early photographic process with slow emulsions on glass plates, the railway companies could, and did, take pictures of trains at speed (Bartholomew & Blakemore, 24). If the image of moving trains had once

Figure 1.1.   Great Northern, North Eastern, and North British Railways, *East-Coast Route*, 1895. National Railway Museum (NRM), 1977–5628.

attracted customers, why did the companies not make use of such images before World War I? The simple answer remains that representations of the brute, material underpinnings of speed, locomotives and trains—moving or not—were no longer enough. Instead, what was preferred, at least until the interwar years, was the scenery of destinations accompanied by the somewhat subdued image of speed, comfort, and luxury: "place marketing" had arrived. As the mechanical presence of trains receded into the background, objective mechanical speed gave way to images in which speed became entangled with a range of other socially desirable characteristics. The presentation of speed here was more than by implication; but it was much less forcefully presented than some theorists of modernity have claimed.

STREAMLINING

Both culturally and practically, railway speed was profoundly affected by the technological development of other means of transport. After World War I the railway companies' old rhetoric of flying—such as the Flying Scotsman—was surpassed by literal reality as airplanes gradually started to be used for civilian purposes. Much more serious competition came from the road. Ownership of cars was rapidly increasing, providing personal speed to mostly wealthy middle- to upper-class travelers, although the cheaper motorcycles found favor with the working class. The combined challenge from increasingly popular bus and coach travel and motoring encroached upon the railways' position in the travel market. This trend was clearly visible by the mid- to late 1920s, and some railway companies saw that they had irretrievably lost the car-owning class as their customers, though they did not, and could not, withdraw from competition altogether (Divall, "Transport"). The strategy to regain some of the lost ground was to widen the net of potential customers from the largely middle class to the mass market. As we have seen, this was by no means a new phenomenon: the railway companies had been developing a popular travel market from the mid-nineteenth century. The changes in the interwar period were intended to expand this customer base still further by treating it not as a homogenous mass, but as a set of diverse groups, each with different tastes and wants. This provided a reason for the increasing importance—and sheer bulk—of railway guidebooks. From numerous destinations and services, customers could choose, combine, and tailor their travel to their liking.

Simply providing options, however, was insufficient to make people take the train. The railway companies needed to present a case for the advantages of railing. The selling points to which they resorted were the traditional triad

of speed, safety, and comfort. But these would no longer "sell themselves"—
salesmanship became much more sophisticated in the interwar years. The
"Big Four" companies, created by statute in 1923, aimed to make every
member of their staff a salesman, to use the contemporary word. These rail
sales(wo)men were to help make potential customers "rail-minded." For
example, the largest of the four, the London Midland and Scottish Railway,
from 1933 circulated a booklet among its employees entitled *Salesmanship
and You* to inscribe the railway's selling points in the minds of the workforce.[10] Lecture series and examinations were held to inculcate salesmanship,
and sales techniques and the knowledge to support the sales activity were
taught and consolidated (Shin). There were even salesmanship competitions.[11] Such sales activities could only be sustained when the sales pitch was
realized, at least to a certain degree, in the delivery of the travel experience.
The advantage of the promised speed was to be achieved through punctual
train operation. The companies did not leave this to the spontaneity of their
workforce; in some cases, the encouragement of punctuality took the form of
intracompany competitions.[12]

Railway publicity in the interwar years reflected these developments. The
London and North Eastern Railway's (LNER) slogan "Quicker by Rail" was
obviously comparative: the railways were quicker than, say, cars. The phrase
was then used in joint publicity by the Big Four. As suggested by its clever
catchphrase, the LNER was possibly the best of the four companies in evoking the image of speed. The language of speed was often accompanied by
visual images heavily tinged by aesthetic modernism, although the LNER's
trains did not always feature in this visualization. The profuse use of smooth
lines in pictorial posters was emphasized by Eric Gill's Sans Serif typeface
of accompanying texts; it was also used in the company's publications and
signs.

As many scholars have pointed out, the most distinctive expressions
of modernist speed were the streamlined trains of the mid-to-late 1930s
(Mullay). Lagging somewhat behind overseas practice, the first British
streamlined steam locomotive was the LNER's A4 class, introduced in 1935
to a design overseen by its chief mechanical engineer, Nigel Gresley. At the
inaugural run of the Silver Jubilee service for which the engines had been
built, the general manager, Sir Ralph Wedgwood, was understandably proud
of the new express train, streamlined "to the shape of a torpedo . . . ."[13] The
war-like metaphor reverberated with the target of the torpedo-train: private
motor travel. The idea was to entice people to long-distance travel, and
then to retrieve the ground over shorter distances.[14] Wedgwood proclaimed:
"Here is the speed, here is the terrific tractive effort." Behind this celebration
of technological achievement, the event was clearly regarded as "a novel

business experiment"; the new express service was accompanied by the re-introduction of supplement fares. With the Silver Jubilee "speed was not an expensive luxury, but a profit earner, when offered to the public under conditions which gave it a strong public appeal."[15] The public face of this project appeared in the official brochure of the Coronation service:

> The travelling public are themselves the soundest judges of new facilities. Their patronage of Britain's first streamline train—"The Silver Jubilee"—has proved that high speed, when it goes with punctuality and comfort, makes a strong appeal. (LNER, *Coronation*)

Moreover the business benefit of the streamlined train was clear: the increase in passenger receipts on the London–Newcastle route served by the Silver Jubilee in the ten months after its introduction was twice that of the preceding ten months.[16]

With hindsight the general opinion about British streamlined trains is that the element of style was more important than the functional benefits of reducing air-resistance (Self, 22). Nevertheless the new design practice was adopted, although in varying degrees, by all four companies. As far as steam locomotives were concerned, the GWR's version was, at best, half-hearted, consisting of nothing more than a few plates experimentally attached to a solitary example of a "Castle" class, a 1920s design. By that decade, the aesthetic of the company's locomotives, received with some horror by traditionalists when the new look had been unveiled in the 1900s, was regarded as well established, conservative even. Here the concept of conservative modernity is useful, for the GWR's application of a "traditional" surface to what by the standards of the early 1920s was a modern machine was consistent with its wider marketing initiatives since at least the turn of the century. The company had long promoted an image of historical English rurality and Celtic otherness in its travel literature and pictorial posters—the modernity of the means by which such places were to be accessed was subsumed under the weight of tradition conveyed in this publicity (Bennett). As the chapter by Alexander Medcalf demonstrates (ch. 3, this book), by the interwar period, and especially after 1930, these "conservative" images were becoming accompanied by a more "modern" image of travel, as the GWR's holiday guidebooks in particular became populated with consumer–travelers enjoying themselves at their destination. But the fundamental point remains: the GWR was adept at mixing "conservative" and "modern" images in whatever proportion it deemed commercially advantageous.

This interpretation is given further support by the GWR's solitary foray into streamlining, in 1934, when it introduced Britain's first streamlined train service, an express diesel railcar on the Birmingham–South Wales route (GWR, *Streamline Way*). The marketing strategy mixed modernist stream-lined visual imagery with an emphasis on the historical landscape through which this highly modern train passed; the publicity brochure described the service as "not only a great saving of time, but also provides a new means of seeing Britain" (10). True to its word, the last half of the brochure was dedicated to a disposition of the sites that could be viewed on the "Stream-line Way." While superficially this might seem to be incoherent publicity, or a half-hearted attitude toward modernity, the incorporation of both machine and traditional landscape struck precisely the kind of balance between past and present that typified the GWR's long-term approach to marketing.

The streamlined trains of other companies can be seen from a similar perspective, although the mix between explicit and conservative modernity was handled differently. The appearance of the streamliners of the late 1930s in publicity materials such as pictorial posters and guidebook photo-graphs was an exception to the general exclusion since the 1890s of visual

Figure 1.2. LMS, *The Coronation Scot Ascending Shap Fell*, 1937. NRM, 1990–7083.

images of trains (Cole & Durack, 25–26). Indeed the early pictorial posters of the Silver Jubilee train did not feature any recognizable landscape;
such machine-centered treatment was the norm in the introductory phase of
streamlined trains. But this did not last long: a far more significant image
appeared in *Holiday by LMS* (1938), "The Coronation Scot near Carlisle."
Again, the precise location of the image was not specified, but in contrast
to the LNER's handling of the Silver Jubilee, it embedded the machine in
a recognizably British landscape. Similar examples of the attempt to merge
the streamlined train into the scenery can be seen in a series of pictorial
posters. Frank Henry Mason's poster for the LNER, *"The Coronation"
on the East Coast Entering Scotland*, employed the sea as a background
softening the presence of the train at speed. Norman Wilkinson's painting
of *The Coronation Scot Ascending Shap Fell* (Fig. 1.2) depicted the train
climbing up a hill. Here, the trail of smoke suggests a slower pace—no
surprise when ascending—but the toning of the blue train with the massive slate-blue mountains in the background arguably connotes the power
that made the movement possible. By placing the streamlined trains *in*
the countryside, not the archetypal urban spaces of "modernity," the
painters manipulated and tamed speed by enclosing it within a "timeless"
landscape.

These images of the assimilation of modern technology and landscape
attest to the continued relevance of conservative modernity immediately
before World War II. But the outbreak of war shattered hope of fully incorporating the streamliners into that kind of marketing, along with Gresley's
planned attempt to raise the world speed record, possibly up to 130 mph.
Under such circumstances, what is really impressive is the swiftness of the
attempt to naturalize the new trains into the British landscape. Historians
have long discussed the advanced aesthetic of the streamlined trains—quite
rightly, as historians usually do not write about what *would have* happened—
but we should not forget that the stories of the interwar period did not have a
neat beginning and end, and many remain unfulfilled.

The more significant point here is that within Britain, the modernity represented by the railways' treatment of speed may broadly be categorized
as a conservative modernity, for all that this took different forms. This is
not surprising given that the companies were facing a common enemy in
the form of road transport, and that they were increasingly cooperating in
their marketing. In this context, the categorization by scholars and others of
individual railway companies as "conservative" (the GWR) or "modernist"
(LNER) misses the fundamental point. This is not to say that the variations
between the companies were unimportant. There was no handbook available to guide railway marketeers in their campaigns, and so to some extent

personal aesthetic tastes or hunches on the part of publicity officers influenced the adoption of specific styles in advertising and industrial design. Above all, these variations may be taken as experiments, albeit only half-understood as such, in trying to create a differentiated market out of a public that had previously been assumed to be largely homogeneous in its tastes. Yet whatever the truth of the matter, all the railway companies now took it for granted that that the majority of their potential customers—apart from some of the growing number of rail enthusiasts—did not have a taste for a monolithic machine modernity.

CONCLUSION: HIGH-SPEED

It was no coincidence that in 1978 the UK's Design Council, a government-supported agency, published an article on the LNER's streamlined trains, refreshing people's memory of the high-speed trains of the interwar period (Self). A new generation of high-speed trains had arrived, with the now-iconic Inter-City 125 entering service in 1976. This train symbolized the culmination of the triumphant transformation of the troubled nationalized British Railways (BR), formed in 1948 from the war-damaged Big Four, into "British Rail," a much more commercially aware and marketing-led enterprise (Gourvish, *British Railways*). The launch of the Japanese *Shinkansen* in 1964 had attracted worldwide attention to high-speed trains, and in 1968 the BR Railway Technical Centre outlined plans for an Advanced Passenger Train (APT), a revolutionary design intended to run at over 160 mph on existing tracks (Potter, 147). Aware of the technical risks of the project, in May 1970 the BR Board authorized construction of an alternative, prototype high-speed diesel-electric train (HSDT), later known as the High Speed Train (HST) and then the Inter-City 125. This prototype, an evolutionary rather than revolutionary advance on existing designs, was completed in twenty-two months (Haresnape, 151; Ford, 20).

The aim of all these projects was to "attract more passengers" when competition from road and domestic air travel was visibly intensifying.[17] But innovative engineering was not enough. Launched in 1965, BR's nationwide Inter-City brand lent the organization a fresh marketing focus, and the coming of the HST encouraged new thinking (Allen, 164–165).[18] While at first the new diesel train was designated "High-Speed Train" within BR, the organization's advertising agent, Greham & Gillies, suggested the use of "Inter-City" for wider consumption.[19] From the agency's report to British Rail, we can see that the use of the description "high-speed train" was intentionally avoided—because it was argued that some people had concerns about speed.[20] Conversely, this description might imply that existing trains were considered "slow."[21] Instead "Inter-City 125" traded on the airlines' use of alpha-numeric names for their equipment, such as Boeing 747, but with the twist that the "125" here referred to the train's maximum speed. As the agency claimed, BR could thereby retain the element of speed without being too explicit.[22] Another pertinent decision was that of not telling passengers in real time of their train's speed (unlike in Japan, where speed indicators were provided in the carriages) because "some passengers might become a little disturbed at the thought of hurtling along at 125 mph."[23] Nearly 140 years after *John Bull* had expressed reservations about the speed of railing, the issue had not disappeared.

But neither were the gainsayers on top. Although we currently lack a full analysis of the effect the new high-speed train had on contemporary cultures of speed, the Inter-City 125 became one of the most prolifically distributed images of passenger trains in the 1970s and 1980s, appearing in brochures and other publicity materials both domestically and overseas. What is striking here was the return of a machine speed which had previously been tamed and carefully managed for decades. The attempts to tame speed through naturalization and enclosure fell away to reveal a still stronger appearance of train speed.

What is less clear is the longer-term effect this has had on our twenty-first-century cultural appreciation of railway speed. In business terms, the Inter-City 125 was an undoubted success, arguably saving the inter-urban network from the worst of road and air competition (Bonavia, 131; Loft, 158; Nash, 82).[24] But despite still running in service, with a projected life that could easily take the train past its fortieth anniversary, the image of the Inter-City 125 is arguably tarnished by association with the remaking of the collective memory of BR in the run up to, and aftermath of, privatization in the mid-1990s. On this narrative, BR was better known for high subsidies and fares, cutbacks, and poor service, HST's success an easily ignored detail (Strangleman). This is, as yet, speculation. But it is tolerably clear that by contrast, a memory of the "Golden Age of Steam" up to 1939, exemplified by stream-lined speed, has come to occupy a powerful place in the cultural imagination of the British railway, even if the nostalgic and "modern" elements have not been resolved, either by enthusiasts or historians. In this sense, Inter-City 125 has arguably failed to make previous limits in the realms of speed "dim memories" (British Rail, *Quest for Speed*).

But what of the future? We seem to be on the verge of another age of "high-speed" trains, even in Britain. This new obsession with high speed can, paradoxically, be understood as a *deceleration*—from jet speed to train speed (but not, note, in the temporal economy of the journey, as the advantages of air speed waste away in the enforced immobility of the airport terminal). While this chapter is not intended to address the politics of tomorrow's high-speed trains, it is worth remembering that "railway speed" has never held one meaning, even in the period commonly known as modernity. "Conservative modernity" reminds us of modernity's diversity and unevenness, and with it the fluctuating fortunes of speed. Furthermore, the determinants of the railways' historical cultures of speed were multiple, including wider cultural trends, politics, and business.

This chapter suggests that the business element, overlapping with these other factors, should continue to be taken seriously. Here, too, history alerts us to challenges ahead. In 1887 the distinguished railway author J. S. Jeans commented on the hidden costs of the great number of express services in Britain, a situation unparalleled in any other country:

> Railway managers profess that these are desiderata that the British public imperatively demand, and for this argument they have ample reason. But if Englishmen will insist upon travelling at the rate of fifty miles an hour, and having more express trains than any other country, they must expect to have to pay somewhat more for the costly facilities thus provided. (Jeans, 267)

This seems to be common sense. Yet when speed is allocated unevenly, whether geographically or socially, the costs are not borne only by passengers, but also, indirectly, by non-users. Historically, the railways' conservative marketing of speed seems to have helped mitigate the tensions of modernity, including the very unevenness of speed, by suggesting that speed and society could exist in a state of symbiosis. In short, if the culture of speed was a crucial component of "modern" society, the railways' commercial culture seems to be an indispensable aspect of our historical understanding of modernity. If the train is set to become an equally important element of late-modernity, then we should do well to attend as carefully to the commercial factors shaping the new paradigm of speed: for now with carbon and climate change inextricably linked, the stakes are even higher.

NOTES

1. Recent criticism of such an attitude can be found in, for instance, Massey's work on the "spatial turn" in social sciences.
2. Although Tomlinson does not clearly describe this, Simmel's insight catalyzed the formation of a group of scholars who paid particular attention to "circulation."

Schivelbusch was clearly one of these. The circulation school has, in fact, a long history with variations including Keynes' velocity of circulation and, not completely separate from economics discourse, the medical theory and literary tradition of "it-narrative" or novels of circulation (Bellamy; Trotter).

3. For a discussion of how ANT might be applied to the techno-cultural history of transport, see Divall and Revill; a revised version is available at http://www.york.ac.uk/ inst/irs/irshome/papers/Cultures%20of%20Transport%20revised.pdf.

4. 7 & 8 Vict. c.89.

5. Some negative opinions about the races to the north can be found in Cecil Parr, "The Disadvantages of Express Trains," *The Times,* 14 August 1888; "The Railway Race to Scotland," *The Times,* 22 August 1895.

6. Great Northern Railway, "Board of Directors Minutes," 7 December 1888, The National Archives, UK (henceforth TNA). RAIL 236/51, fol. 261.

7. Midland Railway, "Minutes of Traffic Committee," 22 September 1892, TNA, RAIL 491/158.

8. For example, the North Eastern Railway's route-map of "Shortest and Quickest Route (East Coast) between England and Scotland," in *Bradshaw*'s 1911 edition. In the previous year, the *Railway and Travel Monthly* congratulated the North-Eastern's Advertising Department for a "traffic-compelling" commercial map poster. *Railway and Travel Monthly*, December 1910: 652.

9. Andrew Dow notes the likely importance of these early diagrammatic maps for the subsequent development of railway route maps, culminating in that of Henry Beck's London Underground map first issued in 1933 (Dow).

10. London, Midland and Scottish Railway (LMS), *Salesmanship and You* (1938, originally published as *Sales Promotion Campaign* in 1933).

11. See the railway companies' official publications such as *Quota News* (LMS) and *Southern Sales* (Southern Railway) issued in the late 1930s.

12. Again, the LMS issued a serial publication, entitled *On Time.*

13. *London & North Eastern Railway Magazine,* 25.11 (1935): 658.

14. The LNER contemplated the introduction of the A4s on London–Norwich route but compromised on streamlining existing locomotives. LNER, "Letter to Sir Murrough J. Wilson," 15 February 1937, "High Speed Trains—Reports on etc.," TNA, RAIL 390/987.

15. *London & North Eastern Railway Magazine,* 26.6 (1936): 332.

16. LNER, "Memorandum: High Speed Trains," 28 October 1936, TNA, RAIL 390/987.

17. British Rail, "Speed for the Seventies," National Railway Museum, York, UK, Forsythe Collection.

18. This trend intensified after the late 1970s (Potter, 155; Gourvish, "British Rail's 'Business-Led' Organization").

19. "Eric Selby to Paul Foulkes," 30 May 1975, TNA, AN 111/933; "Paul Foulkes to Eric Selby," 4 June 1975, TNA, AN 111/933.

20. Greham & Gillies, "Introduction of High Speed Train," 25 February 1975, TNA, AN 111/933: fol. 2.

21. Greham & Gillies, "Introduction of High Speed Train," 25 February 1975, TNA, AN 111/933: fol. 1.

22. The name would also allow for adjustment to future improvements in train speed, which in fact happened with Inter-City 225.

23. "125 mph rail service next week," *The Times,* 1 October 1976.

24. British Rail, "Trends in Inter-City Data," August 1982, TNA, AN 182/393: fol. 1.

BIBLIOGRAPHY

Allen, G. Freeman. *British Rail after Beeching.* London: Ian Allan, 1966.

"The Art of Advertising a Railway." *Advertising* Aug. 1907: 765–768.

Bartholomew, Ed, and Michael Blakemore. *Railways in Focus: Photographs from the National Railway Museum Collections.* Penryn: Atlantic Transport, 1998.

Barton, Susan. *Working-Class Organisations and Popular Tourism, 1840–1970.* Manchester: Manchester University Press, 2005.

Beaumont, Matthew, and Michael J. Freeman, eds. *The Railway and Modernity: Time, Space and the Machine Ensemble.* Oxford: Peter Lang, 2007.

Bellamy, Liz. *Commerce, Morality and the Eighteenth-Century Novel.* Cambridge, UK: Cambridge University Press, 1998.

Bennett, Alan David. "The Great Western Railway and the Celebration of Englishness." University of York, UK: Unpublished D.Phil. thesis, 2000.

Bonavia, Michael. *British Rail: The First 25 Years.* David & Charles: Newton Abbot, 1981.

Brendon, Piers. *Thomas Cook: 150 Years of Popular Tourism.* London: Secker & Warburg, 1991.

British Rail. *Quest for Speed: The Official Story of East Coast Enterprise.* York: British Rail Eastern Region, 1977.

Burchardt, Jeremy. "Rurality, Modernity and National Identity between the Wars." *Rural History* 21.2 (2010): 143–150.

Carter, Ian. *Railways and Culture in Britain: The Epitome of Modernity.* Manchester: Manchester University Press, 2001.

Casson, Mark. *The World's First Railway System: Enterprise, Competition, and Regulation on the Railway Network in Victorian Britain.* Oxford: Oxford University Press, 2009.

Cole, Beverley and Richard Durack. *Railway Posters, 1923–1947: From the Collection of the National Railway Museum, York, England.* New York: Rizzoli, 1992.

Damant, Scott. "Art in Railway Carriages." *Railway Magazine* (Feb. 1898): 158–164.

Daunton, Martin J., and Bernhard Rieger. "Introduction." *Meanings of Modernity: Britain from the Late-Victorian Era to World War II.* Eds. Martin Daunton and Bernhard Rieger. Oxford: Berg Publishers, 2001. 1–21.

Divall, Colin. "Transport, 1900–39." *A Companion to Early Twentieth-Century Britain.* Ed. Chris Wrigley. Oxford: Blackwell, 2003. 286–301.

Divall, Colin, and George Revill. "Cultures of Transport: Representation, Practice and Technology." *Journal of Transport History* 3rd ser. 26.1 (2005): 99–111.

Dow, Andrew. *Telling the Passenger Where to Get Off: George Dow and the Evolution of the Railway Diagrammatic Map.* Harrow: Capital Transport, 2005.

Duffy, Enda. *The Speed Handbook: Velocity, Pleasure, Modernism.* Durham: Duke University Press, 2009.

Esbester, Mike. "Designing Time: The Design and Use of Nineteenth-Century Transport Timetables." *Journal of Design History* 22.2 (2009): 91–113.

Featherstone, Mike. *Consumer Culture and Postmodernism.* London: Sage, 1991.

Findlay, George. *The Working and Management of an English Railway.* 5th ed. London: Whittaker & Co., 1894.

Ford, Roger. "Technology for the People." *The InterCity Story.* Eds. Chris E.W. Green and Mike Vincent. Sparkford: Oxford Publishing, 1994: 17–33.

Foxwell, Ernest. *English Express Trains: Two Papers.* London: Stanford, 1884. Originally published as "Express Trains—Rhapsody." *Macmillan's Magazine,* (Feb. 1883): 264–280.

———. *Express Trains, English and Foreign: Being a Statistical Account of All the Express Trains of the World with Railway Maps of Great Britain and Europe.* London: Smith, Elder & Co., 1889.

Freeman, Michael J. "Introduction." *Transport in Victorian Britain.* Eds. D. H. Aldcroft and Michael J. Freeman. Manchester: Manchester University Press, 1988: 1–56.

———. "Time and Space under Modernism: The Railway in D. H. Lawrence's *Sons and Lovers.*" *The Railway and Modernity: Time, Space and the Machine Ensemble.* Eds. Matthew Beaumont and Michael J. Freeman. Oxford: Peter Lang, 2007. 45–67.

Gaonkar, Dilip Parameshwar, ed. *Alternative Modernities.* Durham, N.C.: Duke University Press, 2001.

Garfield, Simon. *The Last Journey of William Huskisson.* London: Faber, 2002.

Giddens, Anthony. *The Consequences of Modernity.* Stanford, Calif.: Stanford University Press, 1990.

Gourvish, T. R. *British Railways, 1948–73: A Business History.* Cambridge, UK: Cambridge University Press, 1986.

———. "British Rail's "Business-Led" Organization, 1977–1990: Government-Industry Relations in Britain's Public Sector." *Business History Review* 64.1 (1990): 109–149.

Great Western Railway. *Streamline Way: Inauguration of Express Streamlined Rail Car Service between Birmingham and Cardiff, July 1934.* London: Great Western Railway, 1934.

Haresnape, Brian. *British Rail, 1948–83: A Journey by Design.* Shepperton: Ian Allan, 1979.

Harvey, David. *The Condition of Postmodernity: An Enquiry into the Origins of Cultural Change.* Oxford: Basil Blackwell, 1989.

Hermes. *Taxes on Travelling: Interview with Mr George Jacob Holyoake Reprinted from "Commerce."* London, 1899.

Jackson, Peter A., Michelle Lowe, Daniel Miller, and Frank Mort. "Introduction: Transcending Dualisms." *Commercial Cultures: Economies, Practices, Spaces.* Eds. Jackson, Lowe, Miller, and Mort. Oxford: Berg, 2000. 1–34.

Jeans, J. Stephen. *Railway Problems: An Inquiry into the Economic Conditions of Railway Working in Different Countries.* London: Longmans, Green and Co., 1887.

Jeremiah, David. "Motoring and the British Countryside." *Rural History* 21.2 (2010): 233–250.

Kern, Stephen. *The Culture of Time and Space, 1880–1918.* 2nd ed. Cambridge, Mass., USA; London, UK: Harvard University Press, 2003.

Kusamitsu, Toshio. "Great Exhibitions before 1851." *History Workshop* 9 (1980): 70–89.

Leunig, Tim. "Time Is Money: A Re-Assessment of the Passenger Social Savings from Victorian British Railways." *The Journal of Economic History* 66.3 (2006): 635–673.

Latour, Bruno. *We Have Never Been Modern.* New York: Harvester Wheatsheaf, 1993.

Lee, Charles Edward. *Passenger Class Distinctions.* London: Railway Gazette, 1946.

Light, Alison. *Forever England: Femininity, Literature, and Conservatism between the Wars.* London: Routledge, 1991.

Loft, Charles. *Government, the Railways, and the Modernization of Britain.* London: Routledge, 2006.

London & North Eastern Railway Company (LNER). *The Coronation.* London: LNER, 1937.

Massey, Doreen B. *For Space.* London: Sage, 2005.

McKean, Charles. *Battle for the North: The Tay and Forth Bridges and the 19th-Century Railway Wars.* London: Granta Books, 2006.

Mom, Gijs, Colin Divall, and Peter Lyth. "Towards a Paradigm Shift: A Decade of Transport and Mobility History." *Mobility in History: The State of the Art in the History of Transport, Traffic and Mobility.* Eds. G. Mom, G. H. Pirie, and Laurent Tissot. Neuchâtel, Switzerland: Éditions Alphil, 2009: 13–40.

Mullay, A. J. *Streamlined Steam: Britain's 1930s Luxury Expresses.* Newton Abbot: David & Charles, 1994.

Nash, Christopher. "BR's Tale of Two Trains." *High Speed Trains: Fast Tracks to the Future.* Eds. J. Whitelegg, Staffan Hultén, and Torbjörn Flink. Hawes, Yorkshire: Leading Edge, 1993: 78–88.

Nock, O. S. *The Railway Race to the North.* London: Ian Allan, 1959.

Potter, Stephen. "Managing high speed train projects." *High Speed Trains: Fast Tracks to the Future.* Eds. Whitelegg, Hultén, and Flink. Hawes, Yorkshire: Leading Edge, 1993. 145–161.

Revill, George. "Perception, Reception and Representation: Wolfgang Schivelbusch and the Cultural History of Travel and Transport." *Mobility in History: Reviews and Reflections.* Eds. P. Norton, G. Mom, L. Millward, and M. Flonneau. Neuchâtel, Switzerland: Éditions Alphil, 2011: 31–48.

Russell, Thomas. "Picturing the Product." *Advertising World* (Sep. 1924): 550.

Schivelbusch, Wolfgang. *The Railway Journey: The Industrialization of Time and Space in the 19th Century.* Oxford: Blackwell, 1980.

Self, Alan. "Streamlined Expresses of the LNER." *Design History, Fad or Function?* Ed. Terry Bishop. London: Design Council, 1978. 17–23.

Shin, Hiroki. "Business Strategy and Corporate Image: Britain's Railways, 1872–1977." *Railways as an Innovative Regional Factor.* Eds. Heli Mäki and Jenni Korjus. Helsinki: University of Helsinki, Palmenia Centre for Continuing Education and the City of Kouvola, 2009. 63–84.

Simmel, Georg. *The Philosophy of Money.* Ed. David Frisby. Trans. Tom Bottomore and David Frisby. 3rd ed. London: Routledge, 2004.

Simmons, Jack. *The Railway in England and Wales, 1830–1914,* vol. 1, *The System and Its Working.* Leicester: Leicester University Press, 1978.

——. *The Express Train and Other Railway Studies.* Nairn, Scotland: David St. John Thomas, 1994.

Smiles, Samuel. *The Life of George Stephenson Railway Engineer.* London: John Murray, 1857.

Strangleman, Tim. *Work Identity at the End of the Line?: Privatisation and Culture Change in the UK Rail Industry.* Houndsmill, Basingstoke: Palgrave Macmillan, 2004.

Thrift, Nigel. "Transport and Communication, 1730–1914." *An Historical Geography of England and Wales.* Eds. R. A. Butlin and Robert A. Dodgshon. 2nd ed. London: Academic, 1990: 454–486.

——. *Spatial Formations.* London: Sage, 1996.

Tomlinson, John. *The Culture of Speed the Coming of Immediacy.* London: Sage, 2007.

Trentmann, Frank. "Civilization and Its Discontents: English Neo-Romanticism and the Transformation of Anti-Modernism in Twentieth-Century Western Culture." *Journal of Contemporary History* 29.4 (1994): 583–625.

Trotter, David. *Circulation: Defoe, Dickens, and the Economies of the Novel.* Basingstoke, Hampshire: Macmillan, 1988.

Virilio, Paul. *Speed and Politics: An Essay on Dromology.* Trans. Mark Polizzotti. New York: Semiotext(e), 1986.

Watts, D. C. H. "Evaluating British Railway Poster Advertising: The London & North Eastern Railway between the Wars." *Journal of Transport History* 3rd ser. 25.2 (2004): 23–56.

Williamson, Philip. *Stanley Baldwin: Conservative Leadership and National Values.* Cambridge, UK: Cambridge University Press, 1999.

Chapter 2

The Speed of Signs

Train Graffiti, Cultural Production, and the Mobility of the Urban in France and Spain

Benjamin Fraser and Steven D. Spalding

"[T]o argue for the importance of materiality is in fact an argument for apprehending different relations and durations of movement, speed and slowness rather than simply a greater consideration of objects."

—Alan Latham and Derek McCormack ("Moving Cities," 705).

INTRODUCTION

Mobility studies examine the complex set of discourses, economies, and infrastructures governing the movement of individuals, capital, and resources in globalized late-capitalist societies. By analyzing the practice of graffiti and its various cultural valences in those societies, mobility studies has an opportunity to consider how graffiti dialogues with discourses of space and the attendant questions of territorial ownership, legitimacy and identity. Conversely, bringing the concerns of mobility studies to graffiti is an opportunity to re-assess the latter in a way that avoids the pratfalls its handling has encountered in the past. As we shall show, the literature on graffiti has too often displayed a disciplinary parochialism that the interdisciplinary nature of mobility studies can avoid. Scholarship has sought to freeze or capture graffiti in a gesture of figurative "arrest" that ignores the material context of graffiti's production and strips it of one of its greatest critical assets, its posture of critique with respect to the production, movement, circulation and even disappearance of signs in the contemporary political economy.

In the first section of this chapter, we consider what graffiti art means in the context of French culture and point to ways in which both French theory on the one hand, and the French practice and reception of graffiti on the other, have important contributions to make to a mobility studies approach to graffiti. Imported from abroad, graffiti inherited a French legacy of resistance and revolt, as shown in the popular culture by the cult film *La Haine* and in the French political imagination by Chris Marker's documentary, *Chats perchés*. Also, though little scholarly literature on graffiti exists in French (cf. the work of Martine Lani-Bayle and Alain Milon), graffiti shares sympathies with certain strains of French thought. Since contemporary world graffiti largely got its start in New York City, looking at the meanings American graffiti scholars—as well as writers themselves—gave to New York train graffiti in the late '60s and early '70s, when graffiti was on the verge of going global, helps understand its welcome in France. Next, despite frequent reference to the work of Jacques Derrida in the literature on graffiti, we suggest why the writings of Gilles Deleuze, Félix Guattari, and Paul Virilio form a compelling set of theoretical concerns to bring to bear in reading graffiti. Because of their common interest in an ontology of movement, Deleuze and Guattari and Virilio offer complementary elements of a hermeneutics of mobility. This in turn can help inform a more supple grasp of the complexity of graffiti's place in the cityscape. The upshift from French political slogans and graffiti written on the "murmuring walls" of Paris to the tagging of its suburban trains connects the fundamentally oppositional origins of graffiti writing with the nexus of theoretical questions raised by the mobility of the train: what does it mean to put graffiti into movement in the contemporary city? A literal and figural lifeline of cities, commuter rail networks both produce the city and are produced by it. Due to the critical nature of the mobility flows these networks support they play a crucial role in the daily production of the symbolic orders structuring the contemporary *polis*. By troubling those orders, train graffiti causes them to stand out, and creates a unique space of counter-movement that underscores the viewer's own trajectories of speed in the city.

The second section of this chapter delves further into both the philosophical ground of mobility studies and also the literature concerning the production of urban space. In the wake of the emerging "mobility turn" in research (Hannam, Sheller & Urry), non-representational perspectives (Thrift) suggest a new way of reading the city as text. Whereas previous approaches to the city as text have focused on the static, representational capacity of cityspace (notably Barthes)—effectively equating the fabric of the city with the artistic canvas—the act of placing movement prior to signification changes the nature of this type of investigation. As the critical literature on reading the city as a text (i.e., Barthes; de Certeau; Harvey) passes into its third decade, it is important to maintain this important tradition by reconciling it with the recent heightened awareness of the urban as a mobile phenomenon.

As Kevin Hannam, Mimi Sheller, and John Urry (2006) explored in their introductory editorial to the inaugural issue of the journal *Mobilities*, a "mobility turn" in research is emerging.[1] Investigation of mobile urban processes necessarily takes on a multi- and even interdisciplinary character grounded in the intersection of such fields as sociology, geography, economics, tourism studies, and so on. Yet, as the authors go on to argue, in addition to highlighting mobilities as the subject of research, this turn also requires a more mobile method to accompany and subtend such investigation. Significantly, this emerging "mobility turn," while emphasizing the intersection of the various disciplines in the social sciences, has not yet fully recognized the role that humanities scholarship can and should play in the investigation of mobile phenomena. In addition to shedding light on the complex philosophical debates at the core of this methodology (e.g., Fraser "Publicly-Private"; "Manuel Delgado's"), humanities scholarship is in a position to renew interest in the notion of textuality as it relates to city life. Maintaining continuity with the emphasis on French thinkers, we turn to the Spanish context in order to make the argument that graffiti encourages a more mobile approach to urban realities. In its emphasis on temporal process, the ephemeral and even enigma, the study of train graffiti underscores what urban theorists from De Certeau to Lefebvre and Harvey have recognized as fundamental tools in our approach to reading the city.

The goal of this chapter is thus to stake out a claim regarding the contribution of humanities scholarship in the context of mobility starting from the graffiti found on urban trains. Departing from previous analyses of graffiti as a static text to be read, we believe that train graffiti, as legibility in motion, suggests new ways of understanding the city in terms of movement and speed. Just as the "mobility turn" seeks to reconcile various disciplines, here we also seek to intertwine literature with the social sciences, to fuse the acts of reading and writing in a variegated method focusing on mobility, and also to join the Spanish and French contexts. Paying more attention to the art of train graffiti as a mobile urban phenomenon provides a way to recalibrate our approach to the urban itself, envisioning signification as an inherently mobile process and escaping from a static paradigm of cityspace.

FRANCE: IDENTIFYING WITH THE CITY, GRAFFITI AS NOMADIC PRACTICE

Any study of graffiti within a national context begins on shaky ground, due to the international dimensions of the graffiti movement. Graffiti, and its close relative street art are global cultural phenomena, so it is risky to talk of uniquely French or Spanish graffiti art. However, this is one of the very reasons why graffiti and street art are of such enormous pertinence and interest to mobility studies: in its greatly varying forms in city after city, graffiti always already bespeaks the transnational mobility of culture in the contemporary period. That mobility in turn points to the ease with which graffiti has been and continues to be identified as a relevant mode of expression in urban and suburban locales across the globe, able to give voice to types of meanings that individuals have sought to create locally. Graffiti's translatability and apparent inherence to urban environments worldwide is made all the more interesting by its ephemeral nature. Graffiti artists consistently talk of how important it is to see other writers' work, and thus to be constantly moving about the urban environment observing and participating in the work of other writers, and making as much of their own work as possible.[2] No one knows how long a "tag" or "piece" will stay up before being removed. The threat of removal from spaces not designated for such use—which are the very spaces writers prize the most and vie for visibility in—is constant. Except in unusual circumstances, graffiti does not last; and—and this is a defining element of graffiti and train graffiti—its artists do not intend that it should. Graffiti is akin to artistic movements that have rejected institutionalization outright, or at least made a spectacle of feigning to do so, such as the Dada, Surrealist, and Pop Art movements. By its choice of medium, graffiti is largely ensured of its own erasure and is prevented from being commodified into any economy of artistic consumption. Instead, it relies on its translation into other media— video and photography—for anything resembling duration, a highly mediated fixity that underscores its own status as trace of an event. An underground circulation of filmed footage allows writers to show off their exploits, to highlight their audacity in sneaking into train depots and writing on train cars right below the unsuspecting eye of railway personnel.[3] Graffiti photographed and filmed shows what was produced on this spot, once, and in their inability to pass on the effect of the original work photographs are doomed to disappoint traditional aesthetics. In this, graffiti represents a considerable departure from traditional aesthetical and representational norms.

Graffiti is in part an imported cultural phenomenon, and its imported nature speaks of the global circulation of cultures and even sub- or counter-cultures; as such, graffiti must be recognized as a hybrid form. Furthermore, graffiti is a form of expression with an expiration date, largely enjoying a brief existence followed by oblivion. Still, graffiti has special valence in French culture in particular. Carrie Noland has cited some of the reasons why this is so. The cave walls at Lascaux suggest a long-enduring artistic practice of spatial adornment that, taken anachronistically, lends itself almost seamlessly to parallels with graffiti writing. Such parallels result in one's viewing graffiti as a contemporary equivalent of that "primitive" artistic gesture. Indeed, in her article, Noland identifies an analogous treatment of space in the wall paintings at Lascaux and in contemporary graffiti, as both in her view effectuate a layering of space that expands it, multiplying planes of surfaces and suspending viewers' attempts to arrive at a totalized, unified view of the whole. Certain problems do arise from considering Lascaux as a "palimpsest" (305) of contemporary graffiti, however, and Noland's argument showcases one of the dangers of approaching graffiti from the perspective of Derridean "écriture." In following the famous Derridean assertion that "there is no 'outside-the-text'" one is tempted to see everything as text, and from this position one risks eliding critical ontological and phenomenological considerations (Derrida, 158). The context informing viewership of contemporary graffiti—especially with respect to the hip-hop- or gang-related American graffiti Noland refers to before discussing the French—is complex and multi-layered, rich with effects that are inextricable from racial, political, and economic discourses that shape the post-industrial urban cityscape. The cave walls of Lascaux anticipate the city street, the walls of the Paris Métro, the vacant lots of derelict urban and suburban zones, billboards, the sides of buses and trains, and so forth, in only the most abstract of senses. If only by dint of their long survival the cave paintings of Lascaux anticipate the walls of the modern museum much better; though until recently their survival had been more an accident of history than the result of any organized effort at preservation.

Neither the cave paintings of Lascaux nor contemporary graffiti demand their own preservation, and this trait common to each points to another danger of the Derridean perspective: an obsession with permanence. While citing research on gang graffiti, Noland underscores the conclusion drawn from that work that graffiti "cannot ensure territorial boundaries in any permanent way, even within the economy of gang behavior" (312). When Noland identifies the "practices of superimposition and supplementation" involved in graffiti writing she is taking the problematics of Derrida's *supplément*—first written about in his *On Grammatology*, in an essay on Rousseau—and inserting it into a very different context. Derrida's logic of the supplement points out the fallacies of privileging presence and the spoken word over the written; presence acts as a supplement which, though meant to serve as guarantor of effective communication, invariably fails, merely pointing up the inability of any form of supplement to perfect the flawed nature of linguistic communication. Inasmuch as graffiti represents a form of expression which at best is only casually interested in duration the use of the supplement to characterize the interplay between writers, crews, and even gangs brings a set of theoretical concerns that have little currency in the economy of graffiti art.[4] Alternatively,

by viewing Lascaux as a distant precursor rather than as a palimpsest of contemporary graffiti, a different parallel emerges, one that points to thematics
which are more directly a preoccupation of graffiti and which circumscribe
its literal and symbolic place within its (urban) environment. The men and
animals in motion on the walls of Lascaux prefigure the fundamental relationship between graffiti and movement, mobility, and speed.

There is a cultural heritage closer to the contemporary period than Lascaux
that has a greater claim on the attention of graffiti scholars than the caves: the
walls of the subway lines of New York City. New York, the acknowledged
birthplace of contemporary graffiti, also saw the first train graffiti beginning
in the late '60s (Chalfant & Prigoff).[5] As Wimsatt has asserted, graffiti spread
along with hip-hop, rap, and other subcultures to most American cities and,
later, around the world in several waves (134–137 and infra.). Unlike most
French scholarship on graffiti, scholars studying graffiti in New York have
tended primarily to approach the phenomenon as a symptom of some urban
"problem," whether psychological, sociological, or political in nature. It has
taken a second generation of criticism for a more objective eye and ear to be
brought to bear on graffiti in New York, and for the writers' own voices to
be heard. Furthermore, with the notable exception of Miller (2002), few have
looked specifically at train graffiti as a special practice in any way different
from other forms of graffiti writing, with the result that train graffiti becomes
again essentially fixed, viewed as a tableau, its motion arrested. In Miller's
treatment, the train holds exceptional symbolic valences for the graffiti writers. For them, their practice cannot be dissociated from the kinetic properties
of the train, its ability to go everywhere, suggesting that train graffiti is not to
be viewed in static terms.

In a chapter titled "Night Train: The Power That Man Made," Miller argues
that there is a compelling hagiography at the origins of subway train graffiti
in New York and discusses the unique significance of the subway train for
African-American writers from that city's ghettoes. Through interviews with
train writers, Miller reveals the complexity of the writers' relation to the train:
the gesture of writing a train is partly an intricate identification with the train
itself, and partly an homage to an imagined vital force the train possesses.
Further, the train's mobility makes it a privileged site of identification with
the city, an imagined totality otherwise too expansive, too fragmented to contain. For some of the writers Miller interviewed, train writing followed from a
long-held fascination for the universe of the subway train, one of energy and
movement. That universe figures for the city as a whole: one writer speaks
lyrically "of those electric beams running down for miles underground, all
that power in the city, the energy of an antibody in a subway. All of that
energy down underground was like a magnet [. . .] My mentality was shaped

by that energy, the power; the transit, the gamble, the look (fashion), the entire situation" (90). Train graffiti here is an organic grafting onto/graphing the city as social body, an interaction imaginatively situated within its very veins and arteries. Marking trains is leaving one's mark—through the train's mobility—on the social landscape as a whole.

Miller goes on to describe the Yoruba divinity named Ògún, god of iron and patron of blacksmiths, and traces the cultural path of this spiritual figure through from West Africa via the former slave-holding islands of the Caribbean into communities of blue-collar African American and Caribbean populations in New York and its boroughs. In the course of that displacement along the routes of the slave trade—as well as along those of the colonial infrastructures in Africa—Ògún and its power became associated with the iron tools slaves were made to work with and the chains they wore, and later, with the railways and trains they built (92–93). This identification of Ògún with the train connects the latter with both the historical legacy of slavery and exploitation, and with a divine source of power to be drawn upon. Citing descendants of West African cultures in Cuba, for instance, Miller writes: "Enslaved by the very symbols of European progress, the trains and the mills, Lukumi and Kongo peoples used their knowledge of Ògún and Zarabanda to harness its power for their liberation, the breaking of shackles, defense from machetes, and protection from machines" (93). Indeed, some writers believed they worked under the protection of Ògún when they wrote trains (94). Via this mythology the act of train writing becomes inexorably linked with the histories of industrialization, colonization, and the relationships of power, subjugation and resistance that are the legacies of those histories.

Of course, one does not need to look to Santeria for political meanings behind graffiti in New York City: especially in the '60s and '70s race and class politics were central to both the writing of graffiti and the public discourse that grew out of it. In the following quote one writer captures the unique importance of the train to the politics of graffiti writing:

> I identify with the subways as more than just a subway. Maybe because I know that they, just as we, were neglected. Subways are corporate America's way of getting its people to work. It's used as an object of transporting corporate clones. And the trains were clones themselves, they were all supposed to be silver blue, a form of imperialism and control. And we took that and completely changed it. We brought life to them with our paintings. The trains reflected the lives of the painters who were coming up to their sides in the middle of the night. And through us they lived, they came to life! (109)

As graffiti migrated cross-country and abroad, as it traveled with hip-hop and related subcultures into other cities and suburbs, its politics became more diffuse, in the image of its diversifying population of writers. Though it retained the cachet of an expression of political and cultural resistance, despite the best efforts of writers like Wimsatt—whose brilliant graffiti manifesto is very revealingly titled *Bomb the Suburbs!*—its meanings were destined to change. In following graffiti as it migrates into French culture, it will be important to consider how these valences do just that within the new context.

In *Graffiti World: Street Art from Five Continents*, the first of his two large-scale omnibuses of graffiti art, Nicholas Ganz claims that "[n]ationality, race, and sex have no bearing on the graffiti scene" (7; see also Ganz, *Graffiti Women*). Less a keen critical observation about graffiti than an expression that captures the idealism and wishful thinking of many of its supporters, Ganz's assertion speaks to the problem of globalization for local cultures. In an eagerness to imagine graffiti as a pure, universal, truly democratic or "free" *world* art—*the* graffiti scene—in which all that counts is the value of the work itself, Ganz may want to cast graffiti as an antidote to a rigid, institutionalized art *world* that constrains or brakes grassroots expression. But by abstracting nationality, race, and gender Ganz risks abstracting the very grassroots nature of that expression and inoculating its political and social inscriptions. Indeed, as one browses the beautiful, glossy pages of Ganz's compendium, in which a photo of a tagged Paris RER train is followed by that of a graff on a Tokyo wall, the experience becomes more and more akin to reading a coffee-table art book. The artwork is extraordinary; the city is lost into a kind of world urban. Furthermore, according to the writer biographies provided in the book, many of the European writers are professional graphic artists, which attests to the significant transformation in class status among graffiti writers. Ultimately, Ganz's book reflects the reality that at the same time as graffiti has migrated through channels of globalization into local cultures, it has also begun to fashion a globe-trotting, cosmopolitan, parallel art world for itself. A recurring theme in the writer biographies, for instance, is the pilgrimage to New York or Los Angeles to write in those spaces, and alongside those writers, as an integral rite of passage. This particular graffiti world seems destined to ensnare itself in the same problems as the "normal" art world, particularly in the necessity to inscribe distinctions: for instance, which artists get chosen for reproduction in Ganz's omnibuses, and why? When does graffiti cease to be graffiti, and become a potentially commodifiable art object? Does a graffiti artist ever become "just" an artist, and if so, when? The publication of *Graffiti Women*, Ganz's second volume of graffiti photographs seeks, by the author's admission, to "rectify [the] oversight" that has let women's graffiti go unnoticed, and is an important step toward redressing the naïveté of the author's previous assertion (Ganz, 10).

If gender is a meaningful distinction for graffiti, what happens when we look at nationality? Contemporary graffiti in France dates from the early '80s, begun by a small number of writers putting up tags and pieces on the bridges and quays of the Seine in the center of Paris. In *Writers, 1983–2003: 20 ans de graffiti à Paris*, these early founders of "the movement" cite several international influences that spurred graffiti along in the city, none more important than New York. Writers traveled to and from New York, generating legitimacy for the graffiti movement in France and helping to define its "European Style."[6] Several well-publicized events later in that decade lent notoriety to the phenomenon, such as the painting of replicas of art objects in the Louvre Metro station in Paris.[7] While events such as this one likely did little to enamor Parisians of graffiti and its writers, there are important precedents in French cultural history that help to understand why it has tended to be largely tolerated and appreciated in France.[8] To the extent that graffiti is read—correctly or not—as an expression of revolt, it finds support from the French political left. Indeed, in the French cultural imaginary the graffiti writer has something of a romantic, heroic lineage, one that merges with the cultural legacies of the populist revolutions of the nineteenth century, the Resistance and, most importantly, the political and social revolution of May 1968. To discount the weight of this cultural heritage in the perception of graffiti in contemporary France is to limit oneself to the ultimately useless debate—regularly recycled in mass media worldwide—about whether graffiti is good or bad.

The cultural legacy of popular revolt lingers in the Parisian cityscape to this day. When the Ancien Régime undertook construction of the infamous Wall of the Farmers-General around Paris in the eighteenth century—which spawned the famous line "The wall walling Paris keeps Paris murmuring"—it was recognized to be a means of asserting economic control of the city and generated considerable ill-will (Victor Hugo borrowed the popular saying to incorporate it into his *Notre Dame de Paris*, 149). With the overthrow of the monarchy during the French Revolution, much of the wall, too, was toppled. The songs, banners, slogans, and pamphlets of the 1848 French Revolution and the Paris Commune in 1871 were written in the city, were put on view for Parisians on the city's walls. When Nazi Germany occupied France in 1940, the French Resistance went underground, and exploited the large network of catacombs, tunnels, and galleries beneath Paris to circulate beyond the control of the police. In 1968, the youth uprisings spawned a prolific production of posters, slogans, and other artwork and political graffiti painted on the walls of the Latin Quarter. In each of these instances, streets were torn up and walls demolished to form barricades, block circulation, and disrupt state control. This heritage is of two-fold importance: it encourages one to read the otherwise functional elements of the cityscape as potential modes of control, and to read their deformation, whether through graffiti or something else, as an expression of resistance. This hermeneutical posture is analogous to what the Situationists identified in the poetry of Rimbaud by the term "détourne-ment," deflection or re-appropriation, and sought to do through language by taking dominant words, clichés and images and breaking them from their given meanings. (See the issues of the group's journal, *Internationale Situationniste*, republished in 1997; Paris: Fayard.) Indeed, much of the French literary and artistic avant-garde in the twentieth century, from Surrealism to New Realism, called for practices that would re-create "everyday life" in ways that expose and disrupt its ideological discourses.

The practice and reception of graffiti writing in France inevitably summons this cultural legacy. Two contemporary French films show in very strikingly different ways how the city walls are still murmuring, now with graffiti. Mathieu Kassovitz's 1995 film *La Haine* (*Hate*) brought the troubles of Paris's marginalized suburbs into the center of the city and onto the movie screen in dramatic, even controversial fashion. In addition to a scene analyzed below in which one of the film's characters creates a *détournement* with graffiti, graffiti informs the very style with which *La Haine* was shot and edited. The film's abrupt editing, in turns fast and slow camera movements, with highly stylized angles and sequences, mirror what was considered an aesthetic of "youth culture" in its time but that has since pervaded much of popular culture. The film owes as much to the bold and stylized aesthetic of graffiti as it does to Quentin Tarantino and MTV.

The film follows the adventures of three youths, Vinz, Saïd, and Hubert— each representing a different ethnic group largely marginalized by mainstream French society—on a journey from the Parisian *banlieues* into the city and back, against a backdrop of suburban rioting based on events that unfolded in the early '90s. (The film also eerily seems to foretell the events of November 2005.) Vinz, played by Vincent Cassel, has recovered a policeman's revolver, and much of the film's drama is centered on whether he will use it to exact revenge for the police brutality which injured a friend and, we learn late in the film, has caused his death. Saïd is an amiable character, not aggressive like Vinz; indeed, he is not interested in "evening the score" with the police. Next to the threat of rash violence from Vinz, and the cool intensity of the subdued, calm Hubert, Saïd is the jokester. It is no surprise, then, that in stark opposition to Vinz's finding and carrying a weapon, in the latter part of the film Saïd finds and carries a spray can. Saïd is no less thoughtful than Vinz as to when to use his "weapon": in the film's unique graffiti-writing scene, the three main characters are walking the streets of Paris—in a space, therefore, that is not their own, as *banlieusards* often made to feel quite unwelcome in the city—and pass in front of a billboard advertisement that seeks to flatter its target audience with the assertion that "Le Monde est à Vous" ("The World Is Yours"). In a quick gesture, Saïd covers over the V and sprays an N, giving "Nous" ("Us") and altering the sign to read "The World is Ours". Saïd's *détournement* is canny because it disrupts the consumerist message of the billboard to introduce an "us," and in so doing presents an oppositional discourse that will divide those who view the billboard thereafter between those sympathetic to the "us" and those not. This amounts to "graffing" class and identity politics onto consumerism, or at least to pointing out that they were already there. On one level, the "we" of Saïd's message denotes those who would deface such a billboard, those who would write graffiti; on another, it makes an appeal to viewers who sympathize with the rejection of the advertisement's crass message. For viewers of the film, of course, the gesture's meaning is clear, and at the ironic spectacle of the dispossessed claiming possession we are left to wonder if indeed the world does belong to those who participate in the economy of the billboard's former message rather than those who identify with the latter.

By having Saïd, not either of the other two characters, make this idealistic statement in graffiti, the film lends a certain genial image to graffiti writers: that of a benevolent, even naive trickster. His *détournement* turns the ad slogan into a political slogan that solicits viewers to think about the divisions between "us" and "them" that inhabit and are sustained by the city walls—real or virtual. In his documentary video *Chats Perchés* (2004, *The Case of the Grinning Cat*), influential filmmaker Chris Marker goes on the trail of a graffito that persistently rears its head in video footage taken of demonstrations, rallies and marches in Paris in the politically turbulent first years of the current decade. Marker's musings about the cat graffiti and their remarkable presence throughout the cityscape explore connections between the graffiti and social protest and popular expression. As much as *La Haine*, Marker's film conveys a very sympathetic reading of graffiti, at least in this particular manifestation; because it is a film about a specific set of graffiti, *Chats Perchés* is able to put on display a willingness to preserve the essentially unreadable aspect of the graffiti while weighing possible modes of interpretation. The grinning cat of the title turns up everywhere as Marker records the movements of social revolt occupying the streets of the city. Its clever insinuation into the public sphere as a symbolic presence—a kind of detached observer, social conscience, or muse, watching over the marches and demonstrations—is rightly beguiling for Marker, and his meditations as to its meaning are pertinent and compelling. Marker's film is of interest for two reasons: first, Marker performs a reading of graffiti that encapsulates French sympathies for it, at least on the political left—sympathies that have a long history. Secondly, *Chats Perchés* substitutes omnipresence for mobility, for although the cats are not mobile—they merely occupy wall space—they do not need to be. Their omnipresence in the cityscape, in high spots and low ones, on sidewalks and roofs, on T-shirts and picket signs, afforded them a unique ability to circulate in the city virtually.

These examples taken from recent cultural history and popular culture depict the appeal graffiti has in French political fantasy, and help explain its welcome into a cultural heritage of political expression. However, the way graffiti is written—and read—in these examples, runs the risk of circum-scribing graffiti's scope to that of political action and the pursuit of specific political ends. In Deleuze and Guattari's critique of capitalism, elaborated in the two volumes of *Capitalism and Schizophrenia*, and in Virilio's various inquiries into the logistics of speed and mobility in modern political history, there are elements of a typology of agency that can better take account of the meanings of graffiti in the city.

In *A Thousand Plateaus*, Deleuze and Guattari put forth a set of concepts to describe systems—or "regimes"—of signs, various types of forces that operate within them, as well as different ways in which such forces operate. Two pairs of concepts recur in their abstract typology of orders that are of particular interest here, as they offer a new way of framing graffiti that can resist, for a time at least, its reduction to political binaries. In the section of *A Thousand Plateaus* entitled "1227: Treatise on Nomadology—the War Machine," Deleuze and Guattari posit the existence of the nomad, a figure of pure movement, and of the war machine, which they describe as sharing many properties of the nomad (351–453). Both are defined in terms of their fundamental relation to absolute movement (although Deleuze and Guattari come to the conclusion that "only nomads have absolute movement, in other words, speed," 381); both are external to forces of control, such as appara-tuses of state, state logics, state sciences: "It is not enough to affirm that the war machine is external to the apparatus. It is necessary to reach the point of conceiving the war machine as itself a pure form of exteriority, whereas the State apparatus constitutes the form of interiority [. . .] according to which we are in the habit of thinking" (354). As the nomad and the war machine share an exteriority to state forms of order, both are related to the same side of the second pair of concepts, namely "smooth space" and "striated space."[9] Deleuze and Guattari refer to the differences between the games of go and chess as an analogy for the opposition between smooth and striated (353). In their perpetual work of coding urban space for maximum efficiency, order, and the exercise of control, apparatuses of state push out smooth space in favor of striated. Meanwhile, by dint of their exteriority and through their privileged relation to mobility and speed, the nomad and the nomadic war machine are able to disrupt that striation, and turn an environment defined by its utilitarian purposes into a mere support for something else (381).

To cast the graffiti artist as a contemporary form of Deleuze and Guattari's nomad may be the best way to problematize the question of agency and distinguish between those artists who are motivated solely by the breaking of taboos or social rebellion and those who are driven by a nomad-like exteriority, who graff on their own terms and for their own terms. In their definition of war machines, Deleuze and Guattari assert that they can be appropriated and instrumentalized by the state apparatuses; this is how war machines can transform into military institutions (355). So, too, do graffiti artists risk such instrumentalization: by terming their activity as part of a war against the police for instance, they risk accelerating the implementation of further modes of control. Inasmuch as graffiti is most often associated with youth rebellion, rhetoric of "war" is evidenced on all sides (see Yakhlef and Doriath, 40). In turn, such appropriation by state discourses of control would ensure that graffiti art never be really seen as anything other than the sign of an enemy.

Viewed as a nomadic form of representation, graffiti stands a better chance of asserting its exteriority and re-injecting difference into the striated urban environment. Considered from this perspective, the graffiti found on the sides of Parisian subway and commuter trains becomes especially potent: commuter trains with elaborate lettering, abstract shapes and labyrinthine forms running their entire length become something other than merely utilitarian. They present the eye with excess, spillover, jarring colors and highly ramified designs. By capturing the gaze for a single extra moment, the outside logic of graffiti can successfully have asserted itself. The exteriority of graffiti is already very present in the language of French graffiti artists; Bando, for example, at the end of *Writers, 1983–2003: 20 ans de graffiti à Paris*, insists that graffiti "concerns only those who make it; others shouldn't even look." A nomadic practice, graffiti must not be reduced to punctual political goals or predictable Oedipal triangles of rebellion, but rather must constantly redefine the parameters of smooth space within its own realm of representation.

The work of Paul Virilio has had moments of fame outside of France, but has nonetheless been largely overshadowed by the other major figures of French theory. Mobility studies may result in renewed interest in Virilio's work, as they share common central concerns, including how the accelerations of modernity have re-shaped daily life. To highlight the originality of what his thought brings to the question of train graffiti, we point to two critical Virilian concepts. First, his notion of the "dromocracy"—and the concomitant call for a "dromology"—situates the problem of circulation, movement and speed at the core of political and social history. Our understanding of the contemporary state, the rise of cities, and the control and administration of territories must acknowledge the salient importance of the harnessing and deployment of speed. Second, Virilio's thinking about technologies of vision argues for the existence of an economy of perception in which incursions into the visual field are unauthorized, illegitimate, and swiftly eliminated— and their authors punished. As a figure for—and site of—the "dromocratic revolution" the train is a particularly interesting context in which to consider a Virilian reading of graffiti.

Very much akin to the conceptual models of the state and the war machine elaborated in *A Thousand Plateaus* by Deleuze and Guattari, Virilio casts the state itself as a machine that has always first and foremost been preoccupied with the logistics of mobility, ever focused on increasing the speed of certain flows (movement of capital) and slowing or stopping others (city as fortress). In Virilio's view, the technologies and logistics of the state quickly migrate from the battlefield to the city, to become the modalities with which the state sustains a "permanent assault" on capital, labor, and the landscape (*Speed*, 86). The dromocracy, therefore, is in a constant state of war. Foremost among the modalities with which the permanent war is waged are the elements of a logistics of perception, the production and ordering of the "industrialization of vision" (*Vision*, 59). Control of what is seen in the dromocracy has only increased as technology has begun to flatten the city's geography into the screen of the surveillance camera.

> This makes the decisive new importance of the "logistics of perception" clearer, as well as accounting for the secrecy that continues to surround it. It is a war of images and sounds, rather than objects and things, in which winning is simply a matter of not losing sight of the opposition. The will to see all, to know all, at every moment, everywhere, the will to universalised illumination: a scientific permutation on the eye of God which would forever rule out the surprise, the accident, the irruption of the unforeseen. (*Vision*, 70)

In the Virilian war of images the battle is for control of what is seen; in the transit system, the graffiti war is over control of the traveler's field of vision, control of what images the train can make available to the mobile flâneur-voyeur. The train offers passengers a unique, *experiential* vision of the city: how travelers see the city from the platform and from the train cannot be dissociated from their experience of movement. The potency and symbolic importance of this combination lends the train a unique iconic place in the dromocracy's economy of representation, and ensures that the traveler's experience of train perception will be a highly regulated cinematic event.

The Paris Metro has become as iconographically meaningful as any of the monuments of more directly national significance dotting the Parisian cityscape, and representations of Paris never fail to incorporate a Metro train car or the signature Belle Epoque ironwork of a station entrance. Among the loops of early documentary film footage compiled in *Paris 1900*, for instance, one finds an extraordinary sequence filmed from a Metro train car as it crosses over the Seine west of the Eiffel Tower (Védrès).[10] As much as the Baudelairean flâneur could "write" the city of Paris on foot in the nineteenth century, his twentieth- and twenty-first-century equivalents stand out through their deployment of a "battery" of means of transportation, from the car, train, and bus to even the bicycle, using "Vélib," the city's new low-cost bicycle rental system. Like their pedestrian ancestor, the contemporary flâneurs are writer-recorders of the spaces they traverse, and the city is ever more inseparable from, ever more defined by the means with which it is traversed. The Metro sequence in *Paris 1900* captures the new frame, the new screen through which the train traveler henceforth sees the city: the train car window. Virilio's focus on the politics of perception and mobility in the dromocracy urges us to consider the political dimensions of the train car window, which is at once the setting of a logistics of perception and the battleground over control of that perception.

In an economy of signs where the train's field of vision is part and parcel of the city offered up to the consumption of the contemporary flâneur, graffiti is a mischievous interruption, a tear in the sleekness of the city's cinematic representation, and hence is not a mere "accident" but rather an act of symbolic violence. Graffiti visible from the train car window can distort the traveler's perception of the landscape, disrupt and frustrate his or her vision, and misdirect the eye. Painted on top of billboards, graffiti vandalizes and mocks the commercialization of urban space. Sprayed on barriers that section off industrial areas and on walls destined to hide certain "zones" from the traveler's perception, graffiti fills spaces meant to stay empty, invisible, thereby revealing them. Written virtually everywhere, and fast, graffiti proliferates names in a mad parody of the naming and mapping underpinning the apportionment of territories and the distribution and circulation of economic and symbolic capital. Scratched into the train car window itself, graffiti overlays an often labyrinthine visual field on top of the landscape moving past, literally blinding the traveler, thereby foregrounding the very conditions of train perception and frustrating the Godlike will to see with which the train flatters passengers. In the dromocracy's bid for control of the cityscape screen, graffiti signals the trace of an opposition, a graphic reminder of the permanent war over perception in the polis.

Deleuze and Guattari and Virilio offer intersecting elements of a hermeneutics of the city that puts movement, circulation, and mobility at its core. The movements of the nomadic figure within and without the sign regimes of the city are endowed with an alterity able to produce unforeseen, even accidental interruptions within the visual fields of the cityscape and the lines of vision afforded by the train. A special form of *détournement*, train graffiti finds its origins in relations to and of mobility—the prehistoric cave paintings of hunted animals in flight, protests against obstacles to mobility in Paris, the New York writers thriving on the energy of the subway train's movement, so forth—and brings a form of reflexivity to the mobile passenger's gaze, underscoring rough edges in the dromocracy.

SPAIN: TRAIN GRAFFITI, URBAN MOBILITY AND REPRESENTATION

"El graffiti es una forma de vida, un modo de expresión . . . y mancharte las manos de pintura. Mi afán es la creatividad, intentar cosas diferentes. Hacer un tren es distinto, es adrenalina y el reto, no algo artístico o por el placer de pintar."

[“Graffiti is a way of life, a manner of expression . . . and of staining your hands with paint. My desire is to create, to attempt different things. To do a train is different, it is adrenaline and the challenge of it, not something artistic or done for the pleasure of painting.”][11]

Although graffiti has received increased attention, critics have been slow to articulate its deeper resonance with a set of methodological practices of thinking the city. It has been largely evoked as a representation of political identities (McCormick & Jarman; Lamireau; García-Pabón; Genovese; Oliver & Steinberg; Chaffee; Sanchez-Tranquilino; Kim; Hernández) or alternately even as government propaganda (Grieb), while ethnographic research has explored the subculture and terminology of graffiti artists (Gauthier "Confessions," "Writing"; Cooper and Chalfant; Vigara Tauste; Reyes Sánchez) as well as their relationship to music (Milon & Whidden; Trigo). In still other contexts, critics have espoused the benefits of using graffiti in the classroom as realia and as a model of affective writing (Calvin; Edbauer). In Spain, as elsewhere, representational explorations of graffiti have tended to assert its artistic value, leading to the common metaphor of the city as an art gallery (“Las paredes de la ciudad son también una galería de arte [the city walls are also an art gallery],” Delgado Fenoy), thus building implicitly on a metaphor that is common, also, to the world of urban design itself. Nevertheless, it behooves us to remember Jane Jacobs's remark in her monumental work *The Death and Life of Great American Cities* (1961) that “*A city cannot be a work of art*” (original emphasis, 372). Jacobs herself, argued for viewing the city as a complex problem akin to the life-sciences (433). She coined the phrase "sidewalk ballet" to describe the irreducible and multivalent activity of the city streets and opposed this basic complexity to the overly rational approaches of traditional city planning in a modern tradition going back to Ebenezer Howard. Yet although she relies on artistic metaphors in order to communicate the fluid, ever-changing nature of city life, Jacobs is far from approaching the city itself as art (above, 372). Thus she denounces an artistic and representational view of the city many have underscored or taken for granted. If we are to understand graffiti as an urban phenomenon (as Diego suggests is necessary), we must reject the purportedly representational and static character of graffiti itself just as we reject the static views of the urban as an artistic canvas that critics such as Jacobs rail against.[12]

It is significant that prominent urban critics, who by and large have been unconcerned with graffiti itself, have nevertheless articulated a vision of the city that resonates with the urban art form's qualities of ephemerality, movement and enigma, dispensing with the static view of traditional representation. Earlier accounts of the city-text, such as the structuralist analyses that figure in Roland Barthes's mythological project, were largely static in nature. In his famous discussion of the view of the city from atop the Eiffel Tower he notes that it "permits us to transcend sensation and to see things *in their structure*" (9, original emphasis). "[T]o the marvelous mitigation of altitude the panoramic vision added an incomparable power of *intellection*: the bird's-eye view, which each visitor to the Tower can assume in an instant for his own, gives us the world to *read* and not only to perceive; this is why it corresponds to a new sensibility of vision" (9, original emphasis). Reading the city as text was initially a matter of positionality, one of structure, ultimately one of space. Gazing out on the city, the view of the tourist coincides with the photographic mechanism and effectively stops time to allow us to possess the city as a static snapshot. Susan Sontag noted in her epic work *On Photography* that "One can't possess reality, one can possess (and be possessed by) images" (163). And yet, as de Certeau and Harvey were to show, the process of reading the city need not base itself in a static understanding of structure. In chapter 7 of *The Practice of Everyday Life* (1984), "Walking in the City," de Certeau emphasized not merely the static perceived structure of New York as viewed from the World Trade Center but also the mobile character of the city: "The spectator can read in it a universe that is constantly exploding" (91). Nevertheless, a distinction is still maintained between the "practitioners of the city" who write it from below and the voyeur who reads it from above (de Certeau, 92–93). The legacy of this power of the pedestrian to write the city has found its way into notable works of literature, Paul Auster's magnificent *New York Trilogy* (1990) or Argentine Jorge Luis Borges's story "La muerte y la brújula" ["Death and the Compass"] (1970), to give just two intriguing examples. And yet, de Certeau presents a conflict between the mobile city enacted by the real flows of pedestrians and the "clear text of the planned or readable city" (de Certeau, 93), one that figures prominently in the work of Spanish antiurbanist critic Manuel Delgado Ruiz (*El animal, Sociedades*).

It is in David Harvey that the notion of city-text is fully integrated into a dialectical critique of contemporary capitalism. For Harvey, the writing of the city and the reading of the city are not two separate activities but two perspectives on a struggle. This struggle involves, as Lefebvre (1968) was aware, the question of who has "The Right to the City." Harvey begins *The Urban Experience* (1989) with an explicit reference to de Certeau's discussion of the view of the city from above. And yet, in tune with the dialectical reconciliation of the urbanization of capital and the urbanization of consciousness he will advance in the work, Harvey introduces an important corrective to the perspectives of both Barthes and de Certeau. He points out that the view from above is not so different from the view from the streets as has been supposed.

> The relation between such a "God-like" vision of the city and the turbulence of street life is interesting to contemplate. Both perspectives, though different, are real enough. Nor are they independent, in fact or in mental construction. The seeing eye, when it scans the city as a whole, brings to its task a whole set of prejudices, concepts (such as that of the city itself) and even theories built up laboriously out of street experience. [. . .] the eye is never neutral and many a battle is fought over the "proper" way to see. (*Urban Experience*, 1)

In reconciling the bird's-eye view with the view from the streets Harvey consciously unites the supposed heights of theory with the action below, the abstract and the concrete, thinking and doing (2–4). This needs to be seen as an attempt to methodologically mobilize theory. As Lefebvre wrote, "In dialectical materialism the static representation of time is replaced by a vital and directly experienced notion of succession, of the action which eliminates and creates" (*Urban Revolution*, 20). This return to fluid experience, the return to everyday life (Lefebvre Critique, vols. 1–3),[13] requires an effort launched against the analytical and static concepts through which we organize and perceive the world around us (Lefebvre, *Rhythmanalysis*). This rejection of a static paradigm when approaching the city should be all the more appropriate when dealing with the graffiti on trains, which do not merely represent something, but actually do something. Whereas the final section of this chapter will explore in more depth the nature and consequences of this act of *doing*, it is first important to assert the initial importance of releasing the representational bias implicit in common approaches to graffiti. In exploring train graffiti as a necessarily urban phenomenon, we note Bergson's philosophical break with static representation, highlight the temporal character of graffiti in general and of train graffiti in particular, and underscore the enigmatic nature of urban process.

Here a brief introduction to the more contemporary history of graffiti in Spain is in order. An essay on the philosophy of graffiti in the magazine *Letreros* brings out the common observations that graffiti "writers," as they are called (this English word has been borrowed also into Spanish although the literal translation "escritores" is also common), are trying to communicate a message and to gain respect amongst other writers, and that they work in crews ("Filosofía del graffiti," 36). The first public figure of graffiti in Spain was arguably Juan Carlos Argüello, or "Muelle," an active and influential writer who came of age during what is known as "La movida," the cultural explosion that accompanied the transition to democracy following the death of Francisco Franco on November 20, 1975.[14] Of interest is that, in 1987, he was caught tagging the base of the statue of "el oso y el madroño [the bear and the strawberry-tree]," the emblematic representation of the center of Spain located in Madrid's Plaza del Sol and was fined 2,500 pesetas. Because of this he also received much public attention and was able to make the case for what one author calls "la validez de su arte callejero [the validity of his street-art]" through the newspapers. As it is with other writers, this brush with the law did not slow Muelle down—a year later the scaffolding surrounding the statue of Cibeles (then under renovation and also in central Madrid) displayed his signatures (www.valladolidwebmusical.org /graffiti/ historia/05historia_spain.html).

Even while the figure of the graffiti writer as outlaw persists, that is, while graffiti is still illegal, interestingly, there has been an attempt to bring the graffiti tradition more into the mainstream. There is certainly money to be made through the aestheticization of subculture. Take the recent example of a game titled "Mark Eckō's Getting Up: Contents under Pressure," released for the video game console PlayStation 2—"getting up" being the slang used by graffiti artists to refer to the creation of their street art. This broader acceptance or tolerance of the art is also evidenced by fora that selectively and temporarily "legalize" or co-opt street art—the Festival de Arte Urbano [Festival of Urban Art] to give just one example. The Festival, first celebrated in Gran Canarias (Spain), April 1–4, 2004 with a budget of 180,000 euros, saw the creation of graffiti on 30 walls at the same time, and attracted substantial international attention. One pioneer of graffiti art in Germany (Munich) named Loomit remarked that "Ahora mismo, el nivel en España es realmente alto, de lo mejor que puedes ver [At the moment, the level in Spain is very high, it is of the best quality that one can see]" (Gil).

Wall graffiti, both tags such as Muelle's and more extensive murals, are certainly common in Madrid just as they are in other large urban centers (online one can even find maps of graffiti in Madrid, see www.geocities. com/Area51/Crater/2801/portada.html), but there is reason to consider train graffiti as a genre of its own (Cooper & Chalfant). On the Internet, in the form of photographs,[15] YouTube clips, and in published glossy photo-journals, and underground DVD releases,[16] practitioners of train graffiti testify to the popularity and even the marketability of this subgroup of graffiti artists. Jesús Diego's masterful study of graffiti titled "La estética del graffiti en la sociodinámica del espacio urbano [The Aesthetic of Graffiti in the Sociodynamics of Urban Space]" (1997) mentions magazines that range from the high-quality glossy color photographs of GAME OVER and WANTED (Barcelona, 1995, and Madrid, 1995, respectively; see www. wanted.com) to the black-and-white low budget productions of ESTILO URBANO [URBAN STYLE] (Diego, 3, online version). Such magazines (see also NON-STOP) are a necessary source of documentation for what is such an ephemeral form of cultural production—Spain, as have other countries, has worked to repaint what it considers to be vandalized train cars.[17] As it is painted over, either by the city or by other writers, graffiti in general is constantly changing and evolving, disappearing and reappearing, intimately connected with temporal process.

In the graffiti on trains, however, there is another aspect to this temporality of graffiti that goes beyond the problem of documentation and challenges even the moment of perception itself. In the light of non-representational theory (Thrift, *Non-Representational*) and the focus that Lefebvre and Harvey place on relations over things, however, there is reason to see graffiti not merely as an object to be consumed visually or critically, but rather as one point of entry into a more complex assessment of the dialectical process of reading and writing the city. Whereas there is a representational component to the acts of reading and writing, this understanding belies a more complex experience of train graffiti as linked with the immediacy of movement itself. Diego asserts the mobility of graffiti in phrases such as "el factor cinético [the cinematic factor]" (see especially section 10.1 "El concepto de movilidad en el graffiti") and points out that graffiti, even in its purportedly static manifestation on walls, enjoys placement in zones of rapid transit—such as those important to theoreticians of the "mobility turn": "Podemos decir que el observador móvil es el espectador ideal de la mayor parte de las piezas de graffiti [We can say that the mobile observer is the ideal spectator for the greater part of graffiti pieces]" (Diego, 37, online version). As Diego notes, many theorists—even the famed Spanish cinema critic Román Gubern—also tout the mobile nature of even static messages, like graffiti, that are posted on walls: "aunque el cartel contenga una imagen fija sobre una pared inmóvil, el desplazamiento por parte del peatón o del automovilista la convierte en una imagen furtiva, parangonable a la del spot televisivo [even though the poster comprises a fixed image on an immobile wall, the displacement effected by a pedestrian or a driver converts it into a furtive image comparable to the television spot]" (Gubern, qtd. in Diego; see also Chalfant and Prigoff). If, in a shifting urban environment, even static graffiti must be approached in terms of mobility, this mobility seems even more integral to the experience of perceiving train graffiti. And yet, even more than the act of perceiving train graffiti, the act of creating train graffiti is far more dependent on mobility and speed. As Diego writes, reiterating the thoughts expressed by the writer whose words serve as epigraph of this section:

> Un escritor militante, activo en el seno del grupo, intentará dejar su nombre sobre todos los vagones de tren que pueda, en condiciones radicalmente diferentes al graffiti mural. Pintar sobre una pared es un ejercicio de estilo, un soporte rodeado de tranquilas circunstancias de trabajo que le permite experimentar con técnicas, comentar aspectos del graffiti con otros escritores mientras trabajan, ensayar nuevos diseños, etc. Todo esto no existe en el graffiti sobre trenes. [. . .] Un escritor de trenes intenta darse a conocer lo más rápidamente posible.
>
> [A militant writer, active in the core of the group, will attempt to leave his name on as many train cars as he can, in conditions that differ radically from those of mural graffiti. Painting a wall is an exercise of style, a medium characterized by calm circumstances of work that permits him to experiment with technique, to comment on aspects of the graffiti with other writers while they work, to try out new designs, etc. None of this exists in graffiti on trains. [. . .] A writer of trains attempts to get-up as quickly as possible. (Diego, 37–38, online version)

Thus neither in wall graffiti nor in train graffiti should the representational artistic aspect overshadow temporal process—a process that is of utmost importance not only in the creation of graffiti but in its experience by passers-by.

Thus train graffiti should be understood not only from within representational theory or the history of art where the static image reigns supreme, but rather from a perspective theoretically grounded in the urban as a mobile phenomenon. As legibility in motion, train graffiti collapses the acts of reading and writing into one mobile paradigm and supports the view of the urban as a constantly shifting, negotiated and *produced* relationship. In being constantly on the move, such graffiti—in opposition to static graffiti of the city—reaches places and people that are unforeseeable and difficult to document. If it is considered an art at all it is not the art of a privileged instant, but the art of the "any-instant-whatever" (Deleuze, *Cinema*, 1). The audience does not choose the art, the graffiti chooses the audience. It is not the passive site of consumption, of bourgeois art-appreciation, but rather an "invasive" process (Nandrea, 61), an energy, a surge. As a surge, train graffiti is certainly "more-than-representational" a phrase employed by Hayden Lorimer who builds on the work of Nigel Thrift and other non-representational theorists (Thrift *Spatial, Non-representational*; Thrift and Amin). It is not that train graffiti *means* something, but rather that it *does* something. It disrupts the static paradigm of spatial production that obtains in the process of city shaping/urban design just as it "functions with" (Deleuze and Guattari) the critique of that process by Lefebvre, Harvey, and even Marx.

Even if it is a planned activity by a group, train graffiti is opposed to the rational planning of urban design. It is sporadic, rhizomatic, born to disappear. In the case of train graffiti, as Borchard (2005) notes, this disappearance is double, through moving and through erasure (338). Such graffiti reappropriates a commercial space (Borchard, 337) and disrupts the process of canonization working against deliberate attempts to capitalize on the predictability of tourist experience. (Although in some cases train graffiti has been manufactured as a part of model trains; see Borchard.) Whereas wall graffiti can be used to establish or reflect a sense of place, reinforcing a group identity and notions of territoriality, train graffiti turns this process of territorialization on its ear. The nature of the process of viewing train graffiti works against the cult of the artist that can, to a certain degree, only form around art that is stationary, art that allows itself to be quarantined, installed, immobilized according to the spatial logic of the city. Train graffiti is less deliberate, less expected, more fleeting. In this sense it expresses a sympathy with the chaotic, enigmatic, and unpredictable movement of urban life that is taken as the raw material for capitalists and urban developers, who, as Harvey notes, seek to produce "rational physical and social landscapes for capital accumulation" (*Urban Experience*, 29). Thus the mobile nature of train graffiti is evidence for the philosophical claim—here explicit, there implicit in the "mobility turn" in criticism—that movement is prior to immobility and, moreover, that it is the fleeting complexity of enigma rather than the ordered design of rational landscapes that subtends the intellectual approach to space.

This claim is rooted in a literary and philosophical tradition that unites thinkers from both Spain and France. On a visit to Spain in 1916 as part of a diplomatic mission during World War I, Bergson delivered two speeches at the Ateneo in Madrid on May 2nd and May 6th in which he presented this distilled statement of his philosophical contribution: "La inmovilidad es la coexistencia de dos movimientos"["Immobility is the coexistence of two movements"] (*El alma*, 129). The mode of thinking that Bergson consistently denounces as the "intellect" (*Creative*, 306–07) routinely takes immobility to be prior to movement. There is a practical benefit to this conception, in that this intellectual thought allows us to partition experience in order to insert our action into a mobile and fluid reality. Nevertheless, this practice is reductive and, applied to a process of thinking that professes to go beyond immediate concerns, is insufficient to grasp the complex nature of that mobile reality. Staticity is a "view taken by mind" (*Creative*, 157) it is a snapshot of a continuously unfolding time. In order to illustrate that movement is indivisible, Bergson famously turns to the paradoxes of Zeno of the Eleatic school of philosophy. The most notable of these, the tale of Achilles and the tortoise (see Borges, "Avatars"), argues that Achilles will never beat the tortoise in a footrace if the latter is given a 10-meter head start, for example. Even though the tortoise moves one-tenth the speed of Achilles, by the time Achilles has reached the starting position of the tortoise, the latter will have moved yet another meter, and so on. This tale, writes Bergson, follows the tendency of intellect to partition a moving reality, to equate movement with the distance covered. Instead, movement is indivisible, and what seems to be an indivisible immobile state is in fact constituted through movement and only reduced through a process of intellection, intent as it is to replace relations with things.[18] As such—as a temporal process that unfolds, as a quality and not merely a quantity—movement is, the mobile is, an enigma.

As evidenced by a long tradition of Spanish thought and literature, it is enigma which subtends all explanation, time which underlies space. This is in fact the basis of the literary works of engineer-turned-novelist (and literary critic) Juan Benet who goes so far as to state that first comes imagination, and later comes analysis—which can never completely explain its object. Either analysis bases itself on an enigma or else it is "una superchería que difícilmente le podía llevar al descubrimiento de cosas que no conociera de antemano" ["a cozenage that is unlikely to lead to a discovery of things that are not already known"] (Benet, *La inspiración*, 72; see also *Volverás*, *Una meditación*, *Herrumbrozas*, *Del Pozo*, "Un extempore"). Although Benet stands out for his relentless pursuit of this idea in his many essays and novels through compelling and labyrinthine prose, this understanding also undergirds many of the canonical texts of contemporary peninsular Hispanism. From Miguel de Unamuno's novel *Amor y Pedagogía* (1902) and his philosophical essays to the chaotic narrative form of Juan Goytisolo's *Señas de identidad* and the mobile presentation of Madrid in Luis Martín-Santos's *Tiempo de silencio* such literature has rebelled against the static character of rational spatiality in both form and content (also Fraser "Unamuno," "A Snapshot," "Madrid," *Encounters*). Other authors, like Belén Gopegui in *La escala de los mapas* (1993) have more directly confronted the philosophical tension between space and time at the heart of the battles over city-space (also Fraser "On Mental"). This tradition of Spanish letters resonates with philosophers Bergson, Merleau-Ponty as well as with urban critics Lefebvre, Jacobs and others, who all place change before stasis, enigma before analysis. In the Spanish context the deserved attention directed at the urban as process finds its highest expression in the recent work of the Barcelona-based Urban Anthropologist Manuel Delgado Ruiz who recovers explicitly the insights of Bergson, Lefebvre and Jacobs (Delgado Ruiz, *El animal, Memoria, Socie-dades*, "Espacio"; Fraser, "Manuel").

In what they offer to a methodology of process, in the mobility they restore to representational claims of identity formation, moving trains suggest that although onlookers are habitually conceived of as passive voyeurs of a static reality, perception is never as static or as representational as it appears (Diego, Gubern). The judgments and interpretations we advance of purportedly static realities are made from a mere moment in ever-changing subjectivity just as the static realities that capture our attention are likewise not static but mobile phenomena. Visual perception, as Zenon W. Pylyshyn argues in a recent book (*Things and Places: How the Mind Connects with the World*, 2007), evolves through a correspondence between inner and outer experience (interestingly, Pylyshyn uses the phrase "tagging" to describe the correspondence between inner and outer). Pylyshyn starts his book by, in effect, posing an important question of the rift between inner and outer that underlies both theoretical approaches and common-sense worldviews informed by representationality.

> The central topic is the relation between the mind and the world. To a vision scientist this sounds like a strange topic. Isn't all of vision science about this relation? What's wrong with a story that begins with light falling on objects in the world being reflected to the eye where it is transformed into nerve impulses, which encode various properties of the retinal stimulus and transmit them to the visual cortex, where they are transformed once again, in ways that neuroscience is currently making good process studying? (1)

Pylyshyn concludes that this story not merely lacks detail but perhaps is also lacking something far less trivial (1). He suggests that the question of representation is important for cognitive science (7) but points out "the need for a nonconceptual connection between thoughts and things in the world" (9). Thus at a certain level, recent work in visual perception thus squares with (re)emerging work in geography and philosophy (Lefebvre, Bergson) that limits the representational orientation of much structuralist theory to a mere aspect (although an important one) of a wider dialectical relationship. David Harvey's explanation of the entwined categories of abstract space, relative space, and relational space (in "Space as a Key Word," 2004) is instructive in concisely formulating a critique (but not a dismissal) of abstract divisible quantitative space that finds its most modern expression in the work of Bergson. Although the abstract spatiality of representational thought is extensively implicated in the body's action, in the capitalistic production of space explored by Lefebvre, there is thus a relation that makes such representation possible.

CONCLUSION

In this chapter we have begun a project of thinking through the way in which graffiti is evocative of larger questions of shifting identities, temporal process, ephemerality, movement and enigma. The study of graffiti even has much to offer interdisciplinary approaches to questions of urban space that are informed by philosophical, geographical, and cultural investigation. Both graffiti and cityspace show that static conceptual representation is posterior to, and not prior to, a nonconceptual process. Moreover, graffiti on trains are not merely symbols of mobility, they *are* that mobility. They are part of a world to which we have immediate access—one from which we nevertheless abstract static structures in order to prepare our action upon things. In this world, speed and movement mean something in and of themselves—that is, if they do not, in fact, mean everything.

NOTES

1. This turn calls for a renewed interest in content that "encompasses both large scale movements of people, objects, capital and information across the world, as well as the more local processes of daily transportation, movement through public space and the travel of material things within everyday life" (Hannam; Sheller; Urry, "Editorial," 1; see also Urry, Latham & McCormack).

2. This is echoed in interviews with numerous writers; see, for example, Ivor L. Miller, and the film *Writers, 1983–2003: 20 ans de graffiti à Paris* by director Marc-Aurèle Vecchione.

3. By its very nature underground video can confound the archivist's reflex: gathering publishing information is already difficult and approximate for underground video generally. Add to this the penchant among graffiti artists to view conventions like authorship and publishing data as further occasions to splash their writerly sign of authorship, their tag. Ironically, the advent of easy Internet access has facilitated the dissemination of countless titles like *Graff Is Not Dead* (2001), or *Not Another Graff Movie* (2007), lending a virtual ubiquity to these quasi-anonymous productions. The ease of adding subtitles to these files as they circulate helps the videos cross linguistic barriers: one copy of *Graff Is Not Dead* circulating on the Internet is subtitled in both English and French.

4. In *Paris Tonkar*, one of few collections of images of French graffiti in existence, the ephemeral nature of graffiti is a recurrent theme, and is cast as fundamental to its aesthetic value (Tarek Ben Yakhlef and Sylvain Doriath). *Paris Tonkar* is the first book to sketch out a brief history of graffiti in France—major events, places, actors, and styles—elements of which are developed more fully in Vecchione (2004).

5. Henry Chalfant and James Prigoff dedicated their influential book, *Spraycan Art*, to the "spraycan kings of New York City who, in a hostile environment, created and perfected a new art form and, by their example, excited the imagination of young people throughout the United States and across the seas" (4). Ivor Miller dates the beginning of subway graffiti in New York City to 1969 (89).

6. In Vecchione's documentary, it is pointed out that one such influential early graffiti artist and organizer, "Bando," had spent nearly two years in New York City in the early '80s; "Jonone" was a New Yorker who emigrated to Paris, who has crossed over from graffiti art into the legitimate art market.

7. The Louvre Metro station was tagged in May 1991. Television reporting from the era has been posted—with tags of course—on YouTube at the following link: (www.youtube.com/watch?v=Tthk53aAR4A).

8. The vehement discourse in *Paris Tonkar* about the Louvre Metro station incident shows the extent to which it was seen as damaging to public perception of graffiti artists (Yahklef & Doriath, 40). The authors sought to deflect criticism away from graffiti artists and discredit outrage in the media as hype generated in an effort to further criminalize graffiti.

9. Though referred to most often in the "Treatise on Nomadology" these terms reappear elsewhere in the book, and at times seem almost interchangeable with "deterritorialization" and "reterritorialization" (cf. "1933: Micropolitics and Segmentarity," 208–231).

10. *Paris 1900* is a collection of pre–World War I film footage edited by director Nicole Védrès in 1947 depicting various aspects of French political and cultural life during the Belle Epoque (Panthéon Productions).

11. Translation by B. Fraser. www.elmundo.es/laluna/2004/264/1081268436.html.

12. Interestingly there were all-white trains in Spain in the 1980s that implicitly catered to this idea of the city as canvas, inspiring many writers to paint them. See the list of English-language graffiti terms defined for readers of Spanish on the page palabra.nireblog.com/archives/2007/03: "White Trains: Son trenes blancos que circulaban en el 83s. Los writers los adoraban ya que eran como un lienzo en blanco para ellos."

13. See also Henri Bergson's return to experience in *Time and Free Will. An Essay on the Immediate Data of Consciousness*, "Introduction to Metaphysics"; also in cinema Pier Paolo Pasolini's *Heretical Empiricism* and Siegfried Kracauer's *Theory of Film: The Redemption of Physical Reality*.

14. "La Movida" is often characterized as an explosive release following the repressive dictatorship of Francisco Franco (1936–1975; the Spanish Civil War lasted from 1936–1939) that saw a broadening of perspective concerning alternative sexualities and cultural forms such as punk music. Perhaps the most renowned figure of la Movida, internationally, is the director Pedro Almodóvar.

15. One example is mentioned in Spain's *El País* (26-Jan-2008) where the unnamed author notes of a presumed train graffiti artist that "Según la policía, el presunto autor colgaba posteriormente las fotografías de estos actos vandálicos en Internet, 'alardeando de sus hazañas' mediante comentarios en foros visitados por personas con las misma aficiones [According to police, the presumed author posted photographs of these acts of vandalism afterward on the Internet, "boasting of his feats" among comentaries in fora visited by those with the same interests]." Of course, one need not be connected with the police to verify such postings, as such photographs are easily found using an online search engine.

16. The http://ptqkblogzine.blogia.com/2007/julio.ph lists a DVD titled *Night Play* that "Night Play se trata del primer DVD autoproducido (75min. de duración) que muestra la escena de escritores de graffiti sobre trenes en Euskadi . . . [Night Play is the first self-produced DVD (75 minutes long) that shows graffiti writers on trains in the Basque Country]."

17. The cost attributed to the presumed vandal in an above footnote alone (above, "One example [. . .]") was said to be 14,400 euros (No author, "Detenido por hacer 'graffitis' en el tranvía: El acusado, de 18 años, pertenecía a un grupo aficionado a pintar en trenes." *El País*. 26 de enero 2008. online archive).

18. For Bergson, as he explains in *Creative Evolution*, intellect has evolved through an increasing correspondence with things, thus consciousness has molded itself to the seemingly solid borders of matter. In a recent work, Zenon W. Pylyshyn pursues a similar thesis without reference to Bergson in *Things and Places: How the Mind Connects with the World*.

BIBLIOGRAPHY

Auster, Paul. *The New York Trilogy*. New York: Penguin Books, 1990.

Barthes, Roland. *The Eiffel Tower and Other Mythologies*. Trans. Richard Howard. New York: Hill and Wang, 1979.

Ben Yakhlef, Tarek and Sylvain Doriath. *Paris Tonkar*. Paris: F. Massot et R. Pillement, 1991.

Benet, Juan. *La inspiración y el estilo*. Barcelona: Seix Barral, 1970 [1966].

——. *Volverás a Región*. Barcelona: Destino, 1997 [1967].

——. *Una meditación*. Barcelona: Alfaguara, 1990 [1969].

——. *Herrumbrozas lanzas*. Barcelona: Alfaguara, 1999 [1983–1985].

——. *Del pozo y del Numa*. Barcelona: La Gaya Ciencia, 1978.

——. "Un extempore." *Puerta de tierra*. Valladolid: Cuatro, 2003 [1969]. 69–88.

Bergson, Henri. *Time and Free Will. An Essay on the Immediate Data of Consciousness*. Trans. F. L. Pogson, M.A. Mineola. New York: Dover, 2001 [1889].

——. "Introduction to Metaphysics." In *The Creative Mind*, trans. Mabelle L. Andison. New York: Citadel Press, 2002 [1934].

——. *El alma humana. Precedido de un estudio de Manuel García Morente*. Ed. Manuel García Morente. Madrid: Biblioteca <<España>>, 1916.

———. *Creative Evolution*. Trans. A. Mitchell. Mineola. New York: Dover Publications Inc., 1998 [1907].

Borchard, Kurt. "Moving Pictures." In Wright, Will (Ed. and introd.), and Kaplan, Steven (Ed. and introd.), *The Image of the Road in Literature, Media, and Society*. Pueblo, CO: Society for the Interdisciplinary Study of Social Imagery, Colorado State University-Pueblo, 2005. 337–339.

Borges, Jorge Luis. "La muerte y la brújula." In *Borges: Sus mejores páginas*. Ed. Miguel Enguídanos. Englewood Cliffs, NJ: Prentice-Hall, 1970. 89–99.

———. "Avatars of the Tortoise." In *Other Inquisitions 1937–1952*. Trans. Ruth L. C. Simms. New York: Washington Square Press, 1966 [1939]. 114–120.

Calvin, Lisa M. "Graffiti, the Ultimate Realia: Meeting the Standards through an Unconventional Culture Lesson." *Hispania: A Journal Devoted to the Teaching of Spanish and Portuguese* 88.3 (2005 Sept.): 527–530.

de Certeau, Michel. *The Practice of Everyday Life*. Berkeley: University of California Press, 1988 [1984].

Chaffee, Lyman. "The Popular Culture Political Persuasion in Paraguay: Communication and Popular Art." *Studies in Latin American Popular Culture* 9 (1990): 127–148.

Chalfant, Henry, and James Prigoff. *Spraycan Art*. London: Thames & Hudson, 1987.

Cooper, Martha, and Henry Chalfant. *Subway Art*. New York: Holt, Rinehart & Winston, 1984.

Deleuze, Gilles. *Cinema I: The Movement-Image*. Trans. Hugh Tomlinson and Barbara Habberjam. Minneapolis: University of Minnesota Press, 2003 [1983].

Deleuze, Gilles and Félix Guattari. *A Thousand Plateaus: Capitalism and Schizophrenia*. Minneapolis: University of Minnesota Press, 1987.

Delgado Fenoy, Antonio. "Las firmas anónimas." *El País*. 30 November 1993. online archive.

Delgado Ruiz, Manuel. *El animal público*. Barcelona: Anagrama, 1999.

———. *Memoria y lugar: El espacio público como crisis de significado*. Valencia: Ediciones Generales de la Contrucción, 2001.

———. "Espacio público," *El País* (29 mayo 2006), www.elpais.com.

———. *Sociedades movedizas: pasos hacia una antropología de las calles*. Barcelona: Anagrama, 2007.

Derrida, Jacques. *Of Grammatology*. Baltimore: Johns Hopkins University Press, 1976.

de Diego , Jesús. "La estética del graffiti en la sociodinámica del espacio urbano [The Aesthetic of Graffiti in the Sociodynamics of Urban Space]" (1997). Available online at www.graffiti.org/faz/diego.html.

Edbauer, Jennifer H. "(Meta)Physical Graffiti: 'Getting Up' as Affective Writing Model." *JAC* 25.1 (2005): 131–159.

"Filosofía del Graffiti," *Letreros* 75 (2005): 36–38.

Fraser, Benjamin. "The Publicly-Private Space of Madrid's Retiro Park & the Spatial Problems of Spatial Theory." *Social and Cultural Geography* 8.5 (2007): 673–700.

———. "Manuel Delgado's Urban Anthropology: From Multidimensional Space to Interdisciplinary Spatial Theory." *Arizona Journal of Hispanic Cultural Studies* 11 (2007): 57–75.

———. "On Mental and Cartographic Space: Belén Gopegui's *La escala de los mapas*, Bergson and the Imagined Interval." *España Contemporánea* 18.1 (2005): 7–32.

———. "Unamuno and Bergson: Notes on a Shared Methodology." *Modern Language Review* 102.3 (2007): 753–767.

———. "A Snapshot of Barcelona from Montjuïc: Juan Goytisolo's *Señas de identidad*, Tourist Landscapes as Process and the Photographic Mechanism of Thought." In *Spain Is (Still) Different: Tourism and Discourse in Spanish Identity*. Eds. Eugenia Afinoguenova, Jaume Martí-Olivella. Lexington: Rowman & Littlefield Publishers Inc., 2008. 151–184.

———. "Madrid, Neoplasmic City: Disease and the Urban as Process in *Tiempo de silencio*." *Letras Peninsulares* 21.1 (2008): 139–164.

———. *Encounters with Bergson(ism) in Spain*. Chapel Hill: UNC/Studies in Romance Languages and Literatures, 2010.

Ganz, Nicholas. *Graffiti World: Street Art from Five Continents*. New York: Abrams, 2004.

———. *Graffiti Women: Street Art from Five Continents*. New York: Abrams, 2006.

García-Pabón, Leonardo. "Sensibilidades callejeras: el trabajo estético y político de Mujeres Creando." *Revista de Crítica Literaria Latinoamericana* 29.58 (2003): 239–254.

Gauthier, Louise. "Confessions of an Ethnographer: Reflections on Fieldwork with Graffiti Writers in Montreal." *Anthropologica* 43.2 (2001): 273–276.

———. "Writing on the Run: The History and Transformation of Street Graffiti in Montreal in the 1990s." *Dissertation Abstracts International, Section A: The Humanities and Social Sciences* 59.8 (1999 Feb.): 3233.

Genovese, Alicia. "Marcas de graffiti en los suburbios: Poesía argentina de la posdictadura." *Revista Iberoamericana* 69.202 (2003 Jan–Mar): 199–214.

Gil, Pablo. "Artistas del spray." *El Mundo*'s *La Luna* supplement. 9 April 2004. www.elmundo.es/laluna/2004/264/1081268436.html.

Gopegui, Belén. *La escala de los mapas*. Barcelona: Anagrama, 1993.

Goytisolo, Juan. *Señas de identidad*. Madrid: Alianza, 1999 [1966].

Grieb, Kenneth J. "The Writing on the Walls: Graffiti as Government Propaganda in Mexico." *Journal of Popular Culture* 18.1 (1984 summer): 78–91.

Gubern, Román. *La mirada opulent*. Barcelona: Gustavo Gili, 1987.

Hannam, Kevin, Mimi Sheller, and John Urry. "Editorial: Mobilities, Immobilities and Moorings." *Mobilities* 1.1 (2006): 1–22.

Harvey, David. *The Urban Experience*. Baltimore: Johns Hopkins UP. 1989.

———. "Space as a Key Word." *Spaces of Global Capitalism*. London: Verso, 2006. 117–148.

Hernández, Rod. "Battling in L.A.: Chicano Graffiti Poetics and Technologies of Vision." *The Americas Review: A Review of Hispanic Literature and Art of the USA* 22.3–4 (1994 fall–winter): 107–132.

Hugo, Victor. *Notre Dame de Paris*. Ed. Julien Piat. Paris: Collections Larousse, 2003.

Jacobs, Jane. *The Death and Life of Great American Cities*. New York: Vintage, 1992 [1961].

Kim, Sojin. *Chicano Graffiti and Murals: The Neighborhood Art of Peter Quezada*. Jackson: UP of Mississippi, 1995.

Kracauer, Siegfried. *Theory of Film: The Redemption of Physical Reality*. New York; Oxford: Oxford University Press, 1968 [1960].

Lamireau, Clara. "Les Manifestes éphémères: Graffitis anti-sexistes dans le métro parisiena." *Langage et Société* 106 (2003 Dec): 81–102, 142.

Latham, Alan and Derek McCormack. "Moving Cities: Rethinking the Materialities of Urban Geographies." *Progress in Human Geography* 28.6 (2004): 701–724.

Lefebvre, Henri. *The Urban Revolution*, Trans. Robert Bononno. Minneapolis: University of Minnesota Press, 2003 [1970].

———. "The Right to the City." In E. Kofman & E. Lebas (Ed. and Trans.), *Writings on Cities*. Oxford: Blackwell, 1996 [1968]. 63–181.

———. *Critique of Everyday Life, Vol. 1*. Trans. John Moore. London; New York: Verso, 1991 [1947].

———. *Critique of Everyday Life, Vol. 2*. Trans. John Moore. London; New York: Verso, 2002 [1961].

———. *Critique of Everyday Life, Vol. 3*. Trans. Gregory Elliott. London; New York: Verso, 2005 [1981].

———. *Rhythmanalysis*. Trans. Stuart Elden and Gerald Moore. London; New York: Continuum, 2006 [1992].

Lorimer, Hayden. "Cultural Geography: The Busyness of Being 'More than Representational.'" *Progress in Human Geography* 29.1 (2005): 83–94.

Martine Lani-Bayle. *Du tag au graff'art: les messages de l'expression murale graffitée*. Marseilles: Robert, 1993.

Martín-Santos, Luis. *Tiempo de silencio*. Barcelona: Seix Barral, 1997 [1961].

McCormick, Jonathan and Neil Jarman. "Death of a Mural." *Journal of Material Culture* 10.1 (2005 Mar.): 49–71.

Miller, Ivor L. *Aerosol Kingdom: Subway Painters of New York City*. Jackson: University Press of Mississippi, 2002.

Milon, Alain. *L'étranger dans la ville: du rap au graff mural*. Paris: Presses universitaires de France, 1999.

Milon, Alain and Seth Whidden, "Tags and Murals in France: A City's Face or Natural Landscape." In Durand, Alain-Philippe (Ed.), *Black, Blanc, Beur: Rap Music and Hip-Hop Culture in the Francophone World*. Lanham, MD: Scarecrow, 2002. 87–98.

Nandrea, Lorri. "'Graffiti Taught Me Everything I Know About Space': Urban Fronts and Borders." In Wright, Will and Kaplan, Steven (Ed. and introd.), *The Image of the Frontier in Literature, the Media, and Society*. Pueblo, CO: Society for the Interdisciplinary Study of Social Imagery, University of Southern Colorado, 1997. 59–62.

Noland, Carrie. "Graffiti and the Reinvention of Space." *Word & Image Interactions* no. 5 (2005): 305–317.

Oliver, Anne Marie and Paul Steinberg. "A Geography of Revolt." *Public Culture* 3.1 (1990 fall): 139–143.

Olsen, Donald J. *The City as a Work of Art: London, Paris, Vienna*. New Haven: Yale University Press, 1986.

Pasolini, Pier Paolo. *Heretical Empiricism*. Ed. Louise K. Barnett. Bloomington: Indiana University Press, 1988.

Pylyshyn, Zenon W. *Things and Places: How the Mind Connects With the World*. Cambridge, MA: MIT Press, 2007.

Sanchez-Tranquilino, Marcos. "Space, Power and Youth Culture: Mexican-American Graffiti and Chicano Murals in East Los Angeles, 1972–1978." In Bright, Brenda Jo (Ed. and Introd.) and Bakewell, Liza (Ed.), *Looking High and Low: Art and Cultural Identity*. Tucson: Univ. of Arizona, 1995. 55–88.

Sontag, Susan, *On Photography*. New York: Farrar, Straus and Giroux, 1977.

Thrift, Nigel. *Non-Representational Theory: Space, Politics, Affect*. London: Routledge, 2007.

———. *Spatial Formations*. Theory, Culture and Society Series; Sage: London, 1996.

Thrift, Nigel and Amin, Ash (Eds.). *Cities. Reimagining Urban Theory*. Cambridge, UK: Polity Press, 2002.

Trigo, Abril. "Rockeros y grafiteros: La construcción al sesgo de una antimemoria." In Bergero, Adriana J. (Ed.) and Reati, Fernando (Ed. and introd.), *Memoria colectiva y políticas de olvido: Argentina y Uruguay, 1970–1990*. Rosario, Argentina: Beatriz Viterbo, 1997. 305–334.

de Unamuno, Miguel. *Amor y pedagogía*. Madrid: Alianza Editorial, 2004 [1902].

Urry, John. *Sociology Beyond Society: Mobilities for the 21st Century*. London: Routledge, 2000.

Vecchione, Marc-Aurèle, dir. *Writers, 1983–2003: 20 ans de graffiti à Paris*. Resistance Films, 2004.

Virilio, Paul. *The Vision Machine*. Bloomington: Indiana University Press, 1994.

———. *Speed and Politics: An Essay on Dromology*. New York: Columbia University Press, 1986.

Wimsatt, William Upski. *Bomb the Suburbs! Graffiti, Race, Freight-hopping and the Search for Hip Hop's Moral Center*. New York: Soft Skull Press, 1994,

Védrès, Nicole, dir. *Paris 1900*. Panthéon Productions, 1947.

Vigara Tauste, Ana Ma. and Paco Reyes Sánchez, "Graffiti y pintadas en Madrid: Arte, lenguaje, comunicación." *Espéculo: Revista de Estudios Literarios*, 4 (1996 Nov.–1997 Feb.): no pagination.

Part II

On Passengers

Chapter 3

"What to Wear and Where to Go"

Picturing the Modern Consumer on the Great Western Railway, 1921–1939

Alexander Medcalf

Though the railways' relationship with modernity has been analyzed with regard to technological and design elements (Beaumont & Freeman), the reduction of time and space (Schivelbusch), and their representation in cultural production (Carter), their role in the development of modern marketing and advertising practices in the first half of the twentieth-century is largely neglected. The work of Divall, Watts, and Harrington has demonstrated that this is undeserved. These historians highlight the need for, and the value of, further examination of how marketing and advertising were perceived and executed by railway companies through guidebook literature, press releases, posters, and photographic publicity. Taking the latter, one of the most under-analyzed and misunderstood forms of railway marketing, this chapter considers the example set by the Great Western Railway (hereafter GWR). It argues that rather than realistic representations of place, the GWR infused its photographic output with cultural and social meaning in an effort to encourage discretionary travel. The profusion of photographs situated within the GWR's immensely popular travel brochure *Holiday Haunts* allowed the GWR to convey messages about rail travel, the essential character and qualities of destinations, and how they might be consumed. As a prolific producer of such visual messages, the GWR was thus a front runner in the shift from informative advertising to emotional appeals to people's desires, a move which constituted the modern turn in marketing practice during the interwar period.

The title "What to Wear and Where to Go" is used in this chapter to describe the changing nature of the GWR's photographic appeals to potential consumers across the period. Taken from an article in the GWR company magazine, it detailed the collaboration between the railway and the Co-operative retail chain ("Co-operative Advertising Display," 308). Using a shop window display filled with advertising and beach accoutrements, both companies sought to instill the holiday spirit in potential holidaymakers. A useful public relations exercise—but it is not this slogan, but rather what it stood for, that is of interest here. It shows that by the 1930s there was a great appetite for display and conspicuous consumption at the destination. The slogan reflects the broad shift in GWR photographic publicity, which sought to tap into this changing market. The company's marketing appeals at the outset of the 1920s focused on "where to go" based on the perceived qualities of the destination. Through photographic imagery, the GWR augmented this appeal and invested destinations with romantic associations to England's historic past. Responding to change in the market, in the 1930s the dominant visual culture showed passengers idealized visions of themselves, visions that emphasized conspicuous consumption, display and fashion, "what to wear." Both were modern responses to selling travel, but the shift to depicting people and integrating them in lifestyle imagery necessitates reconsideration of the GWR's role in modern marketing that appealed to social fears and desires.

"Modern" marketing is defined here as the move from informative advertising, appealing to reason via bold statements on price and availability, to visual appeals to emotion, which attached products to a range of ideological appeals, portraying them as part of aspirational lifestyles (Ross, 60; Slater, 60). Though businesses, including the railways, experimented with visual publicity in the Edwardian period, this was consolidated in the interwar years with the rise of the photographic image as a highly effective advertising medium. As quality and cost associated with photographic reproduction rose and declined respectively, increasing cinema attendances similarly generated a strong public appetite for, and ability to decode, photographic advertising. Prized for the simultaneous reality and fantasy they conveyed and for their ability to influence consumers more directly than the line drawing or sketch, this chapter is thus underpinned by the identification of photographs as the advertising wonder in the interwar period (Johnson, 1).

Although cultural historians share this viewpoint (Lears, 324–329; Hewitt & Wilkinson, 22–23), the neglect of the railways in this area is surprising considering that they produced enormous amounts of photographic publicity. The GWR possessed its own photographic section attached initially to the Engineering Department, but it recognized early on the value of photographs for publicizing its destinations with more realism as opposed to the artist's hand. The GWR understood the value of carefully selecting and manipulating photographs to appeal to different sections of the market, creating visual narratives to demonstrate how destinations should be thought about and consumed. Every image included in this chapter was initially published in respective annual volumes of *Holiday Haunts*. Such images were the end result of a picturing process that saw thousands of images captured and assessed by the GWR before it published a select number. Each image was thus part of a conscious and calculated effort to imbue destinations with symbolic characteristics and ascribe them greater social and cultural meaning of value to the potential consumer.

The dominance and ubiquity of photographic images in the digital age means that their messages are often taken unquestioningly. Yet it is the ability of photographic publicity to make meanings that this chapter explores, building on the idea that photographs are never innocent windows onto the world, instead interpreting it and displaying it in "very particular ways" (Rose, 2). Historians have recently acknowledged the value of visual sources for analyzing signs and messages (Burke, 30), and have drawn analytical tools from established sociological approaches to questioning the visual. For example, Williamson's seminal text *Decoding Advertisements* forwards the idea that commodities and services carry no inherent meaning. Advertisers locate them in broader systems of meaning through the inclusion of signs (31). Explained succinctly by Leiss, Jhally, and Kline, "a sign is something that has significance within a system of meaning and is constituted of two key elements: the signifier, the material vehicle, and the signified, the mental construct, the idea" (130). Semiotics, the study of signs, has thus been embraced by historians analyzing how companies communicated with consumers, Harrington and Watts using this methodology to read railway posters for their marketing messages. Such approaches can be used to analyze how the GWR perceived its market and constructed meaning based on this within its publicity photograph. As we will see, in the GWR's case, the thatched cottage or horse and cart were intended to represent a timeless rural England under threat from modernity, while attractive individuals crashing through waves stood for success, popularity, and fun. This chapter thus agrees with scholarship that sees the tourist brochure and tourist photography as myths whose function is to transform images of destinations into texts with ideologically potent meanings for holidaymakers (Dann, 61).

Examining photographic meaning builds a greater picture of how the GWR approached its market and how it reconceptualized passengers not as a homogenous consuming mass, but as individuals with wants and desires that required satisfaction. *Holiday Haunts* targeted a growing middle-class market that in reality represented the only ones who could afford lengthy holidays away until the Holidays with Pay Act in 1938 (Walton, 58–59). The images were constructed with this market in mind, anticipating and reflecting what the GWR perceived to be their chief tastes and sensibilities. This chapter thus explores how the GWR approached this market by creating visual narratives based on these perceived tastes. It charts changes within its appeal to consumers while recognizing that to be effective, advertising messages should be updated to meet changes in taste and demand. In exploring GWR's competition against other transport providers in the crowded interwar holiday market this chapter seeks to decipher its attempts as modern responses to marketing discretionary travel.

THE HISTORICAL BACKGROUND OF
RAILWAY MARKETING

It is essential at the outset to understand the roots of interwar marketing developments in Edwardian approaches to selling, both on the railways and in broader terms. The idea of marketing at its most elementary level is that business success is determined by the ability to understand and satisfy customer requirements (Dibb, 5; Solomon, 9–11; Percy, 15–18). The deployment of an understanding of the market to shape services and advertising distinguishes modern practice from the haphazard guesswork of earlier strategies. The Edwardian period and the interwar years have recently seen greater interest from historians of advertising and marketing who view it as the time when these practices became modern. In their studies of Lux and Rowntrees respectively, Schwarzkopf and Fitzgerald demonstrate that though marketing as a term did not appear until the 1930s, approximate cultural practices operated within a range of businesses many decades prior (Schwarzkopf, 8–9; Fitzgerald, 29). Advertising, the means for communicating marketing messages played a key role in this process. Initially viewed as a suspect practice aimed at disguising the quality of a product (Richards, Commodity Culture of Victorian England, 206), it became crucial to marketing in the 1890s and 1900s. Initially advertising copy was lengthy and wordy, or relied on bold statements to make potential consumers aware of new products. Between 1900 and 1915 the view that advertisements simply communicated news to awaken existing wants was gradually discredited in favor of more persuasive approaches. Advertisers increasingly sought to create a necessity in the lives of the people and persuade them to consume (Laird, 279). Images grew in popularity, although expense and reduced quality associated with reproduction inhibited progress. These developments constituted the roots of a process that went from proclaiming that there was a product for sale to explaining *why* the consumer should purchase it.

For the railways the Edwardian period witnessed a similar development away from informative and wordy appeals. Prior to this, in the 1840s and 1850s, handbills and timetables epitomized informative advertising, which did little to persuade potential passengers. Such forms were conditioned by rail's virtual monopoly on travel over all but the shortest of distances and the fact that, at a time when long-distance travel was still a novelty, consumers required little persuasion. By the 1860s and 1870s organizations separate from the railways produced guidebooks and literature to capitalize on a growing appetite for discretionary travel (Martin, 226–227), but the railways were slow to see the benefits of this. Change began in the 1890s, when the railways themselves began to recognize guidebooks and literature as useful means for encouraging patronage. Their quantity and quality still varied by company however (Wilson, 24–25). By the dawn of the twentieth century, there was a growing debate within the railway industry about the appropriateness of advertising for a unique service such as travel. Spurred by the progress made in other industries such as food and tobacco, the railways discussed more prominently the need to "persuade" potential passengers to see travel as a discretionary as well as a necessary good. The benefits of such an approach were encapsulated in the argument of an academic contemporary, Douglas Knoop. He argued that in 1913 the goal of the modern railway was to "induce people who would otherwise not do so, to travel by rail, and to encourage such as would travel a little, to travel more" (Knoop, 235).

The GWR adopted a prominent role in this emerging marketing discourse. Since 1886 the company had undertaken all of its advertising in-house, but in 1894 the Advertising Department was enlarged and transferred to the Traffic Department under the Superintendent of the Line, signaling a reappraisal of the company's advertising policies and practices. Consistently viewed as the best among British railway firms, and among continental ones as well, the GWR believed that advertising was a science and "not a mere game of chance" ("GWR Advertising," 195). The company's staff magazine reveals a preoccupation with the role of advertising and its potential to persuade consumers psychologically (Marks, 99–100; "Railway Advertising," 100–101). The GWR recognized that different people were influenced in different ways, and that more nuanced appeals were best for attracting traffic. The ability to persuade consumers with new methods was thus prized and the company began employing eclectic media to market its services. Thought-provoking and captivating slogans were established alongside experiments with monograms to "brand" the company ("Monogram Competition," 137). Motorbuses toured the countryside filled with promotional material such as posters and postcards depicting famous engines and resorts ("Advertising Motor Car Tours," 163). These initiatives demonstrate a company not content to let the consumer come to it, but one determined instead to reach the consumer.

The use of photography formed a distinct element among these approaches. Though many railways employed company photographers to record new rolling stock and provide evidence in legal disputes (Bartholomew & Blakemore,

12–15), the GWR was the first railway to recognize their commercial value. Included in carriage interiors from 1895 (Timins, 425), it was not long before the publicity-conscious GWR recognized the significance of its own photographs to its literature. The company's first photographic guidebook, *The Cornish Riviera*, was issued in 1904 and was followed two years later by the first of the annual *Holiday Haunts* series. Divided by county and arranged alphabetically, each section of *Holiday Haunts* began with a series of photographic views of principal sites and destinations. These views were updated annually, ensuring that no two were the same. The photographs were followed by a short introductory paragraph describing the main places of interest for each region. Each ended with a tabulated directory of accommodations that indicated distances from the nearest station and facilities offered.

An attractive means of publicizing discretionary travel with allusions to "proper" literature, *Holiday Haunts* was able to make its way into homes and remain there, unlike the poster or the disposable daily press. Eagerly anticipated, consumers strove to complete full sets of *Holiday Haunts* and other GWR guides. Part of *Holiday Haunts'* prestige thus relied on its resemblance to older guidebooks that were viewed as offering a much more educated way of experiencing place. Such literature had long sought to satisfy curiosity, its acknowledged purpose being to inform the traveler (Martin, 226–227). Though *Holiday Haunts* did indeed include descriptive matter written by the eminent travel writer A. M. Broadley (Wilson, 105), it was intended to generate excitement and create the desire to take a GWR holiday.

Far from being an out-of-touch or conservative concern, the GWR was thus a front runner in considering the differential appeal of travel, and considering that passengers could be persuaded to think about travel beyond price and length of journey. *Holiday Haunts'* growth was stunted by the commencement of hostilities in 1914, although it continued to appear annually until 1916, after which time paper and labor restrictions prevented publication until 1921 (Wilson, 112). It is to the 1920s that this chapter now turns: to a drastically different environment economically and socially, and one that saw new approaches to how to meet consumer demands and to reshape advertising.

1920s—A ROMANTIC VISION OF ENGLAND

At the outset of the interwar period it is possible to note a reconsideration of marketing's potential both on the railways and elsewhere. The discourse on advertising as it emerged in the 1920s through specialist publications such as *Advertisers' Weekly* and *The Advertising World* stressed the necessity of carefully planned and coordinated advertising strategies (Hewitt & Wilkinson, 9). Companies were driven both by the need to communicate effectively with an audience and the recognition that this could be achieved through design techniques (Hewitt & Wilkinson, 22–23). The pursuit of realism was extended, putting a high price on photography as advertisers searched for forms of communication that were quickly and easily understood. Already a feature of the GWR's advertising prior to the war, such realism was a concern secondary to that of encouraging consumers to think about railway destinations beyond the ordinary. The ability of photography to develop narratives based on established visual vocabularies allowed the GWR to attach ideological meanings to its destinations that took advantage of both the company's position as the country's most historic travel provider and new social fears about a perceived decline of England. In persuading consumers where to go the company lauded the qualities and characteristics of destinations on its territory as a premodern rural idyll, where the urban dweller could recreate himself or herself and reconnect with a lost past.

The GWR began the 1920s in a position of superiority. The fear that it would lose its pride and prestige when the government handed back control to the railways was unfounded. The GWR was the only company to survive amalgamation with its corporate identity intact. However, the further results of amalgamation meant that discussion of how to persuade passengers continued and was strengthened. There was still no representative body for passengers, and despite the role of two regulatory bodies, the Railway and Canal Commission and the Railway Rates Tribunal, it was up to the railways to develop understandings of the kinds of services that might appeal to consumers (Divall, 110–113). For the GWR, its prewar developmental knowledge concerning advertising and consumers, its unique selling point as Britain's oldest railway, and a history of visual representation of landscape combined to create a dominant visual aesthetic which invested the southwest with the glamour of legend and romance. In countless images and descriptions the company focused on the "picturesque" qualities of a place, a term which had been in use since the eighteenth century. This chapter focuses instead on the GWR's corporate use of this term. Broadly, the company's interpretation of the picturesque was that which highlighted beautiful, charming landscapes devoid of modern intervention. In addition to dramatic landscapes, this could apparently also be found in quaint villages and rural practices taken to have a "timeless" quality. Though each of its territories had a somewhat unique character and regional differences, they were united under the picturesque. The GWR constructed a vision of England as a vast storehouse of premodern and rural Englishness. Rather than an authentic representation of place, this was intended to create a prominent plea to the desires of potential passengers that hinged on their capacity as seekers of the picturesque.

In this way, the GWR used what modern sociologists term the "romantic tourist gaze." Chiefly forwarded by Urry, this is based on the idea that cultural practices of tourism are represented in sets of preferred social activities which are highly structured by distinctions of taste which "lead people to want to be in certain places, gazing at particular objects, in the company of specific other types of people" (66). The romantic gaze describes visual imagery used to communicate the character of a destination in terms of solitude, privacy, and a personal, semi-spiritual relationship with the object of the gaze (Urry, 45). A focus of the nineteenth-century guidebook, this was just as popular in the interwar period. Following the destruction wrought by the new modern warfare, numerous organizations and preservation movements wrote on the condition of England and strove for modernity within limits, employing "binary contrasts of good and evil, order and chaos, beauty and horror" (Matless, 26). While technology advanced at a remarkable pace, people questioned its value and impact on the old orders of society (Rieger, 2). Perceiving its customers as hailing chiefly from the urban middle-class areas of London and the Midlands, both desiring an educated way of seeing place but fearing the encroachment of modernity, the GWR imagined for them a timeless England untouched by modernity. The GWR's photographs focused on rural idylls, supported by text that singled out historical episodes from pre-industrial history and further into the realms of myth.

Detaching from the immediate context of rail and consumption photography, the GWR wanted consumers to see "what hitherto appeared to be a rough heap of stones upon a hilltop" as "the ruins of a castle of great historical interest around which a deal of legend flourishes" (Richards, "Photographs from the Carriage Window," 468). Photography was essential in creating a romantic story and communicating to potential consumers the idea that previously uninteresting buildings or vistas whispered much grander appeal. The benefit of photography in this respect was that while several images together could create a fantastical imaginary landscape, photographic realism ascribed them tangibility and the idea that such experiences existed over the line drawing or sketch.

The images depicting Minehead (Fig. 3.1) and Ilfracombe Lee (Fig. 3.2) were intended to inculcate the romantic idea of an England untouched by modernity. The GWR encoded these outwardly empty signs with value derived from the wider discourses on the disappearance of a traditional England and the encroachment of modernity and industry. For the urban middle classes in their modern, suburban semi-detached houses, the small thatched cottages presented a more peaceful and traditional existence. The roughly cobbled streets connoted permanence and the absence of modern traffic. This was similarly communicated by including older forms of transport, such as

Figure 3.1.   Church Steps, Minehead, 1927.

Figure 3.2.   Swiss Cottage, Ilfracombe Lee, 1927.

the horse and cart. By 1927 a casualty of the internal combustion engine, the heavy horses reinforced this message of timelessness and tranquility and provided visual proof that there were areas where these practices still thrived. Capturing buildings surrounded by nature (as in Fig. 3.2), such photographs created an impression of the comforting embrace of nature, of man and nature in harmony. In the case of Minehead (Fig. 3.1), by this time developed as a bustling family resort, the street scene was intended to connote permanence and wholesomeness. This was supported by text that directed the viewer's imagination, for though no church is depicted, the steps and their ascension tempted allusions in the viewer's mind to pre-existing cultural symbols. Sunlight, a technique widely used in advertising to signify purity and favor from the heavens (Marchand, 276), similarly connoted a favored and natural quality. Such conventions were replicated for all destinations as, even in cities such as Exeter and Bristol, cathedrals, historic buildings, and monuments from an ancestral past were hailed as definitive of the overriding character of the landscape.

The dominant personality for the smaller destinations was that of the idealized English village. Sought time and again in travel literature such as H. V. Morton's *In Search of England*, these all but forgotten centers were advertised as offering the kinds of unity and neighborliness elsewhere effaced by modernity. The GWR was a major proponent of this idea, characterizing such destinations by their difference to modern life. Though Matless illustrates that many organizations and preservation movements wanted modernity within limits rather than no progress at all (25–26), the GWR characterized its publicity fully as lands untouched by modernity. Photography documented the people who inhabited these areas, using them to support the notions of romance and traditional life. Evident in Figure 3.2, the dignity and timelessness of the horse and cart were replicated in other images that detailed scenes of agricultural work or portrayed quaint fishing villages. The success of the GWR myth stood in stark contrast to the contemporary Englishman's experiences of these areas. Though the goal may have been to make the holidaymaker feel that he or she had returned, as in a dream, to the year 1910, rural England was in reality heavily affected by depression. Villages suffered from a lack of investment and an exodus of young labor (Mowat, 255). The situation was similar across the Atlantic, where the idealized small town was a sight more familiar to Americans through the advertising pages than through direct experience (Marchand, 260). This difference does, however, suggest the desire among those who had left for rural and timeless experiences. The GWR played on the fact that customers still perceived or desired ties to these places, and sought to sell the illusion of replacing the various effects of industrialization with a warm and welcoming image of an England that had retained its charm.

The degree of deliberateness in the GWR's representational strategies is evident in what was omitted from the images. Virtually all allusions to tourists and people—except for those who fit within the mythology, such as locals—were actively written out. Despite the fact that the GWR wanted to popularize these areas it realized that in showing them with too many people would limit their appeal to those in search of solitude and the picturesque. This active aversion to humans was extended to elements of the built environment, which made visual allusions to modern human intervention. There was no place for wires, cars, or advertising within the GWR's imagery, except for the busiest London squares, where to omit would have detracted from London's appeal. Modern photographic and advertising practice was used to entrench the appeal of the premodern, carefully constructing narratives that relied on the appetite for, and worry over, rural debasement by modern society's onward march. A facilitator of this as a mass travel provider, the GWR was careful to tie its own image inextricably with such timeless pursuits, a useful defense against the challenges from more modern transport modes.

Figure 3.3.   "The Cornish Coast near the Lizard," 1927.

The third image (Fig. 3.3), builds on a certain tradition of representing the picturesque in painting, now appropriated for advertising. As seen above, to the GWR the picturesque broadly meant nature at its simplest, the kind of beauty that would look good in a picture (Taylor, 17–18). The GWR drew upon the art of the nineteenth-century Romantic movement for its own versions of the picturesque; a logical reference, for it spoke of an appreciation of nature for its own sake and a reaction against the Industrial Revolution (Gold & Revill, 132). Turning landscape into images meant they were objectified and could be owned, captured, exploited, bought, and sold. Gold and Revill recognize a similar process in interwar housing developers. Working in the city was an economic necessity, but living there was regarded as hectic, stressful, and unpleasant. Promoters advertised new estates as retreats to an environment that was greener, pleasanter and, by implication, healthier (Gold & Revill, 201). Such ploys were a large part of the GWR's marketing, which worked on the basis of the healthful and restorative qualities of nature where man could be at his most natural.

Holiday Haunts also played on people's desire to seek out places to photograph for themselves. The GWR actively encouraged passenger photography by running competitions among staff and the public, imploring them not to relegate their cameras to the luggage shelves. Returning to Urry's arguments regarding the ways in which people gaze, he argues that the camera holds the ability to turn everyone into amateur semioticians, as people become comfortable with decoding photographic meaning and actively encode it in their own compositions. To them, the country cottage no longer remains just a building. Rather, a thatched cottage with roses round the door represents "ye olde England," while waves crashing onto rocks signifies wild, untamed nature (Urry, 128). The camera was more effective than painting, because photography required comparatively less skill to replicate whatever was deemed masterly. This comparative ease ensured that more people took up the practice. Encouraging potential consumers to see the GWR's services as a gateway to a vast storehouse of the picturesque relied on this comfort and ability to decode meaning. Inculcating a semi-spiritual relationship with the landscape, the GWR's imagery thus took diverse and outwardly uninteresting places and invested them with cultural meaning. Recontextualized within *Holiday Haunts*, they constituted a dominant visual narrative about consumption, how it should take place, and why it was of value. Idealization of the past, nonmaterialism, and an "English way of life" being the spirit of the age (Wiener, 5–6; Gold & Revill, 138–140), *Holiday Haunts* relayed these messages more thoroughly than the solitary snapshot or pictorial poster.

The novelty in GWR's use of photographic imagery to induce consumption and improve the company's public image is evident when compared to other companies that have attracted the attention of marketing historians. By transferring its publicity from the countryside onto its three thousand petrol tankers, Shell fostered an image of itself as a responsible organization with strong associations with nature and rural Britain (Heller, 202–209). Shell's *County Guides* series similarly focused on the beauty and character of Britain. Matless argues that through a range of literature rural leisure became restyled around the petrol engine (64–66). Though he acknowledges the role of the railways in opening up the countryside, there is no place in Matless's account for a railway pastoral akin to his offer of the motoring pastoral (63–64). The GWR's grasp of rural England as a marketing ploy and its role in the construction of this imagery nonetheless presents an early attempt to integrate these tastes and predilections into selling terms that were part and parcel of the branding of historic England.

Photographic publicity imbued with social meaning thus represented a modern response to the problems of selling travel to a diverse audience that enjoyed an ever-increasing amount of choice in discretionary travel. The GWR's ability to procure large amounts of this imagery, and its developed notions of what consumers wanted, resulted in a prolific depiction of place as a vast storehouse of cultural experiences. This depiction was rarely static, however. While the overarching desire to depict the picturesque remained throughout the 1920s, company photographers were sent to scour the land for new views of destinations eleven months prior to the next issue. The level of construction involved in producing *Holiday Haunts* testifies to the calculated nature of its messages. Throughout the 1920s, both the photographic content and the overall size of *Holiday Haunts* increased, reaching a peak in 1928, when over 200,000 copies were sold (Wilson 115). Though consistently popular with the public, toward the end of the 1920s social and economic developments necessitated that the company revise its advertising strategy.

These challenges came from increasing competition with motor transport. The role of cars and buses was keenly debated in the GWR's magazine and its Traffic Department reports. Starting with losing freight to the roads in the mid-1920s, from 1927 these reports detail the escalating loss of passenger traffic. The 1928 report summed up the problem explicitly, and attributed the decline in passenger train travel to the increase in privately owned automobiles (GWR Traffic Department Annual Report, 1928). The middle classes that the GWR targeted were beginning to shun the railways in favor of their own vehicles, which were now less expensive and more reliable than the cars of the early 1920s (Matless, 64). Competition also came from other railways that innovated in poster and publicity design to mark their services as different from those offered by the GWR. Frank Pick's rebranding of London Transport demonstrated to the railways the benefits that modern design aesthetics could have on patronage (Cole, 8). The LNER was among the first to recognize this, with its Advertising Managers William Teasdale and Cecil Dandridge commissioning posters from avant-garde artists. Tom Purvis' posters for the LNER, along with those of Ethelbert White and Gregory Brown for the Southern Railway, demonstrated that these railways perceived the value of modern designs (Cole, 8–9). Though, as we have seen, not all among the consuming public were fascinated by progress and modern aesthetics, changes in consumer culture, the design of cars, and the influence of America increasingly placed modernity as key to selling strategies.

A perceptible change was also evident in what the "modern" holidaymaker wanted. Greater inroads made by the lower-middle classes, longer and more frequent holidays, and people who desired different experiences became apparent. A prominent example of this was the relaxing of morals surrounding bathing during the late-1920s, which encouraged people to be freer and forgo their usual reticence and reserve. Whereas in the early 1920s segregated bathing was still rife at resorts and the wearing of a bathing costume was likely to incite claims of indecency, toward the end of the decade these beliefs were in decline (Horwood, 659–660). This culminated at the dawn of the 1930s, in the Bathing Boom. Walton describes how developments in the relaxing of morals associated with bathing, the construction of swimming pools, and new beliefs regarding the health benefits of sunbathing were the embodiment of a new ethos of sunshine and freedom (99–101). Walton singles out lidos in particular as the combination of art-deco architecture, blue water, and immaculate lawns, which expressed the burgeoning interwar aesthetic of relaxed modernity (101). Rather than solitude or intellectual tourism, people were invited to become part of the sun-worshipping masses. It was to these masses that the GWR turned. Though its vast romantic storehouse was still popular, to remain competitive the GWR recognized that new appeals had to be made. As opposed to "where to go," the focus was turned onto the consumer, conspicuous consumption, display, and "what to wear."

1930s—THE PEOPLE ARE PARAMOUNT

Following the reconsiderations of the late 1920s, the dawn of the 1930s saw the GWR shift its focus from the landscape to the people who populated it. It was, however, not simply the case that people were pictured in the landscapes or villages. In the new aesthetic turn, consumers were depicted as active and carefree in an attempt to attract and hold the viewer's gaze. They recommended destinations through different visual messages about happiness and success. To communicate these qualities, the GWR used modern picturing

conventions drawn from wider photographic and film culture. Eminent photographers such as Edward Steichen in America demonstrated how photography could be used to create a visual language surrounding consumption,
using people to influence the consumption decisions of others (Johnson, 3–4).
This style was more emotional, more manipulative than photographic realism,
projecting obvious fantasies and ideals, mapping out the way to a happier life
and making an idealized world seem accessible (Johnson, 1). The role of the
commercial photographer increased as advertising photography developed a
distinct professional identity (Hewitt & Wilkinson, 22–23). This, coupled with
the pervasiveness of cinema as chief element of leisure, developed a visual
language surrounding consumption—one that consumers were exceptionally
well equipped to decode. While people did not accept these messages uncriti-
cally, the work of McKibbin and Francis illustrates that cinema's messages
formed a large part of how people perceived their own position and made
moves to better it (McKibbin, 523; Francis, 238). Films were popular because
people could see themselves in an exotic and aspirational form (Francis, 238).
The appropriation of these exotic forms into publicity led to the development
of lifestyle advertising.

Lifestyle advertising, the creation of a precise social setting to evoke a
way of life associated with a given product (Hewitt & Wilkinson, 22–23),
relied on the photographic image to make its aspirational images seem real.
Fashion, beauty, and success were all communicated via youthful models or
celebrity endorsement, as advertisers sought to connect visions of Hollywood
with products and services (Lears, 329). Though historians would not normally associate the railways with such techniques, the astronomical rise of
peopled imagery in *Holiday Haunts* points to the company's own recognition
of the need to appeal to potential consumers' emotions and lifestyles. The
new images contributed to an advertising culture summed up in the GWR's
collaboration with the Newquay branch of the Co-operative whose shop window summed up the importance of looking good. This human element of the
holiday was now as much a prominent consideration as where to go. A modern way of selling the holiday, such marketing reflected fashion, modernity
and glamour more so than famous locomotives or quaint fishing villages, and
represents the GWR's moves to attract the modern consumer.

The GWR's change to lifestyle imagery was also remarkably rapid, suggesting the benefits to a company of having its own photographic pool. In the
space of a few short years landscape imagery was relegated to a secondary
position behind the focus on display and conspicuous consumption. As seen
with regard to the Edwardian period, the GWR was a keen observer of social
trends and developments as well as the need to respond to change. Bennett's
work on the GWR's publicity literature illustrates the terms with which,

at the dawn of the 1930s, the GWR hierarchy debated how a modern turn could be achieved (Bennett, 13, 161). Mr. Penny, a member of the Publicity Department called for a livelier and more dynamic and humorous presentation across the company's advertising media (Bennett, 161). He desired more "friendliness," reducing the amount of cultural information in favor of hedonistic appeals (Bennett, 161). Such comment was also replicated in feedback from consumers. They believed that while information about what happened centuries ago was interesting, they would rather know whether the beach was sandy and the bathing good (Anon, Letter to Maxwell Fraser, 27 May 1935). In the face of such attitudes, *Holiday Haunts'* new photographic turn attempted to address this changing spirit with a marked emphasis on the consumer.

The new imagery pictured holidaymakers as the dénouement of what passengerhood had brought them, happy in their consumption of the destination. Just as wild nature was presented as an adjunct to everyday life in the picturesque imagery of the 1920s, in the 1930s the people were wild and carefree in a different sense. Images of holidaymakers running hand in hand through crashing waves were meant to attract the urban dweller by prompting comparisons of freedom at the destination to the restraint of everyday life at home. The new content was intended to capture this fun and carefree nature through modern advertising conventions that highlighted the qualities associated with picturing people. A range of symbols appropriated from the increasingly visual mass culture was used to convey this. Actions and faces captured close up were meant to speak for the destination. The smile, connoting acceptance and happiness, showed appreciation for the service, but also communicated to the viewer that it was worthwhile and brought fulfillment (Cortese, 28). Advertisers paid increasing attention to psychology in an effort to induce consumption (Leiss, 112). Impelled by dreams and desires, people purchased beauty or health rather than ordinary products or services. Youth, innocence, simplicity, and happiness were the attributes associated with these people and, by transference, with the holiday destination they advertised. Images such as "A Happy Trio" (Fig. 3.4) placed emphasis on bodies and actions and made the idealized holidaymaker the center of the focus. The appearance of anyone who might be defined as conventionally unattractive was rare, and this was also the case for anyone over forty. The obsession with body image was well understood by the GWR and echoed methods used by other advertisers to communicate idealized masculinity and femininity (Zweiniger-Bargielowska, 183). Far removed from rail travel, the GWR's photographs showed not only that it delivered health, happiness, and beauty, but in its depiction of lifestyles it also showed how to become a fashionable consumer or a successful parent.

Figure 3.4. "A Happy Trio," 1935.

The new images anticipated and reflected holiday desires by providing vignettes of consumption, lifestyles, and social settings that were meant to pique the interests of consumers. Boating, beach games, and ordering food were all included, with images such as "Coffee Time" (Fig. 5), a dominant feature of *Holiday Haunts* in the 1930s. Communicating these idealized visions of consumption the GWR sought an active response from consumers. While in reality not available to all they built on fantasies whereby people were encouraged to dream about emulating the lives of the wealthy and beautiful people of the images. The family was appealed to along similar ideological lines. The GWR recognized fully the value of children as salespersons and the appeal to the hearts of fond parents. Images such as "Happy Holidaymakers" (Fig. 3.6) dematerialized the holiday, inspiring the notion that the GWR could create good parents and happy families. The lifestyle associated with an aspirational family holiday was again employed to corroborate this visually. Examples such as Figure 3.6 built on the kinds of imagery that would adorn family photograph albums. The humorous and heart-warming scene of the son pouring sand down father's shirt while his adoring siblings looked on similarly had little to say about the destination itself, but rather what it would help to achieve or make people feel. Other images showed angelic mothers tending to their children or to the whole family unit in which all performed their culturally sanctioned roles perfectly.

Figure 3.5.   "Coffee Time," 1935.

Similar to the desire to personally capture landscape imagery, the new human appeals built in large part on consumers' own fascination with personal photography. Filling photograph albums, which were themselves authored by the selection of only the happiest memories (Spence & Holland, 2), potential holidaymakers were well equipped to decode images such as "Happy Holidaymakers." Yet rather than relying on ordinary tourists or people captured at the destination, the GWR used models and carefully composed imagery to ensure the effectiveness of the photographic message. While an "ordinary" tourist could still connote liveliness, the model packaged these visual appeals more slickly. They also allowed the company to glamorize the holiday by connecting it to the prevalent film culture as well as inculcating perfect visions of consumption. To augment its appeals, the GWR used the Fox Films Model Agency. The authored and constructed nature of these images is revealed in the fact that they are quite clearly posed rather than captured naturally. Capturing models at destinations (Figs. 3.5 and 3.6) or superimposing them onto backgrounds (Fig. 3.7) demonstrates the GWR's commitment to appealing to potential customers along modern lines. In these ways the GWR was also ahead of other companies that relied on stock photography. The expense associated with photographic advertising necessitated that many

Figure 3.6. "Happy Holidaymakers," 1939.

companies wanting to make use of the new appeals of photography purchased stock images. These were produced by specialist companies and made to look as general as possible so that they could be recontextualized to sell almost any product. Such advertising suffered, however, from the fact that designers were divorced from the company and the messages were occasionally lost (Hewitt & Wilkinson, 10–11). Employing its own photographers, and using model agencies only on the company's destinations or carriages, the GWR exercised a great deal of control over the eventual depictions. Thus while it may have built on and made use of established visual languages, its location of these modern appeals on its own territory contributed to the overall better impression of its posed imagery in comparison to stock photography.

Emphasis on consumers in this imagery also meant that market segmentation could be encouraged. While services for sportsmen, families, singles, couples,

Figure 3.7.   "Bathing Belles at Weymouth," 1939.

and hikers had been available for some time, this difference could now be communicated more effectively through photographic conventions. Prominent within current debates among historians regarding railway marketing is the role of women and whether companies recognized them as an individual market worthy of direct targeting (Harrington, 22). The counter to this suggests that such advertising images indicate the availability of women, and thus lend their desirability and animation to the service (Davis, 2–6). Especially in the case of young women, the display of their bodies is held to signal desire and freedom from everyday experiences (Dann, 75). Though such appeals were undoubtedly a successful engagement of the male gaze, Harrington uses pictorial conventions and symbolism within poster art to suggest that the developing social role of women coupled with their increased ability to consume independently was recognized by the interwar railways. Rather than an afterthought, or simply included to attract a male gaze, railways recognized women as individual consumers. This viewpoint is supported in the GWR's photography, which pictured not subservient women, but ones who were active and confident in their consumption. As well as placing them as beautiful and aspirational goddesses, the camera looked up to them and reinforced this message of feminine superiority. The GWR emulated the depictions of women in periodicals such as *Vogue* and *Good Housekeeping*, prominent disseminators of idealized femininity (Zweiniger-Bargielowska, 183–184). Its goal was seemingly to use photographic conventions to align the experience of the holiday with the idea that it could bring health, beauty, and popularity.

Fashion, too, played an important role in reinforcing these appeals, as the title of this chapter suggests. The railways are not commonly seem as communicators of news regarding the fashion world, but in the examples above, the use of models, and the recognition that to some what to wear was as important as where to go, fashion was clearly an important ploy. The people of the GWR images sported modern wear: new rubberized bathing suits imported from America, fashionable suits for the gentlemen, smart skirts for the ladies. Though the company recognized that not all could afford such expensive styles, the fashionable clothes were intended to cultivate desire and the impression that a GWR holiday was socially vaunted. While strained budgets necessitated that consumers shop at the Co-operative as opposed to high-end London retailers, the use of models, fashion, and conspicuous consumption all point to deliberate choices by the GWR in crafting its advertisements very carefully. While holiday lifestyles were often used to sell clothes, the GWR used clothes to sell the lifestyle of the holiday.

As well as holiday destinations, the potential of photography was realized in showing consumers that getting to destinations could play a part in the aspirational experience. Often seen as a low point in the holiday—crammed into aging carriages with many other holidaymakers—the GWR recognized the need to improve the perception of its conveyance. Other transport providers linked themselves inextricably to modern ideas surrounding comfort, speed, and luxury (Rieger, 158–168). Cars and long-distance coaches not only advertised their advantages as taking passengers door to door, but also illustrated them as providers of a more comfortable, more private means of traveling, one which negated some of the commonly held issues associated with rail travel. The Fox Film models were used again to create the impression of rail travel as a convenience of the fashionable and wealthy, connoted both in their clothing and their choice to dine on board the train instead of taking food with them. Again, the models conform to idealized standards seen above. Young and attractive, they subconsciously created the illusion that beauty was an attribute of the service. While Schivelbusch argues for

Figure 3.8.   "The Joy of the Journey," 1939.

the decline of conversation within the rail carriage (74), the GWR's imagery refuted the idea of a solitary experience and assuaged fears of being secluded in a carriage with undesirable individuals. The people of the carriages engaged each other, seemingly excited by their companionship and the journey about to be undertaken (Fig. 3.8). Lifestyle elements, ordering food, and the presence of sporting paraphernalia (in Fig. 3.9) hinted at the pursuits of these people and how the train journey might be useful in improving people's lives not just through holiday but by providing healthy sport or a place to meet friends. The message of comfort and luxury pursued the idea that rail travel was not antiquated but capable of meeting the modern and fashionable standards laid down by aircraft and ocean liners.

The examples from the 1930s photographic turn included here constitute only a brief look at the innovative output that anticipated and displayed consumer desires. Hikers and campers were another prominent group recognized by the GWR and appealed to using an aspirationalized view of the countryside as a place of leisure. While we have seen but one of the photographs aimed at the family market, countless others depicted children playing or embracing parents and innumerable bathing belles basked in both the sunlight and the adoration of their peers. What is clear is that the GWR was a developed user of photographic publicity and lifestyle techniques to ascribe

Figure 3.9.   "By GWR First Class," 1939.

new meanings to its holidays and services. More so than text, these views targeted and appealed to potential passengers based on social desires for fashion, happiness and success. As Harrington recognized, there is a danger that such analysis will see the consumer as a passive cipher, taking in all that is favorably advertised (22). This chapter has not speculated on how consumers interpreted and responded to this imagery, but rather the GWR's perception of them—chiefly that visual advertising could be used to structure consumers' desires. The company's continued success in the face of challenges from cars and other railways and the fact that images of consumers constituted an increasing share of its visual appeals testifies to the value that the company placed on lifestyle and emotive appeals to encourage consumers to consider the GWR above and beyond its role as a provider of transportation.

CONCLUSION

While the marketing efforts of car, ocean liner, and airline companies have been analyzed as icons of modernity, the literature on consumption still neglects the railways as participators in this modern discourse (Marchand;

Gottdiener). This chapter has argued that this neglect is undeserved and that the railways, in this case the GWR specifically, employed advanced marketing techniques led by the need to appeal rather than dictate to consumers. Progressing onward from Edwardian discussions on how to persuade and induce consumption, it is not surprising to find that the GWR had a developed and characteristically modern approach to passenger desires and how to influence these through its marketing. Perceptions of the market drove change. Rather than authentic representations of place, the company constructed visual narratives about consumption at the destination, weaving ideological meanings into its visual narratives to encourage consumers to consider the service beyond its price. Venerating certain images and signs the company first offered a gateway to a romantic rural England. Perceiving an interest in the supposed decline of England as well as widespread unhappiness at the encroachment of modernity, it targeted these appeals to an urban middle class. In the face of changing values and competition from other transport forms the company modernized its appeals by establishing the notion of the GWR as a provider of modern, fashionable, and, above all, aspirational experiences.

Though it may not have used celebrity appeals or rivaled the leading examples of American fashion photography, the GWR's photographic marketing nevertheless echoes much of what has been deemed innovative in studies of American examples (Johnson; Marchand). The case of the GWR also provides a strong example of a British company producing advanced material at a time when other historians see photographic marketing in Britain as "unadventurous and unchallenging" (Hewitt & Wilkinson, 10–11). To the cultural historian wishing to build a fuller picture of how consumption was understood and shaped during the first half of the twentieth century, the railways thus present an interesting comparison to the widely analyzed examples of fashion, foodstuff, alcohol, and tobacco companies. They present an underused source, one able to reveal much about how holiday marketing developed away from informative, text-based appeals and authentic representations of place to emotional visual marketing. To the railway historian, how the railways negotiated modern marketing techniques offers a cultural focus in place of the usual emphasis on statistics and data. The economic performance of Britain's railway companies from the nineteenth century to the twentieth has constituted a popular area of research for many years now (Channon), yet despite this received history the links between economic and cultural factors are conspicuously absent from scholarly literature. Perceptions of the consumer and how they were appealed to through the use of innovative marketing provides an excellent and achievable avenue of research into how the railways as big businesses engaged with and helped shape modern consumption practices.

ACKNOWLEDGMENTS

All images are reproduced with permission courtesy of BRB (Residuary) Ltd and The National Railway Museum, York.

BIBLIOGRAPHY

"A Happy Trio." Holiday Haunts. Paddington. 1935. Print.
"Advertising Motor Car Tours." *Great Western Railway Magazine* (June 1914): 163. Print.
Anon. Letter to Maxwell Fraser. 27 May 1935. Maxwell Fraser Papers. MAXSER F 1–150. National Library of Wales, Aberystwyth. Manuscript.
Bartholomew, Ed, and Michael Blakemore. *Railways in Focus: Photographs from the National Railway Museum Collections*. Penryn: Atlantic Transport Publishers, 1998. Print.
"Bathing Belles at Weymouth." Holiday Haunts. Paddington. 1939. Print.
Beaumont, Matthew, and Michael Freeman (Eds.). *The Railway and Modernity: Time, Space and The Machine Ensemble*. Oxford: Peter Lang, 2007. Print.
Bennett, Alan. *The Great Western Railway and the Celebration of Englishness*. University of York: Unpublished Ph.D. thesis, 2000. Print.
Burke, Peter. *Eyewitnessing: The Uses of Images as Historical Evidence*. London: Reaktion, 2001. Print.
"By GWR First Class." Holiday Haunts. Paddington. 1939. Print.
Carter, Ian. *Railways and Culture in Britain: The Epitome of Modernity*. Manchester: Manchester University Press, 2001. Print.
Channon, Geoffrey. *Railways in Britain and the United States, 1830–1940: Studies in Economic and Business History*. Aldershot: Ashgate, 2001. Print.
"Church Steps, Minehead." Holiday Haunts. Paddington. 1927. Print.
Cole, Beverly, and Richard Durack. *Railway Posters 1923–1947*. London: Lawrence King, 1992. Print.
"Coffee Time." Holiday Haunts. Paddington. 1935. Print.
"Co-operative Advertising Display in a Newport Shop Window: What to Wear and Where to Go—by Great Western Railway." *Great Western Railway Magazine* July 1930: 308. Print.
Cortese, Anthony. *Provocateur: Images of Women and Minorities in Advertising*. Oxford: Rowman and Littlefield Publishers, 2004. Print.
Dann, Graham. "The People of Tourist Brochures." *The Tourist Image: Myths and Myth Making in Tourism*. Ed. Tom Selwyn. Chichester: John Wiley & Son Ltd, 1996. 61–82. Print.
Davis, Simone. *Living up to the Ads: Gender Fictions of the 1920s*. Durham, N.C.: Duke University Press, 2000. Print.
Dibb, Sally (Ed.). *Marketing Concepts and Strategies*. 4th European ed. Boston: Houghton Mifflin, 2001.

Divall, Colin. "The Modern Passenger: Constructing the Consumer on Britain's Railways, 1919–1939." *Railway Modernization: An Historical Perspective (19th and 20th Centuries)*. Pinheiro, Magda (Ed.). Lisbon, 2009. 111–125. Print.

Fitzgerald, Robert. *Rowntree and the Marketing Revolution 1862–1969*. Cambridge: University Press, 1995. Print.

Francis, Martin. "Leisure and Popular Culture." *Women in Twentieth-Century Britain*. Ed. Zweiniger-Bargielowska, Ina. Harlow: Longman, 2001. 229–247. Print.

Gold, John, and George Revill. *Representing the Environment*. New York: Routledge, 2004. Print.

Gottdiener, Mark (Ed.). *New Forms of Consumption: Consumers, Culture and Commodities*. Oxford: Rowman & Littlefield Publishers, 2000. Print.

Great Western Railway Traffic Department. Annual Report 1928. Great Western Railway Secretarial Papers. RAIL 258/425. The National Archives, Kew. Manuscript.

"G.W.R Advertising." *Great Western Railway Magazine* (August 1910): 195. Print.

"Happy Holidaymakers." Holiday Haunts. Paddington. 1939. Print.

Harrington, Ralph. "Beyond the Bathing Belle: Images of Women in Inter-War Railway Publicity." *Journal of Transport History* 25.1 (2004): 22–45. Print.

Heller, Michael. "Corporate Brand Building: Shell-Mex Ltd. in the Inter-war Period." *Trademarks Brands and Competitiveness*. Eds. Da Silva Lopes, Teresa, and Paul Duguid. New York: Routledge, 2010. 194–214. Print.

Hewitt, John, and Helen Wilkinson. *Selling the Image: The Work of Photographic Advertising Limited*. Bradford: National Museum of Photography, Film and Television, 1996. Print.

Horwood, Catherine. "'Girls Who Arouse Dangerous Passions': Women and Bathing, 1900– 39." *Women's History Review* 9.4 (2000): 653–673. Print.

Johnston, Patricia. *Real Fantasies: Edward Steichen's Advertising Photography*. Berkeley: University of California Press, 1997. Print.

Knoop, Douglas. *Outlines of Railway Economics*. London: Macmillan and Co., 1913. Print.

Laird, Pamela. *Advertising Progress: American Business and the Rise of Consumer Marketing*. Baltimore: The John Hopkins University Press, 1998. Print.

Lears, T. J. Jackson. *Fables of Abundance: A Cultural History of Advertising in America*. New York: Basic Books, 1994. Print.

Leiss, William, Sut Jhally, and Stephen Kline. *Social Communication in Advertising: Persons Products and Images of Well-Being*. Scarborough, Ontario: Routledge, 1988. Print.

Marchand, Roland. *Advertising the American Dream: Making Way for Modernity, 1920– 1940*. Berkeley: University of California Press, 1986. Print.

Marks F. C. G. "The Evolution of the Pictorial Poster." *Great Western Railway Magazine* (May 1907): 99–100. Print.

Martin, G. H. "Sir George Samuel Measom (1818–1901), and His Railway Guides." *The Impact of the Railway on Society in Britain*. Eds. Evans, A. K. B., and John Gough. Aldershot: Ashgate, 2003. 225–240. Print.

Matless, David. *Landscape and Englishness*. London: Reaktion Books, 1998. Print.

McKibbin, Ross. *Classes and Cultures: England 1918–1951*. Oxford: Oxford University Press, 1998. Print.

"Monogram Competition." *Great Western Railway Magazine* (August 1905): 137. Print.

Morton, Henry. *In Search of England*. London: Methuen, 1927. Print.

Mowat, Charles. *Britain between the Wars, 1918–1940*. London: Methuen, 1968. Print.

Percy, Larry & Richard Elliot. *Strategic Advertising Management*. Oxford: Oxford University Press, 2009. Print.

"Railway Advertising." *Great Western Railway Magazine* (May 1909): 100–101. Print.

Richards, Thomas. *The Commodity Culture of Victorian England: Advertising and Spectacle, 1851–1914*. London: Verso, 1991. Print.

Richards, T. H. "Photographs from the Carriage Window." *Great Western Railway Magazine* (December 1924): 468. Print.

Rieger, Bernhard. *Technology and the Culture of Modernity in Britain and Germany, 1890–1945*. Cambridge: Cambridge University Press, 2004. Print.

Rose, Gillian. *Visual Methodologies: An Introduction to the Interpretation of Visual Materials*. London: Sage, 2007. Print.

Ross, Corey. "Visions of Prosperity: The Americanisation of Advertising in Interwar Germany." *Selling Modernity: Advertising in Twentieth Century Germany*. Eds. Swett, Pamela E., S. Jonathan Wiesen, and Jonathan R. Zatlin. Durham: Duke University Press, 2007. 52–77. Print.

Schivelbusch, Wolfgang. *The Railway Journey: The Industrialisation of Time and Space in the Nineteenth Century*. Oxford: Basil Blackwell, 1980. Print.

Schwarzkopf, Stefan. "Discovering the Consumer: Market Research, Product Innovation, and the Creation of Brand Loyalty in Britain and the United States in the Inter-war Years." *Journal of Macromarketing* 29.8 (2009): 8–20. Print.

Slater, Don. *Consumer Culture and Modernity*. Cambridge: Polity Press, 1997. Print.

Solomon, Michael (Ed.). *Marketing: Real People, Real Decisions*. Upper Saddle River: Pearson Prentice Hall, 2009. Print.

Spence, Jo, and Patricia Holland (Eds.). *Family Snaps: The Meanings of Domestic Photography*. London: Virago, 1991. Print.

"Swiss Cottage, Ilfracombe Lee." Holiday Haunts. Paddington. 1927. Print.

Taylor, John. *A Dream of England: Landscape, Photography, and the Tourist's Imagination*. Manchester: Manchester University Press, 1994. Print.

"The Cornish Coast near the Lizard." Holiday Haunts. Paddington. 1927. Print.

"The Joy of the Journey." Holiday Haunts. Paddington. 1939. Print.

Timins, D. T. "Art on the Railway." *The Railway Magazine* (May 1900): 417–426. Print.

Urry, John. *The Tourist Gaze*. London: Sage Publications, 2002. Print.

Walton, John. *The British Seaside: Holidays and Resorts in the Twentieth Century*. Manchester: Manchester University Press, 2000. Print.

Watts, D. C. H. "Evaluating British Railway Poster Advertising: The London and North Eastern Railway Company between the Wars." *Journal of Transport History* 25.2 (2004): 23–56. Print.

Wiener, Martin. *English Culture and the Decline of the Industrial Spirit*. Cambridge, UK: Cambridge University Press, 2004. Print.

Wilson, Roger. *Go Great Western: A History of GWR Publicity*. Newton Abbott: David and Charles, 1970. Print.

Zweiniger-Bargielowska, Ina. "The Body and Consumer Culture." *Women in Twentieth-Century Britain*. Ed. Zweiniger-Bargielowska. Harlow: Longman, 2001. 183–197. Print.

Chapter 4

Seen from a Carriage

A Rhythmanalytic Study of Train Travel and Mediation

Rowan Wilken

"Rhythms. Rhythms. They reveal and they hide."

—Henri Lefebvre (*Rhythmanalysis*, 36)

"There should be much to say concerning the arrangement of train seats, timetables, windows, tickets, newspapers, rain clouds, mobile phones, rucksacks, railway cuttings, and all the social and technological flotsam of train travel. Yet, there has been little [. . .]."

—Laura Watts ("The Art and Craft of Train Travel," 712)

" . . . every age has its own carriage, its expressions, its gestures."

—Charles Baudelaire (*The Painter of Modern Life*, 18)

DEPARTURE/INTRODUCTION: RHYTHMANALYSIS

Over the past decade or so, there has been a significant flowering of critical interest in train travel, especially as this dovetails with a range of other concerns, including transport planning issues, temporal considerations (Jain & Lyons; Lyons, Jain, & Holley; Lyons & Urry; Urry), how train travel is experienced by passengers (Bissell, "Passenger Mobilities," "Visualizing Everyday"; O'Dell; Symes), and passenger uses of ICTs (Axtell, Hislop & Whittaker; Ohmori & Harata; Moktarian; Berry & Hamilton; Weight). The present study contributes to this literature. It combines the above strands of enquiry in an exploration of the complex wider forms of mediation that occur within the confined space of the train carriage. In examining this issue, the analysis of this chapter draws together three different approaches: informal observational analysis, Lefebvrian "rhythmanalysis," and engagement with the established critical literature on train travel, everyday public interactions, and contemporary train-based mobile media research.

The central argument of this chapter is that the sociospatial environment of the modern suburban train carriage is routinely experienced and negotiated as a dynamic environment of physical (and "virtual") co-presence that involves complex forms, layerings, and negotiations of different kinds of mediation, including windows (as both mirror and screen), audio public address systems (operated by driver or station staff), analog media (print publications of various forms, as well as advertisements), and digital media technologies (MP3 players, mobile telephones, laptops, train carriage LED displays), and other personal items (makeup compacts, glasses). Furthermore, these intricate mediated engagements also change subtly but significantly according to annual, diurnal, and manifold additional competing rhythms, environmental factors, and other variables, and even according to the socioeconomic makeup of particular suburbs through which the train passes and at which passengers embark or disembark. The conceptual framework that anchors and gives structure to this examination of train travel and mediation is the Lefebvrian notion of "rhythmanalysis."

Rhythms have been understood to take many forms and to operate at a variety of scales and durations. For instance, there are complex social rhythms that, as Edensor and Holloway explain, "can be institutionally inscribed (marked by national festivals, religious occasions, hours of commerce or television schedules), locally organized (via hours of work and local folk customs), or form synchronized collective habits (eating, playing, sleeping and working together)" (484). These are interwoven with cyclical "natural" rhythms, such as "days, nights, seasons, the waves and tides of the sea, monthly cycles, etc." (Lefebvre, 8), and with what Lefebvre designates as "linear" rhythms which he associates with "human activity" as embedded in everyday life, especially "the monotony of actions and of movements" and of "imposed structures" (8). In addition, rhythms, are always "multiple, complex," sometimes harmonious, "often dissonant" (Edensor & Holloway, 484)—or, in Lefebvrian terms (where he draws from the language of medicine), they are both cyclical and linear, but just as commonly characterized by "eurhythmia," "arrhythmia," and "polyrhythmia" (Lefebvre, 16).

Lefebvre developed a particular, generalized, understanding of rhythms in order to be able to attend to them as an "object" of study, and one that consisted of two parts: (1) "everywhere there is interaction between a place, a time and an expenditure of energy, there is rhythm" (15), and (2) all rhythms are characterized by three things: (a) "repetition (of movements, gestures, action, situations, differences)," (b) "interferences of linear processes and cyclical processes," and (c) "birth, growth, peak, then decline and end" (15). In combination, Lefebvre argues, these supply "the framework for analyses of the particular," of "real, concrete cases" (15).

While the scheme of rhythmanalysis is rich with possibility, Simonsen argues that "the scheme of rhythmanalysis should not be overdrawn," as it is "an incomplete project, introduced through a few concepts and hypotheses and employed in very different and diverse examples" (47). Thus, while a generalized science of the study of rhythms has not eventuated (though this was Lefebvre's dream), rhythmanalysis has proven to be a very productive analytical tool with wide application. For instance, it has been employed in examinations of city life (Highmore; Simonsen), domestic technology consumption (Obert), and tourist coach travel (Edensor & Holloway). In the present study it is adopted as a perspective from which to elucidate the complexities of the heavily mediated nature of urban train travel, as studied on the suburban Hurstbridge line in the city of Melbourne, Australia.

Melbourne is a city of around 4 million people and is situated at the southeastern end of mainland Australia. The Hurstbridge line is 38 km in length and runs between the outer northeast of Melbourne from Hurstbridge, a suburb (almost still a village) nestled toward the foothills of the southern most tip of Australia's Great Dividing Range, to Melbourne's central business district (CBD). The first section of this line opened in 1888 (between the inner Melbourne suburb of Collingwood and the middle suburb of Heidelberg); the section between Heidelberg and the outer suburb of Eltham (then a village known as Eltham Town) opened in 1902, and the final section, between Eltham and the line's termination point in Hurstbridge, was completed a decade later in 1912. Two sections of the line, the largest at the Hurstbridge end, are still single-gauge only—a fact that has a significant bearing on the rhythms of the daily commute for passengers traveling in both directions, causing significant flow-on disruptions when there is an incident or when a train is delayed; a further key section (between the suburb of Westgarth and the key inner hub station of Clifton Hill, where this line and the Epping line converge) was only duplicated in 2009.

Motivated by Lefebvre's suggestion that "rhythmanalysis could change our perceptions of surroundings" (17), I undertook to study, via informal participant-observational analysis conducted over a two-year period (2008–2009), the diverse "repetitions and differences" (Lefebvre, 43) that characterized daily commuter travel on this line. As noted at the outset, a key focus of this rhythmanalytic study was a concern for the complex forms, layerings, and negotiations of different kinds of mediation, and the ways that these routinely shape daily train travel.

Thus, the particular rhythms under analysis here are the product of interactions that occur between a place (the carriage of a Metro Trains Melbourne operated X'Trapolis train running the limited express commuter service on the Hurstbridge line), a time (the 42 minutes of travel from 8:06 a.m. to 8:48 a.m.), and an expenditure of energy (an elaborate network of human and nonhuman "actors"—including the train itself, the passengers and their media devices, and so forth).

The specific situational focus of this study, then, is the morning commute between Eltham station—the third stop toward the city from Hurstbridge, and the place where I embark—and the inner city station of Flinders Street, the penultimate stop before the train enters the underground loop running beneath Melbourne's CBD.

Finally, with its focus on the rhythms of an often-crowded carriage, a central preoccupation of this study is with attending to what Lefebvre describes as "bodies as bundles of rhythms." According to Lefebvre, it is necessary to listen to these "bundles" or "braiding of rhythms" (Edensor & Holloway, 484) "in order to grasp the natural or produced ensembles" (Lefebvre, 20) that result from them. Rhythmanalysis, Lefebvre argues, always strives for reason and the sensible. In order to achieve this, that is, "in order to grasp and analyze rhythms, it is necessary to get outside them, but not completely" (27). Thus, in an important passage, with vital methodological implications for the present study, Lefebvre writes:

> The rhythmnanalyst will not be obliged to jump from the inside to the outside of observed bodies; he should come to listen to them as a whole and unify them by taking his own rhythms as a reference: by integrating the outside and the inside and vice versa. (20)

And so, in adopting this approach, I have endeavored, as informal participant-observer (or "auto-ethnographer"), to be a commuter who is attentive to my own cyclical, linear, and dissonant rhythms, as well as to those of my fellow passengers and of the train trip as a whole. I represent these observations as an imagined single journey, beginning in the outer suburbs of Melbourne, and heading inward to the city center.

And so this rhythmanalytic journey begins. But where does it begin? The clear answer is: *in medias res*. This is because the daily commute never begins on or after stepping off the train station platform. Rather, there are manifold other morning rhythms that precede as well as intersect with specific travel rhythms: those associated with rising, eating, and attending to what Goffman might term the presentation of self; there are hurried goodbyes to be made, the interstitial rhythms involved in traveling to the station, and tickets to be purchased and validated, or credit to be added to "smart cards" (Melbourne has a dual ticketing system). There are also a number of other key preparatory rhythms and rituals that have a significant bearing on the discussion to follow, which are associated with the packing of bags and decisions about what to put in them—"media devices," both old and new, analog (printed matter) and digital (phones, laptops, e-readers, MP3 players), and "portable objects" that are harder to classify, such as wallets, keys, and so forth (Ito, Okabe & Anderson).

This examination also begins in the middle of things in the sense that, once the train pulls into Eltham, all those embarking are entering into—disturbing, reconfiguring—the previously settled rhythms of a journey that began three stops prior to this one at the point of origin: Hurstbridge.

ELTHAM 8:06 A.M.

Much could be written about the sociomaterial and spatial relations and decisions that accompany the act of boarding a train. This seemingly simple act is in fact deceptively complex, characterized by manifold microchoices: Where does one stand on the platform to be nearest the opening door? Which carriage is most preferable (both now and at the destination)? Where to sit— forward or backward, window or aisle, does one take the seat in the group of four, even though one is already taken, or the group of six on the other side of the aisle, knowing that they will soon fill up, or does one sit with the group of school students knowing they will likely disembark along the way and, in doing so, vacate a plum seat?

These and other practices Watts refers to as the "art and craft of train travel," a phrase she intends "in the sense of a skilled artistry" that draws on "knowledges, experiences, and perceptions" to create "experiences through social and material practice" (712). In her own "mobile ethnography" of UK train travel, Watts delineates between two broad categories or "configurations" of passengers that are equally applicable here: what she calls the "packed" traveler versus the "unpacked." The packed passenger is highly mobile and is "configured for movement, for walking to the train station, for stepping through a carriage to a seat, for dashing on to a connecting service" (715, 716). In contrast, the "unpacked" involves a "reconfiguration of person and property" and is generally associated with the relative immobility and temporal duration of a longer trip. While these aren't mutually exclusive categories (one needs to travel, "packed," to the train prior to "unpacking" on it), commuters embarking at Eltham, who have 42 minutes' travel time ahead, do tend to be of the unpacked variety.

Thus, as soon as a seat is secured and bodies and bags arranged, a variety of media objects and tools are retrieved and prepared: home-delivered newspapers, extracted with a ripping sound from their cling-wrap cocoons, are unrolled; station-purchased papers are unfolded and refolded into a more manageable and less-intrusive size; books are opened; iPod cords are untangled and earbuds inserted; laptops are opened and booted; and, in my case, a notebook and clutch-pencil are retrieved, as generally are, when I am not observing, a bundle of journal article PDF printouts for reading and annotating. Such a wide assortment of media objects, as Jain and Lyon note, "have become central to the art of equipping travel time and managing the public space of rail [. . .] travel" (89). As has been noted elsewhere, these media objects also serve as "place-making devices" (Berry & Hamilton, 114)—they "help to 'warm' public space, and make it more hospitable to the needs and wants of the individual commuter" (O'Dell, 125).

And yet, *how* one "unpacks," and the motivations for this, are shaped by two further decisional determinations that Jain and Lyons designate as that between "transition time" (defined as "the opportunity for gearing up to the destination's demands," such as the work day ahead) and "time out" (defined, after Goffman, as "'backstage' time to be oneself or [to do] a specific activity," such as reading or listening to music) (Jain & Lyons, 85).

What needs to be noted, however, is that in addition to these material arrangements and rearrangements, other sensory stimuli are also at work—as Watts notes, "the sensoriality of train travel has affects[,] scents and sounds [. . .] that spill out from passengers fill the space and interact in unanticipated ways" (720). There is the auditory, including the polite mutterings as access to seats is negotiated, the sounds of passengers unpacking, electronic doors closing, station announcements, the train horn sounding immanent departure, as well as the screeches of the local bird life (the sulphur-crested cockatoos, corellas, galahs, and eastern rosellas that I strongly identify with Eltham and which serve as aural markers of my departure and return). There is also the olfactory and the oral. "Smells," Lefebvre writes, "are of great importance to the rhythmanalyst" (41). With its own privately operated station coffee cart, at this time of the morning the carriage is permeated by the smell of takeaway coffee, intermingled with the scents of freshly applied perfume and *eau de cologne*. Visual attentiveness is also heightened, both as part of the ritual of securing seats, but also as passengers embarking scan those already seated (and vice versa), and as commuters from Eltham seek out what Stanley Milgram has termed "familiar strangers"—those whom we observe repeatedly but without any direct interaction, such as certain fellow public transport users whom we might encounter on a regular basis in the course of our daily commutes to and from work. So, for instance, while I haven't downloaded Intel's Jabberwocky application (which employs the Bluetooth protocol to search one's surroundings for the ID codes emitted from other proximate Bluetooth-enabled devices, which it then stores, so that the user can search for "familiar" mobile-equipped strangers—see Paulos and Goodman), I do recognize certain "familiar strangers" on my daily travels, such as the bespectacled older gentleman with the *Australia Post* lanyard who reads each day what I assume to be his Bible for the first few stops, before traveling the remainder of the journey with his eyes closed, possibly in prayerful reverie.

This very densely packed and informationally rich data is condensed into a very short space of time, spanning the arrival of the train and its departure a minute or so later at 8:06 a.m.

MONTMORENCY 8:10 A.M.

As the train pulls into Montmorency, the same processes just described are repeated all over again (as they will be at each of the remaining nine stops on this, the limited express service). Even at this comparatively early stage of the journey, the number of seats and the variety of seating positions on offer are already drastically reduced. This has a considerable bearing on what takes place from this point onward in the morning commute. A valuable means of drawing out what occurs in such circumstances as the carriages begin to fill is to turn to the earlier work of Simmel and Goffman.

In a famous passage, Simmel makes the following observations concerning shifts in social interaction brought about by the rise of modernity and associated developments in technologies of mass transport:

> Before the development of buses, trains and streetcars in the nineteenth century, people were quite unable to look at each other for minutes or hours at a time, or to be forced to do so, without talking to each other. Modern traffic increasingly reduces the majority of sensory relations between human beings to mere sight [. . .]. (qtd. in Schivelbusch, 75)

As Schivelbusch puts it, "the face-to-face arrangement that had once institutionalized an existing need for communication now became unbearable" (74). In response, various internal psychic and interactional adjustments have become necessary and have developed over time as a way of ameliorating this sense of discomfort brought about by the proximity of the stranger that is near (Simmel, 402). For instance, Simmel writes that "the metropolitan type [. . .] develops an organ protecting him [or herself] against the threatening currents and discrepancies of [the] external environment" (410). Expanding on this point a few pages later, Simmel remarks that "reserve" becomes the default "mental attitude" of "metropolitans towards one another"—"self-preservation in the face of the large city" demands it (415). Such reserve, Simmel argues, constitutes "the form or cloak of a more general mental phenomenon of the metropolis" (416). A number of years later, Goffman described this in slightly different terms as "civil inattention," by which he means the process of being in public but minimizing the attention one pays to others (*Behavior*, 139).

What is important to note here is that since the earliest days of train travel, media have played a crucial role in facilitating this social distance by acting as an intermediary—as "buffering tools of disengagement" (O'Dell, 125)—between an individual and a wider traveling public. For instance, while Schivelbusch notes that "the idea of reading while traveling on trains is as old as the railroad itself" (64), its rise to prominence in the nineteenth century was for good reason:

> The emergence of the habit of reading while traveling was not only a result of the dissolution and panoramization of the outside landscape due to velocity, but also a result of the situation inside the train compartment. The railroad disrupted the travelers' relationships to each other as it disrupted their relationship to the traversed landscape. (Schivelbusch, 67)

And yet, as Simmel makes clear, while "reserve and indifference" are associated with the isolation that can be seen as characteristic of urban life ("one nowhere feels as lonely and lost as in the metropolitan crowd," 418), it can also provide positive benefits: "it grants to the individual a kind and an amount of personal freedom which has no analogy whatsoever under other conditions" (416). Thus, from the book to the iPod (Bull), media technologies and the sociotechnical adaptations associated with them have, since the nineteenth century, served a vital tactical function in converting "reserve" into a form of (transitory) "personal freedom"—albeit one that some social scientists propose suggests a more concerning "absent presence" (Gergen).

The above insights add a further dimension to Jain and Lyons's conception of "equip time." That is, the time spent preparing and packing for travel "objects such as mobile technologies, work related documents, or leisure reading (or even thoughts and ideas)" as important enablers for the two categories discussed earlier, those of "transition time" or "time out" (85). These carefully selected objects can and often do in fact perform double duty: they assist in the transition from home to work, or in "zoning out" during travel, *as well as* facilitating the maintenance of Simmel's notion of internal reserve.

GREENSBOROUGH 8:13 A.M.

The automated voice-over announces that we are "now arriving at Greensborough." Greensborough, like Eltham, is a bigger "hub" station, albeit one with a very different demographic mix. Over the two-year observation period, this station more than any other tended to cue for me a particular form of visual practice that has been referred to as "anticipatory watchfulness," where "passengers actively perceive, evaluate, and appropriate objects of vision, particularly in relation to corporeal risk and personal security" (Bissell, "Visualizing Everyday," 52). These observations are significant in that they draw attention to the fact that civil inattention rarely (if ever) implies a lack of attention. Rather, on some occasions it can be an active and open scanning, and on others it can be more covert alertness, "masked" by an apparent retreat into "backstage" time via our engagement with the protective shield of various forms of analog and digital media.

Passengers embarking at Greensborough trigger certain reconfigurations of settled rhythms of each carriage in another sense also (which is not necessarily negative). This is the first stop where seated passengers need, by necessity, to rearrange and shift their packed and unpacked belongings in order to free up the few remaining available seats. This process, too, has been understood to be dense with meaning, despite its apparent mundanity. Recounting one occasion when a fellow passenger had (somewhat reluctantly) moved her book bag to make room for him, O'Dell reflects on how the two of them had "entered a vaguely defined guest-host relation" insofar as that passenger had opened to him "part of the space she had staked out for herself" (127).

Leaving Greensborough, the train turns left heading south on its journey toward the city. Along this section of track, the carriage is elevated so that one can see above and across the tightly subdivided housing that is arrayed alongside the track and continuing to the north. Sitting on the right side of the carriage, as I like to do, I find the window is "sucking me outside the train" (Watts, 718), drawn by the "infectious pull of the view" (Adey, qtd. in Bissell, "Visualizing Everyday," 52). What I am describing is an experience with a long history in the scholarship on train travel, where it has been suggested that, in the early days of train travel, "the train window accentuated the processual and mobile qualities of landscape perception" (Bissell, "Visualizing Everyday," 42).

What I encountered, in short, was the train window experienced as a media screen of sorts "displaying" or "containing" the flickering suburban landscape within it. A great deal has been written about the apparent parallels between vehicular windows of one form and another and media (usually cinematic) screens. For instance, commenting on the "private telematics of driving," Baudrillard suggests that "the vehicle now becomes a kind of capsule . . . the surrounding landscape unfolding like a televised screen" (qtd. in Friedberg, 203, n. 1). In a similar vein, Virilio remarks that "what goes on in the windshield is cinema in the strict sense" (qtd. in Friedberg, 203, n. 1). According to Schivelbusch, however, trains present a somewhat different case. Unlike the driver of the train, or the driver of a car for that matter, train travelers "had a very limited chance to look ahead: thus all they saw was an evanescent landscape" (55). Nevertheless, the screenic associations continue. For instance, writing on contemporary train travel, Bissell ("Visualizing Everyday") makes mention of the "widescreen presentation" (47) of windows, the way windows produce a "cinematic effect" (46), the "filmic, kinesthetic dynamism" of train travel at speed, and how sonic portable media devices, such as iPods, add to the "cinematic effect" of landscape apprehension. Of key importance here, though, is the admission that landscape experienced through the window (as "media screen") is not viewed as a seamless scrolling or unfolding. Rather, our often distracted engagement with the world through the train window is more akin to "snapshot images" (46). That is to say, rather than a visual "gaze," "looking through the window of a fast-moving train constitutes a travel 'glance'" (46; Larsen, 87).

The fractured nature of our "screenic" perception of track or roadside landscape is captured superbly in Jean-Luc Godard's 1958 cult film *Breathless* (*A Bout de Souffle*) through his strategic deployment of the jump cut. In contrast to the more conventional "forced logic" cut, Godard's use of jump cuts in *Breathless* is deliberately jagged. Far from flowing smoothly, these jagged cuts function to disorient the spectator; they create disruption, calling attention to shifts in time and space (Baumbach, 362). A particularly memorable instance of the use of this technique is during a brief scene in which Michel Poiccard (Jean-Paul Belmondo) and Patricia Franchini (Jean Seberg) travel across Paris in a stolen convertible. The idle conversation of the pair, and Patricia's distracted glances at the passing scenery, are punctuated by abrupt cuts to the roadside cityscape. This disruption of time and space contributes to an overall sense of time, and, most importantly, *landscape* as perceived in fragments. In this particular scene, Godard's use of the jump cut captures economically the precise way in which we, as regular and often distracted train commuters, experience landscape visually when transported through it at speed: fleeting, almost disinterested glimpses that are disrupted and disjointed.

The more expansive external view just described is abruptly foreshortened as the train approaches Watsonia station, which is situated at the valley of a steep cutting.

WATSONIA 8:16 A.M.

The composition of passengers on the train changes noticeably; numerous school students disembark and city commuters continue to pile on, filling the few remaining seats and, with standing room available only, the central isle. With this, as Lefebvre would have it, "the interaction of diverse, repetitive and different rhythms animates" (30) the train carriage and become increasingly sensorially intermingled. For instance, I, along with the two fellow travelers opposite me share (whether we wish to or not) the sounds emanating from nearby headphones; at the same time, I guiltily watch over the arm of the teenage boy to my left as he checks his Facebook on his iPhone; and, in between these stolen glances, I, along with others with a shared sight line, watch the woman diagonally opposite us with her makeup compact held up close to her face as she goes about, in Baudelaire's rather poetic description, "applying herself to the task of fostering a magic and supernatural aura about her appearance" (Baudelaire, 46).

On a prior occasion, one memorable scene which captivated me and others nearby involved an older, gray-haired gentleman in a well cut suit across the isle from me who was glued to his fire-engine red Sony PlayStation Portable (PSP) 3000 console as he sent a portly Luigi or Mario leaping and running back and forth within the diegetic world of the game that was unfolding on the screen in front of him. What was striking about this scene was the man's evident attentive dedication to his portable media device. He played uninterrupted for a full 30 minutes—at least. Even when seats became available beside him and were eagerly sought by other passengers, he did not pause in his game play or even look up. Rather, for each occupant leaving or claiming a seat he would turn his body to one side and raise his gaming console off his lap and up, out of the way, in order to let them pass, before swiveling back—still playing—to resume his original position. He performed this maneuver three or four times in the period I observed. My own fascination and that of those nearby presumably was a mix of curiosity at a perceived generational mismatch of an older man playing a bright red portable game often associated with a much younger consumer, *and* the deep level of his commitment to his game play in the midst of such distraction and movement and competing rhythms.

In contrast, a very different state of temporal and attentive interaction has been attributed to mobile phone use: "mobile phone engagement is characterized by interruption, and sporadic or split attention in the midst of other activities" (Richardson 71)—"behaviour quite distinct [. . .] from handheld console game-play" (71), as was described above. Richardson's arguments about the distracted nature of mobile phone use were witnessed repeatedly

over the two-year duration of my observations. For example, the aforementioned teenage boy checking his Facebook on his iPhone would punctuate
glances at the screen, held in his left hand and which he scrolled through
vertically by flicking his thumb downward, with glances through the windows and, from time to time, around the carriage. This, it would seem, forms
the default mode of mobile phone engagement, which Heidi Rae Cooley has
characterized as an increasingly "material experience of vision" by mobile
phone users, where "hands, eyes, screen, and surroundings interact and blend
in syncopated fashion."

MACLEOD 8:20 A.M.

A shortish distance further along at Macleod, the rhythms of the carriage are
further reconfigured as passengers embark and, notwithstanding the school
students noted above, disembark in significant numbers for the first time,
despite this being a smaller station. Many are, presumably, making transfers
by bus to La Trobe University to the north-west.

Jain and Lyons write of train travel as a "liminal process," one in which
"time and place of departure and destination" can become "blurred" and
where the journey thus becomes a "nebulous boundary" (85). They approach
this liminality as a positive thing, insofar as it provides the traveler with "the
temporal opportunity to translate, adjust or prepare [. . .] for a different social
setting and social identity at the destination" (86).

This "nebulous boundary" can be extended in other ways, however, that
are far less commonly seen as productive, especially during times of delay
or technical failure—an increasingly common occurrence given the stress
Melbourne's train system is said to be under (Weight, 2). (On one occasion I
overheard a woman remark to the coffee cart operator at Eltham station, while
discussing train delays and cancellations, "I've only managed to not be late
to work once this week.")

Macleod is a key station in this respect, especially for evening services traveling from the city. With stabling facilities on the west (Hurstbridge-bound)
side of the platform, trains can have their journey terminated here prematurely
if there are difficulties further down the track. (I have been caught here on at
least two occasions.)

I do recall one instance of system failure during the observation period,
however, that produced great mirth rather than consternation. This involved
the internal train automated public address system, which states the names
of the stations in advance of the train's arrival at them. On this particular
occasion, the audio track had been reversed so that, while the train was an

outbound service, the audio was running as if it were an inbound service, with the result that each announcement was out of sync with the forthcoming station; instead of approaching Macleod, we were told we were approaching Jolimont.

Continuing this discussion of outward journeys, by early to-mid-autumn, with the days getting shorter, the train tends to approach Macleod around dusk. These seasonal changes draw attention to Lefebvre's point that, often, "other, less lively, slower rhythms superimpose themselves on this inexorable rhythm" (30) of the daily commute. One of these slower rhythms is annual: the changing of the seasons. At dusk, the transition point between day and night, the train window shifts from functioning as a transparent "screen" to that of a reflective media surface. Accordingly, visual attention is directed from the train's exterior to its interior, a refocusing with is accompanied by other necessary adjustments (such as how to conduct discrete "person-watching" via reflection while maintaining some level of civil inattention).

ROSANNA 8:23 A.M.

For those passengers who embarked at Eltham, it was around Rosanna—just before the midway point of the journey—that, for unknown reasons, a high proportion of phone calls tended to be made.

On one occasion I actually attempted to log precisely how many ring tones and other alerts I heard sounding over the duration of the entire trip. The sheer number of alerts that sounded made this too difficult an exercise to persist with. What I was able to observe and confirm over the two-year period, however, were a number of the observations and findings I was familiar with from much of the established mobile phone research: the prevalent use of mobiles in "micro-coordination" of everyday activities and, in particular, of basic daily travel arrangements; the "where are you?" question, asked in order to establish "some sense of shared context" (Laurier); the whole gamut of social responses to negotiating incoming mobile phone calls that Plant documents in her typology of response behaviors; and, the sort of complex juggling of travel and communications demands—such as simultaneously carrying packed bags while responding to a call while exiting the train—that Light has documented.

The most striking (because so recurrent) of the many things I observed, however, relates to "notifications," such as ringtones and the sounds associated with incoming text or voice messages. According to Licoppe, "notifications, occur, appear, and surge up in our environment, and their occurrence is understood as a possible source of interruption" (289). For Licoppe, our "'connected presence' seems to call for ways to make the call recipient less obligated by the ringing of his or her phone" (294). He refers to this as a "'connected-presence'-related 'crisis of the summons'" (294). Two ways by which phone users manage this, Licoppe argues, are by (1) "weakening the summative force of the ring," often by replacing it with a musical tone and (2) "facilitating the decision to answer by personalizing the sound extract to the callers" (294). From my observations, however, this was in fact far less common than the decision to go with popular factory or downloaded options—such as the old-fashioned phone ringer sound for ringtones, and the Tour de France car horn for SMS alerts. On the return leg home I identified at least four male phone users with this last notification type, which on a number of occasions, when sounded, added an additional layer of complexity to the "crisis of the summons" described by Licoppe as four sets of hands reached for phones.

HEIDELBERG 8:26 A.M.

In his detailed study of visual practices on UK train travel, Bissell delineates three different forms of vision that he sees as characteristic of the modern day passenger experience ("Visualizing Everyday"). The first of these is "sublime vision," which Bissell draws from Schivelbusch's acclaimed account of nineteenth-century train travel to refer to "a cinematic style of visuality and the embodied experiences of passivity that emerge" (44) when viewing a panoramic landscape. The second he calls "attentive vision," where "vision is enlisted in order to achieve specific ends" (44) and which require concentration, such as reading. The third and final form is termed "mediation of vision," which emphasizes the relationship between visuality and the materiality of the carriage and is concerned with visual practices that are "intensified or quiesced by the presence of other passengers and the spatiality of the carriage itself" (44). On this journey, the only true instance of sublime vision occurs on the approach to Heidelberg, where the view opens up momentarily to reveal the expanse of eastern suburban development and the Dandenong Ranges rising behind them on the horizon. For the most part, given this is an intracity commuter service, vision is more commonly experienced in Bissell's terms as "structured and mediated by the materiality of the carriage itself" (52).

Heidelberg station services two of Melbourne's largest suburban hospitals, which loom large on the west side of the platform. Given its proximity to this vital health infrastructure, when the train draws to a halt, there is a significant reconstitution of the rhythmic composition of the carriage as passengers embark and disembark. The significant influx of passengers—not to mention the aroma of coffee once again as here, too, there is a platform-situated coffee cart—filling the isles and doorways leads to a significant "narrowing of the visual field" (Bissell, "Visualizing Everyday," 54) inside the carriage. Internal vision is no longer unimpeded. Given the low-level seating in X'Trapolis trains; seat design is not a significant mediating factor for vision in the same way that it is in Bissell's UK study (where all the seats had high backs that blocked lines of sight). Rather, here the key factor in mediating vision is other people. As a result of the near-full carriage, the overall internal visual field of the carriage is dramatically foreshortened. Sightlines are contracted, and longer lines of vision are only available on oblique angles in the gaps that open up momentarily between standing and seated passengers, more surreptitiously via angled reflections in the train windows, and, as I observed on many occasions and practiced myself, from behind the protective "mask" of sunglasses. What this suggests is that while "particular arrangements of people, space and technology must be employed to allow spectatorship" (qtd. in Bissell, "Visualizing Everyday," 51), adjustments are often made to accommodate changes in these arrangements that continue to facilitate spectatorial forms of vision.

In other words, in such restricted visual settings, sight is heavily mediated; it is also characterized by a shift from the gaze toward that of the glance. Thus, for writers like Bissell, it is not only our engagement with the passing landscape that is characterized by fleeting, disrupted glimpses (as discussed above), but *all* travel vision is "cultivated only through particular prompts, such as a stop at a station, a person walking through the carriage, the glance at a wristwatch and so on" (Bissell, "Visualizing Everyday," 52).

From Heidelberg, the train passes through Eaglemont before arriving at Ivanhoe.

IVANHOE 8:28 A.M.

The name Ivanhoe, from the novel by Sir Walter Scott, was first given to a farm established in the area in the 1840s, and was subsequently perpetuated through a series of later land donations (Garden). Almost half a century later, "during the 1880s land boom there was a spate of speculative subdivision which established Ivanhoe as an area of high socio-economic status with pretensions to be the 'Toorak of the north'"[1] by providing "comfortable residences for affluent businessmen" (Garden). In the post-WWII period, "lower socio-economic estates were opened in the north," but development around the Yarra River to the south "was more affluent, perpetuating Ivanhoe's reputation as a suburb of comfortable housing, leafy streets, and private (independent) schools" (Garden).

Ivanhoe's longstanding reputation for comparative affluence is confirmed when one considers the current Australian housing market. Drawing on April 2011 data, the median house price in Ivanhoe is AUD$915,000, which then drops in steady increments as you travel north back along the Hurstbridge, whence we have come via Heidelberg (AUD$792,000), Rosanna (AUD$695,000), Macleod (AUD$613,000), and Watsonia and Greensborough (AUD$505,000), before climbing again as we enter the increasingly prized bushlike suburban settings of Montmorency (AUD$552,000) and Eltham (AUD$602,000). Not surprisingly, these housing price differentials also reflect key differences in occupation, with a higher proportion of professionals and managers in Ivanhoe than in, say, Greensborough, which has a greater number of tradespeople and clerical, sales, and services workers.

What these statistical differences point toward is the significance of remembering that the particular (and shifting) rhythms of suburban train travel are part and parcel of a very different set of (often slower) rhythms associated with land development, class position, and socioeconomic status. Over the course of my two-year observations I have come to understand how these larger ("macro") rhythms have a significant, if at times rather subtle, impact on the composition of the more focused ("micro") rhythms of daily commuter train travel.

An ex-colleague of mine once half-jokingly declared that, as he went away from the city on a different Melbourne train line to this one, there was an observable shift in the general physiognomy of passengers which increased the further he traveled outward. What was intended at the time to be a deliberately provocative remark does, however, find a degree of support in Baudelaire's statement that, "In a unity we call a nation [. . .] the social classes [. . .] introduce variety not only in gestures and manners, but also in the general outlines of faces" (Baudelaire, 18). In his introduction to rhythmanalysis, Lefebvre, too, picks up on a related point, when he suggests that "the rhythms of dressage"—that is, the ritualized ways that we learn to hold ourselves, to present ourselves to others—"seem particularly worthy of analysis" (Lefebvre, 40). In the context of my travels, these rhythms of which Lefebvre speaks were evident both through forms of deportment that subtly differentiated the educational and class status of those embarking at Ivanhoe from those who had gotten on at earlier stations, and through more direct and outward displays of affluence, such as an at times quite overt "stylistic self-consciousness" (Featherstone, 81) in male and female dress, and through media consumption practices. For instance, as regards the latter, it was at Ivanhoe that I first recall seeing a

Kindle e-reader in use, and, on a subsequent trip, an Apple iPad after its initial Australian release.

As the automated carriage voice announcement states, after leaving Ivanhoe, the train runs express from Ivanhoe, in the process bypassing a number of suburbs, some well-established and generally affluent like Ivanhoe (such as Alphington), others more recently gentrified (Darebin, Fairfield, Dennis, and Westgarth), before arriving at the key hub station of Clifton Hill (where the Hurstbridge and Epping lines meet).

CLIFTON HILL 8:36 A.M.

Considerable passenger movement takes place here, albeit with passengers embarking for the city leg in generally greater numbers than those disembarking for connections back along the Epping line, or, more commonly, for those later stops that are bypassed as this is an express service. The net result is a crowded train carriage that is filled near to capacity (indeed, it is not uncommon to see additional passengers remaining on the Clifton Hill platform with bemused looks as they determine to wait for a later service which, it is hoped, will have more room). The impact of this crowdedness is twofold. First, close bodily proximity restricts the kinds of media devices that it is possible to interact with to a series of "micro-gestures" involving that which can be handheld, such as a novel, or, more commonly, a mobile phone or MP3 player. Second, as Bissell notes ("Visualizing Everyday," 56), "on crowded services, where passengers have reduced personal space, the visual field becomes constricted and even uncomfortable, since there is nowhere to look" other than at the floor, people's backs, up at the roof, seat or window trim, or wall-mounted advertising and warning notices. These are just a few of the examples of a range of "nonverbal indices of avoidance" (Evans & Wener, 90) and "civil inattention" (Goffman, *Behavior*, 139) that have been noted, such as turning one's body "towards the side of the car and away from people" (Evans & Wener, 90).

From Clifton Hill, the train passes without stopping at a series of inner suburban stations (Victoria Park, Collingwood, North Richmond, West Richmond) as it makes a south and then westward arc toward Jolimont. For someone fortunate enough to have secured a window seat, such as myself, this express leg of the trip becomes one characterized by "waymarking"—that is, identifying key landmarks on the run-in to the city, such as the partially obscured but quite beautiful origami bird graffiti that adorns a wall just before Clifton Hill, the multistory block of artists' studios immediately following

Clifton Hill, where you can sometimes see a glimpse of a painter standing alone in a room before an easel, the warehouse apartment/office where I often glimpse through bifold glass doors a man attending to the morning ritual of espresso making, or the enigmatic phrase "senile oils" that has been written in graffiti ("tagged") high up on a wall nearby.

Also marking the approach to Jolimont is a series of two small tunnels through which the train passes close to the city side of West Richmond station. Seasoned train commuter-mobile users are aware of these tunnels and tend to alert those they are speaking to of impending signal dropout. What we have here, is one small example of "a complex intermingling of material objects, including wireless transceiver towers, mobile devices, [. . .] human bodies, [and] building materials," all of which exert a "qualitative force" on the train traveler's ability to make or take a phone call, and on the clarity of the signal should he or she wish to do so (Sutherland, 80).

JOLIMONT 8:41 A.M.

As the penultimate stop before the city, the arrival at Jolimont prompts a further series of rhythmic reconfigurations to the patterns already described. The squeeze of passengers' bodies eases somewhat as travelers disembark in substantial numbers. Many do so in order to walk the remainder of the way through the surrounding parkland. Other mediated reconfigurations occur. There are those passengers who prepare for imminent arrival by "micro-coordinating" (Ling & Haddon) the activities to follow via phone and text message. Others, like myself, begin the task of packing what has hitherto been unpacked. The putting away of various media (books, newspapers, laptops, MP3s, etc.) results in natural greater visual attentiveness, albeit in ways that are "managed"—or, in Bissell's terms, "quiesced" ("Visualizing Everyday," 56)—by the close proximity of other passengers on the still crowded carriage.

It was toward the end of the observation period on the approach into Flinders Street that I overheard two ladies performing their own form of "waymarking," such as that described earlier. Over the two-year duration, an older, somewhat portly man had been having regular morning sessions with a personal trainer in the strip of parkland adjacent to the train line. On viewing this scene one day, one of these ladies said to her companion, "Oh, he's getting thinner, you know." This forms a striking example of what Lefebvre would describe as "the interaction of diverse, repetitive and different rhythms," all working together to "animate" the commuter experience (30).

FLINDERS STREET 8:48 A.M.

Finally, 42 minutes after I embark, I ready myself to disembark, as do many hundreds of others, at one of Melbourne's busiest stations, Flinders Street. "Packed" passengers prepare themselves to step off the train and all its associated rhythms and enter the many "streams" and "currents" of other converging urban rhythms. For me, this tended to involve catching a connecting train service to a different location with a remarkably different confluence of rhythms—but that is a tale for another time.

ARRIVAL/CONCLUSION

This chapter has attempted a rhythmanalytic study of train travel on one suburban line within the city of Melbourne, Australia. What should be stressed at the conclusion of this examination is that it has been quite restricted in scope, and very specific in its spatial and temporal focus. Thus, while some observations and insights to emerge from this study might be generalized across Melbourne's wider train transport network, it is also acknowledged that, in key respects, a different spatial and temporal focus would likely produce quite different outcomes.

For example, the 7:44 a.m. Eltham train constitutes a very different journey and "braiding of rhythms" than the 8:06 a.m. service examined here. This is because the earlier service carries both larger numbers of school children (commuters with their own quite specific sets of rhythms—see Symes) and workers who aim to be in the city by 9:00 a.m. Because of this dual use, the 7:44 service is quite often so full that all seats are taken before it even leaves Eltham! This carries with it a quite constricted spatial and visual environment from the outset and, from experience, can often lead to heightened levels of stress (Evans & Wener) and potential for confrontation, as physical proximity can no longer be regulated easily. In a similar way, later departures, such as the 8:17 a.m. Eltham limited express or the 8:35 a.m. Eltham express service, are characterized by their own particular rhythmic patterns.

Recording what occurs during the late afternoon return leg that departs from Flinders Street at 5:04 p.m. would also produce very different results. This journey, preceded by the rhythms of the workday, involves quite distinct forms of mediation from the trip in. There is the ubiquitous presence of the free newspaper, *mX*, which is produced specifically for the evening commute. There is also the growing prevalence of business use of "smart phones" as part of what Middleton refers to as "work extension practices" in an "always-on environment" (28–29). On one occasion, I noted down the following snippet of conversation between a casually attired businessman sitting beside me talking on his mobile to his still office-bound colleague: "It's been a bloody busy week this week. I tell you, if it wasn't for this Blackberry I'd be way behind." After this particular call, this gentleman went on texting and calling for the entire trip home, continuing to do so even as he disembarked. And, in addition, to business specific calls there is the almost constant sounding of SMS alerts, and ringtones, and then more domestically oriented calls made at various (often carefully timed) locations and intervals as part of the evening micro-coordinations concerning pickup from train stations, meal plans, and so forth.

These qualifications notwithstanding, the key aim of this investigation has been twofold. First, to draw out how the sociospatial environment of the modern suburban train carriage is routinely experienced and negotiated as a dynamic environment of physical (and "virtual") co-presence that involve complex forms, layerings, and negotiations of various kinds of mediation. Second, to emphasize how our experience of these detailed and complex mediated engagements also change subtly yet significantly according to a range of competing, intersecting and combining rhythms, as well as other influencing factors. What emerges from this study is a specific account of one example of the train carriage as a crucial site for what Thomas Misa has aptly termed the "compelling tangle of modernity and technology."

NOTES

1. The southern suburb of Toorak is commonly regarded as Melbourne's most prestigious address, and domiciles the city's business and social elites.

BIBLIOGRAPHY

Axtell, Carolyn, Donald Hislop, and Steve Whittaker. "Mobile Technologies in Mobile Spaces: Findings from the Context of Train Travel." *International Journal of Human-Computer Studies* 66 (2008): 902–915.

Baudelaire, Charles. *The Painter of Modern Life*. Trans. P. E. Charvet. London: Penguin, 2010.

Baumbach, Jonathan. "*Breathless* Revisited." *Great Film Directors: A Critical Anthology*. Eds. Leo Braudy and Morris Dickstein. New York: Oxford University Press, 1978: 361–364.

Berry, Marsha, and Margaret Hamilton. "Changing Urban Spaces: Mobile Phones on Trains." *Mobilities* 5.1 (2010): 111–129.

Bissell, David. "Visualizing Everyday Geographies: Practices of Vision through Travel-Time." *Transactions of the Institute of British Geographers* 34 (2008): 42–60.

———. "Passenger Mobilities: Affective Atmosphere and the Sociality of Public Transport." *Environment and Planning D: Society and Space* 28 (2010): 270–289.

Breathless [*A Bout de Souffle*], dir. Jean-Luc Godard (1958).

Bull, Michael. *Sound Moves: iPod Culture and Urban Experience*. London: Routledge, 2007.

Cooley, Heidi Rae. "It's All about the *Fit*: The Hand, the Mobile Screenic Device, and Tactile Vision." *Journal of Visual Culture* 3.2 (2004): 133–155.

Edensor, Tim, and Julian Holloway. "Rhythmanalysing the Coach Tour: The Ring of Kerry, Ireland." *Transactions of the Institute of British Geographers* 33 (2008): 483–501.

Evans, Gary W., and Richard E. Wener. "Crowding and Personal Space Invasion on the Train: Please Don't Make Me Sit in the Middle." *Journal of Environmental Psychology* 27 (2007): 90–94.

Featherstone, Mike. *Consumer Culture and Postmodernism*. London: Sage, 1991.

Friedberg, Anne. *Window Shopping: Cinema and the Postmodern*. Berkeley: University of California Press, 1993.

Garden, Don. "Ivanhoe." *eMelbourne: The City Past and Present*. Parkville, Victoria, Australia: School of Historical Studies, Department of History, The University of Melbourne, 2008. www.emelbourne.net.au/biogs/EM00768b.htm.

Gergen, Kenneth. "The Challenge of Absent Presence." *Perpetual Contact: Mobile Communication, Private Talk, Public Performance*. Eds. James E. Katz and Mark A. Aarhus. New York: Cambridge University Press, 2002. 227–241.

Goffman, Erving. *Behavior in Public Places: Notes on the Social Organization of Gatherings*. New York: Free Press, 1966.

Goffman, Erving. *The Presentation of Self in Everyday Life*. London: Penguin, 1990.

Highmore, Ben. "Street Life in London: Towards a Rhythmanalysis of London in the Late Nineteenth Century." *New Formations* 47 (2002): 171–193.

Ito, Mizuko, Daisuke Okabe, and Ken Anderson. "Portable Objects in Three Global Cities: The Personalization of Urban Places." *The Reconstruction of Space and Time: Mobile Communication Practices*. Eds. Rich Ling and Scott W. Campbell. New Brunswick: Transaction Publishers, 2009. 67–87.

Jain, Juliet, and Glenn Lyons. "The Gift of Travel Time." *Journal of Transport Geography*, 16 (2008): 81–89.

Larsen, Jonas. "Tourism Mobilities and the Travel Glance: Experiences of Being on the Move." *Scandinavian Journal of Hospitality and Tourism* 1.2 (2001): 80–98.

Laurier, Eric. "Why People Say Where They Are during Mobile Phone Calls." *Environment and Planning D: Society and Space* 19 (2001): 485–504.

Lefebvre, Henri. *Rhythmanalysis: Space, Time and Everyday Life*. Trans. Stuart Elden and Gerald Moore. London: Continuum, 2010.

Licoppe, Christian. "The 'Crisis of the Summons': A Transformation in the Pragmatics of 'Notifications,' from Phone Rings to Instant Messaging." *The Information Society* 26 (2010): 288–302.

Light, Ann. "Negotiations in Space: The Impacts of Receiving Phone Calls on the Move." *The Reconstruction of Space and Time: Mobile Communication Practices*. Eds. Rich Ling and Scott W. Campbell. New Brunswick: Transaction Publishers, 2009. 191–213.

Ling, Rich, and Leslie Haddon. "Mobile Telephony, Mobility, and the Coordination of Everyday Life." *Machines That Become Us: The Social Context of Personal Communication Technology*. Ed. James E. Katz. New Brunswick, NJ: Transaction Publishers, 2003. 245–265.

Lyons, Glenn, Juliet Jain, and David Holley. "The Use of Travel Time by Rail Passengers in Great Britain." *Transportation Research Part A* 41 (2007): 107–120.

Lyons, Glenn, and John Urry. "Travel Time Use in the Information Age." *Transportation Research Part A* 39 (2005): 257–276.

Middleton, Catherine A. "Illusions of Balance and Control in an Always-on Environment." *Mobile Phone Cultures*. Ed. Gerard Goggin. Routledge: New York, 2008. 28–41.

Milgram, Stanley. *The Individual in a Social World: Essays and Experiments*. Reading, MA: Addison-Wesley Publishing Co., 1977.

Misa, Thomas J. "The Compelling Tangle of Modernity and Technology." *Modernity and Technology*. Eds. Thomas J. Misa, Philip Brey, and Andrew Feenberg. Cambridge, MA: MIT Press, 2003. 1–30.

Mokhtarian, Patricia L. "Telecommunications and Travel: The Case for Complementarity." *Journal of Industrial Ecology* 6.2 (2003): 43–57.

Obert, Julia C. "Sound and Sentiment: A Rhythmanalysis of Television." *Continuum: Journal of Media & Cultural Studies* 22.3 (2008): 409–417.

O'Dell, Tom. "My Soul for a Seat: Commuting and the Routines of Mobility." *Time, Consumption and Everyday Life: Practice, Materiality and Culture*. Eds. Elizabeth Shove, Frank Trentmann, and Richard Wilk. Oxford: Berg, 2009. 115–132.

Ohmori, Nobuaki, and Harata, Noboru. "How Different are Activities While Commuting by Train? A Case in Tokyo." *Tijdschrift voor Economische en Sociale Geografie* 99.5 (2008): 547–561.

Paulos, Eric, and Elizabeth Goodman. *The Familiar Stranger: Anxiety, Comfort, and Play in Public Places*. Berkeley, CA: Intel Research, 2002.

Plant, Sadie. "On the Mobile: The Effects of Mobile Telephones on Social and Individual Life." *Receiver* 8 (2002): no pag. www.receiver.vodafone.com.

Richardson, Ingrid. "Pocket Technospaces: The Bodily Incorporation of Mobile Media." *Mobile Phone Cultures*. Ed. Gerard Goggin. Routledge: New York, 2008. 66–76.

Schivelbusch, Wolfgang. *The Railway Journey: The Industrialization of Time and Space in the 19th Century*. Berkeley: The University of California Press, 1986.

Symes, Colin. "Coaching and Training: An Ethnography of Student Commuting on Sydney's Suburban Trains." *Mobilities* 2.3 (2007): 443–461.

Simmel, Georg. *The Sociology of Georg Simmel*. Ed. and trans. Kurt H. Wolff. Glencoe, IL: The Free Press, 1950.

Simonsen, Kirsten. "Spatiality, Temporality, and the Construction of the City." *Space Odysseys: Spatiality and Social Relations in the 21st Century*. Eds. Jørgen Ole Bærenholdt and Kirsten Simonsen. Aldershot, Hants, UK: Ashgate, 2004. 43–62.

Sutherland, Iain. "Mobile Media and the Socio-technical Protocols of the Supermarket." *Australian Journal of Communication* 36.1 (2009): 73–83.

Urry, John. "Travelling Times." *European Journal of Communication* 21.3 (2006): 357–372.

Watts, Laura. "The Art and Craft of Train Travel." *Social & Cultural Geography* 9.6 (2008): 711–726.

Weight, Jenny. "Phones and Trains: How to Subvert Industrial Time." *ANZA08: Power and Place: Refereed Proceedings*. Wellington, NZ: Massey University, 2008. http://anzca08.massey.ac.nz

Part III

City Networks

Chapter 5

Urban Railways, Industrial Infrastructure, and the Paris Cityscape, 1870–1914

Peter Soppelsa

The Paris Metro was discussed and debated long before the rail network was a reality, and many scholars have puzzled over why Paris did not develop urban railways sooner. The earliest plans for the Metro come from the 1840s to 1850s; Paris developed horse-drawn streetcars in the 1870s. With nearby London (often imitated by the French since the 1700s) opening its Underground in 1863, it has surprised many that Paris's Metro did not open until 1900. The struggle to establish the Metro from 1872 to 1895, accompanied by Paris's early experience of streetcars, shows how difficult it was to integrate urban railways into the city, for cultural reasons both material and symbolic. Yet scholars have tended to explain Paris's stalled railways in wholly *political* terms: the local and national governments fought for jurisdiction, the right to design and control the railway.

This would be fine if only engineers, transit tycoons, and politicians took part in the so-called "long debate" or "battles" over the Metro. But the Metro was an object of public concern, debated by journalists, intellectuals, landlords, local business owners, workers, and citizens in addition to politicians and engineers. The Metro was not only a valuable prize to be fought over, but also a controversial object to be fought *about*. Each bid for control of the railway was also a bid to define what kind of railway it would be. Even after it opened in 1900, the Metro remained controversial.[1] To capture this broader debate, we need to show why urban railways were objects of cultural concern for both designers and users. This chapter shifts the analytic frame from "the Metro" to "urban railways" in general (including streetcars), and from politics to *cultural politics*. In order to fit the city with railways, I argue, both concepts of railways and concepts of the city had to be socially reconstructed. Paris offers a compelling example of this process. Paris's urban railways were never solely technological or political objects, but also intersected with many currents in urban life, social, cultural and spatial.

Railway development sprang from postwar reconstruction in Paris, following the 1870 Franco-Prussian War and the 1871 Paris Commune. In January 1872, Prefect of the Seine Léon Say called a special commission of engineers to study "local interest railways and tramways" for the department of the Seine, the provincial territory including Paris. Since Say's predecessor Baron Haussmann, the Prefecture had been associated above all with public works, owing to Haussmann's massive reconstruction of Paris in the 1850s and 1860s. Like many bourgeois Parisians, Say spent the turbulent years of the war and Commune in exile, traveling around the Western world. Historian Hippolyte Taine and poet Arthur Rimbaud, for example, went to London, where they admired the world's first subway, the "Underground."[2]

Say returned to Paris in late 1871 convinced that Haussmann's modernized city, otherwise a beacon of modern development, had fallen behind in terms of transportation.[3] London had its subway, New York had elevated trains, and cities around the world were developing horse-drawn streetcars. Soon San Francisco and Istanbul would have cable cars. While France's Second Empire collapsed in the fires of international and then civil war, other major cities had been busy following Haussmann's example, equipping themselves with networked infrastructures like gas lighting, water supply, and sewage systems, in addition to urban railways. Anthropologist James Scott cited Haussmann as a prime example of rationalist, authoritarian "high modernism," and geographer David Harvey called mid-nineteenth century Paris the "capital of modernity."[4] Haussmann's example has been so widely imitated—from Berlin to Budapest, Buenos Aires, and Bangkok—that urban geographers Steven Graham and Simon Marvin credit him with helping define a "modern infrastructural ideal," the "notion of the ordered, unitary city, mediated by standard ubiquitous infrastructure networks,"[5] a notion otherwise known by the term "networked city."[6] Haussmann made networked infrastructure a hallmark of urban modernity.

One thing Haussmannization did not do was fit Paris with a "metropolitan" railway like London's. Paris embarked on that journey with San Francisco, New York, Berlin, and Istanbul in the 1870s. Although Say's 1872 commissioners believed that Paris should remain a model modern, networked city, they struggled to imagine railways that fit the city's needs. They worried about financing such a large project, especially because Paris was deep in debt, still paying off Haussmann's public works. Equally worrisome were the social and spatial questions of whether railways were compatible with urban spaces and urban life. Railway engineer Flachat thought streetcars could never work in Paris because they were confined to their rails, offering little flexibility of travel, and thus being out of step with "our customs."[7] Although the commissioners knew of pneumatic (or compressed air) and funicular (or cable) traction, they assumed Paris's railway would be powered by steam locomotives, whose noise, smoke, sparks and steam would be unsightly and dangerous in the city's bustling streets. To protect surface traffic flows, they rejected street-level and elevated railways. Finally, they were concerned about what they called "the beauty of the capital," Paris's legendary streetscape, showing a patriotic attachment to France's architectural patrimony. Standard-gauge, steam-powered railways didn't fit neatly into the Paris they knew and loved, and so they imagined an underground network to bypass it.

These concerns and London's example encouraged the commissioners to imagine an underground network. Though they made few definitive decisions, they recommended a mixed system, with horse-drawn streetcars (light rail) in the peripheral districts, and a standard-gauge subway in the historic city center (source of traction pending). Their report referred throughout to a *réseau Métropolitain* or "metropolitan network," ultimately the Paris Metro. The report thus reveals tensions between deep-set cultural ideas about the nature of the city and the technical demands of railways.

Planners *expected* problems. With their modernizing ideology and France's war-battered national pride cutting against their skepticism of urban railways, Paris's engineering corps met one of the foremost urban and technological challenges of their era, what Wolfgang Schivelbusch called "tracks in the city." In the early decades of railway development (1830–1870), railways traveled *between* cities, not within or across them. Having originated in Britain's industrializing coal mines, railways seemed like loud, dirty, heavy machinery—fit for a factory, perhaps, but not for the civilized spaces of a monumental Western capital city.[8] Haussmann's Paris helped make this idea commonplace. He famously buried fresh water and gas pipes in the sewer mains to hide them from the cityscape, so they could, as he put it, "maintain public health without troubling the good order of the city and without spoiling its exterior beauty."[9] Haussmann thought the city needed the practical benefits of such infrastructure, but that it was unsightly, generally incompatible with architectural aesthetics; this became a common principle in Paris planning.

Schivelbusch saw similar tensions embodied in railway station architecture. Stations functioned like city gates. Typically located outside the historic central districts of European cities, but facing in, their façades were made of cut stone in the historical style to blend in. Arrival halls and other "industrial" sections, by contrast, were made of iron and glass like factories and exhibition halls and hidden in the rear, facing away from the city. Stone façades hid the industrial parts of stations that clashed with traditional cityscapes.[10] As architectural theorist Siegfried Giedion put it, "In every field the nineteenth century cloaked each new invention with historicizing masks." Citing Paris's *Gare du Nord* as an example, Giedion wrote, "The architect Hittorff's façade in the style of Roman public baths is soon forgotten," as one moves from the station's historicist front to its industrial rear.[11] Though modern building materials like brick and concrete were introduced during Haussmannization, they were also hidden behind cut stone.

These aesthetic tensions were joined by technological friction between rails and streets. Traditionally trains stayed on track via a mechanical "lock" between grooved wheels and flanged rails. Hence rails stood up above the pavement, potentially encumbering roadways and damaging coaches' wheels. Until the system was reversed—with grooved rails and flanged wheels, sinking rails under the pavement—roads and rails were technically conflicting. This problem was solved in the early 1850s by a French engineer named Loubat, who designed some of New York's first horse-drawn streetcars and then returned to France to install the first such line in Paris in 1853.[12] This remained Paris's only streetcar line until 1873, when construction of Leon Say's new streetcars began. Hence Parisians long referred to horse-drawn streetcars as "American railways," both exogenous and exotic.

While Parisian visions of underground railways modeled England, visions of streetcars modeled the United States. As many cultural historians have argued, France's jealous regard for the Anglophone world was a response to being embarrassed by Prussia in 1870.[13] Many nationalists suffered an inferiority complex, hence one journalist: "We won't forget that our great city, which has so often taken the initiative of perfecting and embellishing [itself], has remained 25 years behind in adopting American railways."[14] But construction began in 1873 and service in 1874–1875. Between 1874 and 1879, forty-nine new streetcar lines were installed in the department of the Seine, forty-six of them horse-powered, two steam-powered, and one electric.[15] This was Paris's first streetcar boom, spurred by fear of being embarrassed before an international audience with out-of-date or inadequate means of transport at the Universal Exposition of 1878, where the young Third Republic planned to show the world France's recovery since the Second Empire's collapse. What historians of technology call "techno-nationalism" was an essential part of the Third Republic's political culture.[16]

Along with their rapid development, however, horse-powered streetcars brought their own problems. As popular science author–editor Émile Gauthier put it, "animal traction is the ruin of the streetcars. Thus all cities are preoccupied with replacing it with various methods of mechanical traction."[17] The Prefecture tested steam-powered and compressed air streetcars throughout the 1870s, but none were fully satisfying. Safety was the main concern—and not only for passengers. Planners feared these engines would produce noise, steam, smoke, or sparks, frightening or blinding horses, causing accidents with Paris's many horse-drawn coaches, omnibuses, and streetcars. Comparing animal to mechanical traction, one local politician later noted, "I know well that mechanical traction is destined to replace animal traction: 'the one will kill the other.'"[18] The Prefecture also outfitted existing trams with "body catchers," sheet metal skirts that made accidents less lethal for passengers and pedestrians. Local newspapers offered sensationalized accounts of gory accidents; contemporaries estimated two accidents each day in the 1870s.[19]

These safety concerns were complicated by a peculiarity of streetcar practice. Like Paris's omnibuses—ancestors of the twentieth-century bus, comparable to stagecoaches—streetcars did not pick up passengers at fixed stations or stops, but could be flagged down anywhere and boarded ad hoc. Conductors were officially required to stop trams to pick up passengers, but in practice, they often just slowed down. Hence images of Parisians running to catch the tram were quite popular in literary and visual culture.[20] Many passengers also complained of conductors being careless, lazy, or rude. In 1878 a conductor named Vallet spent eight days in jail after punching a passenger in the eye when he complained that Vallet made him run to catch the tram. Streetcars were new to Paris, and the practices of streetcar use were as uncertain and unfinished as the technology of streetcar traction.[21]

The coming 1878 exposition also inspired more plans for the future Metro, though none were ever realized. When plans emerged to use the Metro to link up the separate networks of the five powerful nationwide railway companies, Paris's increasingly left-wing municipal council vetoed them. The council members wanted a local network for the benefit of common Parisians, not lucrative contracts handed out to already powerful companies. This conflict led in time to two dominant visions of the Metro: one a locally controlled, passenger-centered, and socially oriented light rail network, and the other a nationally controlled, mixed-use, and privately operated network on standard-gauge tracks, with commercial and military applications. These two visions spawned a battle for jurisdiction over the network between left-wing locals and center-right nationalists that raged for twenty years, replaying the bitter lines of conflict from 1871's civil war. If politics is war by other means, then the battle over these competing visions of the Metro replayed the local socialist and national conservative conflict behind the Commune. When the municipal government finally won control in 1896, it was a victory for "local democracy," as historian Alain Cottereau put it, and a major factor in the development of a local welfare state for municipal employees.[22] The Metro finally opened in 1900. This political battle has been at the center of all scholarly accounts of the Metro, but the Metro was never merely an instrument in, or object of, political struggles. Like the streetcars, it suggested important social, spatial, symbolic, and technological problems of its own. In negotiating what kind of Metro Paris needed, Parisians were also wrestling with whether the city could handle an urban railway.

In the late 1870s architect Louis Heuzé published an elevated Metro plan, following New York's example, arguing that it would relieve street traffic while improving pedestrian traffic, ensuring a "double circulation." He envisioned ornate, wrought-iron viaducts above Paris's avenues and boulevards, forming a roof over a "special street" for pedestrians, protected from the weather. It could be embellished with lamps, benches, gates, and other street furniture, or the classic iron and glass storefronts of Paris's shops and arcades. Heuzé thought railways could be durably integrated into Paris's social routines, traffic patterns, and architectural aesthetics. Viaducts and streets could be tightly stitched together.

By contrast, Heuzé thought underground tunnels might be vulnerable to flooding, pollute the groundwater, collapse the city above, damage monuments, or bring down property values. He found subways rather morbid, writing: "For the adjective *metropolitan*, Parisians will soon substitute that of *Necropolitan*, for a railway obliging the public to descend by way of long staircases into veritable catacombs!"[23] Another critic used the term "sewer train."[24] These epithets reflect a deep-seated public uneasiness about the underground plans of the 1870s, a sign that not everyone envied London. Like many others, Heuzé argued that Parisian passengers preferred to ride in daylight and open air. In fact, the upper decks of omnibuses and streetcars were both popular and fashionable places to ride. Other contemporary critics suggested subways might make passengers bored, anxious, or even sick.[25]

Underground trains collided with a common cultural image of the spaces beneath Paris as fearsome catacombs, depicted famously in Victor Hugo's *Les Misérables* and Gaston Leroux's *Phantom of the Opera*. Here, the underground stood for crime, revolution, filth, disease, and ultimately death—a monstrous netherworld of specters cast out by civilization, what historian Rob Zaretsky called "labyrinths of the unthinkable or unspeakable."[26] Just as the social norms of street life made surface-level railways problematic, so the cultural image of the underground discouraged subways.

While politicians, engineers, and architects were struggling to imagine a workable Metro, Paris's remarkable streetcar boom was slipping into an equally remarkable bust. The two streetcar companies chartered in 1873—one connecting the north suburbs with Paris, the other the south—began to see deep financial trouble after 1878. Like all railways, the streetcars required heavy initial investment that could ideally be recouped in ticket sales. Smelling lucrative speculation, capital was provided by big financial interests like the Paris Financiers' Society, the Franco-Italian Bank and several Belgian firms, amid contentious chatter in the press about unsavory mergers and acquisitions.[27] This was a good, old-fashioned nineteenth-century investment craze, and when growth plateaued in 1878, the gamble was lost. The South Tramway Company lost 3 million francs between 1879 and 1881; soon the North Tramway Company was in trouble, too.[28] Despite rising sales and public demand for transport, use of streetcars was not yet heavy enough to cover initial investment or operating costs. Ticket prices were not yet cheap enough to be within everyone's reach; practices and routines were still uncertain for passengers.

These financial troubles reveal important problems of Paris's transport organization and regulation. In 1860, when Haussmann expanded the city limits, he granted the General Omnibus Company (hereafter CGO) a fifty-year "monopoly" on all public transport in Paris. This was a vague pronouncement indeed, but an immensely powerful one. In practice, it meant a monopoly of horse-powered, large-capacity vehicles, though the CGO often interpreted it more liberally in an attempt to block competition from new means of transport. The CGO was one of the loudest opponents of tramway and Metro development, and no small contributor to delaying development, a fact many contemporaries recognized.[29]

Because the streetcars crossed from the suburbs into Paris, their 1873 charters specified that the CGO would maintain all rails within the city limits, and the streetcar companies would rent them. On top of small maintenance rates per franc and per kilometer, the companies also paid the CGO an indemnity for compromising its monopoly.[30] As public demand for streetcars gradually increased in the 1870s, the streetcar companies expanded their networks, thus increasing what they owed the CGO. This expense was compounded by a technological detail: CGO streetcars rode on rails without metal or iron bars in the ballast to increase resistance and keep rails evenly spaced. The CGO's Loubat-style "American" rails were simply sunk in the pavement. As the CGO was responsible for constructing tracks within the city limits, it installed them to its own standards. But these tracks did not match the North and South Tramway Companies' cars, "un-derailable" because their axles did not pivot, making them vulnerable to smaller changes in rail height and width. The streetcar companies, therefore, spent extra money—according to one source, over 2 francs per meter—retrofitting CGO tracks to their cars. Conveniently, CGO trams had no trouble circulating on the modified tracks.[31]

In 1881 the CGO proposed the acquisition of the failing streetcar companies, but the local government and the public were uncomfortable with extension of the CGO's already unwieldy monopoly, and the bid was denied. Failing companies brought contract violations and roadways crumbling from wear and tear. Struggling to trim the fat, the streetcar companies cut some meat from their operations as well: numbers of trams and employees sagged; passengers waited longer for trams as pavement was slowly rattled to bits. The North and South Tramway Companies steadily demanded to be bailed out by the authorities but went bankrupt in 1884, and were replaced by two new companies in 1887.[32]

The 1880s were slow for streetcar development, so negotiation of urban railways shifted back toward the Metro. While the municipal and national governments continued to vie for jurisdiction, organized blocks of interests began to form as the struggle spilled onto the terrain of civil society. In 1883, the Paris Society of Civil Engineers began an organized campaign for an elevated Metro, amid a flurry of elevated plans by architects, engineers, and contractors. In 1884 civil engineer Jules Garnier imagined an elevated Metro riding on slender, double-decker wrought-iron viaducts clad in cut stone to match the Haussmannized streetscape. By stacking two tracks on top of each other, he hoped to ensure a continuous, simultaneous flow of traffic in two directions, reminiscent of Louis Heuzé's "double circulation."[33] In 1887, engineer Eugène Chardon imagined viaducts creating new shopping arcades in Paris, thus claiming they could become a "veritable work of art."[34]

The partisans of elevated trains saw four distinct advantages. First, no land would have to be expropriated, because tracks could be built atop existing streets, where the city already owned the land. Second, elevated trains would bypass street-level traffic, and could add meaningful architectural and aesthetic detail to the streetscape. Third, viaducts would offer a ride in the daylight and open air, and travel along elevated tracks would offer a new, stimulating vantage point from which to view the cityscape. Finally, viaducts offered less restriction on traction than underground trains, thus easing the contemporary project of experimenting with mechanical engines.[35] By 1887, the campaign blossomed into a civil association called the "Parisian League for an Elevated Metro."

But the Metro's opponents were also organizing themselves. In 1884 the "Society for the Friends of Parisian Monuments" was founded, a historical preservation society concerned that the Metro would damage Paris's architectural patrimony.[36] Specifically, they worried about structural damage from construction and rumbling trains, the possibility of tunnels collapsing, and elevated tracks visually disrupting monuments and streetscapes. The group waged an opinion campaign against both underground and elevated plans, though elevated trains were particularly odious. In 1883 engineers at the Prefecture of the Seine rejected several elevated plans on grounds that they "caused an uproar" because they would require "making major cuts through houses" in Paris.[37] Haussmann's heavy hand had made expropriation of land for public works a sore subject; many Parisians feared being evicted by a government buyout. Soon the Paris Landlords Association emerged as another organized opponent of the Metro. There was also concern that viaducts and/or construction might interrupt life on the city's surface. Elevated tracks would pass by the windows of houses, making noise, perhaps depressing property values or violating the privacy of the indoor world.

In 1886, the Metro's opponents were joined by Albert Robida, science fiction author, illustrator, and editor-in-chief of satire magazine *La Caricature*. That June, Robida ran his own drawing of "The Embellishment of Paris by the Metro" on the magazine's front cover, depicting Paris as a queen, crowned and crowded, her body entangled in a knot of elevated railways, which enter and exit her body through various orifices. Robida's claim was clear: the Metro would violate lady Paris, in all her architectural splendor.[38] In 1889, conservative member of the National Assembly Madier de Montjau opposed all sides in the Metro dispute, insisting that "the Metro is anti-national, anti-municipal, anti-patriotic, and detrimental to the glory of Paris." In 1895, a municipal councilor embellished the idea, claiming that the Metro would stifle business, culture and intellectual life until "there will no longer be a Paris."[39]

These conservative, traditionalist voices of protest saw any urban railway as inimical to Paris's architecture, culture, and economy. Among wealthy, educated traditionalists, aristocrats, and academics was a small segment of Parisians who simply could not accept the novel notion of "tracks in the city." Ultimately, theirs was a losing battle. Between the 1870s and 1890s, just over 100 distinct plans for the Metro were published, and in spite of the decades-long struggle to decide what kind of railways could work in Paris, the vast majority of Parisians agreed that railways would benefit the city, if properly designed.

In 1889, with the streetcar companies struggling to survive and the Metro question stalled by this many-sided dispute, a critical junction had been reached. 1889 was the year of another Universal Exposition in Paris, this one the centennial celebration of the French revolution with the Eiffel Tower as its showpiece. Paris held a world's fair like this every eleven years between 1855 and 1900 (1855, 1867, 1878, 1889, and 1900), and 1889 was the only one not preceded by a burst of transportation development.

Minister of Public Works Yves Guyot tried to pull the streetcars out of their slump by creating a new "Tramway Control Service" for the department of the Seine, which would make regular inspections. The first issue facing inspectors was the rails themselves. Having previously been wholly incompatible, rails and streets were slowly worked together, a process which accelerated the shift in Paris from cobblestones to asphalt and cement paving.

Whereas rails laid between cobblestones rattled the stones apart over time, compromising both roads and rails, asphalt and cement hugged the rails, integrating pavement and rails as a single surface.

Guyot's inspectors also attended to a common litany of complaints from passengers: agents were coarse and violated rules, there were too few street-car lines, and too few trams on existing lines, lines didn't go to or from the right places, the interior of the cars was uncomfortable, smoky, stinky, or cold, and so on. A common anecdote was that one's feet got wet and cold while waiting too long for trams. As newspaper *Le Rappel* put it, "The street-cars and omnibuses are a never-ending subject. What improvements doesn't the public demand, whether in the time-table of trains, or in the renovation of cars?"[40] Departmental councilor Gauthier later said, "From all sides, they demand the expansion and improvement of our ways and means of transport, as well as a reduction of fares."[41] These were chronic problems that became embarrassing before an international audience in 1889, and that were not durably addressed until well after 1900.

The 1889 exposition also included a conference on the Metro, where engineers, politicians, planners, and concerned citizens discussed how to solve the nagging problems of urban railways. As one speaker put it, "What the population wants is that we finish with this question."[42] Hétier, chief engineer for the department of the Seine, added the following year, "We don't have to establish the utility, one could say the necessity, of constructing a metropolitan railway." He said the same for the streetcars: "For more than eight years now, we have recognized the urgent necessity of completing the network of tramways which serves Paris and its suburbs so insufficiently."[43] In the early 1890s, engineer Paul Villain published plans called "The Metro we can do" and "A Metropolitain that won't cost and won't trouble anything," while another Parisian noted that "the philosophy of the Metropolitan is done." There was a good deal of frustration about the slump and stalemate which had stalled the Metro question since the mid-1870s. By 1896, Guyot was calling it "shameful" that Paris didn't already have a Metro, arguing that "the best metropolitan is that which will get done."[44]

The pressure of the impending 1900 Exposition finally ended the battle over the Metro, when the municipal government declared that it would not pay its share of the exposition costs unless the Metro was legally defined as municipal property.[45] The prospect of a failed exposition was more than the national government could bear, and the municipality prevailed. Planning began in 1895–1896 and construction in 1898. The Metro was opened as a showpiece in the 1900 exposition, the world's fourth underground electric railway after London, Budapest, and Boston. After decades of tentative, unsuccessful experiments with mechanical traction, electricity emerged as the clear alternative to horsepower, promising faster and more frequent service, increased passenger capacity, and cheaper fares. Electricity seemed like a technical fix for Paris's ongoing problems, especially the failing streetcar companies, burdened by the cost of animal and mechanical traction, and consistently unable to keep up with growing public demand.[46] In addition, electricity was a major theme of the 1900 exposition, identified with the coming twentieth century.

But electric traction also brought cultural problems. In the 1880s, electricity enabled a global streetcar boom based on the trolley, a conductor dragging or rolling on overhead wires. Parisians knew the trolley, at least after the Siemens & Halske demonstration tram at Paris's 1881 electrical exposition, but it always remained exotic and controversial. French technical journal *L'Électricien* called trolleys "totally anti-aesthetic," while engineer Paul Dupuy called them "impossible in major cities," blaming "the ugly aspect of the wires, which destroy the aesthetic of streets. . . ."[47] The notion was repeated endlessly by politicians, intellectuals, architects and engineers: the cheap, efficient, and practical trolley was simply too ugly for a monumental capital like Paris. According to savant Georges d'Avenel, the trolley's ugliness outweighed its practicality: "Paris knows how to suffer to be beautiful," because "[t]he noble passion for aesthetics dominates all our building enterprises."[48] Exploiting the homophony between "trolley" and the French phrase "too ugly" (*trop laid*), a British technical journal cleverly punned, " . . . to the French the overhead system carries its own condemnation. Apparently they do not distinguish between *trolley* and *trop-laid*."[49]

In the mid-1890s, with the 1900 Universal Exposition looming, local authorities and newspapers continued to stress that new streetcars were "impatiently anticipated."[50] Meanwhile, Paris's several streetcar companies recognized trolleys as the cheapest form of electric traction, and, hoping to capitalize on growing demand, they petitioned the municipal and departmental governments to install them throughout the department of the Seine. In 1896, a future of electric traction and cheaper fares seemed almost predestined, and the so-called "ten-cent streetcars," accessible to a mass public for the first time, became an issue in the senatorial election. The Prefecture of the Seine responded by beginning planning for a new "complementary" network of streetcars. Between 1890 and 1900, sixteen new streetcar companies went into business, and twenty new lines were quickly approved in 1899 and 1900 for the exposition.[51]

Paris's electrical network was quite limited until preparations for 1900 began, but because electricity was an important theme of the exposition, many exhibits needed wiring. Expanding transportation and communication to "upgrade" the city for the exposition thus jump-started development of

Paris's electrical network more generally. But as electric and telephone wires were gradually installed, they were bundled with gas and water pipes in the sewers, following Haussmann, and thus hidden from the cityscape.[52] Grooming Paris for the exposition thus unleashed contradictory impulses. Paris's perceived need to modernize through infrastructural development clashed with the perceived need to preserve its architectural patrimony. How could the city accommodate modern traffic and the influx of foreign visitors in 1900, remaining both classically beautiful and technologically cutting-edge?

Excluding the trolley for aesthetic reasons, and accumulator batteries for cost and efficiency reasons, left only one possible system of electric traction: conductors mounted on or in the pavement. These could take several forms: a trolley-like device dragging in a charged furrow (rejected for its cost), a third rail (rejected for safety), or charged plates on the pavement, known as *contacts superficiels* or "surface contacts." Rushing to prepare for 1900, Paris opted for surface contacts.[53] In this system, magnetic conductors hung from the bottom of each tram, picking up current from charged "plots," conductors mounted in cement boxes buried in the pavement between the rails. Its low profile, flush with the pavement, made it an ideal aesthetic alternative to the trolley, though the trolley would have satisfied Paris's purely technical needs just fine. This shows that technical choices could never be pursued in a cultural vacuum. Even for engineers, the aesthetic of the streetscape was never an afterthought, but part of the design process.

As construction of the new streetcars began, some bourgeois Parisians began to protest the torn-up cityscape. In January 1900 construction of the new *Bourse-Opéra* line was stopped by angry neighbors protesting the "barbarian tramway." Newspaper *Le Temps* echoed them, arguing streetcars would spoil the iconic beauty of the ritzy neighborhood around the Opera, one focal point of Haussmann's renovations.[54] Urban historian Gérard Jacquemet, however, argued that protesters more likely feared the "barbaric" working classes of east Paris would invade their upscale neighborhood on the streetcar. These same two fears—dangerous social mixing and monumental architecture at risk—had previously motivated neighbors to refer to a line crossing the Champs Elysées as "barbarian" in 1897. For these critics, streetcars were a danger to French civilization; one critic implicated them in Americanization.[55] Ultimately, several lines in Paris were called "barbarian tramway" between 1897 and the 1910s.

Construction was not the only problem. In 1900, other popular epithets like "murderous tramways" and "tramway of death" emerged, reflecting safety concerns.[56] Once the tramways became operational, Parisians found that the new surface contacts were electrocuting both humans and horses—and because iron horseshoes were good conductors, horses (unlike humans) could be killed. One prominent American visitor had already criticized Paris's "inadequate streetcar system," but these accidents more directly questioned the electrophilic messages broadcast by the exposition.[57] By the fall of 1900, local newspapers and authorities were in an uproar. Newspaper *Le Temps* contrasted theory and practice, noting that surface contacts worked well "in drawings," but not in the street: who could ignore pedestrians and horses, lying unconscious or dead on the tracks? The public was growing uneasy, so the police and the departmental government began to investigate.[58]

The departmental investigation uncovered three technical issues. First, plots often remained improperly charged after trams passed. Second, hoping to prevent electrocutions, the streetcar companies began equipping trams with a second magnetic foot designed to deactivate plots. Ironically, these safety devices themselves often caused short circuits, setting off small fires that damaged plots, making electrocution even more likely. Third was the problem of moisture: the small cement boxes that housed surface contacts often filled with rainwater, another invitation to short circuits. As one councilor put it, "no one knows how the surface contact system will behave with snow and rain." December and January were snowy months, and over forty more horses were electrocuted.[59] Surface contacts were a bad match for Paris's humid climate, dense traffic, and continuing reliance on horse traction. They were relatively cheap and efficient, and obviated overhead wires, but they were also fragile and dangerous.

The Metro was no stranger to accidents, either. According to a Municipal Council study, the Metro witnessed more than 1,000 accidents that injured passengers and employees between 1900 and 1903. The streetcars were slightly less dangerous, killing 112 and wounding 937. The Metro caused more injuries, the streetcars far more deaths.[60] While the surface contact accidents of 1900–1901 were a turning point for the streetcars, the Metro had its turning point in the accident of August 10, 1903, which caused an underground fire that killed 84 and threw the network into a full decade of architectural and technological overhaul between 1903 and 1914. As one historian of transportation technology has put it, as a result of this accident, daily operation of the Metro finally shifted "from improvisation to method," as operating routines firmed up.[61]

Metro ticket sales declined by half the day after the accident, and when news of the Paris accident reached London, a similar panic broke out on the subway there. The event sent shockwaves of fear and panic through a broad Western public dealing with the new prominence of railways and electricity in the city. Paris catholic newspaper *La Croix* saw the accident as an indictment of electrified modernity, suggesting that the hellish fire was heavenly retribution for the hubris embodied in the Metro. *La Croix* also criticized the company responsible for operating the Metro as "notoriously beneath its task," reminiscent of the failing streetcar companies. Center-left *Le Temps*, meanwhile, evoked the 1897 *Bazar de la Charité* fire—sparked by another risky modern technology, film—which killed 126 and wounded 200.[62]

The most strident response came from sharp-tongued, non-conformist magazine of left-wing political cartoons *L'Assiette au Beurre*, which ran a special issue called "Le Metro-Nécro," resurrecting Louis Heuzé's term nec-ropolitan. Like *La Croix*, with which it otherwise had very little in common, the staunchly anti-clerical *L'Assiette au Beurre* took the Metro Company to task for cutting costs and endangering workers and the public. While *La Croix* blamed modern technology for the dangers of contemporary urban life, *L'Assiette au Beurre* blamed modern capitalism. In the public sphere, the 1903 accident became a vehicle for fears about the dangers of modern life and a prop for critiques of capital and the state.[63] It collided with the dominant technophilic idea of the Metro, electrical showpiece of the exposi-tion, adding fuel to the fire of popular fears, reservations, and doubts about electrical technology, urban railways, film, and other dangers of high-tech urban modernity.

The London *Times*, however, found the accident curious because Parisians were already so loyal to the Metro. "The Metropolitan now forms part of the daily life of many thousands of Parisians," having "completely changed the mode of living of the working population," because the public "got accus-tomed to this new means of locomotion in an amazingly short time." David Pike has shown that Metro ticket sales grew much faster than did subway sales in London. So Parisians' love and devotion for the Metro made the acci-dent traumatic. It challenged the otherwise hegemonic notion of the Metro as a technological advance and a practical convenience, causing friction between attitudes about, and the realities of, the network. It was not easy for Parisians to accept the accident's indictment of the system they had grown so quickly to love.[64] In addition to being just another accident, then, the tragedy of 1903 indicates some budding solutions to the problems of urban railways, their gradual integration into Paris's daily life and booming popular (mass) demand.

In the early 1900s, in the wake of these frequent and occasionally spec-tacular streetcar and Metro accidents, the authorities began to substantially rework the station architecture, business organization, government regula-tion, and technologies of urban railways. Although free enterprise was a key value in the Third Republic's official, national political culture, the number of socialists in government, especially Paris's municipal government, was grow-ing, and failing streetcar companies inspired many heated council meetings about municipalizing Paris's privately operated transit networks. Beginning in 1902, the municipal council also began to relax its opposition to the trolley, first allowing trolleys only in the periphery, but often on a so-called "trial" basis that later became permanent. One dissenting councilor screamed in session that if trolley wires were installed in his district, "I will cut them down with my own hands."[65]

This gradual introduction of the trolley only emboldened its more resolute opponents to resist harder, and organized campaigns against trolleys began to emerge. Now that the battle for the Metro was over, the opponents of urban railways turned their attention to the streetcars. In 1904, the Commission of Old Paris, the municipal government's organ of historical preservation, passed a resolution against trolleys anywhere in Paris.[66] In 1907, Ernest Levallois, mayor of Paris's 2nd district, formed a civil association called "The Parisian Association for Art in the Street," whose mission was to protect his iconic neighborhood from a new streetcar line he called "the criminal tramway." It was yet another organized attempt at the level of civil society to oppose streetcar development. Complaining of noise, stalled traffic, dangerous accidents, unsightly construction and neighbors who "lose their clientele, lose air, [and] lose sleep," Levallois published a polemical pamphlet illustrated with photographs of the neighborhood, showing roads torn up by construction and vacant buildings for rent.[67] In these same years, his epithet "criminal" was joined again by "barbaric" in several sessions of the municipal and departmental councils.[68] But these defenders of architectural tradition were already losing their battle, outnumbered by Parisians who accepted the trolley's practical and economic benefits. Like the Metro, the streetcars were gradually being integrated into Parisian routines and expectations in spite of their problems, as trolleys crept slowly into Paris from the outside.

Construction of the first Metro network—the original six lines approved in 1898—continued until 1910, and the accident of 1903 inspired significant renovations of station architecture, rolling stock and electrical equipment which continued until 1914. Twenty-four of forty-one kilometers of this network were underground.[69] The Metro's shallow, cut-and-cover construction removed roadways and then replaced them atop finished tunnels, leaving the streetscape an obstacle course of scaffolds, pits and detours, and leaving damaged buildings and slowed business in its wake. Complaints of dusty or muddy roads, potholes, heaps of paving stones, open trenches and tools or waste left in the streets deployed a language of "vandalism," "sabotage," "barbarity," and even "ruins."[70] Novelist Jules Romains said construction was "strangling" the streets.[71] All of these terms suggest violence to the city, and the pain felt by patriotic Parisians. Although many critics continued to complain that this was fulfilling dark prophecies of railways ruining Paris, they were, like the opponents of streetcars, increasingly a vocal minority.

Public demand for the railways was simply booming. From 1879 to 1895, annual streetcar ridership nearly tripled; from 1895 to 1928, it quadrupled. Metro ridership grew even more dramatically: from 1901 to 1910, annual first-class ticket sales grew from about 6.5 million to almost 27 million (over four times), and second-class from 34.5 million to 164 million (closer to five times).[72]

The Metro became durably integrated into Paris's everyday life in the twentieth century. In 1911, Franz Kafka visited Paris and wrote in his diary, "Because it is so easy to understand, the Metro is a frail and hopeful stranger's best chance to think that he has quickly and correctly, at the first attempt, penetrated the essence of Paris."[73] The streetcars, by contrast, would continue to suffer for their nagging problems. Although they were widely used until the 1920s, they ultimately could not compete with the Metro and the autobus, first introduced in the 1910s after the CGO "monopoly" expired. By 1938, all Paris streetcars were shut down. Given their difficult debuts, the long-term success of Paris's urban railways is remarkable, though the divergent fates of the Metro and the streetcars suggest how fragile and contingent this success was. The city was outfitted with urban railways between 1870 and 1940, but their fit was never perfect.

One classic genre in the history of technology is narratives of adopting new technologies. Seen through this lens, the case of Paris's engagement with urban railways seems a rather difficult story with a bittersweet end—the streetcars struggled, while the Metro flourished. In the four decades between the 1870s and the 1910s, Parisians did manage to find ways to work railways into the city, but not without a good deal of difficulty, and some major adjustments to the social construction of railways and the social construction of the city. It took decades of work, both material and symbolic. The case of Paris thus sheds light on what historians of technology Mikael Hård and Andrew Jamison call the "appropriation" and "domestication" of new technologies, showing that new technologies can never be *adopted* without being *adapted*. Paris was around 2,000 years old when authorities first sought to introduce urban railways. Existing spatial forms, social routines, and customs created significant problems of retrofitting. Railways could not be overlaid whole onto the fabric of the city, but had to be painstakingly woven into it. As the railways were socially reconstructed to fit Paris, images of the city were symbolically reconstructed as well.

In spite of all the fears, conflict, accidents, failing transit companies, bureaucratic inefficiency, and so on, overall Parisians continued to desire railways, and to identify them with modernity and the future—whether these were envisioned in utopian or dystopian terms. In the process of working railways into the city, Parisians showed themselves committed to remarkably divergent values, conflicting scripts about how technology ought to work in the city. Flights of technophilic, utopian fancy were paired with dark fears of modernity. Commitments to modernization and to preserving tradition were equally strong. Technonationalism cut against significant technophobia. Political economy and class differences played a significant role as well. While powerful foreign investors licked their chops at the prospect of Paris's massive ticket sales, local capitalists like the Paris Landlords Association and the CGO tried to protect their economic interests by preventing railway development. Meanwhile, the working-class and middle-class public clamored for expanded means of transport, more accessible and affordable, hungry for mobility and the practical benefits of railways, little concerned with bourgeois outcry over architectural aesthetics and civilization.

Many of these tensions reflect the specificity of Paris's role as a capital city, the capital of a nation historically known for its nationalism and "civilizing mission," which prized Paris's streetscape as a trophy case of achievements in French and Western civilization. But Schivelbusch reminds us that it was "tracks in the city" *in general* that were new and challenging after the 1870s. Thus Paris was not alone in seeing controversy and opposition around urban railways. Historians have uncovered similar friction in Berlin, Brussels, Budapest, Dresden, Vienna, Chicago, Louisville, Philadelphia, New York, San Francisco, Washington, D.C., Toronto, Rio de Janeiro, Seoul, and Beijing.[74] In this historiographic context, I hope that this study of Paris's engagement with urban railways adds to a broad dialog in cultural history and the history of technology dealing with technology and modernity in the years around 1900. In particular, I have tried to put focus on what historians and sociologists of technology call "heterogeneous engineering"—the idea that technological decisions can never be made in a vacuum, but become necessarily tangled up in society, culture, politics, economy, and ecology. Urban railways caused concern in Paris about architecture, commerce, government, modernity, nationalism, noise, public health and safety, traffic, and many other problems—and these problems had to be resolved before railways could be durably integrated into city life.

NOTES

1. Louis Biette, *Le Métropolitain de Paris* (Paris: Chaix, 1906); Norma Evenson, *Paris: A Century of Change 1878–1978* (New Haven: Yale, 1979), 91–105; Benson Bobrick, *Labyrinths of Iron: Subways in History, Myth, Art, Technology, and War* (New York: Quill, 1986), 133–168; Alexandre Ossadzow, "Les Pères du Métropolitain: l'Intervention des Ingénieurs," Sheila Hallsted-Baumert (Ed.), under the direction

of Francois Gasnault and Henri Zuber. *Métro-Cité: le Chemin de fer Métropolitain à la Conquête de Paris, 1871–1945* (Paris: Paris-Musées/RATP, 1997), 57–72; Pascal Desabres, "The Parisian Subway, 1880–1900: A Local or National Interest Line? On the Concept of Globalization," *Business and Economic History On-Line* 1 (2003): http://www.thebhc.org/publications/BEHonline/2003/Desabres.pdf; Alain Cottereau, "Les Batailles pour la Création du Métro: un Choix de Mode de Vie, un Succès Historique pour la Démocratie Locale," *Revue d'Histoire du XIXe Siècle* 29 (2004): 89–151; Nicholas Papayanis, *Planning Paris before Haussmann* (Baltimore: Johns Hopkins University Press, 2004), 201–226; David Pike, *Subterranean Cities: The World beneath Paris and London, 1800–1945* (Ithaca: Cornell University Press, 2005), 47–68.

2. Hippolyte Taine, "Lettres de Londres," *Le Temps* (8 January 1872); *Tables du Journal Le Temps*, vol. 3, 1871–1875 (Paris: Editions du Centre National de la Récherche Scientifique, 1968), 643; Michael Spencer, "A Fresh Look at Rimbaud's 'Métropolitain,'" *The Modern Language Review* 63 (October 1968): 849–853.

3. Georges Michel, *Léon Say: Sa Vie, Ses Oeuvres* (Paris: Calmann Lévy, 1899), 177–181.

4. James Scott, *Seeing Like a State: How Certain Schemes to Improve the Human Condition Have Failed* (New Haven: Yale University Press, 1998), 59–64; David Harvey, *Paris, Capital of Modernity* (New York and London: Routledge, 2003).

5. Stephen Graham and Simon Marvin, *Splintering Urbanism: Networked Infrastructures, Technological Mobilities and the Urban Condition* (New York and London: Routledge, 2001), 49, 52, 62.

6. Joel A. Tarr and Gabriel Dupuy (Eds.). *Technology and the Rise of the Networked City in Europe and America* (Philadelphia: Temple University Press, 1988).

7. Société des Ingénieurs Civils, *Mémoirs et Compte Rendu des Travaux* (Paris: Librarie Scientifique, Industrielle et Agricole, 1872), 269.

8. Wolfgang Schivelbusch, *The Railway Journey: The Industrialization of Time and Space in the 19th Century* (Berkeley: University of California, 1987), 178–188.

9. The quote has been reproduced several times. See John Reader, *Cities* (New York: Grove Press, 2006), 213–214; David Jordan, *Transforming Paris: The Life and Labors of Baron Haussmann* (Chicago: University of Chicago Press, 1995), 274; Jean-Pierre Goubert, *The Conquest of Water: The Advent of Health in the Industrial Age*, trans. Andrew Wilson (Cambridge, UK: Polity, 1989), 67; Donald Reid, *Paris Sewers and Sewermen: Realities and Representations* (Cambridge, MA: Harvard University Press, 1991), 29; Jeffrey Jackson, *Paris under Water: How the City of Light Survived the Great Flood of 1910* (New York: Palgrave Macmillan, 2010), 14.

10. Schivelbusch, 171–178.

11. Schivelbusch, 178–187. Siegfried Giedion, *Building in France, Building in Iron, Building in Ferroconcrete*, Trans. J. Duncan Berry (Getty Research Institute, 1996), 85, 114–115.

12. Evenson, 80; John McKay, *Tramways and Trolleys: The Rise of Urban Mass Transport in Europe* (Princeton, NJ: Princeton University Press, 1976), 14.

13. Bertrand Taithe, *Defeated Flesh: Medicine, Welfare, and Warfare in the Making of Modern France* (Lanham, MD: Rowan and Littlefield, 1999); Robert Nye,

Crime, Madness, and Politics in Modern France: the Medical Conception of National Decline (Princeton, NJ: Princeton University Press, 1984); Eugen Weber, *France Fin de Siècle* (Cambridge, MA: Harvard University Press, 1986).

14. "Communications et Avis Divers," *Le Temps* 6 September 1872.

15. Yves Guyot, Tramway Statistics (1894), Archives Nationales F/14/8588.

16. On technonationalism, see Thomas Hughes, *Networks of Power: Electrification in Western Society, 1880–1930* (Baltimore, Johns Hopkins University Press, 1983); Jeffrey Herf, *Reactionary Modernism: Technology, Culture, and Politics in Weimar and the Third Reich* (Cambridge University Press, 1984); David Nye, *American Technological Sublime* (Cambridge, MA: MIT Press, 1994); Gabrielle Hecht, *The Radiance of France: Nuclear Power and National Identity after World War II* (Cambridge, MA: MIT Press, 1998); Mikael Hård and Andrew Jamison (Eds.). *The Intellectual Appropriation of Technology: Discourses on Modernity, 1900–1939* (Cambridge, MA: MIT Press, 1998); Mikael Hård and Andreas Knie, "The Grammar of Technology: German and French Diesel Engineering, 1920–1940," *Technology and Culture* 40.1 (1999): 26–46. Connecting this idea specifically to Third Republic France, see Eugen Weber, *Peasants into Frenchmen: The Modernization of Rural France, 1870–1914* (Palo Alto: Stanford University Press, 1976); Alice Conklin, *A Mission to Civilize: The Republican Idea of Empire in France and West Africa* (Palo Alto: Stanford University Press, 1997).

17. Émile Gautier, *l'Année Scientifique et Industrielle* 39, 1895 (Paris: Hachette, 1896), 310; historian of technology John White found the same in the United States, writing: "Almost from the day it collected its first fare the street railway industry searched for a way to replace the horse." See: "War of the Wires: a Curious Chapter in Street Railway History," *Technology and Culture* 46.2 (April 2005): 374–384, quote 374.

18. Councilor Duval-Arnould, see: *Bulletin Municipal Officiel*, 16 December 1900, 4081.

19. M. L. LeHir, *Réseau des Voies Ferrées Sous Paris* (Paris: Mémorial du Commerce et de L'industrie, 1872); *Précis sur la Locomotive sans Foyer* (Paris: Boyer, 1875); Société des Ingénieurs Civils, *Discussion sur L'emploi de l'Air Comprimé pour la Locomotion Mécanique par la Procédés L. Mékarski* (Paris: Imprimerie Viéville et Capiomont, 1876); *La Lanterne*, yr. 3, no. 770 31 May 1879; materials related to motor testing and safety concerns can be found in Archives Nationales F/14/9189.

20. *La Clé des Omnibus et Tramways* (Paris: Administration d'Affichage, 1876); "Les Tramways de Paris," *Le Magasin Pittoresque* 47 (1879): 113–114.

21. Letter from Rousseau to the Prefect of Police, 29 October 1878. Archives Nationales F/14/15000.

22. Allain Cottereau, "Les Batailles pour la Création du Métro"; Edmund James, "Conditions Relating to the Treatment of Employees and Laborers Imposed by the City of Paris upon the Company to Which the Metropolitan Road Was Leased" *The American Journal of Sociology* 5.6 (May, 1900): 826–828.

23. Louis Heuzé, *Chemin de Fer Transversal à Air Libre dans une Rue Spéciale. Passage Couvert pour Piétons* (Paris: A. Lévy, 1878), 5.

24. Quoted in Evenson, 93.

25. Evenson; Bobrick; Pike.

26. Rob Zaretsky, "The Sewers of Paris," *The Engines of Our Ingenuity*, episode 1966 (University of Houston KUHF), www.uh.edu/engines/epi1966.htm.

27. Alberte Martinez Lopez, "Belgian investment in tramways and light railways: An international approach, 1892–1935," *The Journal of Transport History* 24.1 (March 2003): 59–77.

28. Sérafon. *La Vérité sur les Tramways Nord & Sud de Paris* (Imprimerie de la Publicité, 1882), 17.

29. Paul Vibert, *La Concurrence Étrangère: les Transports par Terre et par Mer*, 2 vols. (Paris: Berger-Levrault, 1896–1897) vol. 2, 83–84; L. de Laere, "La Question des Tramways," *Le Courrier Bleu de Neuilly-Boulogne* (17 October 1897).

30. Compagnie des Omnibus. *Tramways dans Paris: Cahier des Charges* (Paris: Ch. De Mourgues Freres, 1873), Article 22, 12–13. Archives Nationales F/14/14999.

31. See Sérafon, 5–6.

32. E. Van Imschoot-Roos, *Vérités Nécessaires! . . . Protestation de M. Marsoulan, . . . Lettre de MM. Bayard et Van Imschoot-Roos, du 3 Novembre 1879, aux Membres du Conseil Général* (Paris: Imprimerie Moderne, 1879); Em. Lemoine. *Etude sur la Formation et l'Emploi des Capitaux Engagés dans les Tramways-Nord & Sud de Paris* (Paris, Imprimerie de la Publicité, 1881); Sérafon, *La Vérité sur les Tramways*, 22; Jean Robert, *Les Tramways Parisiens*, 3rd ed. (Paris: RATP, 1992), 29–30; *Bulletin Municipal Officiel* (2 July 1885), 1311.

33. Jules Garnier, *Avant-Projet d'un Chemin de Fer Aérien à Voies Superposées* (Paris: Imprimerie Chaix, 1884).

34. Eugène Charon, Letter to M. Charles Garnier, 30 April 1887. Bibliothèque Nationale 8-V Piece-6342.

35. Société des Ingénieurs Civils, *Mémoires et Compte-Rendu des Travaux* (Paris: Société des Ingénieurs Civils, 1883); Jules Garnier, *Avant-Projet d'un Chemin de Fer*; Eugène Chardon, Letter to M. Charles Garnier; Bobrick, 142–143.

36. Evenson, 103–104.

37. J. Frémaux. *Rapport de l'Inspecteur Général. Chemins de Fer Métropolitain de Paris. Avant-Projet. Résultats de l'Enquête d'Utilité Publique, Sept. 12, 1883* (Archives Nationales F/14/9154), 25.

38. Albert Robida, "L'Embellissement de Paris par le Métropolitain," *La Caricature: Journal Hebdomaire* no. 338 (19 June 1886); Elizabeth Emery, "Protecting the Past: Albert Robida and the Vieux Paris Exhibit at the 1900 World's Fair" *Journal of European Studies* 35 (2005): 65–85.

39. Evenson, 93.

40. See Yves Guyot, *Trois ans aux Ministre des Travaux Publics: Expériences et Conclusions* (Paris: Léon Chailley, 1896), 96–97; "Le Chauffage des Tramways," *Le Parti National,* 5 December 1892; *Le Rappel,* 12 November 1892; Arsène Lopin, "Omnibus et Tramways," *Le Radical* 7 December 1892.

41. "Les Tramways à Dix Centimes," *l'Éclair* (24 October 1897); Conseil Général de la Seine, *Rapport* No. 5, 2 April 1897 (Paris: Imprimerie Chaix, 1897).

42. *La Question du Métropolitain. Conférence a l'École des Hautes Études Commerciales* (Paris: Administration des Deux Revues, 1889), 9.

43. Conseil Général de la Seine, *Chemins de Fer Métropolitains. Tramways. Rapport de l'Ingénieur en Chef du Département* (Paris: Imprimerie Chaix, 1890). Quotes 57 and 78, respectively.

44. Paul Villain, *Le Métro qu'on Peut Faire* (Paris: Grande Imprimerie, 1891); P. Villain and E. Mauger. *Un Métropolitain qui ne Coûte Rien et ne Trouble Rien* (Paris: Grande Imprimerie, 1892); Max de Nansouty, *La Question du Réseau Métropolitain de Paris et le Projet de la Cie des Etablissements Eiffel* (Paris: Génie Civil, 1891), 4; Guyot, *Trois Ans au Ministère des Travaux Publics*, 84.

45. Guyot, *Trois Ans au Ministère des Travaux Publics*, 96–97.

46. N. N. Petitjean, *Les Grands Travaux de Paris: l'Exposition de 1900, le Métropolitain, la Démolition des Remparts, la Nouvelle Enceinte, le Tout-à-l'Égout* (Paris: L. Thouvenin, 1895), 19; Vibert, *La Concurrence Étrangère*, 107; Georges d'Avenel, *Le Mécanisme de la Vie Moderne* vol. 5 (Paris: Librarie Armand Colin, 1905), 182; Léon Francq, *Chemin de Fer Métropolitain: Recueil des Articles Publiés dans le Journal le Métropolitain à propos de la Traction du Métropolitain Parisien* (Paris: E. Bernard et Cie., 1892).

47. William Dierman, "La Traction Électrique des Tramways à Paris," *L'Électricien; Revue Internationale de l'Électricité et de ses Applications* Ser. 2, 4.87 (27 August 1892): 137–141, quote 137. Paul Dupuy, *La Traction Électrique: Tramways, Locomotives et Métropolitains Électriques* (Paris: Librairie de sciences générales, 1897), 150.

48. D'Avenel, *Le Mécanisme de la Vie Moderne*, 191–192.

49. "Notes," *The Electrical Engineer* (30 October 1896), 477.

50. "Les Tramways à Dix Centimes," *l'Éclair* (24 October 1897); Conseil Général de la Seine, *Rapport No. 5* (1897).

51. Gauthier, *Rapport de l'Ingénieur Ordinaire* (Paris, 18 November 1896), Archives Nationales F/14/14999; Paul Vibert, *La Concurrence Étrangère*, vol. 2, 107: "a great national movement is taking shape today and which will impose itself imperiously tomorrow, thanks to the truly miraculous progress of electric traction"; *Tramways Concédés dans la Département de la Seine de Juin 1899 à Juin 1902* (Archives Nationales F/14/15024); Robert, *Les Tramways Parisiens*, annexes, 526.

52. Alain Beltran and Patrice Carré, *La Fee et la Servante: la Société Française Face à l'Électricité* (Paris: Belin, 2000), 188–189.

53. Most, but not all, lines in Paris were equipped with the Diatto system. The Dolter, Claret-Vuilleumier and Védovélli systems were also used. Henry Maréchal, *Les Tramways Électriques* (Paris: Librarie Polytechnique Charles Beranger, 1902), 117–145; Louis Barbillion and G. J. Griffisch, *Traité Pratique de Traction Électrique* (Paris: E. Bernard, 1903), 451–513; Robert Henry Smith, *Electric Traction* (New York: Harper, 1905), 167–206.

54. Elisabeth Hausser, *Paris au Jour le Jour: Les Événements Vus par la Presse, 1900–1919* (Paris, Les Editions de Minuit, 1968), 15; "Le Tramway de Romainville" *Le Temps* (11 January 1900), 2, and "Le Tramway de la Rue du Quatre-Septembre" *Le Temps* (18 January 1900), 1.

55. E. Mouchelet, "Doléances du Photographe Contre les Excès de la Civilisation," *Photo-Gazette* (25 September 1900): 201–205; Jules Claretie, *La Vie à Paris 1897* (Paris: Charpentier, 1898), 110; "Flâneuries et Curiosités," *Gazette Anecdotique, Littéraire, Artistique et Bibliographique* 1 (1897): 212–214; Gérard Jacquemet, "Voirie, Transports, et Equipement Urbain à Belleville de 1860 à 1914" in *Paris et Ile-de-France: Mémoires Publiés par la Fédération des Sociétés Historiques et Archéologiques de Paris et de l'Ile-de-France* 33 (1982), 249.

56. "Les Tramways Meurtrières" *Le Petit Parisien* (5 October 1900), 1; "Les Oeuvres et les Hommes," *Le Correspondant* 198 (1900), 416.

57. Edmund James, "The Inadequate Street Car System of Paris," *Chicago Daily* (22 April 1900), 51.

58. "Mésaventures Électriques" *Le Temps* (19 October 1900), 2–3.

59. *Bulletin Municipal Officiel* (16 December 1900), 4081–4096; *Rapport de l'Ingénieur Ordinaire* (Paris 25 December 1900). Both sources Archives Nationales F/14/14999.

60. Conseil Municipal de Paris, *Rapport au Nom de la Commission du Métropolitain sur l'Accident du Chemin de Fer Métropolitain du 10 Août 1903 et sur les Améliorations à Apporter à l'Exploitation, Présenté par Félix Roussel, Conseiller Municipal* (de Paris: Imprimerie Municipal, 1904), 32, 37.

61. Jean Tricoire, "L'Exploitation du Métropolitain: de l'Improvisation à la Méthode," in *Métro-Cité*, 103–116.

62. "Cri de Douleur" and "Le Métro en Feu," *La Croix* (12 August 1903), 1; "Lendemain de Catastrophe" *La Croix* (13 August 1903), 3. See also: "La Catastrophe du Métropolitain," *Le Temps* (12 August 1903), 2; "La Catastrophe du Métropolitain," *Le Temps* (13 August 1903), 1–2; "La Catastrophe" *Le Temps* (14 August 1903), 1–2.

63. *L'Assiette au Beurre* 125 (22 August 1903).

64. "The Fire on the Paris Underground," *The Times* (13 August 1900), 3.

65. McKay, 86.

66. Commission du Vieux Paris, *Procès-Verbaux* 1903 (Paris: Imprimerie Municipal, 1904), session of June 11, 198.

67. Ernest Levallois, *Paris Propre!* (Paris: Edouard Cornély et Cie, 1910), 5–40.

68. Conseil Municipal de Paris, *Procès-Verbaux* 1st sem. (Imprimerie Municipal, 1906), 682; Conseil Général de la Seine, *Procès-Verbaux* vol. 103, 2nd–3rd sessions 1906, 2nd part (Imprimerie Municipal, 1907), 393; Ibid., *Procès-verbaux* Vol. 106, 2nd session 1907, 2nd part (Imprimerie Municipal, 1908), 112.

69. "Le Métropolitain" *Le Temps* (26 March 1896), 3.

70. As I have elsewhere shown, see Peter Soppelsa, "Finding Fragility in Paris: The Politics of Infrastructure after Haussmann," *Proceedings of the Western Society for French History* 37 (2009): 233–247, 243–245, http://hdl.handle.net/2027/spo.0642292.0037.016; Peter Soppelsa, "The Fragility of Modernity: Infrastructure and Everyday Life in Paris 1870–1914" (Ph.D. dissertation, University of Michigan, 2009), 238–248.

71. Quoted in Pike, 51, and Rosalind Williams, *Notes on the Underground: An Essay on Technology, Society and the Imagination* (Cambridge, MA: MIT Press, 1992), 79.

72. Annual tramway passengers increased from 58,370,878 (1879) to 166,236,000 (1895) to about 700,000,000 (1928). See Jean Robert, *Les Tramways Parisiens*, 36 and appendixes; "Chemin de fer Métropolitain: Notes Diverses relatives à l'Évalutation de la Dépense," mid-late 1880s (Archives Nationales F/14/9154); for Métro statistics, see statistics and accounting records in Archives de Paris V1O8 13.

73. From Kafka's diary. See Steven Barclay, ed. *A Place in the World Called Paris* (Chronicle Books, 1994), 43.

74. McKay, *Tramways and Trolleys*; Eric Schatzberg, "Culture and Technology in the City: Opposition to Mechanized Street Transportation in Late-Nineteenth Century America," in Gabrielle Hecht and Michael Allen (Eds.). *Technology and History: Essays in Honor of Thomas Parke Hughes and Agatha Chipley Hughes* (Cambridge, MA: MIT Press, 2001), 57–94; Min Suh Son, "The Technology of Protest: Streetcar Riots, Race and Public Activism" (conference paper, Society for Social Studies of Science, October 2007, Montreal).

BIBLIOGRAPHY

Barbillion, Louis, and G. J. Griffisch. *Traité Pratique de Traction Électrique*. Paris: E. Bernard, 1903.

Barclay, Steven (Ed.). *A Place in the World Called Paris*. Chronicle Books, 1994.

Beltran, Alain, and Patrice Carré. *La Fee et la Servante: la Société Française Face à l'Électricité*. Paris: Belin, 2000.

Biette, Louis. *Le Métropolitain de Paris*. Paris: Chaix, 1906.

Bobrick, Benson. *Labyrinths of Iron: Subways in History, Myth, Art, Technology, and War*. New York: Quill, 1986.

Charon, Eugène. *Letter to M. Charles Garnier* (30 April 1887). Bibliotheque Nationale de France 8-V Piece-6342.

Claretie, Jules. *La Vie à Paris 1897*. Paris: Charpentier, 1898.

La Clé des Omnibus et Tramways. Paris: Administration d'Affichage, 1876.

Commission du Vieux Paris. *Procès-Verbaux* 1903. Paris: Imprimerie Municipal, 1904.

Compagnie des Omnibus. *Tramways dans Paris: Cahier des Charges*. Paris: Ch. De Mourgues Freres, 1873.

Conklin, Alice. *A Mission to Civilize: The Republican Idea of Empire in France and West Africa*. Palo Alto: Stanford University Press, 1997.

Conseil Général de la Seine. *Procès-Verbaux* vol. 103, 2nd–3rd sessions 1906, 2nd part. Imprimerie Municipal, 1907.

Conseil Général de la Seine. *Procès-verbaux* vol. 106, 2nd session 1907, 2nd part. Imprimerie Municipal, 1908.

Conseil Général de la Seine. *Chemins de Fer Métropolitains. Tramways. Rapport de l'Ingénieur en Chef du Département*. Paris: Imprimerie Chaix, 1890.

Conseil Général de la Seine. *Rapport* no. 5, 2 April 1897. Paris: Imprimerie Chaix, 1897.

Conseil Municipal de Paris. *Rapport au Nom de la Commission du Métropolitain sur l'Accident du Chemin de Fer Métropolitain du 10 Août 1903 et sur les Améliorations à Apporter à l'Exploitation, Présenté par Félix Roussel, Conseiller Municipal. de* Paris: Imprimerie Municipal, 1904.

Conseil Municipal de Paris. *Procès-Verbaux* 1st sem. Imprimerie Municipal, 1906.

Cottereau, Alain. "Les Batailles pour la Création du Métro: un Choix de Mode de Vie, un Succès Historique pour la Démocratie Locale." *Revue d'Histoire du XIXe Siècle* 29 (2004): 89–151.

"Cri de Douleur" La Croix (12 August 1903): 1.

D'Avenel, Georges. *Le Mécanisme de la Vie Moderne* vol. 5. Paris: Librarie Armand Colin, 1905.

De Laere, L. "La Question des Tramways." *Le Courrier Bleu de Neuilly-Boulogne* (17 October 1897).

De Nansouty, Max. *La Question du Réseau Métropolitain de Paris et le Projet de la Cie des Etablissements Eiffel.* Paris: Génie Civil, 1891.

Desabres, Pascal. "The Parisian Subway, 1880–1900: A Local or National Interest Line? On the Concept of Globalization." *Business and Economic History On-Line* 1 (2003). www.thebhc.org/publications/BEHonline/2003/Desabres.pdf

Dierman, William. "La Traction Électrique des Tramways à Paris." *L'Électricien; Revue Internationale de l'Électricité et de ses Applications* Ser. 2, 4.87 (27 August 1892): 137–141.

Dupuy, Paul. *La Traction Électrique: Tramways, Locomotives et Métropolitains Électriques.* Paris: Librairie de *Sciences Générales*, 1897.

Emery, Elizabeth. "Protecting the Past: Albert Robida and the Vieux Paris Exhibit at the 1900 World's Fair." *Journal of European Studies* 35 (2005): 65–85.

Evenson, Norma. *Paris: A Century of Change 1878–1978.* New Haven: Yale, 1979.

"The Fire on the Paris Underground." *The Times* (13 August 1900): 3.

"Flâneuries et Curiosités." *Gazette Anecdotique, Littéraire, Artistique et Bibliographique* 1 (1897): 212–214.

Francq, Léon. *Chemin de Fer Métropolitain: Recueil des Articles Publiés dans le Journal le Métropolitain à propos de la Traction du Métropolitain Parisien.* Paris: E. Bernard et Cie., 1892).

Frémaux., J. *Rapport de l'Inspecteur Général. Chemins de Fer Métropolitain de Paris. Avant-Projet. Résultats de l'Enquête d'Utilité Publique,* 12 September 1883 (Archives Nationales F/14/9154).

Garnier, Jules. *Avant-Projet d'un Chemin de Fer Aérien à Voies Superposées* (Paris: Imprimerie Chaix, 1884).

Gautier, Émile. *l'Année Scientifique et Industrielle* 39 (Paris: Hachette, 1896).

Giedion, Siegfried. *Building in France, Building in Iron, Building in Ferroconcrete.* Trans. J. Duncan Berry (Getty Research Institute, 1996).

Goubert, Jean-Pierre, *The Conquest of Water: The Advent of Health in the Industrial Age.* Trans. Andrew Wilson (Cambridge, UK: Polity, 1989).

Graham, Stephen, and Simon Marvin. *Splintering Urbanism: Networked Infrastructures, Technological Mobilities and the Urban Condition* (New York and London: Routledge, 2001).

Guyot, Yves. *Trois Ans aux Ministre des Travaux Publics: Expériences et Conclusions* (Paris: Léon Chailley, 1896).

Hård, Mikael, and Andrew Jamison (Eds.). *The Intellectual Appropriation of Technology: Discourses on Modernity, 1900–1939* (Cambridge, MA: MIT Press, 1998).

Hård, Mikael, and Andreas Knie. "The Grammar of Technology: German and French Diesel Engineering, 1920–1940." *Technology and Culture* 40.1 (1999): 26–46.

Harvey, David. *Paris, Capital of Modernity* (New York and London: Routledge, 2003).

Hausser, Elisabeth. *Paris au Jour le Jour: Les Événements Vus par la Presse, 1900–1919* (Paris, Les Editions de Minuit, 1968).

Hecht, Gabrielle. *The Radiance of France: Nuclear Power and National Identity after World War II* (Cambridge, MA: MIT Press, 1998).

Herf, Jeffrey. *Reactionary Modernism: Technology, Culture, and Politics in Weimar and the Third Reich* (Cambridge,UK: Cambridge University Press, 1984).

Heuzé, Louis. *Chemin de Fer Transversal à Air Libre dans une Rue Spéciale. Passage Couvert pour Piétons* (Paris: A. Lévy, 1878).

Hughes, Thomas. *Networks of Power: Electrification in Western Society, 1880–1930* (Baltimore: Johns Hopkins University Press, 1983).

Jackson, Jeffrey. *Paris under Water: How the City of Light Survived the Great Flood of 1910* (New York: Palgrave Macmillan, 2010).

Jacquemet, Gérard. "Voirie, Transports, et Equipement Urbain à Belleville de 1860 à 1914." *Paris et Ile-de-France: Mémoires Publiés par la Fédération des Sociétés Historiques et Archéologiques de Paris et de l'Ile-de-France* 33 (1982): 225–253.

James, Edmund. "Conditions Relating to the Treatment of Employees and Laborers Imposed by the City of Paris upon the Company to Which the Metropolitan Road Was Leased." *The American Journal of Sociology* 5.6 (May 1900): 826–828.

James, Edmund. "The Inadequate Street Car System of Paris." *Chicago Daily* (22 April 1900), 51.

Jordan, David. *Transforming Paris: The Life and Labors of Baron Haussmann* (Chicago: University of Chicago Press, 1995).

"La Catastrophe du Métropolitain." *Le Temps* (12 August 1903), 2.

"La Catastrophe du Métropolitain." *Le Temps* (13 August 1903), 1–2

"La Catastrophe" *Le Temps* (14 August 1903), 1–2.

L'Assiette au Beurre 125 (22 August 1903).

LeHir, M. L. *Réseau des Voies Ferrées Sous Paris* (Paris: Mémorial du Commerce et de L'Industrie, 1872).

Lemoine, E. *Étude sur la Formation et l'Emploi des Capitaux Engagés dans les Tramways-Nord & Sud de Paris* (Paris, Imprimerie de la Publicité, 1881).

"Le Métro en Feu" *La Croix* (12 August 1903), 1.

"Le Métropolitain" *Le Temps* (26 March 1896), 3.

"Lendemain de catastrophe" *La Croix* (13 August 1903), 3.

"Le Tramway de la Rue du Quatre-Septembre" *Le Temps* (18 January 1900), 1.

"Le Tramway de Romainville" *Le Temps* (11 January 1900), 2.

"Les Oeuvres et les Hommes." *Le Correspondant* 198 (1900), 416.

"Les Tramways Meurtrières" *Le Petit Parisien* (5 October 1900), 1.

"Mésaventures électriques" *Le Temps* (19 October 1900), 2–3.

"Les Tramways de Paris." *Le Magasin Pittoresque* 47 (1879).

"Les Tramways à Dix Centimes." *l'Éclair* (24 October 1897).

Levallois, Ernest. *Paris Propre!* (Paris: Edouard Cornély et Cie, 1910).

Lopez, Alberte Martinez. "Belgian Investment in Tramways and Light Railways: An International Approach, 1892–1935." *The Journal of Transport History* 24.1 (March 2003): 59–77.

Maréchal, Henry. *Les Tramways Électriques* (Paris: Librarie Polytechnique Charles Beranger, 1902).

McKay, John. *Tramways and Trolleys: The Rise of Urban Mass Transport in Europe* (Princeton, 1976).

Michel, Georges. *Léon Say: Sa Vie, Ses Oeuvres* (Paris: Calmann Lévy, 1899).

Mouchelet, E. "Doléances du Photographe Contre les Excès de la Civilisation." *Photo-Gazette* (25 September 1900): 201–205.

"Notes." *The Electrical Engineer* (30 October 1896).

Nye, David. *American Technological Sublime* (Cambridge, MA: MIT Press, 1994).

Nye, Robert. *Crime, Madness, and Politics in Modern France: the Medical Conception of National Decline* (Princeton, NJ: Princeton University Press, 1984).

Ossadzow, Alexandre. "Les Pères du Métropolitain: l'Intervention des Ingénieurs." Sheila Hallsted-Baumert (Ed.), under the direction of Francois Gasnault and Henri Zuber. *Métro-Cité: le Chemin de Fer Métropolitain à la Conquête de Paris, 1871–1945* (Paris: Paris-Musées/RATP, 1997).

Papayanis, Nicholas. *Planning Paris before Haussmann* (Baltimore: Johns Hopkins University Press, 2004).

Précis sur la Locomotive sans Foyer (Paris: Boyer, 1875).

Petitjean, N. N. *Les Grands Travaux de Paris : l'Exposition de 1900, le Métropolitain, la Démolition des Remparts, la Nouvelle Enceinte, le Tout-à-l'Égout* (Paris: L. Thouvenin, 1895).

Pike, David. *Subterranean Cities: The World beneath Paris and London, 1800–1945* (Ithaca: Cornell University Press, 2005).

La Question du Métropolitain. Conférence a l'École des Hautes Études Commerciales (Paris: Administration des Deux Revues, 1889).

Reader, John. *Cities* (New York: Grove Press, 2006).

Reid, Donald. *Paris Sewers and Sewermen: Realities and Representations* (Cambridge, MA: Harvard University Press, 1991).

Robert, Jean. *Les Tramways Parisiens*, 3rd ed. (Paris: RATP, 1992).

Robida, Albert. "L'Embellissement de Paris par le Métropolitain." *La Caricature: Journal Hebdomaire* no. 338 (19 June 1886).

Schatzberg, Eric. "Culture and Technology in the City: Opposition to Mechanized Street Transportation in Late-Nineteenth Century America." Eds. Gabrielle Hecht and Michael Allen. *Technology and History: Essays in Honor of Thomas Parke Hughes and Agatha Chipley Hughes* (Cambridge, MA: MIT Press, 2001): 57–94.

Schivelbusch, Wolfgang. *The Railway Journey: The Industrialization of Time and Space in the 19th Century* (Berkeley: University of California, 1987).

Scott, James. *Seeing Like a State: How Certain Schemes to Improve the Human Condition Have Failed* (New Haven: Yale University Press, 1998).

Sérafon, F. *La Vérité sur les Tramways Nord & Sud de Paris* (Imprimerie de la Publicité, 1882).

Smith, Robert Henry. *Electric Traction* (New York: Harper, 1905).

Société des Ingénieurs Civils. *Mémoirs et Compte Rendu des Travaux* (Paris: Librarie Scientifique, Industrielle et Agricole, 1872).

Société des Ingénieurs Civils. *Discussion sur l'Emploi de l'Air Comprimé pour la Locomotion Mécanique par la Procédés L. Mékarski* (Paris: Imprimerie Viéville et Capiomont, 1876).

 Société des Ingénieurs Civils. *Mémoirs et Compte-Rendu des Travaux* (Paris: Société des Ingénieurs Civils, 1883).

Son, Min Suh. "The Technology of Protest: Streetcar Riots, Race and Public Activism" (unpublished conference paper, Society for Social Studies of Science, Montreal, October 2007).

Soppelsa, Peter. "Finding Fragility in Paris: The Politics of Infrastructure after Haussmann." *Proceedings of the Western Society for French History* 37 (2009): 233–247. http://hdl.handle.net/2027/spo.0642292.0037.016.

Soppelsa, Peter. "The Fragility of Modernity: Infrastructure and Everyday Life in Paris 1870– 1914" (Ph.D. dissertation, University of Michigan, 2009).

Spencer, Michael. "A Fresh Look at Rimbaud's 'Métropolitain.'" *The Modern Language Review* 63 (October 1968): 849–853.

Taithe, Bertrand. *Defeated Flesh: Medicine, Welfare, and Warfare in the Making of Modern France* (Lanham, MD: Rowan and Littlefield, 1999).

Taine, Hippolyte. "Lettres de Londres." *Le Temps* (8 January 1872).

Tables du Journal Le Temps 3, 1871–1875 (Paris: Editions du Centre National de la Récherche Scientifique, 1968).

Tarr, Joel A., and Gabriel Dupuy (Eds.). *Technology and the Rise of the Networked City in Europe and America* (Philadelphia: Temple University Press, 1988).

Tricoire, Jean. "L'Exploitation du Métropolitain: de l'Improvisation à la Méthode." Sheila Hallsted-Baumert (Ed.), under the direction of Francois Gasnault and Henri Zuber. *Métro-Cité: le Chemin de Fer Métropolitain à la Conquête de Paris, 1871–1945* (Paris: Paris-Musées/RATP, 1997), 103–116.

Van Imschoot-Roos, E. *Vérités Nécessaires ! . . . Protestation de M. Marsoulan, . . . Lettre de MM. Bayard et Van Imschoot-Roos, du 3 Novembre 1879, aux Membres du Conseil Général* (Paris: Imprimerie Moderne, 1879).

Vibert, Paul. *La Concurrence Étrangère: les Transports par Terre et par Mer*, 2 vols. (Paris: Berger-Levrault, 1896–1897).

Villain, Paul. *Le Métro qu'on Peut Faire* (Paris: Grande Imprimerie, 1891).

Villain, Paul, and E. Mauger. *Un Métropolitain qui ne Coûte Rien et ne Trouble Rien* (Paris: Grande Imprimerie, 1892).

Ville de Paris. *Bulletin Municipal Officiel* (various dates).

Weber, Eugen. *Peasants into Frenchmen: The Modernization of Rural France, 1870–1914* (Palo Alto: Stanford University Press, 1976).

Weber, Eugen. *France Fin de Siècle* (Cambridge, MA: Harvard University Press, 1986).

White, John. "War of the Wires: A Curious Chapter in Street Railway History." *Technology and Culture* 46.2 (April 2005): 374–384.

Williams, Rosalind. *Notes on the Underground: An Essay on Technology, Society and the Imagination* (Cambridge, MA: MIT Press, 1992).

Zaretsky, Rob. "The Sewers of Paris." *The Engines of Our Ingenuity*, episode 1966 (University of Houston KUHF). www.uh.edu/engines/epi1966.htm.

Chapter 6

Subways and Cell Phones

Seoul as a Network City

Samuel Gerald Collins

It's December 2010 in Seoul. A woman in her twenties has taken a seat in the part of the subway reserved for the elderly and physically disabled (*noyak chwasŏk*). An elderly man approaches, expecting her to relinquish the seat (*yangbo*) to him. Instead, she refuses. "I'm sitting here—sit somewhere else!" An argument ensues. As luck would have it, a passenger sitting across from the disturbance taped the whole episode on his cell phone, and within a short time, uploaded the video onto the Internet, where it quickly gets cross-posted across hundreds of forums and blogs. The incident of "Rude-Speech Girl" (*panmal nyŏ*) focuses attention on several perceived problems in Korean society: the alienation of the city, the generational divide, and the replacement of the multigenerational household with the nuclear family.

There is a long tradition in the social sciences of theorizing the city as the epicenter of alienation and anomie in modernity (Berman). Writing in response to the pivotal work of Georg Simmel, Stanley Milgram catalogs the compensatory strategies urban dwellers have developed to adapt to the essential problem of urban living: the psychic stress of a large population of strangers interacting together (Milgram). The carefully maintained boundaries of "familiar strangers," the avoidance of eye contact, together with the use of a variety of "filtering devices" (books, newspapers, magazines) that discourage unnecessary social intercourse: all technologies for maintaining distance.

But Milgram, together with the many lines of urban research he inspired, saw the city as a problem that needed to be overcome. That is, implicit in the kinds of questions he asked was a distinction between "the country and the city," as Raymond Williams called it in his 1973 survey, where "the city" appears as the negation of the more multiplex relationships said to inhere in "the country" (Williams; Gluckman). But, what if we construed the city as less of a problem and more of an opportunity? That is, rather than start from a baseline defined by nostalgic references to a pastoral existence, why not examine the urban as a novel way to be human, where "human" is less a given set of characteristics than an emergent project?

Urban environments present opportunities to interact with a variety of people in distinctly different ways—from ignoring them altogether to "hooking up" with them. If we think of the city from something of a Baudelarian perspective, then we might think about life in the city as less about compensatory strategies and filtering devices than as the utilization of a broad range of technologies and techniques for the generation of new and varied social relations: technologies of flânerie (Berman).

As cell phones give way to handsets with multiple applications, media theorists have begun to concentrate on "convergence," "the flow of content across multiple media platforms" (Jenkins). Indeed, the rapid development of mobile devices offers, from the perspective of consumers, a revolution in media convergence, allowing unprecedented access to television, movies and internet browsing. At the same time, though, there is something altogether too scripted about academic writing on "convergence"—we are, after all, merely following in the footsteps of advertising copy that promises instant media synergy. "Convergence" is the academic version of smart phone advertisements promising integration of multiple platforms. And that advertising copy promotes a reified—and misleading—image of information and communication technologies (ICTs) as a cumulative, linear process of invention and product development, the ongoing progress of "next generation" technologies continuously feeding consumer appetites in the speed-up of advanced capitalism.

But that is only one way to think about "convergence." Another way might be to examine technologies in their sociotechnical contexts, as inextricably enmeshed in social and cultural meanings and practices. The more radical approach to this would be something like Latour's "assemblage," where humans and technologies conceived as nonhuman agents (momentarily) connect together in accomplishing meaningful action. In this, Latour delights in confounding the usual casuistries that privilege the human over the nonhuman, as in his point that guns don't kill people, and people don't kill people, but the assemblage formed by gun and humans is, ultimately, what kills: "You are different with a gun in your hand; the gun is different with you holding it. You are another subject because you hold the gun; the gun is another object because it has entered into a relationship with you (Latour, 179). Latour's assemblage has devastating consequences for linear narratives of technological development—it demands that we follow the trail formed by technosocial action and refrain from granting any agency a priori outside the chains of association they form (Latour, *Reassembling the Social*).

An actor-network is an important anodyne to a distressing trend in analyses of ICTs to see them as ultimately following linear teleologies that construct spurious chronotypes. For example, Urry writes: "Whereas trains and pocket watches were early modern twins, mobile phones and cars are the late modern twins in an era where social networks are dispersed and coordination and travel are necessary for social life" (174). Here, he constructs a linear narrative where the pocket watch and train ineluctably give way to the mobile phone and automobile. But, here, Urry's analysis ignores (1) the actual periods during which these technologies gained popularity and (2) the stubborn coexistence of all four in the world today. The better approach instead would be to examine the synchronic sociotechnical systems of which all of these technologies form a part. Looking at ICTs in their complex association not only challenges narratives of progress but also serves to suggest alternative narratives and, ultimately, alternative futures. Seeing the cell phone and the automobile as the central characteristics of a mobile society as Urry does projects the automobile into the future—indeed, by yoking it to ICTs, Urry extends the automobile into the future, connecting the rise of the smart phone to the continued hegemony of the automobile.

The point is not just that cell phones have little meaning outside of their practice, but that mobile handsets form variegated assemblages with other machines and other technologies and that, furthermore, these do not need to follow some linear chronotype where 4G handsets can only combine with other 4G technologies. As Michael writes,

> [T]he claims of epochal transformations supposedly wrought by exotic technologies can be criticized in terms of the argument that these transformations will be minute, piecemeal in the context of the continuing, stabilizing, inertial mundane technologies that enable them [. . . .] We do not, for example, become hypertextual beings (in the dual sense of constantly jumping across texts and of becoming largely "disembodied" beings) because we will sit on seats, change light bulbs, maintain plugs and cables. (132)

And more than just an admonition of the salience of the past, "older" technologies form part of the assemblages made up of diverse human and nonhuman agents; hence it is entirely appropriate to analyze a "flexible" cell-phone/subway "system." To examine Seoul as a truly mobile city means including different nonhuman agents and different temporalities. Mobility is not unidirectional; it includes mobility in space and time.

In order to sketch the contours of this mobile city, I begin with the subway, turn to the cell phone, and then consider both together. Rather than imply causality (or even chronology), I allow subways to help interrogate the cellular phone, and cellular phones to illuminate the subway, moving back and forth over this sociotechnical system in order to pick up the pieces of alternative meanings and practices. In so doing, I sketch the twin asymptotes of an inquiry into a sociotechnical system on the move, networking itself into my search even as it allows human agents to network with each other.

First, however, there are logistical problems: how should one study this assemblage, the collision of people, machines, communications, visual perspectives, and social networking? For one thing, "blackboxing" renders these technologies all but invisible. As Latour writes in *Pandora's Hope*,

> The way scientific and technical work is made invisible by its own success. When a machine runs efficiently, when a matter of fact is settled, one need focus only on its inputs and outputs and not on its internal complexity. Thus, paradoxically, the more science and technology succeed the more opaque and obscure they become. (304)

Rendered seamless by design and practice, the quotidian technologies of urban survival—the subway and mobile handset—are at once unremarkable and unremarked. How do we gather data? We may be able to analyze people's tweets, and to some extent even map their movements. But we can't see them engaged in the complex exchanges of a multi-agent system, the minutiae of the mobile device/ subway encounter. Research on sociotechnical systems has generally used two methods: (1) interviews and focus groups with users who are asked to discuss their technology practices and (2) journals that "log" technology usage over the course of a day (Bull; Lally). Both are possible methods, but both grant a kind of ontological primacy to the cell phone—it is the mobile device that creates the conditions of meaning in the research, and the research question devolves into the use of the cell phone.

My own efforts to interview people about their phones in spring 2007 yielded laconic responses—testament not only to the ubiquity of cellular devices but also to the unarticulated habitus that makes social life through the phone seamless, second nature. People use their cell phones. A lot. On subways, buses, in cars. Even while they're biking. What of it? If one indication of hegemony is silence, then we might conclude these technologies are very powerful indeed. Taken for granted by academics and informants alike, the subway–cell phone system represents what Ehn and Löfgren call the "backyards of modernity," unacknowledged places where modernity is freely produced and reproduced.

I had better luck with other narratives—blog posts, film, essays, and literature—where subways and handsets are elements of mise-en-scène for other activities. Seldom articulated as standalone meditations on the mobile handset/subway system, these vignettes incidentally sited encounters in the context of these technologies. The following, then, represents some of the results of this ongoing research—research that develops questions and gestures to more inquiry, but that is not, in the end, the last word on this subject.

THE SUBWAY

Subways have always represented the very height of modernity, and it is no mistake that the Paris Metro opens in 1900 during the *Exposition Universelle*. It functions to (literally) support ideologies of state progress. And it is no surprise that Seoul's #1 line (*il ho seon*) opened a year after it's "*Ch'eollima*" counterpart in Pyongyang, nor that Seoul's new subway featured prominently in mid-1970s textbooks trumpeting the technical advances of the capitalist South versus that of the communist North. Transportation has a powerful, nationalist function that extends over the span of Korean development—whether trains, subways, or automobiles (Jeon). And as Marc Augé has described, one of the functions of the metro is to reference the national in the names of stops, and in its pageantry and public art (Augé). Seoul's subway has—besides gallery spaces built within the subway itself—various gestures to Korean media, history, and so forth. The Chungmuro station pays homage to the Korean film industry; there even used to be a stained glass window installation at the Dongdaemun stop. But the subway performs a part of the nationalist project in another way, too. As Marshall Berman wrote of Haussmann's Paris, there was a reciprocity of vision in the boulevards: one that allowed both a knowledge of the class and ethnic other as well as a mutual identification of each as citizens, that imagined community most often identified with written technologies rather than the built environment (Berman). As in Haussmann's Paris, the subway is a way of rendering the city visible and knowable, a way of inscribing social practice onto the warp and weft of the urban built environment. Unlike Parisian boulevards that celebrate state power, subways render the city into an abstract network—connected subway stations crisscrossing the city, an order achieved through the physicality of tunnels and galleries, conveying "a general sense of structure" and working to "establish points of interaction" (Vertsei, 25). The Seoul subway structures the city—in the sense of a network society that both connects and disconnects—channeling people, ideas, and practices toward certain stops, connections, perambulations while making others more difficult. Thus, opening new lines is not only an economic issue, but also a cultural, political, and historical one—literally altering the imagination of the city.

And what can be easier to meet at than the subway (or points near the subway)? In Seoul, individual buildings aren't numbered sequentially like their Western counterparts, resulting in occasional confusion for Koreans and non-Koreans alike. In this urban labyrinth, even people who drive may still meet in front of subway stops.

> When people make appointments or give each other directions, subway stations play an important role. So do nearby bookstores, the lobbies of department stores. The entries to shopping malls and fast-food restaurants surge with people waiting to meet each other. This is because the lines and stops of subways are universally known meeting places. There's no need for any explanation and certain subway stops are part of the universal route map that everybody knows. (Song, 61)

In a city that shifts vertiginously with every redevelopment scheme (*chaekaebal*), subway stops remain ironically permanent, islands in a stream of perpetual, creative destruction. Yet, however permanent it is, the subway is perpetually strange and anonymous—places where people's ties to place have been rendered most tenuous.

> Even though we're in the same compartment, it's rare that we meet someone we know. Hardly a word passes between people—it's mainly faces we've seen for the first time. In contrast to buses we board at the same time, where we may become accustomed to people's faces, on the subway there's almost no one we see who becomes more than a stranger. (Song, 59)

That is, nothing could be contrasted more to the subway than the neighborhood *maŭl* bus, where driver and passengers are as familiar as the people on one's stairwell. But, that said, people on the subway, courtesy of the 9 million riders who board each day, pass their time in often extremely close proximity to each other. Allison describes this intimacy in Tokyo (the busiest metro in the world):

> Certainly, the connected disconnectedness of Tokyo train travel breeds intimacies all its own. The density and proximity of flesh alone, for example, can be intense [. . .] . People tend to endure their commutes in silence, and talk between strangers rarely occurs, even when (or precisely because) bodies are jammed next to each for long stretches. Yet boundaries of other kinds are more fluid. When commuters sleep, which is commonplace, flopping heads often come to rest of neighbors' shoulders. (72–73)

The same technologies that "make strangers" by allowing people to travel the city together without actually interacting simultaneously structure intimacies that would only otherwise occur between friends or lovers. The contradiction becomes most obvious with something like "chikan," the improper touching that is reportedly rampant on Tokyo subways. In Seoul, the term is Koreanized as "ch'ihan" and there is ongoing debate as to where in Korea it is most rampant. But this contradictory quality of anonymity and intimacy itself constitutes a kind of knowledge and mutual recognition built not upon first-hand acquaintance, but on a knowledge of types in Simmel's sense of the stranger. In Simmel's formulation, "the stranger" as a social type has several functions in society, among them "mobility" and "objectivity," characteristics generated out of the tension between intimacy and distance:

As such the stranger is near and far *at the same time*, as in any relationship based on merely human similarities. Between these two factors of nearness and distance, however, a peculiar tension arises, since the consciousness of having only the absolutely general in common has exactly the effect of putting a special emphasis on that which is not common (Simmel, 188). In Simmel's terms, subways are "stranger machines" par excellence—technologies for producing the categories of stranger and strangeness. It is in the subway that we can confront people as "the other," as an unrelated not-self to be observed and objectified into a kind of social knowledge that is only possible in the city, knowledge of the stranger "not really perceived as individuals, but as strangers of a certain type" (188). In Seoul's subways, this combination of anonymity and familiarity gives people knowledge of several types that form the dramatis personae of social concerns and moral panics. It is here, in other words, that one can detachedly (but also passionately) mark the breakdown of Confucian social mores that is at the core of the "panmal nyŏ" incident explored in the introduction to this chapter.

In a 1998 poem, Jiwoo Hwang gestures to the category of that abstract knowledge of types:

On the stairway down to the subway / The Seated Bodhisattvas crouch there at the entrance / Selling dried squid, fresh corn, kimbap, and rice cakes wrapped in cellophane,
A leper who once stood in the Unju Temple valley—one stone Buddha, / Stands dozing off halfway down the steps. (110–111)

Urry argues that trains transform nature into an object of "*visual* consumption by those visiting by train from towns and cities" (101). Submerged beneath the spectacle of nature, subways transform other passengers into both subjects to be avoided and objects to be spectatorially consumed. As in Hwang's poem, mass transit systems make it possible for someone to sell vegetables and cuttlefish and be regarded as a "seated Bodhisattva." Accordingly, encounters in Seoul subway are generative of many other character types that, however, stereotypical, constitute an urban knowledge of the Other.

THE FOREIGNER

One source of disquietude lies in the explosion in the "foreign" population (now estimated at over 1 million), along with the usual stereotypes that, for example, link crime to foreigners. Whatever the feelings individual citizens may have regarding people who migrate to Korea to work in "DDD"

(Difficult, Dirty, and Dangerous) jobs generally eschewed by Koreans, their presence in the city raises the specter of a Korea that is no longer coterminous with ethnic Koreans: a multicultural Korea.

> Now there's a foreigner in on the subway in his mid-40's. He's white, but he seems like a laborer—not from Europe or the United States. He's eating a big bag of popped corn in hand and drinking a can of mango juice. I think he's drunk because he keeps milling about, hitting his hand against the ceiling making a loud sound. He doesn't seem to know how strange it looks and continues [. . .] I try to understand his situation. If you come to a foreign country you've got to have the proper preparedness and determination. But to be drunk on a subway in a foreign land with this bizarre behavior! (Ch'oi)

Seoul's foreign population is growing, but highly concentrated into a few, urban neighborhoods clustered according to social class—Western foreigners readily spotted in wealthier neighborhoods in Kangbuk and Kangnam (the areas north and south of the Han River), and Central and Southeast Asian immigrants in neighborhoods clustered around urban markets or industrial centers: Dongdaemun, Seongbuk, Guro. And yet, foreign immigrants and laborers are also peripatetic—traveling far beyond their homes to other far-flung neighborhoods in Seoul (Kim & Kang). There are few places where the stranger is rendered as visible as on the subway—it is there that impressions can be confirmed, and, particularly for foreign populations not strongly represented in media, a kind of knowledge attained.

THE ELDERLY

In a society where the multigenerational household is a thing of the past, with 82.5% of families living in what might be called "nucleated" households in 2005 (according to Kim), there is a huge (and perhaps irredeemable) gap between older and younger generations (Lee). On the subway, it comes down to "*yangbo*," the (theoretically) obligatory surrendering of one's seat to elderly people (and, by extension, the differently abled).

> I was super-tired after work, and boarded the subway at Seongdaeyeok. I was in 9–30 when I heard a noise from 9–4 . . . . An elderly woman had fallen. But it looked like she had tripped over a student's backpack. This was subjective rather than objective but it looked like she was trying to find an empty seat. . . . But then there was a sharp noise and it looked like she gave the boy a hard slap on the face. I think the violence was pretty extreme. I could see the boy for a moment with a look of hatred on his face, thinking "this old woman is crazy."

Next to me an old man spoke up, "Why hit the child? The parents taught them wrong—why hit the child?" (IYLF)

The subway brings people up against the generational divide as well as the demographic realities of Korea as a rapidly aging society experiencing negative population growth. As with "*panmal nyŏ,*" the city focuses the tensions between older and younger generations along multiple binaries: a Confucian past contrasted with a highly individuated present, the rural village contrasted with the urban present.

THE POOR

The subway is also a place to experience the reality of Korea's growing economic disparities (on the rise since the 1990s and spiking sharply during the IMF crisis), no more typified than by the heretofore almost unknown homeless population (*nosukja*) (Song). Seoul Station, for example, has become one of the most highly visible places where homeless people seek shelter.

A few days before I was getting off the train around 10 o'clock. There was a really strange, strong smell. The next day, the smell was even stronger. "Wow, what a smell," I said. There was a homeless woman there who scared me so I went back out, but she followed me. I was scared that she was following me, so I ran, but she ran after me. She followed me all the way back to the front of my house. I was really scared so I went in and got the building attendant, and he called my Mom. (Anonymous)

Structured like a dream (or a nightmare), the narrative expresses both the pleasures and the dangers of the subway—the chance to consume the image of the (class) other, on the one hand, plus the danger that the essential anonymity of the encounter could give way to more familiarity.

Indeed, the "types" encountered on the subway suggest what Allison calls "intimate alienation," "In that, even though people are solitary and anonymous, it is also a place that is familiar, habitual, and shared" (71). On the one hand, peopled by stereotypical "types," the subway becomes a spectatorial space—a *tableau vivant* of Seoul society. In the above example, the *frisson* of the subway is that the observed may wish to interact with the observer. But this voyeuristic intimacy defines a latency that might develop into actual social relationships. The subway can also be a place where people might meet, belying the anonymity of the experience.

I'm half-way to the subway station when I decide that TODAY I'M GO-ING TO GIVE UP MY SEAT TO EVERY ADULT TODAY—grandfathers, grandmothers, pregnant people. Next to me on the subway, this foreign woman sits down. Surely I've seen her before? I think I saw her on the sidewalk next to the university chanting "Believe in Jesus Christ and go to heaven!" And least, she was that kind of type. I eyed her suspiciously as she took out a piece of gray paper and started to look at it. What's this? The paper had the word "homework" at the top and was printed with Korean language problems! (P'a-talk)

In a charitable mood, he helps her complete her Korean homework. They begin to chat:

The woman said, "Korean is too difficult," and I said, "For me, English is too difficult."
    Finally, when we got off at the station, we exchanged names and goodbyes. She lives in Itaewon, so I explained that the place where I live is kind of far away. If you intend on studying you're pretty . . . . If you really want to study Korean, we can get together later and have a conversation. We exchanged cell phone numbers. (ibid)

In the end, the cell phone number picks up where, literally, the subway lets off. If the subway confronts an individual with the co-presence of urban types, then the cell phone defines a virtual co-presence where people might languish in varying degrees of urban alienation or where more intimate relationships might emerge. Will the Korean and the foreigner ever talk again? Will the number drift amidst hundreds of others in their handset contact lists? Here, the cell phone is a kind of subway of the mind—cohabitating strangers that nevertheless admit the possibility of more intimate encounters.

THE CELL PHONE

The cell phone begins in much the same way as the subway—as a state-supported technical project stimulating business profits in order to (at least putatively) support the public good. As Lee writes, "In Korea, the major drive of informatization has been not only the state's desire to support domestic conglomerates, but also its desire to regulate the citizens by normalizing control of network technology" ("Globalization," 11). And, he reminds us, the first computerization effort was the 1975 national ID system—a massive, integrated plan to bring the citizenry under panoptic control. The organization—if not the spirit—of technological development survived into Korea's telecommunications revolution during President Kim Dae-jung's "second national building," where building a telecommunications and information infrastructure was linked to "re-creating" Korea as a knowledge-based economy. Both the national ID system and the development of Korean IT combined a characteristic public–private cooperation with a strong element of ideological coercion—in the first, to police citizens, in the second, to create a knowledge-based citizenry.

Whatever one's feelings about the politics behind its develop, it would be hard not to see efforts to develop a cell phone industry as a huge success. With the number of mobile phone subscribers exceeding the entire population of South Korea, the cell phone is a ubiquitous technology embraced by Koreans of all ages. It is now difficult to conceive of Korea outside of its varied data ecologies. As one German woman on the popular television talk-show program, *"Minyodŭl Suda"* (*The Chatter of Pretty Women*), opined:

> If you go to a restaurant or bar, the first thing people do is put their cell phones down on the table. I was really surprised to see students answering the phone in the middle of class, but the professor does it too! I'm not kidding! "And it's really irritating when I'm eating with a friend who pauses every five minutes to send off a message from her phone." (Kim, 62)

The phone is so indispensable that it has taken on some of the qualities of an indispensable human right—for example, in the 2008 campaign to help North Korean youth in South Korea navigate cell phones. Handhelds are as much a "survival skill" in contemporary capitalist society as being able to using banks and credit cards.

Over the past two decades, there has been a dramatic growth in scholarship on cell phones—much of this has dealt with the explosion of handheld technologies in Asia (Glotz & Bertsch; Hjorth; Ito et al.; Kim, *Hyudaep'oni Malhada*). Among researchers, there has been a certain level of consensus about what the cell phone does, and what it will do, to identity and social life: a range of possibly contradictory claims about the impact of cell phones on the fabric of urban life that are both descriptions of the present and prognostications about the future. Many of these involve specific claims about cell phones as a form of urban practice. For example, our mobile devices are said to

1. Utterly disconnect us from space: That is, cell phones bring together things and people widely distributed across space, and turn heretofore public spaces into private enclosures encased in media.
2. Annihilate boundaries: All of the temporal/spatial boundaries that order our daily rounds (home/work/school/leisure) are said to bleed into each other until there is no longer any sharp distinction between having fun with your friends and, say, attending an academic conference.

3. Help create "interspaces": Accord new importance to "third spaces" positioned in the interstices of home, work and school, placing new importance on intervals of commuting, waiting, and walking (Urry, 250).
4. Isolate people from the world around them: By "parochializing" or "cocooning" people in social networks of their own devising, the complex, stochastic world in which we live is replaced by a homogenous "non-place" of ubiquitous media distraction.

But despite this emphasis on spatial practice, the specificity of place is lost. Indeed, the metaphor of mobile phone applications is particularly apt here. If we think of apps as materializations of various theories of social networking—that is, software solutions to the problems of creating and maintaining social relationships—then we might see these theorizations on cell phones as a kind of academic app: a theoretical shorthand for articulating the significance of cell phones in urban life. In creating this hermeneutic shortcut, however, we simultaneously "cut" the network: truncate the networked field of meanings. As Strathern writes of genetic patents, the potentially endless accretion of nodes in networks of scientific discovery is "cut" by the legal assignation of property rights to a bounded group of patent holders (Strathern). Similarly, the possibility for different, aberrant or emergent meanings for cell phones in social life is "cut" by the insistence on reified affect.

But as my opening vignette suggests, mobile devices in Seoul are inextricably embedded in Seoul—that the citizen–mobile device–subway–city forms a sociotechnical system that is not reducible to a single, set of *a priori* signifieds. An analysis informed by Actor Network Theory (Latour, 2005) seems a much more natural fit for research on cell phones in Korea for several reasons: (1) mobile devices embed a host of variously lively agencies that combine with us in various ways, and (2) mobile devices are about social network and social network problems—and not in the sense of classic social network theory with its ossified *tableau vivant* of edges and vertices, but in the sense of an emergent, even stochastic, revelation of human and nonhuman agencies unfolding across a built environment made up of overlapping visual and audio landscapes.

Consider the coordination of a Saturday happy hour somewhere in Sinchon—five friends board the subway from their homes and offices in five different parts of the city without specifying in advance where they will meet. Along the way, ample text messaging, perhaps some locational applications, together with the transportation systems, enable a meeting to emerge from the (loosely) coupled actions of a variety of agents.

Out of an interest in recognizing the importance of place on the one hand, and revisiting the place of mobile devices in Korean life on the other, I began to examine media representations and, in particular, television programs. Korean television dramas spend a lot of time representing cell phones—testament to relentless product placement and the ways the cell phone has been deployed for all sorts of narrative crosscutting. I considered them for at least two reasons: (1) they present cell phones in an agential, dramaturgical sense—as *deus ex machina* devices for the twenty-first century. (2) I wanted to use clips from television dramas to both better understand the data I had already gathered in research in Seoul in 2007 and 2009 and to help prompt people to discuss their own cell phones practices in future research.

My Sweet Seoul (*Naui TalKom Han Dosi*) is a popular drama that aired on SBS in 2008, based on a 2006 novel by Jeong I-hyeon. Self-consciously patterned after the popular U.S. series "Sex in the City," this television drama follows the lives of three friends who have all passed the age of 30, the age at which they are supposed to have been married. As the friends navigate the city, they also navigate various, male friends: in particular Eun-soo, who juggles multiple suitors, linking to one, breaking off ties to another, while endeavoring to keep the skein of relationships from tangling at inopportune moments. Here, the cell phone appears to be key to these efforts, and "My Sweet Seoul" stands apart as devoting astounding amounts of airtime to cell phones—in some episodes as much as 23% of the program is devoted to people fiddling with their mobile devices.

Analyzing the first eight episodes of the series yielded up over sixty minutes of cell phone time, almost 100 situations that combine cell phones, people, and parts of the city in different constellations.

But how is one to analyze/interpret these instances? We can see them as the application of a function, in which case we simply mimic marketing researchers who base their newest campaigns on consumer behavior.

Table 6.1.   Total seconds of airtime in "My Sweet Seoul" involving cell phones (by episode).

Episode (each episode ~3,000 seconds long)	Total seconds devoted to cell phones
#1	659 (21.96%)
#2	690 (23%)
#3	354 (11.8%)
#4	395 (13.17%)
#5	625 (20.8%)
#6	141 (4.7%)
#7	514 (17.1%)
#8	266 (8.9%)

Table 6.2. Cell phone use in first eight episodes of "My Sweet Seoul" broken down by application.

Function	Voice	Text	Phone Book	Voice Mail	Ringtone	Caller ID	Other
Frequency	38	24	5	5	4	3	7
Time	1,516 sec.	909 sec.	439 sec.	180 sec.	147 sec.	134 sec.	193 sec.
Average Time	40 sec.	38 sec.	88 sec.	30 sec.	37 sec.	45 sec.	27 sec.

Instead, I have chosen to engage them dramaturgically and, by tracing the way hand-sets work to weave together narratives, I evoke the palimpsest of scapes that coheres briefly in the space of the drama. The following instances of "voice" and "text" functions suggest this broader approach:

Voice

1. Tae-oh uses a call as a pretext to leave an awkward dinner. Since he is the youngest, Tae-oh can't refuse going to dinner with Eun-soo's friends, even though he doesn't know them. When they begin quarreling bitterly over long-term disagreements, Tae-oh takes advantage of a phone call to get up and leave the group.
2. Demonstrates/enables cocooning. Eun-soo can use her friends as a sounding board for all of the conundrums she faces as a single woman.
3. Enables surveillance of call recipient. Cell phones enable Eun-soo's mother to pursue an affair with an old friend, but they also allow Eun-soo to eavesdrop on text messages and discover her mother's infidelity.
4. Allows friends to get advice from each other.
5. Allows private conversations separate from work or home.
6. Allows for greater intimacy.
7. Allows one to check on friends through calling other friends.
8. Allows friends to come between friends (by calling them at inopportune moments). Eun-soo is continuously interrupted by phone calls from her live-in boyfriend, Tae-oh, when she meets with her other romantic interest, Yeong-soo. She shields her screen from Yeong-soo to conceal the name of her boyfriend.
9. Allows one to deceive others about your location.
10. Tae-oh keeps Eun-soo on the line while he rushes to her house. Eun-soo is awakened by a woman's screams coming from the apartment above her. Terrified, she calls Tae-oh and leaves a voice-mail message.

Checking the message, Tae-oh takes a cab to Eun-soo's apartment, and tries to comfort her over his phone on the ride over. He continues to talk to her as he gets out of the cab and runs down the narrow street to her door.

11. Hanging up on someone shows anger.
12. Allows people to negotiate meeting places.

Text

1. Reminds friends about appointments.
2. Renew connections with old acquaintances/weak ties.
3. Allows one to contact friends without disengaging from other, social interaction. Eun-soo can still remain in contact with Yoo-hee, even when she's on a date with Tae-oh.
4. Allows one to disengage from a social situation.
5. Eun-soo and Tae-oh walk together in her old neighborhood. Because of their age differences, Eun-soo is particularly reticent about her new relationship with Tae-oh. When he accompanies Eun-soo to her old neighborhood, she's particularly concerned that one of her old neighbors might see them and tell her parents, so the two walk apart and text each other about the beautiful flower blossoms along the street. They meet one of her parents' neighbors and Tae-oh hangs back, pretending not to know her.
6. Allows someone else to discover, or eavesdrop on, your secret relationship.
7. Eun-soo texts and erases messages to Tae-oh. After a particularly serious fight with Tae-oh, Eun-soo sits in her office alongside her co-workers and contemplates contacting him again. She starts to text him several times, but erases her text and never sends it.
8. Allows one to hesitate without replying.
9. Eun-soo texts Yeong-soo an innocuous message. Eun-soo is interested in Yeong-soo, but is cautious about approaching him directly. Instead, she sends him a simple, ambiguous text message that maintains her connection to him without pushing him toward any specific action and without requiring his reply.
10. Allows one to send reminders.
11. Allows one to receive communications without breaking a professional context.
12. Allows one to indicate interest in a new relationship.

What these suggest is the broader networks of human and nonhuman agencies implicated in cell phone practice. We can look at the cell phone as primarily about relationships—indeed, Eun-soo uses her phone to manage her relation-ships with friends, family, and potential suitors. But we can only see mobile phone practices as primarily about social relations by abstracting social com-munications from the other technological agencies put into association. I would argue that it is more useful to think of the cell phone as part of a connecting/disconnecting machine that includes people, transportation, and the city itself in shifting assemblages of connection and disconnection. When Eun-soo sits on a bench to manage her phone book, the agencies that form into a momentary association include (in addition to Eun-soo and her phone) the bench, the park, and the people. When she walks in front of Tae-oh texting him, her neighbor-hood and neighbors all come together into a machine assemblage that in turn structures the kinds of texts that Eun-soo and Tae-oh will share.

By "machine," I mean a Deleuzean departure from a sterile antinomy that makes up popular understandings of information and communication tech-nologies, between technologies as primarily extensions of the human body on the one hand, and the machine transcending a superannuated humanity on the other. One scholar terms the Deleuzean machine as follows:

> [It i]s no longer a matter of confronting man and machine to estimate possible or impossible correspondences, extensions and substitutions of the one or the other, or ever new relationships of similarity and metaphorical relations between humans and machines, but rather of concatenations, of how man becomes a piece with the machine or with other things in order to constitute a machine. The "other things" may be animals, tools, other people, statements, signs or desires, but they only become a machine in the process of exchange, not in the paradigm of substitutions. (Raunig, 32)

The machine sets into motion what Raunig calls "a strange theory that deals with the mutual exchange, the flowing of atoms, the particles of matter; and this means not only the flowing *within* precisely delimited bodies and identities, but rather the unbounded flow *between* bodies that touch or close to one another, that merge into one another in neighboring zones." That is, the machine exists in the temporary space of networked exchanges, where agents swap information, communication and characteristics in variously coupled exchanges along lines of affinity, rather than filiations and genealogy.

THERE IS NO THIRD SPACE

One way of interpreting cell phones in urban life has been to concentrate on their role in the creation of a "third space," the places that emerge between work, school, and home and that are thought to include cafés, PC *bang* (rooms), bookstores, and other places that proliferate in urban Seoul (Hjorth). We can see cell phones accomplishing this through connecting and disconnecting nodes along a social network—indeed, a "third space" implies a kind of networked sociality that is as much about including a circle of friends as it is excluding an infinitely large, outside world. But this is not what the dramaturgical reading of cell phones would suggest. Instead, the cell phone acts as a catalyst in the concatenation of multiple elements, including (but never limited) to the phone, the people contacted, the people not contacted, the spaces in which the communication is enacted, the communication itself, and the presences and absences that the cell phone enables. That said, neither human nor nonhuman agents are specified in advance, and new agencies always threaten to intrude. "Cell phone," "city," "interlocutor," "message"— none of these are *a priori* determined—all of them are spun together in the course of the encounter.

> Yesterday when I got off work I took a company bus. I was really tired, so as soon as I got on board, I feel asleep. While I was sleeping my phone went off. My friend sent me three messages. First, "Are you still angry about last time? I was so late that you barely got to see my face. I'm sorry." The second, "You're not . . . Are you still angry? This is really difficult." The third, "You're really still angry? I should have asked your opinion . . ." It went on like that, so I sent a message: "It's not like that. I fell asleep on the bus." (Kŏn-ppang)

The machine—as temporary and chiasmatic as a ride on the bus from downtown Seoul to the Kyeonggi-do suburbs—involves people, a bus (with its gently rocking motion and slow progress through Namsan tunnel downtown), cell phones, unspoken rules about the proper times for returning text messages, and a great deal of articulated and tacit discourse. If we try to limit the circuit of communication to people, or to phones and people, we still have not evoked the full machine, as much about human and nonhuman agents connecting and disconnecting. The end result, therefore, is something altogether more emergent—that is, both something that cannot be predicted from supervenient parts, on the one hand, and something that exerts—through downward causation—new opportunities for emergence. This may not have revolutionary significance; in the difference capitalism associated with neoliberalism, novelty and consumer production have been readily appropriated into what Guy Debord called "the society of the spectacle."

As in Japan, the cell phone in Korea followed a similar development trajectory—first the pager (BiBi) was initially subscribed to by businessmen, following by its widespread adoption by youth by the late 1990s. Cell phones similarly spread through society, but additionally (and eventually) included groups never really penetrated by the pager—housewives, the elderly. Still, though, the generational differences become evident. The landline is generally represented in television and film as the domain of elderly people at home; in television dramas, for example, elderly people are often represented as answering the phone together. This is in contrast to the individuating properties of the cell phone, which are said to undermine family relationships:

> The use of the mobile phone has caused concern about increasing dislocations of young people from the Korean norms of harmonious sociality, which derives from the idea that new communication technologies are likely to both defamiliarize and individualize human relations and consequently that the mobile phone may destroy collective and affective relationships. (Yoon, 328)

But that is not quite what happens—that is, the universal adoption of mobile handsets is not a one-way road to Putnam's alienated society (Putnam). Rather, the cell phone allows people to form and maintain a hierarchy of relationships. As Ichiyo Habucki writes of *keitai* in Japan:

> In other words, *keitai* is a medium with contradictory connotations that reflect the characteristics for particular users. The increase in encounters between with strangers through *keitai* corresponds to the increase in population one encounters, a factor related to urbanization. On the other hand, *keitai* can serve as a means of maintaining existing relationships when it is used to strengthen ongoing collective and social bonds. (167)

On one end of the spectrum, the cell phone brings with it the heavy burden of perpetual contact with people defined as intimates, as in the bus example above. But the cell phone also allows one to differentiate between social relationships—consigning some to never-dialed numbers in a phone book, and a lucky few to a speed dial. And like the subway, it also brings the possibility of contact with strangers. In Japan, this brought about a full-blown moral panic in the 1990s with the revelation that older mean were using *keitai* Internet to contact young girls to date (*enjo kousai*). In Korea, there is the phenomenon—prominent up until a couple years ago, of "text friends," cell phone pen pals who may text intimate details of their lives but who may never actually meet in person.

> A woman of such-and-such an age wanting a male of the same for a text friend. My number is 010-xxxx-xxxx . . . I'm surprised at how many blog postings say this. And it's not surprising to see the same kinds of replies to these postings: "Why is this person writing this on the internet? To a totally unknown person? Lonely? Aren't there many people around you can text with?" [. . .] But, really, I think the same thing, too. When things are tough you want to talk to someone who will coddle you. Before college, I had three, really good friends. But now

that I'm in college? Three close friends? Not that many. And they're all men. Sometimes, I want to speak frankly to a woman. (Wingy)

The cell phone holds out the possibility of virtual intimacies—conversation, but still sufficiently distant to maintain a safe distance. Like their subway counterparts, the cell phone reinforces societal divisions, family structures, friendship cliques, but it also initiates any number of shadowy, virtual networks, edges that define some future network: virtual relationships that could grow.

SUBWAY + CELL PHONE MACHINE

On one level, the combination of subway and cell phone suggests the ultimate anonymity.

> If you sit on the subway for a long time you observe people. I had to and I couldn't help looking around. Finally, my earphones broke so I couldn't listen to music. To my surprise, everyone was watching TV on their cell phones. Out of the 7 people sitting around me, 5 were watching TV! OK, that's not really surprising. In my third year of college, people who boarded the subway would tiredly communicate on their cell phones, or take a nap, or just sit listlessly. I began to think how I don't like Seoul. Today everyone seemed suddenly pathetic. People totally staring at their small screens. (Pang-a)

In this, media apps available on handsets extend the alienating and individuating aspects of subway travel. Now—beside the other technologies one might use to mitigate the forced intimacy of subway (and, by extension, urban travel)—those books, newspapers of yesteryear, as well as that old standard, feigned or real sleep, one might now utilize DMB (digital multimedia broadcasting) to keep people at arm's distance. One of the unifying themes behind many of the apps currently popular on Korean handsets is that all of them offer ways to disengage from crowds of strangers in an (almost) entirely private way.

But there are other possibilities as well. One of the earliest problems of the subway is that people might act in ways that cross the line from the "intimate stranger" to other levels of intimacy. As the anthropologist Song writes, special critique is reserved for "People who treat the subway like their bedroom" (72–73). And special censure is reserved for two levels of intimacy: (1) eating and drinking on the subway and (2) cell phone conversations. Although different in Japan, where large-scale public campaigns and laws have targeted cell phone conversation on subways (Koreans are always surprised by the level of vehemence seen in Japan), people nevertheless express embarrassment when their phones go off on the subway: "This morning on the way to work my cell phone went off in my backpack. On the subway it kept ringing and ringing. Looking in the direction of another person my fingers poked through my backpack. Finally, my fingers closed on it" (Suri). Other modes of blurring such lines would include something like "up-skirt photography." In their examination of *keitai* as a moral panic, Kato *et al.* point out that:

> The newly ubiquitous image-capture functions of *keitai* cause concern today similar to the concerns surrounding *keitai* manners in the mid-nineties. Then, *keitai* was perceived as violating the boundaries of public and private space, particularly in public transportation. Just as voice calls were gradually regulated out of existence on Japanese public transportation, we are seeing the efforts to regulate and discipline uses of *keitai* cameras. (Kato *et al* 308)

As Song points out, it is precisely that central contradiction between anonymity and forced intimacy that makes these kinds of sexual harassment possible (72).

There are other times when the cell phone becomes something else—neither a tool for anonymity nor an unacceptable, unwanted intimacy. In one heavily cross-posted instance, subways riders used their mobile devices to photograph an encounter between an elderly woman and a woman dressed as a Buddhist nun (*pikuni*).

> Inside the subway an elderly woman dressed like a Buddhist priest comes in begging. Then the elderly woman sitting in front of the begging woman tries to comfort the sad, uncomfortable woman by giving her shoes. The people who have taken this photo have spread it all over, and I'm happy that it warms my heart. (Sarang)

Here the cell phone camera and the subway come together to form neither intimacy nor anonymity—instead, intimacy through anonymity.

THE THIRD SPACE IN BECOMING

Urry's main thesis is that mobility breeds interspaces—these liminal spaces that lie between work, home and school. These paraspaces—spatiotemporal mobilities—become surplus time to be exploited for labor or used for social networking. Korea in many ways anticipates the development of interspaces in other places. With Seoul's long commutes, in addition to the general tendency of children to live with their parents until marriage, the development of "pang munhwa" (room culture) has stimulated the mobile socialities favored by younger generations. For the youth of Korea, these third spaces operate to connect to other like-minded people. These spaces—semiprivate zones where islands of intimacy can be carved out of more urban anonymity, are at the end of a process that begins with complex coordinated movements through the city—through a negotiated process of text messages and phone calls that precede the face-to-face encounter and continue afterward. On the one hand, in Seoul, where traffic, work, and school schedules may keep one from making an exact appointment time, and where finding meeting places may sometimes be a challenge, the cell phone and the subway need to be used together. On the other, we can see the cell phone and the subway initiating a network that begins with home or work and that, by degrees, carves intimacy out of the anonymity and flux of urban space.

Thus, on one level, we might see the subway as a space of the "intimate stranger," but this, I think, ignores its role in the kind of cell phone–subway sociotechnical system described here. In this system, the role of the cell phone and subway may be to connect people and places, an edge connected nodes in the network of the city, yet it also sets up a serious of virtual points around which new spaces of sociality may emerge. Like weak ties in general, the role of the system is to define a degree of potentiality in the anonymous city.

Commentators on Korea often stress the importance of the group (*chip-dan*), but what is apparent in Korea is the importance of weak ties—referring, of course, to the pioneering work of sociologist John Granovetter, who demonstrated that people rely on distance acquaintances, rather than members of their intimate circle, for job leads (Granovetter). In urban Seoul, where family ties are rarely (outside of television dramas) used in marriage, and where one's immediate circle of friends is of little help in landing your first postgraduation job, the cultivation of weak ties has never been so important. Indeed, modern social history can almost be rewritten as the cultivation of weak ties.

Urry points out that in societies characterized by mobility, weak ties proliferate. Indeed, research on networks suggests that urban people forge more weak ties than their rural counterparts. But, importantly, these weak ties require periodic face-to-face encounters to be useful. In order to facilitate these, particular social spaces are required. Here, Korea (as in many other things), is a trendsetter for other places, and it is no surprise that Urry also stresses the centrality of face-to-face meeting for the cultivation and maintenance of networks of weak ties (239). Koreans have gone to great length to structure just these kinds of spaces: "membership training," hobby groups, Internet communities. These are the "spaces" (whether physical, dialogical or conceptual) where people drawn together through weak ties might share dialogues, ideas, and resources, and where there is at least the potential that relationships may be mobilized in other, more intimate ways.

But these "third spaces"—that is, the spaces between home and work— require additional steps, nuanced mobilities both transitioning between spaces as well as suggesting emergent possibilities. What Ito and Okabe (264) write about text messaging might be said of the whole subway-cell phone machine:

> These messages are predicated on the sense of ambient accessibility, a shared virtual space that is generally available between a few friends or with a loved one [. . .] As a technosocial system, however, people experience a sense of a persistent social space constituted through the periodic exchange of text messages [. . .] The analogue is sharing a physical space with an other whom one is not in direct communication with but whom one is peripherally aware of.

CONCLUSION

Throughout 2011, incidents continued to proliferate along Seoul's subways. The opening salvo of "*panmal nyŏ*" continued with "cigarette man" (January), "rude man" (June), "mask man" (June), and "ignorant woman" (July), each abrogation of Confucian mores dutifully recorded by subway passengers for later networked consumption and discussion. What did it all mean? That moral codes were breaking down in Seoul? That Western individualism had finally annihilated any trace of Korea's traditional, social graces? Perhaps—but there was something else going on as well. Each of these instances was enabled by the subway and the handset, each the (unfortunate) result of a complex, sociotechnical system bringing together people, objects, representations, dialogue, and technologies. I expect the remainder of 2011 to bring more incidents, and more soul-searching, in Korean popular media. And not all of these assemblages need end in violence. For example, as an OhMyNews contributor, Yun Tae, recounts:

> Through an older friend, my wife and I were given each other's cell phone numbers, and we decided that we should meet. We decided that we should try a 'subway meeting" (*jihacheol ting*). At that time, my office was at Yangchaeyeok on the third line, and my wife's at Nambuterminal station. We would board the same train, her on the very car, me on the very first, and then get off at Sinsa station. After that we would wait on the platform for one minute. We thought this would be an easy way to find each other and there would be no need to know what clothes the other person was wearing, whether or not they were wearing glasses, etc. After one minute, all of the people had passed by, and I saw a shape at the end of the platform. We started to walk in each other's direction. My heart

was pitter-pattering; what would she look like? My heart ready to explode, as she we got closer and more distinct, we burst out laughing. When we got within three meters of each other and were face-to-face, we laughed aloud and clapped our hands.

The subway + cell phone machine may generate new pleasures for Korean society as well. In any case, whether romantic or unfortunate, the combination of technologies, spaces, and people is generative of new socialities and new forms of representation.

BIBLIOGRAPHY

Allison, Anne. *Millennial Monsters*. Berkeley: University of California Press, 2006.

Anonymous. "Ossak ossak Kongp'o Pang" (Shivering Horror Room). http://cafe.daum.net/ok211, 2007.

Auge, Marc. *In the Metro*. Minneapolis: University of Minnesota Press, 2002.

Berman, Marshall. *All That Is Solid Melts into Air*. New York: Penguin, 1982.

Bull, Michael. *Sound Moves*. New York: Routledge, 2008.

Ch'oi, Hyŏn-suk. "Taehanminguk K'ŏming Authara!" (The Republic of Korea Coming Out). 2007. http://blog.naver.com/bebreaking/150023253027.

Ehn, Billy, and Orvar Löfgren. *The Secret World of Doing Nothing*. Berkeley: University of California, 2010.

Fischler, Stanley. *Moving Millions*. New York: Harper and Row, 1979.

Glotz, Peter, and Stefan Bertsch (Eds.). *Thumb Culture*. Piscataway, NJ: Transaction Publishers, 2005.

Gluckman, Max. *Essays on the Ritual of Social Relations*. Manchester, UK: Manchester University Press, 1963.

Habuchi, Ichiyo. "Accelerating Relativity." Eds. Mizuko Ito et al. *Personal, Portable, Pedestrian*. Cambridge: The MIT Press, 2005. 165–182.

Hwang, Jiwoo. "Stone Buddha Leaning against a Wall in the Subway." *Azalea* 1 (2007 [1998]): 110–111.

Hjorth, Larissa. *Mobile Media in the Asia-Pacific*. New York: Routledge, 2009.

ILYF. "Ŏje Chiachŏlesŏ Pon Sagŏn" (Incident seen on a subway yesterday). 2009. http://bb3.agora.media.daum.net/gaia/do/story.

Jenkins, Henry. "Welcome to convergence culture." *Receiver* [www.receiver.vodafone.com], 2005.

Jeon, Chihyung. "A Road to Modernization and Unification." *Technology and Culture* 51 (2010): 55–79.

Kato, Fumitoshi, Daisuke Okabe, Mizuko Ito, and Ryhei Uemoto. "Uses and possibilities of the Keitai Camera." Eds. Mizuko Ito et al. *Personal, Portable, Pedestrian*. Cambridge, MA: The MIT Press, 2005. 300–310.

Kim, Ch'an-ho. *Hyudaep'oni Malhada* [*The Cell Phone Speaks*]. Seoul: Chisikŭi Nalgae, 2008.

Kim, Choong Soon. *Kimchi and IT*. Seoul: Ilchokak, 2007.

Kim, Eun Mee, and Jean S. Kang. "Seoul as a Global City with Ethnic Villages." *Korea Journal* 47.4 (2007): 64–99.

Kŏn-ppang. "Sanŭn Yaegi" (Living Word). 2006. www.okjsp.pe.kr/seq/75021.

Lally, Elaine. *At Home with Computers*. New York: Berg, 2002.

Latour, Bruno. *Pandora's Hope*. Cambridge, MA: Harvard University Press, 1999.

Latour, Bruno. *Reassembling the Social*. New York: Oxford University Press, 2005.

Lee, Kwang-Suk. "Globalization, Electronic Empire and the Virtual Geography of Korea's Information and Telecommunications Infrastructure." *The International Communication Gazette* 70.1 (2008): 3–20.

Lee, Myŏng-jin. *Han'guk 2030 Sinsedaeŭi Ŭsikkwa Sahoe Chŏngch'esŏng* [*The Beliefs and Social Identity of the Korean 2030 New Generation*]. Seoul: Samsŏng Kyŏngje Yŏnguso, 2005.

Michael, Mike. "Between the Mundane and the Exotic." *Time & Society* 12.1 (2003): 127–143.

Milgram, Stanley. "The Experience of Living in Cities." *Science* 167 (1970): 1461–1468.

Pang-a. "Somewhere." 2006. http://blog.naver.com/jiji348/30027711295.

P'atalk. "P'atalk P'atalk Tŏpbab" (P'atalk Smothered Rice). 2008. http://sirox.egloos.com/3540141.

Raunig, Gerald. *A Thousand Machines*. Los Angeles: semiotext(e), 2010.

Sarang. "Chiach'ŏl Kŭnyŏ" (Subway Woman). 2009. http://blog.daum.net/apple5103.

Song, Jesook. *South Koreans in the Debt Crisis*. Durham, NC: Duke University Press, 2009.

Song, To-yŏng. *Illyuhakcha Song To-yŏngŭi Seoul Ilgi* [*Seoul Readings of Anthropology Song To-yŏng*]. Seoul: Sohwa, 2005.

Suri. "All That Line Dance." 2008. http://cafe.daum.net/allthatlilnedance.

Urry, Jon. *Mobilities*. Malden, MA: Polity Press, 2007.

Vertsei, Janet. "Mind the Gap." *Social Studies of Science* 38.1 (2008): 7–33.

Williams, Raymond. *The Country and the City*. New York: Oxford University Press, 1975.

Wing. "'Munja Ch'ingu'lŭl P'ilyolo Hanŭn Sesang" (A world where a "text friend" is needed), 2009. http://flierfelix.egloos.com/2200296.

Yoon, Kyongwon. "Retraditionalizing the Mobile." *European Journal of Cultural Studies* 6.3 (2003): 327–343.

Yun, Tae. "Meeting through a White Day Subway-ting." OhMyNews [www.ohmynews.com], 2004.

Part IV

Inside the Station

Chapter 7

Brief Encounters and Lasting Impressions

Contemporary Train Station Architecture

Agata Morka

Instead of the flying cars and personal jetpacks imagined by science fiction authors, transportation at the end of the twentieth and the start of the twentieth first century was marked by the renaissance of a nineteenth-century technology—the railroad. Thanks to advances in high-speed rail technology, trains, almost forgotten in the fifties and sixties as they were replaced by cars and airplanes, in the last decades of the twentieth century became the most efficient, ecologically friendly, and fast, in terms of door-to-door trip time, means of medium-distance travel. Research in high-speed rail technology, conducted simultaneously by Japan and France, resulted in the introduction of a new generation of trains, capable of reaching speeds faster than 300 mph and ensuring a comfortable and safe travel experience.

This new technology needed a new infrastructure, leading to the construction of high-speed tracks, bridges, viaducts, and new train stations across all of Europe. Starting with the success of the TGV lines in the nineties, new train stations became important structures within the urban fabric of their cities, frequented by a significant amount of people, yet usually for an insignificant amount of time. The train station, in order to be remembered and associated with a specific city, thus needed to be an aesthetically engaging space. This particular condition of the train station as a space usually experienced in a hurry and at the same time as a space of first and last interactions with the city demanded brave architectural gestures and often resulted in some of the most exciting architectural adventures of the late twentieth and the beginning of the twentieth first century. It was here, at the railroad station, where the city in which the station stood had a chance to manifest its modernity, either to foster an image to which it aspired or simply to confirm its status as a cutting-edge metropolis of the future.

This chapter will investigate the question of the architectural identity of the contemporary train station, proposing to read this structure as a space of condensed, and intensified, modernity, or even *supermodernity*, as theorized by Marc Augé. The contemporary train station, remaining a space of ever-faster movement, can arguably be seen as a structure marked by the most intense architectural decisions, as it acts as a showcase for the city and has to rely on rather noisy solutions in order to convey the desired first impression of an exciting destination to travelers. The result, as will be shown through an analysis of stations such as Lille-Europe by Rem Koolhaas, the Lyon Saint-Exupéry TGV (formerly named Lyon Satolas) and the Liège TGV by Santiago Calatrava, the Florence TAV by Sir Norman Foster, and the Naples Afragola by Zaha Hadid, is contemporary railroad architecture that enacts the drama of unleashed mobility and the poetics of the modern railway travel experience.

TRAIN STATIONS AND MODERNITY

In the final scene of the classic British film *Brief Encounter,* the leading character Laura Jesson is sitting by the table in a train station bar, trying to calm down after a dramatic split-up with her lover Alec Harvey, who has just left to catch his train back home. Laura, ignoring a friend who has unknowingly deprived the lovers of their proper goodbye, listens to the noises of the departing train, praying for Alec to come back. When that does not happen, Laura sinks deeper and deeper into despair until she hears the whistle of the station-master announcing the passage of the express train. She springs out of her seat, rushing toward the platform with a sudden urge to end her life. The viewer sees a quick shot of the approaching speeding locomotive and then the camera focuses on Laura's face, as she changes her mind and stays on a platform watching flickering lights of the express rushing in front of her.

The story of Laura, a suburban housewife, taking the train to go shopping and find entertainment in the cinema in the nearby town, and Alec, a doctor commuting to a local town hospital, explicitly shows the transformative power of the railroad, which revised previous ideas of distance, and opened new spaces unreachable and unimaginable for many before its coming. The particular shrinkage of distances, a phenomenon also referred to as an "annihilation of space and time," was a crucial effect of rail travel (Schievelbusch, 33). Trains, rushing through the landscape at previously unknown speeds, introduced a different, "condensed" geography, where the traveler was deprived of the sense of relationship with the space he or she traveled through, a relationship which he or she would have time to establish if he or she was slowly traversing space using previous transport technologies. The introduction of rail disrupted previous understandings of time and space as a continuum, favoring the fleeting, the ephemeral, and the transient. For the rail passenger this space in between destinations, so strongly experienced, even savored, in the prerail era, was reduced to a series of fleeting images, fragmentary and ungraspable, culminating in the bustling termini of train stations. Focusing on the disjunctive, momentary meetings of its main characters, the movie captures the poetics of this new public space brought by the arrival of the trains in city centers, a space of brief encounters, flickering lights from passing trains and rushing crowds.

The train station, as a building type, from the very beginning of its existence in the first half of the nineteenth century remained an ambiguous structure, oscillating somewhere in between a city monument and a strictly functional building. The train station, as it emerged in the 1830s and 1840s, was a building with no precedent, a byproduct of technological development, a new structure which had to be invented from ground zero and whose architectural form was a subject of often-heated discussion.[1] The station had to embrace both the urban realm, to which it showed its usually imposing stone façade with allegorical figures, and the realm of the travel, to which it opened its intricate train sheds rendered in iron. By the 1860s César Daly in his *Revue Générale de l'Architecture et des Travaux Publics* referred to the train station as an ultimately "modern building," which, in the eyes of this influential architect was just about "the highest monumental and artistic expression of industrial and commercial genius, which so profoundly characterizes the époque in which we live."[2] By the end of the nineteenth century most big cities could impress travelers with their new monumental gateways, whose architectural form ranged from the classicizing arcades of Gare de l'Est in Paris and the neo-Gothic decorations of Saint Pancrass in London to the imposing towers of the first Grand Central, opened in New York in 1871.[3] If at the turn of the century railroad architecture flourished around the world and train stations could indeed be seen as embodiments of technological progress and modernity, their position, as well as the status of the railroad in general, was deeply undermined in the first three decades after World War II.

The two facets of the train explored in the movie *Brief Encounter*—its speed and the transformative mobility that it brings—are also two key themes in the history of rail, themes which came to be embodied in the aesthetics and design of the material environment of the railroad. The 1945 film straddles a pivotal point in the history of this speed and mobility, when the railroad had become firmly established in European life, yet was about to be overshadowed by air and automobile travel.

It was the relative comfort of travel and the timesaving elements that were identified as major factors attracting clients to planes or cars, as a member of *Académie Française*, Louis Armand, pointed out in his analysis of the problem of rail transportation in France in 1964.[4] These modern, ultrafast means of transportation not only provided the practical advantage of saving time, but they also brought excitement and a thrill of novelty. A growing fascination with planes and cars, combined with the stable economic situation that made them relatively accessible, pushed more and more people to taste new adventure as they bought cars and plane tickets. The plane, especially in the early sixties, was *à la mode*, introducing a new way of living, a new way of spending free time, as immortalized in the iconic 1963 song by Gilbert Bécaud *Un Dimanche à Orly,* a number one on French playlists in the sixties. The song presents the typical life of a young man, still living with his parents, "enjoying" the modest comfort (an elevator, a bathroom, and a distant view of the capital) of their HLM in a Parisian *banlieue*. Rather bored with his repetitive existence, the young boy looks for a more exciting space, something that would tickle his imagination, and he finds this desired thrill every Sunday when he sneaks out of the house to go to Orly. The airport becomes therefore an alternative space, a space of dreams, open possibilities, and longing. In the second half of the twentieth century the airport took over much of the popular imagery up to then associated with the steamy platforms of the grand rail termini, so often used as the location for dramatic and romantic stories, from *Anna Karenina* to *Casablanca*. In the sixties drama, romance and adventure no longer remained attributes of the rail world, shifting instead toward air and road travel, forging the car and plane as new symbols of modernity and freedom. If the railroad was to survive, if the train station was to sustain its status as an ultimate monumental expression of modernity, it had to reinvent itself.

In Europe this situation resulted in an increased interest in developing high-speed train technology, able to compete, at least for medium-distance travel, with both the car and the plane. Responding to the challenge of this competition the French National Rail Company (SNCF), as early as the 1960s, started a determined technological research program whose goal was to construct a train capable of achieving speed so high that it would enable it to become a threat to both plane and car (Meunier, passim). The research gained favorable attention from the state, which at that time was especially interested in the development of new technologies, a desire strengthened when the Japanese launched their first high-speed train, Shinkansen, in 1964 (Guigueno; Meunier). The first high-speed rail in France, linking Paris and Lyon, was inaugurated in 1981, and in response to its success, by the early 1990s France had a plan for developing high-speed train technology throughout the country, ultimately connecting not only the furthest parts of eastern, southern, northern, and western France with the capital, but also expanding beyond French borders. Simultaneous efforts undertaken by other countries of western Europe, such as Italy, Spain, and Germany, resulted in the construction of a truly European international network connecting such distant destinations as Barcelona and London. The growing popularity of high-speed trains, reflected in the increased number of passengers seduced by its comfort and speed, witnessed a renewed interest in this mode of transportation and, by the end of the twentieth century, introduced the "second rail era" (Batisse, 35).[5]

The eventual success of the high-speed train can however best be mirrored by the 1996 movie *Mission Impossible*, in which Tom Cruise, surrounded by a substantial amount of technological gadgets, overcomes yet another obstacle in order to successfully complete his impossible tasks. The movie marks the victorious comeback of the train into the popular imagination, as the actor, trying to save the world, struggles to keep his balance on the roof of none other than a speeding French high-speed train. The appearance of this record-breaking train, along with other cutting edge high-tech devices, ultimately confirms that the train, at the end of the twentieth century, had become yet again en vogue, providing its users with an apt sense of thrill and adventure. Thanks to advances in high-speed train technology, the railroad reemerged as a competitive, ultramodern means of transportation, and the train station, hosting these new fast machines, regained its status within the city fabric as a bustling epicenter of movement.

The quest for speed, so strongly pronounced in the evolution of rail travel, is seen by several scholars as one of the important characteristics of modernity in general. Supporting her argument with Zygmunt Bauman's writings, Dorthe Gert Simonsen claims that the development of rail, with its transient and fleeting character, might be seen as a "prerequisite for conceiving and 'performing' the idea of the modern" and the formation of modern society (Simonsen, 98). Bauman, however, distinguishes in his recent writings between two types of modernity: the old one, which he describes as "solid," "heavy" and "constructed," and a new type of modernity, with no strict framework, defined by a constant flow of information, globalized communication, and general "liquefaction" of old, solid systems. Putting this melting quality at the core of the modernity concept, Bauman proposes to look at the contemporary social condition in terms of "liquid modernity" (2). Similar reflections are expressed by Marc Augé in his book *Non-places: Introduction to an Anthropology of Supermodernity*, where he meditates upon the nature of "our times," seeing them in terms of two oppositional ideas—places and non-places (Augé, 79). Like Bauman, who in his analysis of the contemporary urban realm points toward nonplaces as unidentified, nowhere zones, Augé defines them as places of transit, always in a state of becoming and never completed (see Augé, 75–115). He contrasts them with "anthropological places," such as churches, which can be characterized by their history, set of relations, and identity. *"Non-places"*—train stations, airports, hotels and supermarkets—marked by anonymity and a certain detachment, are nevertheless in his eyes the "real measure of our times," crucial embodiments of the contemporary human condition, to which he refers as "supermodernity" (Augé, 29–41, 79).

In the Augeian reading, then, the train station, a building defined by the constant flow of travelers, the movement of people and machines, belongs to a realm of uniquely liminal spaces of which one is used to thinking in terms of transition rather than destination, in terms of a temporary space rather than a real place. Circulation, movement, the fleeting and the ephemeral—all give the train station its conflicted identity, a certain "suspended condition" placed somewhere in between here and there, between a place of departure and destination, epitomizing the fragmentary, liquid, ever-changing character of both liquid and super modernity.

How then, does this supermodern and liquefied condition translate into the built environment? How does the architectural form of the train station, particularly of these most recent ones, erected in the last decades of the twentieth century and at the beginning of the third millennium, account for the alleged placelessness of contemporary transportation hubs, stressed in the Augeian reading of the train station? The following analysis of a few strategically chosen examples will show that the contemporary train station is a space marked by a struggle between anonymity and identity, local presence and global ambitions, and the contrasting functions of efficient transportation hubs and civic monuments, all crucial questions of the contemporary condition, as theorized by both Bauman and Augé. Yet rather than thinking of the train station in terms of a non-place deprived of any specific characteristics, this analysis presents contemporary train stations as buildings, which, despite their inherently liminal character, are being constructed as vibrant public spaces, whose function shifts from mere accessibility and focus on travel toward a versatility of uses geared to travelers and residents alike. It will be shown here that contrary to Augé's analysis, recently built stations not only do not exhibit a lack of memorable features, but in fact take the question of memorability to be their crucial design component. Due to its position as the first and last structure that a traveler sees en route to a destination, the train station is here presented as a space of intensified architectural expression, determined by an accelerated mode of experiencing the building, and employing an architectural idiom based on momentary yet powerful gestures.

A PLACE, A NON-PLACE? THE CONTEMPORARY TRAIN STATION AS EXPRESSION OF SUPERMODERNITY

In Europe, it was France that first launched experimental research in high-speed rail technology, and it was also in France that some of the first high-speed train stations were built. Departing from the previous modernism-inspired architectural solutions of the sixties widely applied in French and worldwide railroad architecture (of which one of the most telling example remains the Montparnasse station, whose generic façade could indeed epitomize the Augeian idea of a non-place), these new train stations were conceived of not as purely functional structures, but rather as pivotal elements of the urban tissue, and as visual markers of a desired status of ultramodern metropolis. The chosen cases of high-speed rail stations opened over the span of the last two decades, with Lille-Europe (1994) and Lyon Satolas (1994) as examples of some of the first European high-speed rail stations, and more recent structures such as Liège Guillemins (2009) and Napoli Afragola and Florence TAV (as of this writing, not yet opened), show very different architectural responses to the contemporary train station problem, ranging from the exhibitionist display of delirious movement to oversized sculpturelike statements. All of them, nevertheless, can be looked at as particularly rich and conflicted territories, metonymies of the contemporary liquefied condition, driven by the contradictory forces of local presence and global ambitions, oscillating somewhere between a place and a non-place, constantly negotiating their liminal condition.

Global Soul, Local Ambitions

The clashing interests between the local and the global, in the case of contemporary train station commissions, play an exceptionally important role in terms of both economics and public relations.[6] Contemporary train stations are often used as structures that are to express local ambitions and enhance or even forge regional identities. These tendencies can be inscribed into a broader idea defined as the "Europe of Regions," which emerged with the establishment and strengthening of the European Union.[7] The precept of European integration, based on the idea of blurring the borders between member countries, departing from the divisions of nation and state, leaned toward an idea of Europe in which regions as subnational entities acquired more territorial power and could be seen as new economic, social, and cultural centers. The challenge of a globalized rather than state-based economy pushed regions to find ways of establishing interregional relations, also putting them in competition against each other, as they had to fight in order to draw both investments and tourism. In response to these new circumstances many local authorities launched widespread campaigns advertising their regions on the market as ultimately modern, dynamic, and attractive products (Paasi, 137). The question of a certain shared regional identity in this case remained crucial for the local authorities. In this context architectural commissions for public spaces were treated as one of the numerous ways of confirming local particularities, or creating tangible embodiments of a desired future for the newly established regions. Train stations, then, acting as the first or last structures that a traveler sees approaching or leaving the city by train, emerged as a particularly important site of self-promotion, and the question of the choice of a particular project and its architect grew to be treated as a strategic decision.

The tendency to value global rather than local architects is well exemplified by the Euralille project, opened in 1994 as a multifunctional urban development which was to evolve around a new high-speed train station, Lille-Europe, hosting the TGV Nord line and ensuring connections between the United Kingdom and continental Europe through the Channel Tunnel.[8] At the beginning of the eighties Lille found itself in desperate need of reinvention, as in the late seventies it had been struck by a severe economic crisis. The textile factories and coal mines that had for over a century made up the heart of the region's economy were closed, causing the unemployment level to jump dramatically over the span of only fifteen years, reaching 13% in 1990, compared to 3% in 1975.[9] The city's mayor, Pierre Mauroy, a Lille native, made the transformation of the decaying economy of the Nord Pas-de-Calais an absolute priority in his political agenda (Dufour). It was hoped that with the TGV line crossing the city center, Lille would have a chance to redefine its image and to transform from a decaying industrial city once powered by its coal mines into a blossoming, modern European metropolis. The arrival of the TGV line was, in the context of the deep recession, a chance that the region "simply could not afford to miss" (Mandrelli, 32).

When in 1988 the city of Lille announced a competition for the master plan for an entire new district of Euralille, four French architects were chosen— Vasconi, Macary, Lion, Viguier/Jodry—to compete in a final round against three other European architects—Sir Norman Foster, Gregotti and Ungers, and Rem Koolhaas. It seems, however, that the selection of the competing architects was from the start marked by a certain lack of balance as the entries of the four French architects were treated with less excitement by the jury, as one of the commentators noticed:

> This selection was carried through by a slim margin. In addition to not being notably "urban" architects, our four fellow countrymen adhered to the rational

end of the spectrum of approaches to the city. It was thus not very likely that they would deliver *a brutal surprise, a strong and symbolic response that would involve the European ambition of the metropole.* (original emphasis)[10]

Koolhaas, on the other hand, as a foreigner and an already famous theoretician of "urban chaos," was expected to deliver this "brutal surprise" which would be able to face the challenge of the wholesale reinvention of Lille. Jean-Paul Boietto, responsible for the overall quality of the project, justified the unanimous decision of the jury by the fact that Koolhaas defined a certain "vision of the city" which in his opinion the other propositions lacked, as they only proposed a "vision of the project" (Doutriaux, 98). Other than being determined by the purely personal aesthetic preferences of the jury, it was clear that the choice of this internationally recognized architect, a theoretician known for his fascination with chaos and urban "delirium," fit perfectly into the ambitious program of Euralille, into the almost "visionary character" its developers wished it to have. Mauroy himself admitted that the decision was deeply strategic, explaining: "The choice of Rem Koolhaas shows our ambition. The architect could have been French; we wanted somebody of international renown."[11]

In the Euralille project Koolhaas, whose architectural sensibility since the very first years of his career had been profoundly shaped by the metropolis, technology, congestion, and what he saw as the delirious speed of contemporary life, could face the challenge of putting his postulates of "density without architecture" and "bigness" to life (Koolhaas, *Delirious*, 10; "Bigness," 84). His presence as the head of the entire project promised an exciting, cutting-edge urban intervention and immediately attracted the attention of the media, which, long before the last scaffoldings were taken off at the construction site, had already promoted Euralille as one of the most important projects of the late twentieth century, partially validating Lille as "a radically contemporary city" and therefore fulfilling the initial expectations of the city authorities.[12] Euralille and the TGV Nord line which it was to host benefited from the press campaign for the Channel tunnel, adding to it its own strong presence in the press, fashioning itself as a center of innovation and creativity, "one of the largest and perhaps one of the most mysterious projects in Europe" (Edelmann, paragraph 1). In the early nineties the Euralille project took up a great deal of space on the pages of architectural magazines, which devoted to it not only hundreds of articles, but also entire dossiers and special issues, where it was described as "an enormous and unreal project (Doutriaux, 158), a "tertiary turbine" (Mandarelli, 32) and "a radical experiment in new thinking" (Sudjic, 22).[13] The later engagement of Jean Nouvel as the head architect of the Euralille commercial center and Christian de Portzamparc

and Richard Rogers for the design of the station's roof towers further
followed the logic of accumulating projects by "starchitects," transforming
the district of Euralille into a veritable showcase of contemporary architecture
superstars.[14]

Lille-Europe, as the *raison d'être* of the entire operation, was to act as
a response to the city's decaying status and, both through the choice of
a global starchitect and the audacious architectural form for the station,
was to evoke the ultimately modern character of Lille. Similar ambitions
drove representatives of the Rhône-Alpes region, who also chose a globally
renowned architect to design the high-speed train station, located on the
outskirts of Lyon, by the Lyon international airport. The station was to
become a regional landmark and was supposed to act as a new referential
point for the travelers and for locals, confirming Lyon's status as the
second biggest French city, and fashioning it as a modern, if not futuristic
metropolis.

In the eighties and nineties Lyon, just like Lille, was a city in danger, as it
had to fight to sustain its position as the second biggest metropolis in France
and the leading city of the Rhône-Alpes region. The disintegration of the
coal industry based in St. Étienne on one hand and the speeding development
of other cities such as Grenoble and Chambéry within the region on the
other threatened its position and indirectly stimulated a search for ways of
reinventing the city and fulfilling its "Eurocity" ambitions (Thompson, 31).
After the arrival of the TGV in Lyon in 1982, the city's status as *métropole
européenne* was still questioned and, while acknowledging the city's
importance within the region, some insisted that it could not yet be compared
to such other metropolises in Europe as Barcelona or Munich. While the
potential was there, Lyon lacked efficient infrastructures, a highly animated
cultural life, and international-scale institutions and investments (Labasse,
150). Lyon needed yet another asset, and a new TGV station, located right
by Lyon Satolas international airport, at the time the fourth-busiest airport in
France, seemed to promise the possibility of creating one.[15] The question of
giving the new station an adequate architectural form which could express
the city's aspirations became pivotal from the start, when the local authorities
requested changes in standard SNCF procedures. Rather than accepting an
in-house design by one of the SNCF architects, they decided to look for
a leading architect elsewhere and launched an international architectural
competition.[16] This insistence on organizing a competition on an international
scale rather than accepting the standard SNCF design was seen by the Conseil
Régional as a highly appropriate choice, given the region's importance in
France and the world. Trying to create a certain international image, local
authorities insisted on treating the "*portes d'entrée*" to the region as public

spaces of great importance, feeling that Rhône-Alpes deserved exceptional treatment, and that it was worthy of having a new monument designed by a renowned architect.

Symbolically evoking a sense of opening toward the future, the station was expected to act as a showcase of all the qualities the region wanted to be known for. The municipalities called for an ultramodern transportation hub that would link different modes of transportation and ensure full comfort and accessibility for its users, yet at the same time keep much of the traditional symbolic dimensions of the monumental stations of the nineteenth century, acting as a metaphorical gateway to the city. Satolas was thus conceived as a regional monument, as a visual reference point for the city and the region.[17] The station was to forge a certain image of modernity and creativity, and this very image was pronounced as the first of the ambitions of the architectural contest program. As one reads in some of its first lines: "The placement of the future TGV station on the site of SATOLAS (. . .) should allow in time the renovation of the image of the SATOLAS site, an image that is strong, modern and open towards the future (. . .)."[18]

From the original fifty-four entries submitted for the competition, the Region chose seven teams to compete in the final: Rogers and Partners, Santiago Calatrava, Jourda et Peraudin, Pierre and Pascal Sirvin, Noel Baduel and Pierre Monmarson, Curtelin and Ricard, Gimbert and Vergely.[19] Symptomatically, only the two starchitects from the short list remained to compete in a final round, beating all other local entries. Santiago Calatrava's presentation relied strongly on the symbolic qualities of his design, its ability to attract attention and become a memorable first impression of the region. In order to highlight these qualities of his project Calatrava brought to his session with the jury Salvador Dali's painting "Melting Watches" stating: "Our building is like this painting. Once you've seen it, you'll never forget it" (Metz, 90).

The jury, however, after secret voting found the two projects—by Rogers and by Calatrava—equal and was unable to clearly determine a winner.[20] The decision could then have been made by the president of the Conseil Régional, Charles Millon, who preferred Calatrava's proposition, yet, rather than making the final decision by himself, he wanted the question to be discussed by all of the Conseil members (Lagrange). The case, to Charles Millon's surprise, caused heated discussion during the assembly meeting, as the voters split into two groups: "*le plus spectaculaire*," who opted for Calatrava's proposition, and "*le plus rationnel*," who praised Roger's idea for its feasibility and less financially risky character (da Fonseca, 1).[21] After numerous discussions and one failed vote followed by even more passionate debates, the assembly meeting concluded in a final vote. Garnering 80 out of 149 votes, the "more spectacular" project by Calatrava was officially accepted by the Region (da Fonseca, 1). The SNCF commented on this choice as being strictly dictated by the desire to create a new "image" for the region, concluding: "The final architectural project was chosen for the impact that it could have in service of the image of the region" ("Conséquences financières," 1) [22]

Both Euralille and Lyon Saint Exupéry witness a trend of granting train station commissions to globally appreciated architects, atop the contemporary architectural Parnassus. As one looks at recent railway station commissions it becomes clear that local authorities are more and more interested in big names in architecture and tend to favor global over local architects, as they recognize the possible benefits coming from associating a "starchitect" project with their cities. Most architectural competitions for new train station projects have an international character and, although submissions from lesser-known local architects are welcomed, it is only very rarely that their projects make it to the short list, let alone are actually pronounced winners. In recent competitions for five new high-speed train stations in Italy held at the beginning of the third millennium, most of the chosen projects were contributed by such recognizable architects as Jean Nouvel, Lord Norman Foster, Arata Isozaki, or Zaha Hadid, to name just a few. A glance at the short list of ten competitors for the Florence Belfiore train station commission clearly shows the preference given to the starchitects' projects, as, along with the local architects' propositions, one finds three podium places secured by none other than Santiago Calatrava, Arata Isozaki, and Lord Norman Foster, whose 450-meter-long station, covered with a semi-cylindrical roof with changing patterns created by the supporting beams, was ultimately selected (Kucharek, 48).

The boom in railway-connected "starchitect" projects started in the early nineties with such iconic buildings as Sir Nicolas Grimshaw's Waterloo International Terminal in London from 1993, with its tubelike translucent silhouette, or Calatrava's all-white, lacy Lisbon Oriente Station, opened in 1998.[23] The trend continued strongly into the first decade of the twentieth century with numerous railway urban projects as "starchitects" were hired to both interfere with nineteenth-century grand termini (such as in the remodeling of Saint Pancras station in London by Foster and Partners, opened in 2007, or Sir Nicolas Grimshaw's Melbourne Southern Cross Station extension, with its unique wavy roof, opened in 2006) and to create completely new buildings (the airy and ethereal Liège Guillemins by Santiago Calatrava, opened in 2009, or the strong and sensuous bridge station Napoli Afragola by Zaha Hadid, scheduled to open in 2012).

The examples discussed above depict the larger tendency shown by "cities in danger" to take interest in large-scale high-speed railway projects. Frequently it is the very cities whose economies are decaying and who have lost much of their previous grandeur that are ready to invest large amounts of money in a "starchitect" project, counting on repeating the miraculous "Bilbao effect" in their own backyard and provoking a massive change in the fate of their cities and regions.[24] Both the earlier and latest railroad projects have tended to be charged with high expectations toward their possible beneficial economic impact on the territories in which they are implanted.[25] Such was the case of Lille and Lyon, and such is also the logic behind more recent interventions, such as the urban development of the neglected Guillemins district in Liège, Belgium. Here the national rail company SNCB decided to replace the outdated train station and build a new one capable of receiving high-speed rail connections, making the most of Liège's potential as an international railway node due to its strategic geographical position between France, Germany, and the Netherlands. Euro Liège TGV, responsible for conducting the project in 1996, issued a request to European architects for the design of the future station, a competition yet again won by Santiago Calatrava, who in the final round competed anew against other starchitects, this time Nicholas Grimshaw and Aldo Rossi (Minutillo, 87). The city of Liège, immediately recognizing the project's potential—calling it "a true window of opportunity for the region"—developed a larger urban intervention around it which sought to reinvigorate Guillemins and transform a district until this point known mainly for its high crime rates and noisy brothels into one of the most desirable and modern parts of the city, with new residential and commercial zones accompanied by cultural facilities.[26] These examples show that cities and, on a smaller scale, underprivileged city districts in need of reinvention have shown interest in bringing high-speed rail infrastructure into their urban tissue. The way this rail infrastructure looks, however, in what architectural form it is wrapped, remains a crucial factor, *"une question centrale"* in the words of Eurogare TGV Liège creators, as it is to mirror the city's status, and create a desired image of it ("La dimension architecturale"). The semiotic values of contemporary railway architecture are highly valued by their sponsors since train stations are thought of as symbols of desired or acquired respected position, acting as powerful instruments in the "politics of appearance," as theorized by Joan Ockman (235). Local authorities and railway companies therefore tend to promote these new investments by pointing out this very symbolic character of the structure, which is to help them create an impression of "ultramodernity" as the SNCB tries to convince one in leaflets about Calatrava's project, stating: "with a majestic station symbolizing its development, Liège is moving forward."[27]

Instantaneous Places: Architectural Identity of the Contemporary Train Station

The complexity of the contemporary train station problem lies not only in the multiplicity of actors involved in the construction of the project and the clashing interests of local authorities and railway companies, but also in the inherent liminality of train station space and its dual identity as an efficient transportation hub and a civic monument. The suspended condition of this building type, referred to as an "interregnum space" by Pico Iyer, seems to not allow for more than just brief encounters (40). At the beginning of the twenty-first century the accelerated mode of experiencing the train station—itself reminiscent of the "annihilation of time and space" brought about by the railroad in the nineteenth century—reached an unprecedented level, turning contemporary train stations into zones of condensed architectural expression based on the arresting tension between the mobile and the static.

The Euralille station designed by Rem Koolhaas, and expected to be a "brutal surprise" in its final form, took the shape of a transparent rectangular box encompassing six TGV tracks located in the lowest level and covered with an undulating roof whose lower side pointed toward the city's historic center (Fig. 7.1). The second level—a concourse—ran parallel to the tracks and housed all of the station services: ticket counters, shops, a waiting room,

Figure 7.1.   Lille Europe train station, with a wavy roof, opened in 1994. As seen from Le Corbusier Viaduct. Photo by author, May 2010.

an exchange office, a restaurant and the restrooms. The highest level acted as a viewing platform, from which one could admire the entire station and from which one was immediately conducted to the concourse level by a series of elevators. The station's design, based on the logic of "exacerbated complexity," offered a number of rather vertiginous views. At Lille-Europe one was confronted with hardly any spatial anchors or points of reference, as, despite the concourse level with its services located in closed mini-boxes, there were no solid elements in the station's interior. Instead, the traveler was meant to be arrested by a composition of juxtaposed tracks, elevators and bridges floating in an unbounded space of permanent movement (Fig. 7.2). This impression was further intensified by the level differentiation and by the series of balconies suspended above the platforms, offering a panoramic view on the trains speeding below, cars passing behind the TGV windows, and passengers moving on the elevators. The subtle presence of structural elements such as roof supports did not really compete with the overall experience of the ephemeral, undefined, and ever-changing. The building did not cover anything, honestly putting on display its inner business, making the absence of rigidly defined space a constitutive factor of its architectural design.

Lille-Europe's sense of openness and airiness was even more strongly accentuated by the curved, translucent roof, which provided for excellent

Figure 7.2.   Lille Europe train station, opened in 1994. Exacerbated complexity as a design principle. Interior. Photo by author, May 2010.

light penetration and, despite its significant heft, seemed to float above the train hall. Koolhaas was interested in constructing in Lille-Europe a building which would affect the viewer not by its strong presence in the city, but rather by its absence, a building which would let the space be in a constant state of becoming, a space not defined by the walls which cut it off from the cityscape, but instead defined by the complexity of its ambiguous inner relations, mirroring Koolhaas's theories of the liminal character of the contemporary metropolis.

The introduction of big "TGV windows" partially erased a border between the station's building and its surroundings, allowing the city to penetrate the station while simultaneously permitting the station to invade the city (Fig. 7.3). The further opening in the wall sheltering the two middle tracks in the form of arches supported by pillars and recalling a shape of a window allowed for even more profound penetration of the station's interior, again both for the passengers on board a TGV passing the station, who were confronted with the speeding view of the city, and for the *Lillois* who could almost see through the transparent façade, far inside the station, almost recognizing its opposite end. This sequence of openings and multiple, juxtaposed views, with virtually no solid architectural elements, created an experience of absence, of void, of a disturbing lack of shelter. The TGV window not only did not obstruct the

Figure 7.3.   Lille Europe train station, opened in 1994. TGV window. Photo by author, May 2010.

Figure 7.4.   Blurring boundaries between the realm of the city and the realm of the travel. Lille Europe train station, opened in 1994. Photo by author, May 2010.

view of the interior space of the station but acted as a showcase, displaying the building's inner dynamics (Fig. 7.4). It transformed the station's façade into an ever-changing spectacle of movement and speed, placing the train— arriving, departing, or passing—in surprising closeness to the window's sur- face, one of its decisive elements. The heavy use of glass in the construction of the station allowed it to enter into an intimate relation with its surround- ings, almost transforming the building into a prolongation of the street, as there were no strong demarcation lines between them.

The station was conceived of as a multifunctional transportation hub, and nowhere was the juxtaposition of infrastructures more brutally pronounced then in the meeting point of the station's structure and Le Corbusier Viaduct leading to Lille-Europe. The viaduct hits the station building itself, literally cutting its upper level in halves and brutally dividing it into what seems from the highest level to be two separate buildings, with two separate roofs (Fig. 7.5). Initial plans to continue the roof structure above Le Corbusier Viaduct were not realized, leaving the gap shamelessly exposed and by doing so contributing to the overall liminal character of the Lille-Europe TGV station, marked by the drama of its colliding infrastructures ("La halle aux trains").

The Le Corbusier Viaduct, leading one from the monumental façade of the nineteenth century Lille Flandres station toward the transparent silhouette of Lille-Europe, acts as a symbolic transition between the city's past and its

Figure 7.5.   Le Corbusier Viaduct, cutting the station's building in halves. Lille Europe train station, opened in 1994. Photo by author, May 2010.

Figure 7.6.   Le Corbusier Viaduct piercing the station, view from the ground level. Lille Europe train station, opened in 1994. Photo by author, May 2010.

visionary future, between the solid and the liquefied. It offers a monumental vista toward the train station, just as the Rue de la Gare did in the nineteenth century, piercing the city fabric and ending right in front of Lille Flandres's imposing arches. Although based on a very similar idea of offering access and visual guidance, the Le Corbusier Viaduct is no longer a street, but an automobile route, which, rather than politely stopping in front of Lille-Europe, collides with it, aggressively piercing the station itself and disappearing in the distant suburbs of Lille, marking its new "supermodern" identity—as a bustling, accessible and borderless European city (Fig. 7.6).

The chosen project for Lyon Satolas, signed by Santiago Calatrava, employed a different strategy, operating with strong, sculpturelike forms, accentuating the presence rather than absence of the building, as it was in the case of Euralille, which took the idea of the void to be its design principle. This "more spectacular" proposition by Calatrava, as the SNCF referred to it, stressing its important image-making characteristics, was based on his earlier sculpture of an eye. Calatrava expanded on the idea and translated it into a large-scale, wide central station hall placed above the tracks (Fig. 7.7).[28] The main hall took on a trapezoidal form, delineated by a rear adjacent building called the "sac-à-dos" from the airport side and two lateral screen walls resting on concrete arches spanning the width of the hall. The main entrance to the hall was located on the narrowest side of the building, also rendered in steel and glass. In front of it there was a massive concrete two-part buttress supporting the entire structure of the hall. The lateral parts of the building served as platforms for the winglike glazed forms that sprang from them far above the train shed, strengthened by diagonal steel ribs recalling the shapes of wings poised to take flight. The interior of the hall was covered by a lacy concrete vault, intersected at an acute angle by the lateral curtain walls of the station, creating the impression of receding perspective crowned by the narrowing silhouette of the buttress and its tip, which almost hits the ground (Figs. 7.8, 7.9). Operating according to the gradual loss of density within the project, the central building remains the heart of the structure, the element of largest physical as well as symbolic weight.[29] Its closed character, accentuated by the presence of dark colors, heavy materials, and an eye-catching form seems to dissolve the further one goes from the center into the lacy horizontal lines of the platforms, whose outermost ends open to the countryside, into the unbounded landscape (Fig. 7.10).

The juxtaposition of the transparent and the opaque, the light and the weighty, results in an arresting tension between the mobile and the static, embodied by the wings of the main hall springing in the sky, yet grounded by a massive central buttress (Figs. 7.11, 7.12). Even the most liminal parts of the station received a distinct architectural treatment and, together with the dramatic *bâtiment voyageurs*, create a station which radically departs from the Augeian definition of a *non-lieu*, as not only does it not exhibit a lack of memorable features but in fact takes the question of memorability to be its crucial design component.

The unusual shape of the roof, as well as the mass and weight of the central buttress, further emphasize the monumental character of the main hall and, combined with the extensive use of steel supports, create the impression of a large-scale object, a sculpture rather than a building. These sculptural

Figure 7.7. Lyon Saint-Exupéry (formerly named Lyon Satolas) by Santiago Calatrava, opened in 1994. Photo by author, May 2010.

Figure 7.8. Main hall, interior. Lyon Saint-Exupéry by Santiago Calatrava, opened in 1994. Photo by author, May 2010.

Figure 7.9.   Main hall, vaulting system. Lyon Saint-Exupéry by Santiago Calatrava, opened in 1994. Photo by author, May 2010.

Figure 7.10.   Platforms level, train shed disappearing into landscape. Lyon Saint-Exupéry by Santiago Calatrava, opened in 1994. Photo by author, May 2010.

qualities of the central building were also recognized by the Region, and stressed even on the information boards in the station, where the building is referred to as no other than "Calatrava's sculpture," casting it not just as a train station, but also as a work of art.[30] For its well-pronounced architectural form Lyon Satolas became a destination in its own right even before it was officially inaugurated in 1994. Four months before the design was completed, the Bird, as it came to be called, was visited by 30,000 sightseers attracted as much by the monumental architecture of the station as by its functional high-speed rail services. In order to promote the site and introduce it to travelers, the Rhône-Alpes region arranged special guided tours, highly frequented not only by the residents of Lyon but also visitors from the entire country (Stungo, 35). Fulfilling the local authorities' original wishes, the station did function to a large extent as a monument, a work of art, and a new tourist attraction, provoking enthusiastic reactions typical for sightseers, as expressed by one of the tourists interviewed inside the central building: "I had already been through the aerodrome in Singapore, but . . . but . . . (looking around) [this is] a hundred times better" ("La nouvelle gare TGV de Lyon Satolas"). Lyon Satolas exemplifies a growing phenomenon in contemporary railroad architecture, in which starchitects are hired to design train stations in the hope that they will become easily recognizable, memorable, and remarkable buildings, bearing witness to the modernity and creativity of the place in which they are located. Where the "Bird" relied on the compact, internal sculptural silhouette of the main hall, Calatrava's most recent design for the city of Liège achieves a similar monumentality by employing more airy, ethereal, and open shapes. In the Liège TGV station it is the roof that is responsible for the overall architectural expression, as the building has virtually no façade (Fig. 7.13). A massive 518-foot-wide vault, placed 115 feet above the track level, encompasses five platforms and nine tracks ("Santiago Calatrava"). Services and shops do not invade the station's space as they are covered on the ground level, arranged along the main aisle into series of esthetically coherent circular booths (Fig. 7.14). A sense of openness and lightness is provided by the extensive use of glass, as the massive, yet transparent, vault, rather than covering the station, blurs the limits between the interior and exterior, allowing for the mutual interpenetration between the city and the TGV terminal. The structure, with both its striking shape and white color contrasting with the surrounding, mostly brick, buildings, is well visible from afar, announcing the city of Liège to incoming travelers. The platform level, placed fifteen feet above the ground, acts as a sort of viewing platform immediately confronting travelers with the city's panorama, framed by the vault's arches (Figs. 7.15, 7.16, 7.17). The building, with its exuberant, lyrical form, evoking the idea of movement, is already referred to in terms of a new civic monument, rather than just a functional space of travel,

Figure 7.11.   The buttress, seen from the main entrance to the station. Lyon Saint-Exupéry by Santiago Calatrava, opened in 1994.

Figure 7.12.   The mobile and the static: the buttress. Lyon Saint-Exupéry by Santiago Calatrava, opened in 1994.

Figure 7.13.   Liège Guillemins by Santiago Calatrava, opened in 2009. Photo by author, May 2010.

Figure 7.14. Liège Guillemins by Santiago Calatrava, opened in 2009. Interior, with shops and services. Photo by author, June 2010.

Figure 7.15. Liège Guillemins by Santiago Calatrava, opened in 2009. Panoramic views of the city from the platform level. Photo by author, May 2010.

Figure 7.16. Liège Guillemins by Santiago Calatrava, opened in 2009. Calatrava's white structure contrasts with its surroundings. Photo by author, June 2010.

Figure 7.17. Liège Guillemins by Santiago Calatrava, opened in 2009. Vaulting system. Photo by author, June 2010.

fulfilling the ambitions of sponsors who wish to see it as "a symbol of the redevelopment of the city and as one of its most prestigious calling cards."[31]

The lyrical, almost oneiric quality of the Liège Guillemins station could not be more different from strong, sensuous lines of the yet-to-be-opened Napoli Afragola high-speed station by Zaha Hadid. Although both buildings aim to capture and evoke the idea of movement, Hadid does so with a robust and compact zigzag-like building hanging above the tracks. Here the tension between the fluid and the static reaches its most arresting dimension, as the building is designed to be a bridge, an ultimately transitory zone, yet its eye-catching, expressive form constitutes it as a landmark, departing far from placelessness and anonymity of transportation hubs, as seen by Marc Augé. The interior, organized on three levels, with the platforms at the bottom and restaurants and shopping areas at the top, further emphasizes the idea of movement, as the spaces seem smoothly interconnected.

As I have sought to argue, contemporary train stations with their eye-catching architecture often promoted by starchitects display many of the characteristics that Marc Augé uses to define his *lieux,* rather than *non-lieux.* Train stations, alongside supermarkets and airports, were in his interpretation the ultimate embodiment of *non-lieux.* A closer investigation of several indicative cases sheds some light on the question of the inherent placelessness of train stations, revealing that, starting from the last decades of the twentieth century, they have been conceived of as expressive and often symbolic monuments, not anonymous transitory zones as Augé and Iyer see them. The crucial questions concerning contemporary railroad architecture identified in the course of this discussion—stations as image-makers, stations as parts of larger multifunctional urban projects, stations as multimodal platforms, and stations as urban signals—remain indicative of a worldwide phenomenon of the "second rail era." The recent railroad renaissance, determined by the introduction of high-speed rail, resulted in a profound transformation in railroad-related design, calling into question the Augeian reading of the train station as an in-between zone, deprived of identity, oblivious toward history, and incapable of entering in meaningful relations—be it with its location, or with its users. If Augé sees places and non-places as oppositions, contemporary train station architecture compromises this view, creating stations which address their inherent liminality, grasping large numbers of passengers and even adding to their transitory character by creating multimodal platforms encompassing different forms of transport, while simultaneously aiming at anchoring the building in its specific location through memorable architectural forms indicative of regional ambitions or by an increased number of versatile services geared toward both transitory and local clients. As this discussion aimed to show, the duality of the stations' space and the tension it provokes lie at the core of their design and may be the key issue in attempts to grasp both the ephemeral and lasting qualities of railroad architecture.

With their insistence on treating the train station as a crucial self-promotional commission, as a multifunctional place of gathering for both passengers and residents and with their particular attention toward creating memorable architectural forms, all of the examples presented here call for a rethinking of the train station and a more nuanced understanding of it than the propositions of the Augeian "non-place" or Iyer's "interregnum." The reading advanced in this discussion, which focused on the contradictions in train station space and tensions between its simultaneous rootedness and detachment, and the way these are translated in their architecture, has stressed the fact that contemporary train stations are conceived of as easily recognizable public spaces, with their own set of well-pronounced characteristics, renouncing their alleged placelessness yet still remaining ambiguous territories, palimpsests of clashing trajectories.

The condition of the train station as a building through which one crosses or passes in a hurry does not encourage any lasting relations and is based on a series of disjunctive ephemeral impressions that are hardly contemplative or focused. Instantaneity marks the experience of train station space and for that very reason, if the station is to fulfill its contemporary role as a symbolic "business card" and an urban signal evoking regional or municipal ambitions, it requires instantaneously recognizable and memorable architectural gestures. Contemporary train stations, as spaces of architectural audacious experimentations, are capable of arresting one's attention, compromising their inherent transitory character, forcing one to recognize their role as destination points in their own right. Those *instantaneous places*, combining characteristics of both Augeian places and non-places, might just remain some of the richest constructs in contemporary architecture, indicative of the uprooted condition of the "global soul," whose parameters are constantly being renegotiated, oscillating between the static and the mobile, the global and the local, the nomadic and the settled.

NOTES

1. For some of the debates about appropriate railroad architecture and the problem of the train station, see John Ruskin's writings, particularly his *Seven Lamps of Architecture*, where he ferociously opposes any attempts to adorn railroad architecture, seeing train stations as some of the most miserable urban spaces that should be designed, so that one could leave them as soon as possible. His discussion concludes in a powerful statement: "Better bury gold in the embankments than put it on ornaments on the stations" (101).

2. Originally in French (all translations by the author unless otherwise indicated); *"la plus haute expression monumentale et artistique du génie industriel et commercial qui caractérise si spécialement l'époque où nous sommes."* Daly, César, *Revue Générale de l'Architecture et des Travaux Publics*, XIX 1861, col. 79.

3. For more about Gare de l'Est, see Bowie; for Saint Pancras, see Lansley; for Grand Central, see Schlichting.

4. Originally in French: *"Il faut ajouter que, dans l'accélération continuelle du progrès technique, certains autres modes de transport peuvent paraître à priori privilégiés. C'est ainsi que les jeunes se passionnent plus pour les records de vitesse des voitures de sport ou des avions supersoniques que pour les performances des dernières locomotives électriques"* (Armand, 1964).

5. In 1998 TGV in France transported more than 70 million passengers, covering 45% percent of total intercity passenger traffic and 60% of freight traffic. In the same year the French were reported to travel an average of 480 kilometers per year on board the TGV (Batisse). For more about the second rail age, see, for example, two issues of *Built Environment*: "Railways in Europe: A New Era?" (2009) and "The Age of the Train," (1993); see also Binney; Thorne; Ringen; Moore.

6. For TGV effect on cities and regions see for example: "La gare. . . . Collection collective"; Gonzalez.

7. See, for example, Andrew Donaldson (2075–2092), Susana Borrás-Alomar, Thomas Christiansen, and Andrés Rodríguez-Pos (1–27).

8. For the most thorough account of the Euralille project, Menu and Vernandel, "Espace Croisé" (1996).

9. www.lilletourism.com/histoire_de_lille-1–0–8-fr.html.

10. Originally in French: *"Cette sélection portait en elle une faible marge de décision. Tout en n'étant pas des architectes modestement 'urbains,' nos quatre compatriotes appartiennent à une mouvance acceptable de la raison face aux enjeux de la cité. Il était donc peu probable qu'ils apportent une surprise brutale, la réponse forte et symbolique qu'impliquait l'ambition européennne de la métropole"* (Edelmann, paragraph 3).

11. *"Le choix Rem Koolhaas montre notre ambition. L'architecte aurait pu être français, nous voulions quelqu'un d'envergure internationale."* As quoted in Rambert, 17.

12. Dossier about Euralille in *L'Architecture d'aujourd'hui*, April 1992, the entire issue is devoted to Rem Koolhaas.

13. To name just some of these publications: "Chunnel City"; "Euralille"; "Euralille, Lille, France"; Rambert; "TGV station, Lille 1994"; Treiber.

14. Richard Rogers later withdrew from designing his tower for the station's roof, as he felt budget restrictions harmed his original idea to an unacceptable extent.

15. Development of transportation was seen as one of the crucial factors that would help Lyon to acquire the desired "eurocité" status; see, for example, SEPAL, Lyon 2010.

16. This decision was exceptional, as previously no city authorities had specifically requested a non-SNCF architect to design their station, something that was true of the Euralille project as well. Even though partially designed and thoroughly coordinated by Rem Koolhaas, it was still executed by the SNCF architect Jean-Marie

Duthilleul, who was named the architect on location of the Lille-Europe station and who, together with Koolhaas, is credited with the final design.

17. These motivations were clearly stated in the SNCF report about Lyon Satolas, which explained: "We considered the most efficient way for the architect to create a signal of high symbolic value to be to associate it with a specific building. France is full of symbols of similar types and attitudes, the Notre Dame de PARIS, the pont d'AVIGNON, the ramparts of CARCASSONNE, SAINT CHARLES station, . . .

"We chose the central building of the station giving it a very strong and easily recognizable form that one could associate with the region, visible from the ground and from the sky. The symbol itself resembles an idea of flight, that of passage, of the Alpine countryside, as well as the *élan* of progress.

"*Nous avons considéré que la manière la plus efficace, en tant qu'architecte de créer un signal de haute valeur symbolique est de l'associer à un bâtiment concret. La France est pleine de symboles du genre et d'attitudes semblables, Notre Dame de PARIS, pont d'AVIGNON, remparts de CARCASSONNE, gare ST CHARLES, (. . .)*

"*Nous avons choisi le bâtiment central de la gare en lui donnant une forme très forte, facilement reconnaissable, et associable à la région, tant vu du sol, que des airs. Le symbole ressemble lui-même une idée de vol, celle de passage, de paysage alpin, ainsi que l'élan du progrès'*," Cinq gares TGV, les espaces quais, SNCF archives p. 3.

18. Originally in French: "*L'implantation de la future gare TGV sur le site de SATOLAS (. . .) doit permettre à terme : De renouveler l'image du site de SATOLAS : image forte, moderne, ouverte sur l'avenir (. . .)*" Rapport de synthèse de la commission téchnique, Concours Satolas, 1989, SNCF archives.

19. Although seven competitors went through to the final round, only six teams actually competed, as one of the contestants Viguier Jodry withdrew his candidacy; see *Concours Satolas*, juin 1989, SNCF archives, 1.

20. The jury, composed of twenty-seven members, was at that day missing one—a representative of Isere, who failed to attend. Lacking one member, the jury, in a secret vote, delivered a score of thirteen for Rogers versus thirteen for Calatrava. In this case, Charles Millon was entitled to make the final decision; see Sorgue.

21. This Regional Assembly session was widely described in the press as an example of "democracy which turned into cacophony" (Sorgue, 4); "une effervescene peu habituelle au sein de l'assemblée des Charbonnières" (Lagrange, 2) or "une zone de turbulence" (da Fonseca, 1).

22. "*Le projet architectural retenu (a été) choisi pour l'impact qu'il pourra avoir au service de l'image de la région,*" Conséquences financières du choix du projet Calatrava pour la gare de Satolas, 11/07/89, SNCF archives, 1.

23. A good overview of the "starchitect" phenomenon can be found in Davies and Schmiedeknecht; McNeill.

24. On starchitecture and the Bilbao effect, see, for example, Egan, Nakazawa & Brantley; Long; Smith.

25. On the impact of TGV on regions, see Bonnafous; Vickerman.

26. "A New Ultramodern Station and District in Full Expansion, Les perspectives de developpement du site de Guillemins en lien avec la gare TGV, juin 2006, le nouvel axe urbain, Guillemins, Médiacité," Liège promotional leaflet.

27. For a description of the city fathers' hopes, see the leaflet SNCB, "A New Ultramodern Station and District in Full Expansion," www.liegeonline.be/en/ medias/ pdf/gareguilleminsEN.pdf.

28. A similar case of translating a sculpture into a building took place in 1999, when a Swedish developer—captivated by Calatrava's marble sculpture "The Turning Torso"—asked him to translate it into a skyscraper.

29. Calatrava explains this idea further in one of his interviews, see "Santiago Calatrava Valls," 1994.

30. Information board at Lyon Satolas station, as seen in May 2010.

31. For a thorough description of the project, as well as the client's expectations, consult www.euro-liege-tgv.be/fr/gare-de-liege.html?IDC=17.

BIBLIOGRAPHY

Armand, Louis. "L'avenir des chemins de fer." *Revue Générale des Chemins de Fer* (April 1964): 205–212.

Augé, Marc. *Non-places. Introduction to an Anthropology of Supermodernity.* London: Verso, 1995.

Batisse, F. "*La grande vitesse dans le monde.*" RGCHF (février 1999): 34–44.

Bauman, Zygmunt, *Liquid Modernity.* Cambridge, MA: Blackwell, 2000.

Binney, Marcus. *The Architecture of Rail: The Way Ahead.* London: Academy Editions, 1995.

Bonnafous, A. "The Regional Impact of the TGV." *Transportation* 14 (June 1987): 127–137.

Borrás-Alomar, Susana, Thomas Christiansen, and Andrés Rodríguez-Pos. "Towards a 'Europe of the Regions'? Visions and Reality from a Critical Perspective." *Regional Politics and Policy* 4.2 (1994): 1–27.

Bowie, Karen. *Polarisation du territoire et développement urbain: les Gares du Nord et de l'Est et la transformation de Paris au XIXe siècle.* AHICF archives.

"Chunnel City." *Blueprint* 108 (1994): 22–24.

Davies, Paul, and Thorsten Schmiedeknecht (Eds.). *An Architect's Guide to Fame: A Collection of Essays on Why They Got Famous and You Didn't.* London: Architectural Press, 2005.

"La dimension architecturale du projet, Une architecture contemporaine de grande qualité." http://www.euro-liege-tgv.be/fr/la-dimension-architecturale.html?IDC=41.

Donaldson, Andrew. "Performing Regions: Territorial Development and Cultural Politics in a Europe of the Regions." *Environment and Planning A* 38.11 (2006): 2075–2092.

Doutriaux, L'Architecture d'aujourd'hui (April 1992): 98.

Dufour, Jean-Paul. "Trois questions à. . . . Pierre m Mauroy." *Le Monde* (31 mai 2003).

Edelmann, Frederic. "Pierre Mauroy inaugure le nouveau centre commercial de la métropole du Nord; Euralille ou le génie de la transfiguration." *Le Monde* (21 September 1994).

Edelmann, Frederic. "Le Nord passe à la grande vitesse." 1993.

Egan, Nancy, Paul W. Nakazawa, and William Brantley. "Starchitecture: Cities Are Using High-Image Architecture to Give Form to a New Generation's Concepts of Identity and Civic Order—and Sense of Economic Stability." *Urban Land* 62.11–12 (Nov.–Dec. 2003): 52–58.

"Euralille." *Arca* (February 1996): 30–43.

"Euralille, Lille, France." *GA Documents* 41 (1994): 36–65.

Fonseca da, Manuel. "L'architecte de la future gare TGV de Satolas s'appelle Santiago Calatrava," *Lyon Matin*, 7 juillet 1989.

"La gare. . . . Collection collective." *Architecture Intérieure Crée* (November 1994): 76–93.

Gonzalez, Xavier, "TGV cities." *A10. New European Architecture* 26 (March 2009): 66–68.

Guigueno, Vincent. "*Building a High-speed Society, France and the Aérotrain, 1962–1974.*" *Technology and Culture* 49.1 (2008): 21–40.

"J'avais déjà passé par l'aérodrome de Singapour, mais . . . mais . . . cent fois mieux, La nouvelle gare TGV de Lyon Satolas," showed on JA2 on 28th of July 1994, INA archives.

Koolhaas, Rem. *Delirious New York: A Retroactive Manifesto for Manhattan.* New York: Oxford UP, 1978.

"La halle aux trains." *L'Architecture intérieure crée* (1994): 44–49.

Labasse, Jean. "Lyon, métropole?" *Revue de Géographie de Lyon* 57.2 (1982): 145–153.

Lagrange, Catherine. "La gare se pose à Satolas," *Le Figaro* (7 July 1989).

Lansley, Alastair. *The Transformation of St Pancras Station.* London: Laurence King, 2008.

Long, Kieran. "It's Official: Star Architects Can Revive Flagging Cities." *World Architecture* 106 (May 2002): 12.

Mandrelli, Doriana O. "Euralille, interview with Pierre Mauroy." *Arca* 101 (1996): 30–43.

McNeill, Donald. *The Global Architect; Firms, Fame and Urban Form.* New York; London: Routledge 2009.

Menu, Isabelle. Vermandel Frank, *Euralille: poser, exposer*, Espace Croisé. Lille, 1995.

Menu, Isabelle, and Frank Vernamdel (Eds.). *Euralille: The Making of a New City Center: Koolhaas, Nouvel, Portzmparc, Vasconi, Duthilleul, Architects.* Basel, Boston, Berlin: Birkhauser, 1996.

Metz, Tracy. "Return to the Heroic, interview with Santiago Calatrava." *Architectural Record*, 182.10 (October 1994): 88–95.

Meunier, Jacob. *On the Fast Track: French Railway Modernization and the Origins of the TGV, 1944–1983.* Westport, CT: Praeger, 2002.

Minutillo, Josephine. "Liège-Guillemins TGV Railway Station." *Architectural Record* 198 (March 2010): 87–91.

Moore, Rowan. "The New Age of the Train." *Blueprint* (May 1993): 21–26.

"Le Nord passe à la grande vitesse." *Le Monde* (23 May 1993).

Ockman, Joan, "Bilbao and the Global Imagination." *Architecture and Tourism: Perception, Performance, and Place.* Eds. Lasansky, D. Medina, and Brian McLaren. Oxford: Berg, 2004. 227–241.

Paasi Anssi. "Bounded Spaces in the Mobile World: Deconstructing 'Regional Identity.'" *Tijdschrift voor economische en sociale geografie* 93.2 (2002): 137–148.

Rambert, Francis "Koolhaas ne fait pas de quartier." *Architectes* (avril 1989): 16–17.

Rapport de synthèse de la commission téchnique, "Concours Satolas," 1989, SNCF archives.

Ringen, Jonathan. "Station to station." *Metropolis* 21 (December 2001): 71–74.

Ruskin, John, *The Seven Lamps of Architecture, The Lamp of Beauty.* Mineola, NY: Dover Publications, 1989.

Rybczynski Witold. "The Bilbao Effect." *The Atlantic Monthly* 290.2 (September 2002): 138–142.

"Santiago Calatrava, Liège–Guillemins TGV station, Liège Belgium." *GA Documents* 111 (2010): 74–93.

"Santiago Calatrava Valls, *Escale à Satolas: Rhône-Alpes à grande vitesse.*" Glénat 1994.

Schlichting, Kurt C. *Grand Central Terminal: Railroads, Engineering, and Architecture in New York City.* Baltimore: Johns Hopkins University Press, 2001.

Schievelbusch, Wolfgang, *The Railway Journey, The Industrialization of Time and Space in the 19th Century.* Berkeley: The University of California Press, 1986.

SEPAL, Lyon 2010 un projet d'agglomération pour une métropole européennee, Documentation Francaise, 1988.

Simonsen, Dorthe Gert. "Accelerating Modernity: Time-space Compression in the Wake of the Aeroplane." *The Journal of Transport History* 26.2 (2005): 98–117.

Smith, Terry. *The Architecture of Aftermath*, University of Chicago Press, 2006.

Sorgue, Pierre. "Region: la gare de Satolas fait dérailler la session." *Libération*, 7/07/89.

Stungo, Naomi. "Lyons made." *RIBA journal* 101.8 (August 1994): 32–37.

"TGV station, Lille 1994." *A+U* (1997): 110–117.

Thompson, Ian B. "High-Speed Transport Hubs and Eurocity Status: The Case of Lyon." *Journal of Transport Geography* 3.1 (1995): 29–37.

Thorne, Martha (Ed.). *Modern Trains and Splendid Stations: Architecture, Design and Rail Travel for the Twenty-First Century.* New York: St. Martin's Press, 2001.

Treiber, Daniel. "Oma a Euralille: una angosciata modernità." *Casabella* (May 1995): 18–33.

Vickerman, Roger. "High-Speed Rail in Europe: Experience and Issues for Future Development." *The Annals of Regional Science* 31.1 (1997): 21–38.

Chapter 8

Digging Madrid

A Descent into Madrid's Subway Museum, Andén 0 [Platform 0]

Araceli Masterson-Algar

"Metro is Madrid, and Madrid is Metro." With this statement, Alberto Ruiz Gallardón, the city's Mayor, inaugurated Andén 0 [Platform 0], the museum for Madrid's subway (known as just 'Metro') on March 24, 2008. Comprising an investment of 6.3 million Euros, and under the direction of architects Pau Soler and Miguel Rodríguez, Andén 0 is the "restored" version of the old station of Chamberí, in disuse since 1966, and popularly known as the "estación fantasma" (ghost station). The museum's mission is to serve the Metro-City, becoming "*the* point of reference in the interpretation of the history of Madrid's Metro and its ties to the city" (original emphasis, video presentation).[1]

Since its inauguration in 1919, Madrid's subway has become a symbol of the city's progress, order, and international competitiveness. Metro is a site for the articulation of the local and global, as well as for residents' definitions and (re)constructions of Madrid. Its successful "packaging" through the museum Andén 0 dialogues with the concept of "selling place" (Harvey, *Urban*; Philo and Kearns; Zukin, *Loft, Cultures*), whereby the city turns into a site of consumption (rather than production) through more flexible forms of capital accumulation. Indeed, global economic forces influence both the production and construction of Madrid's now 317-kilometer underground network. A strong symbiosis between the government and private corporations such as Iberdrola, real estate agencies such as Sacyr Vallehermoso, ACS, Ferrovial, and private cleaning and security companies such as Securitas and Prosegur, has fueled Metro's frenzied growth, particularly after the approval of the 1998 *Ley del Suelo*[2] and its stated prioritization of public works and real state over industry (Calvo López et al.; Rodriguez López). Yet, backed by a celebratory coverage in the media after the inauguration of each new station, the ferocious expansion of underground Madrid has encountered little opposition, echoing Metro's successful self-representation as a company/technology that "cares" about history, the environment, and culture.

Analyzing Madrid's subway as a process means taking into account the relations between physical, mental, and social space (see Lefebvre, *Production*; Soja, *Thirdspace*) in order to articulate the connections between the representation of Madrid's subway in the "official" discourse and metanarratives of development, and the ways in which its users imagine it (and thus (re)produce it). While in previous work I have focused on the social practices that make Metro through everyday use (Masterson-Algar "Madrid"), my current focus is on the physical and mental representations of Metro through the analysis of its museum Andén 0. An approximation of the museum's content and form, as well as to the visitors' responses to its display, reveals how much of the support for the city's largest public work is rooted in ideologies of modernity that fueled the extension of rail transport to the underground while redefining the relations between technology, nature, and culture.

John Urry, in his research on mobility, defines modernity as "that moment when enormously powerful machines are imbricated within human experience" (*Mobilities*, 93). Metro holds such power, (re)articulating the relations between technical changes and social processes in Spain's capital. Various press releases on the museum's opening day quote Mayor Ruiz Gallardón's address to Metro as "not only as an answer to attain competitiveness through mobility, but also as the city's introduction into modernity" ("Museo," "Una estación," "De estación"). Yet, social and cultural scholarship on trains rarely addresses their underground forms. Various scholars have shown a specific interest in the simultaneous implications of trains and tracks on modern subjectivities (Urry, *Mobilities*; Thrift; Huyssen; Dennis; Williams; Bailey; Bissell), and on the landscape they "conquer" (Bailey 12) through "flattening and subduing" (Urry, *Mobilities*, 94). Focusing on the implications of trains as constitutive and constituting of modern consciousness, these authors emphasize the implications of trains on definitions of time and space, following Harvey's observations on the "annihilation of space by time" (*Urban*). Andreas Huyssen highlights the central role of the railroad in the transformation of consciousness. While he extends his analysis to the airplane, and even to cyberspace, he overlooks systems of underground transportation. Focusing specifically on New York City, Richard Dennis shows the key role of the elevated railway on the urban consciousness, and identifies underground networks, namely the sewer system, as central to notions of the urban. Yet he overlooks underground trains and tracks. Even

Urry, who describes the railway expansion as movement "over, under, and across" (*Mobilities*, 51), preferences horizontal movement "across" over underground trajectories. Rosalind Williams, in her seminal work *Notes of the Underground*, offers a framework to understand the entwinement between trains' movement "across" and their trajectories "under."

Linking technologies of the above and of the below, and working from the European context, Williams explains that at its inception, the steam engine was meant to drain the groundwater from the mines (57). But mostly, Williams establishes the ties between surface and underground showing how mining, geology, and transportation were constitutive and constituting of the notion of "deep time" from the eighteenth-century onward. According to Williams, "deep time"—that is, the awareness of the earth as a succession of layers of strata laid down in regular and predictable ways—is tied to the history of transportation networks, first through the development of canals, roads, and the railroad beginning in the eighteenth century, and later through the emergence of underground planning beginning in the last half of the nineteenth century. Under this light, the ties between transportation and modernity involved speeding "across" space while "digging" its crust, and underground trains offered movement not only *across* space, but *into* time.

This double journey is key to understanding the role of Metro in Madrid's urban consciousness as represented through its museum Andén 0. Williams describes the journey into the underground as "one of the most enduring and powerful cultural traditions of humankind, a metaphorical journey of discovery through descent below the surface" (34). But while Williams looks at nineteenth-century narratives to better understand the intersections between the imaginary and physical spaces of the underground and modernity, this chapter turns to narratives of the museum Andén 0. The official website of Andén 0 describes Metro not only as an underground train, but also as the "machinery" that would lead to social and urban change through its architecture, engineering, technology, advertisement, and design. Andén 0 and its surrounding discourse embody this crisscross of technology, science, and aesthetics, presenting Metro as a technological wonder, part of the physiognomy of the city and the conduit of the capital's cultural patrimony. As stated by Williams, "the subterranean environment is a technological one—but it is also a mental landscape, a social terrain, and an ideological map" (21). It is precisely the combination of all three, as manifested in the form and content of both the museum and the narratives surrounding its visit that we find much of the ideological terrain to understand Metro's unquestioned support amongst the citizenry.

ANDÉN 0: TIME MACHINE

During the museum's inaugural ceremony, Manuel Lamela, counselor of transportation, described Andén 0 as a means to "travel in time," and "enter into" "the history of the city" ("De estación"). The transformation of the abandoned station of Chamberí into the "in situ" museum Andén 0 entails both metonym and mimesis. It becomes a part that stands in a contiguous relation to two absent wholes, Metro and Madrid. As explained by Barbara Kirshenblatt-Gimblett, "the art of metonym is an art that accepts the inherently fragmentary nature of its object." Showing it in all its partiality enhances the aura of its "realness" (20). If, as the Mayor added, "Metro is Madrid and Madrid is Metro," what better way to "recuperate" the memory of the city than to penetrate *into* the city?

Metro's museum claims "realness" from the premise that human experience can be re-created (Hutton, xxiii) or, as stated by Michel Foucault, transformed from a "document" (past transmitted) to a monument (past reconstructed) (*Archaeology*, 8). Pierre Nora explains this process as the turn from history to places of memory (lieux de memóire), and Kirshenblatt-Gimblett ties this transformation to the conversion of the museum from an exhibit to a place of/to "experience." As a result, visitors to Andén 0 become "travelers" in a "journey" that necessarily entails a recreation of Metro's memory through the production of "hereness" (Kirshenblatt-Gimblett, 153), thus merging past, present, and future. Such "accumulation of time in an immobile place," write Foucault and Miskowiec, "belongs to our modernity" (26), and sets the ideological grounds from which Andén 0 emerges as a "capsule of time," birthplace and destiny of the Metrocity.

Presented as a container of the city's "patrimony," Andén 0 joins the long list of Madrid's sights for the production and consumption of "heritage." But while Hewison denounces heritage as a simulacra of the past, Harvey sees it as a process in the present, and thus as an "instrument of cultural power" (*Heritage*, 327). The latter approach turns to the "presentness of the heritage processes and practice" (*Heritage*, 324), tying "representations" of the past with decisions about the future. Thus, despite the imagery of Andén 0 as an anchor to the past, its "origin" folds into its present and future. As stated in the museum's information pamphlet, Andén 0 offers a "journey" through space and time by means of "a sentimental trip through the history of Metro" from the turn of the nineteenth century to its current "expansion" "beyond the city limits."

The choice of the word "sentimental" in the quote above addresses the significance of nostalgia as the tool to (re)create a desired past and future with Metro as protagonist. The museum then, and in dialogue with Goss, offers a "hypernarrated" space for commemoration through a discourse of the loss and restoration of the "authentic" (56). To be "sentimental" thereof, Andén 0 must make a claim that the history it presents is the same for *all* of the city's residents, while sustaining a narrative of the "recuperation" of that which is "lost." Under this light, the "rescue" efforts of the museum are not so much for documenting Metro's history as for (re)presenting it as a metonymy for the solidity of the city and nation in the past, present, and future. As stated by Mayor Alberto Ruiz Gallardón, Andén 0 "has opened for us a window into the past, through which we recognize the magnificent reality of the city of Madrid" ("La antigua estación").

To uncover the ideologies embedded in the production and consumption of Metro through its museum, parallels must be drawn with the popularity of nineteenth century excursions to the underground, either through cave tours, or through tours of Haussmann's underground Paris (Williams; Shortland). Williams explains how Modernity increasingly resorted to a vocabulary of sublimity commonly associated with nature to describe technical "wonders." As she states, "the image of artificial infinity gradually shed its aura of terror and assumed the mantle of enchantment" (95). Most importantly, Williams shows the technological determinism emerging from this narrative, which underpins the uncontroversial expansion of Madrid's underground network.

Thus, while Metro becomes the agent for the city's "growth," the station of Chamberí becomes its shelter. The appeal of Andén 0 is not only its location "in situ," and its recourse to a myth of origins and glorious destiny, but the fact that this "truth" emerges from a descent *into* history. Urry indicated the resemblance between the objects of tourist gaze and "religious pilgrimages in traditional society" (*Mobilities*, 144). This is intensified in journeys to the world below, which Williams describes as "inherently sacred" (8), thus adding to the capacity of Andén 0 to produce "hereness," and "truth." Further, the abandoned station of Chamberí was the scenario of popular imagination *prior* to the plans for the museum.

In an article for *El País* from August 10, 2003, de Cózar and Gutiérrez describe this underground space as a "place of worship" for many citizens longing for its "recuperation." Supporting their claim are multiple entries in the blog Andén 2,[3] providing cues as to how to "see" the space despite its closure to the public. Recommendations range from information on how to reach the station on foot, to step-by-step descriptions of where and how to stand inside the train in order to get the best "view" possible in a time frame of one second. Bloggers' descriptions of the abandoned station echoed those of de Cózar and Gutiérrez, who portrayed it as an apocalyptic site of "sepulchral" silence and rust, absent of any contact with the outside world—a place "where not even rats nest." Narratives of the abandoned station as a "space for worship" accompanied demands for Mayor Ruiz Gallardón to follow his promise and build Metro's museum from this "mountain of dust and ruins."[4]

The Mayor's above reference to "ruins" cannot be overlooked, given their connection in the public imagination to a "former pristine state" (Kirshenblatt-Gimblett, 18). Part of Metro's public relations includes its presentation as a space to find, rescue, and protect "the origins" of Madrid and its people. In 2007, for instance, the company launched a short advertising documentary that included a celebration of Metro as an archaeological site and caretaker of the city's buried pasts (*Anuncio*). One month after the opening of the museum in March 2008, the local and international press announced Metro's new "finding" of fossils dating back 13 million years ("Hallan"). With such an accumulation of "findings," it is not all that surprising that on March 23, 2011, Metro crowned its discourse as the city's "archaeologist" with the inauguration of the largest archaeological underground museum in the country, part of the rehabilitation plans for the Metro stop "Ópera" ("Inaugurados"). Prior to this display, most of the archaeological findings dug out during Metro's construction works were transferred to the city's science museum, further speaking to the entwinement between technology and science. Hence, Metro, as the company that "cares," transforms the destruction attached to "drilling" and "perforating" into an exercise in archaeology and preservation of the past.

At the juncture of the sacred and the archaeological, Chamberí leaps from phantasmagoric station to "sanctuary." As posed in an article for the *Washington Post*, Andén 0 "emerged from the ashes of an abandoned 'ghost station'" (Dell'Amore). Supporting Williams's description of the underworld as "inherently sacred" (8), Andén 0 emerges as a sanctuary for Metro, a space for a descent not only through space, but *in* time. This journey *into* Madrid and Metro's history leads the visitor through a double ride of remembrance and oblivion.

The journey/ritual to Madrid/Metro's underground responds to Augé's description of "oblivion" as a journey between memory and expectation that "organizes the passage from a before to an after, of which it is at once the interpreter and the landmark" (55). As the 'Centro de Interpretación del Metro de Madrid,' Andén 0 offers such a ritual. In its official website it describes the museum as a "time machine," through which "visitors will be able to travel through the history of Metro and the history of the city, beginning in the first decades of the twentieth century, continuing with the Civil War and Metro's transformation into a refugee for citizens against bombing raids, and arriving to its present phase of expansion beyond the city limits."

Visitors reinforce the description of the museum, addressing Andén 0 as a journey in time. Even the aforementioned article about the museum in the *Washington Post* commented that "time travel has never been so fast and easy" (Dell'Amore). Similarly, a scan through the entries for the museum in the blog Andén 2 reveals a consensual image of Metro's museum as "time machine," although its destinations in time vary from blogger to blogger: "It carries you to the fifties," "a perfect trip to 1966," "a journey back in time to the Madrid of the 1920s," "a trip through the imagination."

The above inconsistencies in the museum's "interpretation" of Metro's history reveal the fine lines between memory and imagination, or as David Cohen put it, "the combing of history." The museum's materials describe the historical trajectory of the station in three stages: the first comprises the period from its opening as part of the Metro's first line on October 17, 1919, to its closure in 1966; the second, from 1966–2008, is simply the station's *descent* to "oblivion" which earned it the name of "*estación fantasma* [ghost station]"; and finally, the third period initiated through its *rescue* after forty-four years in the "dark" and its entitlement as Metro's "center of interpretation." But as noted in the visitors' responses, in Andén 0 all these time frames overlap. Much of its furniture dates back to Metro's inauguration, and the visitor is led to believe that, despite half a century of activity, the station remained "in its original state" up to its closure in 1966. The tile advertisements along the platform support this claim. Dating from the 1920s, they were an unexpected finding buried under layers of paint, graffiti, and paper publicity spanning fifty years. Furthermore, the opening documentary, and the visual projections down by the platform include images of pre-Metro Madrid, as well as "timeless" symbols (Cibeles) and traditions (Fiestas de San Isidro) of the city. Ultimately, and under the banner of patrimony and preservation, Metro's history is as infinite as its future expansion.

A central element to the "feel" of descent in space and time—deeper into truth—is the visit's trajectory. The journey into Metro begins at the entrance of the museum across from its original access in the Plaza de Chamberí. Although the museum presents itself as a "careful" reproduction of the original station, its main access differs entirely from its original, displaying a "futuristic" structure of steel and glass. Reminiscent of an obelisk, the entrance attempts to mark the difference between the entrance to Metro's museum and those of other "functioning" Metro stops, while celebrating Metro's monumentality (Figs. 8.1–8.4).[5] The descent into the museum takes place through a spiral staircase, an architectonic choice that increases the feeling of depth and distance from the surface. Once inside, museum personnel lead the visitor to what used to be the original "boca" of Chamberí station (the entrances to the subway are popularly known as "bocas" or "mouths"), which has been turned into a small room with a staircase structure from which visitors can sit and watch a short film. This setting marks the former entry to the station, while the video projection works as an entry *into* the history of Metro, and the "frame" for the subsequent steps in the visit.

Figure 8.1.   Boca de Salida de la Estación del Metro de Chamberí, 1966. Colección particular de César Mohedas. [Exit opening of the Station of Chamberí, 1966. Courtesy of César Mohedas (private collection).]

Figure 8.2.   Construction site for the Museum Entrance. Courtesy of "Andén 1. Asociación de Amigos del Metro de Madrid."

Figure 8.3. Construction site for the Museum Entrance. Courtesy of "Andén 1. Asociación de Amigos del Metro de Madrid."

Figure 8.4. Entrance to the Museum "Andén 0." Photograph by Miguel A. Sandoval.

Rather than revealing Metro's entwinement with Madrid's processes of capital accumulation, the museum presents itself in its audiovisual materials as the outcome of the city's commitment to *rescue* the past from oblivion: "The purpose is to bring the citizens closer to their history, and to recuperate a part of the collective memories and of the spaces that conserve it" ("Andén 0—Museum Information Guide"). The attempt to *rescue* the past from oblivion is unavoidably tied to a process of framing the history for conservation *in* the present. As Tony Bennett describes in his genealogy of the public museum, museums become machines for the exercise of power, framing "patrimony" as detached from politics. Nowhere is this more overt than in the seventeen-minute film that begins the tour (*Andén 0*). Tracing the history of Metro decade by decade, the short documentary, reduces the complexity of Spain's historical turmoil to "changes," which never interfered in Metro's plans. In fact, there is no mention of the dictatorship of Primo de Rivera (1923–1930), much less that of Francisco Franco (1939–1975), nor of the country's dynamics under either dictatorship. As the film's voiceover proclaims, "[a]lthough the country lived important social and political *changes*, Metro continued its expansion" (my emphasis). According to the film, the Civil War (1936–1939) was the only event capable of "putting the break" on Metro's expansion. The film's voiceover describes Metro's response to the needs of the citizens; it reconfigured itself, turning its trains into ambulances, and its network into a refuge against air raids: "[s]ome of the coaches were turned into ambulances of the Red Cross for the transportation of the wounded," while "women, children and the elderly found refuge in Metro's installations."

Following the projection of the film, a guide leads visitors into a "dimly lit" area displaying the "original" ticket disposers, narrow metal turnstiles, and the ticket attendant's booth (see Figs. 8.5–8.6).[6] The combination of "light bulb replicas" from the period with the white Sevillian tile covering the walls and vaults irradiate "an almost ethereal glow" (Dell'Amore) that after its inauguration in 1919 had been compared to the radiance of candles in Semana Santa Processions ("Los primeros"). Museum guides stop at this location to explain the choice of white tile as evidence of Metro's careful design at the hand of Antonio Palacios, author of some of the most emblematic projects in the capital, including the Edificio España, the Torre de Madrid, and the planning of the Gran Vía Diagonal. Palacio's choice of white tile as both aesthetic and functional was a response to widespread fears of descent into the underworld predominant during the nineteenth century (Fig. 8.7). The journey continues in final descent to the Platform—Andén 0 (Fig. 8.8), where the visitors can admire the tile advertisements from the 1920s and watch the mixed images projected onto three screens on the other side of the platform.

A combination of advertisements for events, news reels, and emblematic images of Madrid, past and present act as testimonials of Metro's history and relevance *regardless* of time—omnipresent.

Figure 8.5. Marker of the access to the subway. Original ticket attendant's booth and turnstiles. Photographs by Miguel A. Sandoval.

Figure 8.6.   Marker of the access to the subway. Original ticket attendant's booth and turnstiles. Photographs by Miguel A. Sandoval.

Figure 8.7.   Original ticket disposers and metal turnstiles. Photograph by Miguel A. Sandoval.

Figure 8.8.   Descent to the platform—Andén 0. Photograph by Miguel A. Sandoval.

Yet, despite the apparent lack of any chronological order, and absolute absence of any documentation other than the station itself, visitors show a conviction of the museum's "authentic" past rooted in their physical responses to the journey, and which respond to Urry's description of travel as a corporeal movement (*Mobilities*). For the imagination to generate "memory," Andén 0 must appeal to the senses. Thus, although the trip is a "visual" spectacle,[7] visitors comment on the "textures" of the floor and walls, express feeling the "smells" of the Metro of their childhood, and above all, share their impression on its most powerful generator of "here/hereness"—Metro itself ("Andén 1," blog). The presence of Metro on Platform 0 (the origin of origins) is "felt" each time it cuts through the museum following its regular, continued, and unaltered course from infinite past to infinite future (Fig. 8.9).

The effect of Metro's dash through the museum cannot be overstated, and features in a majority of blog entries following the visit to the museum. Metro's presence gives "life" to Andén 0, while silencing the film, and threatening the vocal chords of the museum's guides. Every few minutes, the museum's protagonist, Metro itself, breaks through the dark, generating a feel of anticipation, and a sensorial rush that (in)corporates Metro as the ultimate evidence of the museum's "authenticity." The references to Metro as a living entity illustrate modernity's gradual turn to narratives of nature to describe technological wonders (Williams). Under this light, Metro becomes a natural landscape, and Andén 0 its landmark.

Figure 8.9.   Beam of light produced by the passing of the subway through the station. Photograph by Miguel A. Sandoval.

ANDÉN 0: NATURAL LANDSCAPE

On February 11, 2011, a dispatch of state figures, including Mayor Ruiz Gallardón and the President of Madrid's region Esperanza Aguirre, gathered in Atocha station to await the emergence of the "tuneladora," the tunneling machine after nine months of drilling the underground passage between the city's two largest train stations, Chamartín and Atocha. The press described the event as the welcoming of a star, who as one engineer described, had labored "as gentle as a caterpillar, despite having the size of a dragon" (Álvarez). Numerous metaphors describe Metro and its system as "natural." In the above references, Metro overlaps the force of the dragon, with the gentleness of a caterpillar, aided by a coincidental nine-month period (gestation), which (re) frames the "emergence" of the "tuneladora" into the scenario of a "birth." But revealingly, labor itself is absent from the description of such a "natural" scene. Like this piece of news, the museum Andén 0 "interprets" the history of Metro as a "natural" one, through a total erasure of the human labor and labor dynamics involved in its construction and maintenance.

Underpinning the conversion of Metro from "humanmade" to "natural" are ideologies of power fostering technological determinism. In the absolute absence of the social or political context of the Metrocity, Andén 0 emerges as a place to pay one's respects to Metro, not to analyze it. The entwinement of discourses of nature and technology cater to the popular image of Metro as "environmental," [9] while fostering a general understanding of its expansion as "natural growth." This parallels the representation of Metro inside the museum as a living organism that works diligently for the benefit of all citizens.

In order to better understand the perception of Metro as a species, and of the museum as its "shelter" it is helpful to return to Williams's analysis of the transformations of the underworld from a space of fear to a natural marvel, which she describes as inseparable from changes in the perception of time and space that accompanied modernity. On the one hand, technological development resulted in the effervesce of sciences invested in researching "deep time," particularly geology, and led to a widespread popularity of "cave tours." On the other, the compression of time and space vis-à-vis technological developments resulted in descriptions of the city as an organism.

Williams shows how the initial association of the underground with hell and technology—as reflected for instance in H. G. Wells's *The Time Machine* (1895) and Fritz Lang's *Metropolis* (1927)—gradually led the way to its celebration as a "pristine" environment, and thus *the* "natural" space for the expansion of technology. This went along with descriptions of technology that drew from a discourse of nature, particularly through the concept of the sublime. At this juncture, it is not surprising to find references to Andén 0 as a landscape of "undisturbed natural beauty." Descriptions of the station of Chamberí prior to its makeover into Andén 0 also resorted repeatedly to "natural" imagery. One of the entries in the blog Andén 2 illustrates this perceived parallel between technology and nature, as it describes Chamberí's closure to the public in 1966 as "a clock that stopped, just like an insect inside a drop of amber." Other entries compare the abandoned station to "a natural cave," and wish they could have "entered" it when it was still abandoned, for it would have been "like entering a cave in its natural state."

The film at the museum defines Metro as "one more element of the urban physiognomy," a description which resonates with Lewis Mumford's address of underground planning as inextricably linked to the city's development:

> City Planning began to involve not only disposition of the surface but also an "underground system of functions that form as it were the *physiological apparatus* of the new city . . . the modern city plan involves a co-ordination of the super-surface city with the sub-surface city." (qtd. in Williams 52, my emphasis)

Richard Dennis (drawing from the work by Fraser and Sutcliffe) comments on the paradox whereby while cities are associated with civilization and humans' transformation of nature, there was a growing discourse paralleling the workings of the city to those of a natural system, added to an emergent protagonism of the city as a locus of circulation rather than production (Trotter). Andén 0 elaborates on the image of Metro as the circulatory system for the city in multiple ways.

Most notably, Metro runs through the museum in its uninterrupted course, pumping citizens throughout the city through its "vessels." On the other, the film at the museum visually charts the "unstoppable" extension of Metro, through an animated delineation of its path on the screen, independent from political and social processes. The pulse of the subway is free from social and political context—a history of eternal expansion. This becomes evident in the film's transitions from images of passengers entering and exiting ticket gates and getting on and off the subway to mappings of Metro's growth during each period. Thus, the takes marking the transitions to each of Metro's "stages" are accompanied by an animation showing the moving trajectories of Metro's map, reminiscent of both an electric circuit, and neural connections. The nodal branch is Línea 1, with Chamberí at its core. As it "naturally" branches out, Metro's connective tissue outlines a system of "paths" connecting the social body, and which (re)articulate Metro into a means to "make citizenry." The voiceover of the museum's film concludes with a reminder of this role—Metro's ultimate mission: "Madrid's Metro was born to unite its citizens"—while the footage displays a succession of shots indexing connectivity and movement: cogs and gears, crane shots of successive stations, and bodies ascending and descending through a system of elevators and escalators that index "precision," "rigor," and social "order."

In an analysis of the connections between the mines and social fabric of the Mexican state of Guanajuato, Elizabeth E. Ferry describes the (re)presentations of the caves—most converted to tourist sites—as embodiments of the region's glorious past, "whose dispersal or decay would lead to a dispersal or decay of the collective itself" (301). Similarly, in its conversion from technology to "patrimony" Metro is (re)presented as the vehicle for common memory, and thus emblem of social unity. Working through the continuity between technology-nature and culture, Andén 0 offers "nostalgia"—a space to a promised destiny through the imagination of a common past.

ANDÉN 0: VEHICLE TO THE "COAL(TURAL) TOWN"

Jules Verne's *The Underground City* (1877), known for a variety of titles including the revealing *Les Indes Noires* (Black Indies), narrates the success story of "Coal Town," an ideal mining community inside a mine in Aberfoyle, Scotland. Through careful planning, persistence, and reason—and because they are "morally" on the right *place*—the characters overcome a series of impediments posed by human envy and malice. "Coal Town" is an illustration of modernist thought rooted in the belief that the careful interventions in space—planning—would solve social inequalities.

Andén 0 welcomes the visitor to "a piece" of the Madrid's "Coal Town," a space cut off from social conflict, or, as Richard Morley describes it in his popular blog on Madrid's tourist destinations, a "refuge" from "today's frantic bustle." But the representation of the museum as absent of conflict draws from larger ideologies underpinning Metro as a catalyst for social change since its inauguration in 1919. Immersed in the teleology of biological and social "evolution," whereby technology, and nature, "progress," it follows that Metro's growth is a necessary path to social advancement. Madrid's popularly used slogan, "From Madrid to Heaven," feeds precisely from the idea that, when it comes to progress, the sky is the limit.[10]

The website for Andén 0 describes Metro not only as a time machine, but also as "part of the machinery for social change" after the industrial revolution. From its beginning, the subway was tied to a modernist-based plan, which sought to respond to the city's shortcomings, and offered solace to fears brought by the growing numbers of people arriving to the city. The

Metro company, *Compañía Urbanizadora Metropolitana,* initially a private enterprise, purchased land along subway stops in the peripheries. Its stated goal was to transform "lower-class neighborhoods" into residential areas with "the ultramodern criteria of other European nations" (Gómez-Santos, 88). Lack of hygiene and poverty in these areas, was, in the Modernist view, largely a result of their isolation from the city center and poor urban planning. Today, the current campaigns for Metro draw largely on its presentation as the vehicle for a more inclusive "citizenry," aligned with Madrid's popular slogan "Madrid, la suma de todos [the sum of all]." As a metonym for the MetroCity, Andén 0 becomes part of the machine for social change. Tony Bennett describes the museum as a machine that shapes social behaviors, which he traces to Modernity's fascination with architecture as a moral science. The belief that much desired social change will result from the overlap of scientific truth and technological power feeds the narrative of Metro in the museum, and the museum itself.

As a catalyst for social change, Metro is believed to bring citizens "closer," allowing the poorer classes to access "middle class" spaces and lifestyles. The tile advertisements along the platform (Andén 0), in addition to those projected onto its screens, remind the visitor (and user) that Metro is a track not just to move faster, but to achieve the middle class status associated with modernity. Ranging from the 1920s through the 1960s, the advertisements display the marketing of products, places, and events associated with middle class indulgence and "taste": the food distributor "Gota de Ámbar," food products (cookies, anise liquor, cognac, cigars, coffee, soda), brands for personal hygiene and care (perfumes and soaps, toothpaste, laxative water, medicines), a shopping center, leisure activities (film magazines, circus, night clubs, sports clubs), and technologies (light bulbs, watches, cement, explosives) (Figs. 8.10–8.11).[11]

Of all of the above, the advertisement for "Longines," "The best watch" is particularly telling (Fig. 8.12). Inseparable from the ideology of "deep time," modernity is framed by the invention of the clock, which Urry describes as "more important even than the steam engine" (*Mobilities*, 4). Incorporated in 1832, Longines became a symbol of tradition and elegance, recognized to the present for its emblem of the winged hourglass. Metro also prides itself on "flying through time" as indicated in its popular logo "Metro vuela." Lefebvre identifies the "measurement" of time as central to ideologies of modernity, and de Certeau shows the implications of the compartmentalization of time in the formation of "collective myths" (de Certeau, 25). Describing how this looks *culturally*, Sharon Zukin addresses the "reconstruction of the city" as "spectacle" for visual consumption ("The City," 21). The watch and the train turn time into a resource that can be measured, while Andén 0 becomes a

Figure 8.10. and Figure 8.11.   Tile advertisements. Photographs by Miguel A. Sandoval

Figure 8.12.   Advertisements for café "La Estrella," and for Longines captured immediately after Metro's crossing through the platform. Photograph by Miguel A. Sandoval.

stronghold for Metro as a "collective myth" of technological, environmental, and social "progress." Through its packaging as "visual" spectacle, a place that "speaks for itself," it illustrates Williams' observations that the transfer of properties of nature to technology was inseparable from the emergence of a canon of beauty that included technological environments (Williams, 83).

The (re)creation of memory in Andén 0 is, above all else, an exercise in aesthetics, and the space to "interpret" Metro's beauty, through the refurbishing of Chamberí's "dusty treasure" ("La estación"). Bennett describes the museum as a technology of modernity that runs on the effective combination of technology and culture in shaping social behaviors beginning in the nineteenth century. The architecture of the formerly abandoned station, its furniture, and the collection of imagery of its film, advertisements, and screens offer "culture."

The modernist belief of Metro as the vehicle to a "cultured city" remains as strong as ever, now accompanied by Andén 0, Metro's "cultural center." Andén 0 connects citizens to the history of the Metrocity, and also to its cultural sites. In addition to its inclusion in major cultural guides to the city, Andén 0 is a recommended stop during the Madrid's annual "Day of the Museums," where it has even become the scenario for live reenactments of Metro's inauguration ("Metro celebrará"). On November 7, 2010, *TeleMadrid* announced Metro's invitation to Madrileños to visit its "entrails," through a program that featured a visit to Andén 0 ("Los madrileños"). Seven months before, Metro had announced its collaboration with the Spanish Foundation for Technology and Science (FECYT) for the program "passport to science" whereby visitors received a stamp in the Metro stops corresponding to different museums, Andén 0 included ("Del Metro").

The (re)presentation of "Metro as culture" allows, on the one hand, its affirmation as a "monument," and, on the other, its perpetuation as part of the city's patrimony. James Young indicated the centrality of the monument in the modern era, "at the intersection between public art and political memory" (234). The construction of Metro as monument of Madrid's regional splendor is a par to Spain's controversies regarding the "monuments" of its national past, namely the removal of the last of Franco's statues in Santander in 2008 ("Tiran") and in Melilla in 2010 ("Retiran"), as well as current debates surrounding the destruction of the Valle de los Caídos outside Madrid—for some "national patrimony," while for others former internment camp (Martín-Cabrera). In a context where celebrations of nationhood are tinted with the memories of Spain's past dictatorship, Metro emerges at the intersection of historical memory, nature, and culture, to show a "monumentality" rooted in technological accomplishments—progress and expansion. The recent advertisement of Metro as the object of envy of a large Egyptian sphinx and of the Statue of Liberty is reminiscent of the celebration of the Brooklyn Bridge in 1883 as the "eighth wonder of the world, more powerful than the pyramids" (*Harper's Weekly*, qtd. in Dennis, 6).[12] Drawing from the same ideological quarry, Madrid's Metro has become a symbol of human power over nature, the "natural" landscape of progress, and part and parcel of Madrid's configuration as a sight for "culture." The descent into Metro signals the way to Madrid's "Coal Town," a (coal)tural capital of citizens with the moral integrity of Verne's protagonists.

An approximation to Metro through its museum is a window onto not only Madrid's past and future, as Gallardón announced at its inaugural event, but a better understanding of the ideologies "packaging" Metro as "cultural space," and "selling" it as an image of "public space" (Logan & Molotch). While undoubtedly an excellent form of transportation, and a legitimate source of regional pride, an active citizenry should turn a "watchful eye" to the economic motives underpinning much of Metro's rhetoric of commitment to history, nature, and culture.

Williams describes how the everyday experience "of looking down into the abyss" shaped technological and social consciousness through the Modern period. Andén 0, a cultural ambassador for Metro, wishes "to bring citizens closer to their history, and to recuperate a part of the collective memory and of the spaces that contain it" (*Andén 0*). But while Madrileños peek into their own abyss, Metro drills the way for Madrid's (coal)tural ascent to a global city.

NOTES

1. All translations mine unless indicated.

2. Preceded by the *Ley Boyer* and the *Plan para el transporte en las grandes ciudades* (1990–1993), the *Ley del Suelo* declares all space as subject to urban development, with the exception of national environmental reserves (and this, of course, is quite a malleable condition for most administrations).

3. The blog is provided by the Andén 1 Asociación de Amigos del Metro de Madrid. It is the only blog with a thread dedicated exclusively to Andén 0, which dates back to August 28, 2006, with a total of 688 messages. The author is grateful for the continuous assistance provided by the association Andén 1 and the members of its blog.

4. The municipal government announced the plans for the future reconstruction and restoration of Chamberí in 2006 ("El metro"), to be completed by 2007. In March 2008, the press announced the museum's definite opening for that spring (Villaba), one year after the anticipated deadline.

5. On two out of my six visits, I witnessed confused tourists who had descended into the museum thinking it was a "regular" Metro stop.

6. I have visited the museum on six occasions, and guides were present for half of my visits. In the absence of guides, the visitor can walk through the museum while surveillance cameras assure the guards at the entrance (normally two people) that he or she follows the "prescribed" route.

7. The pervasive visual consumption associated with Disneyland travels, for instance, emerges in responses to the museum in the blog Andén 2, specifically in suggestions on how to improve it. Various visitors to Andén 0 commented on the possibility of including a "ride" inside one of the older trains as part of the visit, "something like the train at Warner Amusement Park, or at a Renaissance Festival."

8. Most histories on Madrid's Metro do not elaborate the social and political contexts underlying Metro's construction and continuous expansion. Marino Gómez-Santos made the first attempt to write a book on Metro's history, incorporating some primary sources and historical references to outline the "evolution" of Metro from 1919 to 1969. Francisco Azorín narrates the various phases of Metro's expansion, but focuses more on the relations between each station below and its neighborhood above, drawing heavily on popular culture and on the "anecdotal." The most comprehensive coverage of Madrid's subway was published by Mohedas et al. (2010) to commemorate ninetieth anniversary of Metro (see bibliography). This book shows a careful gathering of primary materials (pictures, press coverage, maps, legal documents, and sections of urban plans), and offers a window to begin inquiring about the historical dynamics constitutive and constituting of Metro's journey. In addition, Juan Carlos Zamorano, current president of Andén 1 Asociación de Amigos del Metro, has two forthcoming books on the history of Metro.

9. The references to the environmental consciousness of Madrid's subway are central to its public image. Celebrations of Metro as the mode of transportation of a "clean" city run a par to news releases comparing the pollution of other means of transport to that of Metro. Following its role as a scientific and technological emblem,

Metro's image always resorts to "hard data." For instance, and specifically regarding the environment, a press release announced that each underground traveler equals planting thirty new trees in Madrid ("Un usuario").

10. Michael Saler describes the development of London's subway as a "model of aesthetic integration and communal service, a catalyst for a more harmonious London of the future" (124). Similarly, Matti Siemiatycki describes how these same ideas underpin the generalized support for Delhi's subway.

11. The company "Gota de Ámbar" was particularly strong during the 1930s. The advertisements for food products and brands include cognac "Domeck," cigars "Hija del Toro," Cookies "Patria," Anise liquor "San Fernando," the coffee brands "Nescafé" and "La Estrella," sodas "Fanta," soaps and perfumes "Gal," the toothpaste "Pepsodent," and the light bulbs Phillips (present in Spain since March 1926). Advertisements for leisure activities include the "Circo Segura," "Noche tropical," the "Real Hockey Club de Jérez," and the "Escuela española de equitación." The company Gal, still active today, is particularly relevant for its association since 1898 with a building considered a "masterpiece" of Madrid's Modernist architecture, the "Moncloa" building. The company was known for its advertisement, and for pioneering the study of consumer behaviors at the turn to the twentieth century. The tile advertisement for the shopping center "Almacenes Rodríguez" is also particularly relevant. The company was one of the first referents of its kind in the city, and its building one of the first to stand along the Gran Vía, now demolished. On its former location in Gran Vía 19, now stands the Court for Contentious Administrative Proceedings.

12. Both advertisements are part of a larger campaign by the company McCann Erickson for Metro in 2008 and appear in numerous websites, including the following site for the blog on marketing and advertisement "B-Make": www.agencia-de-publicidad.es/blog/publicidad-metro-de-madrid.

BIBLIOGRAPHY

Álvarez, Pilar. "La tuneladora emerge en Atocha." *El País* February 11, 2011. www.elpais.com/articulo/espana/tuneladora/emerge/Atocha/elpepuesp/20110211elpepunac_24/Tes.

Andén 0. "Andén 0—Museum Information Guide." *Estación de Chamberí-Nave de Motores*. 2008.

Andén 0. Museum film.

"Andén 0. Centro de Interpretación del Metro de Madrid. Página oficial." www.esmadrid.com/anden0/.

"Andén 1 valora positivamente los primeros meses de Andén 0 y aporta sugerencias para su mejora." "Andén 1." June 1, 2008. www.anden1.org/comunicados/36.

"Andén 2." Asociación de Amigos del Metro de Madrid. "Andén 2." www.anden1.org/anden2/foro/viewtopic.php?f=33&t=102.

Anuncio Metro Madrid Plurirreportaje. July 28, 2007. www.youtube.com/watch?v=knZYEw-3taA&NR=1.

Augé, Marc. *Oblivion.* Trans. Marjolijn de Jager. Minneapolis: University of Minnesota Press, 2004.

Azorín, Francisco. *Madrid y el Metro caminan juntos*. Madrid: Rubiños, 1997.

Bailey, Peter. "Adventures in Space: Victorian Railway Erotics, or Taking Alienation for a Ride." *Journal of Victorian Culture* 9.1 (2004): 1–21.

Bennett, Tony. *The Birth of the Museum. History, Theory, Politics*. New York: Routledge, 1995.

Bissell, David. "Conceptualising Differently-Mobile Passengers: Geographies of Everyday Encumbrance in the Railway Station." *Social and Cultural Geography* 10.2 (2009): 173–195.

"B-Make. El blog de marketing y publicidad." www.agencia-de-publicidad.es/blog/publicidad-metro-de-madrid/.

Calvo López, Rodrigo, Patricia Molina Costa, Natalia Rieznik Lamana, Almudena Sanchez Moya y Eva Garcia Pérez. "La explosión urbana de la conurbación madrileña." *Madrid, ¿la suma de todos? Globalización, territorio, desigualdad*. Ed. Observatorio Metropolitano. Madrid: Traficantes de Sueños, 2007. 223–316.

de Certeau, Michel. *The Practice of Everyday Life*. Berkeley: University of California Press, 1984.

Cohen, David William. *The Combing of History*. Chicago: The University of Chicago Press, 1994.

de Cózar, A. and V. Gutiérrez. "Los grafiteros destrozan la estación de Chamberí, cerrada hace 37 años." *El País* August 10, 2003. www.elpais.com/articulo/madrid/grafiteros/destrozan/estacion/Chamberi/cerrada/hace/37/anos/elpepiespmad/20030810elpmad_1/Tes.

"De estación fantasma a museo." *El País* March 24, 2008. www.elpais.com/articulo/espana/estacion/fantasma/museo/elpepuesp/20080324elpepunac_10/Tes.

Dell'Amore, Christine. "Step Back in Time to the Birth of Madrid's Metro." *The Washington Post* February 15, 2009. www.washingtonpost.com/wp-dyn/content/article/2009/02/13/AR2009021301531.html.

"Del Metro a los museos." *El Mundo* April 26, 2010. www.elmundo.es/elmundo/2010/04/26/madrid/1272278420.html.

Dennis, Richard. *Cities in Modernity: Representations and Productions of Metropolitan Space, 1840–1930*. Cambridge, UK: Cambridge University Press, 2008.

"El metro tendrá en 2007 un museo en la 'estación fantasma' de Chamberí." *El País* February 19, 2006. www.elpais.com/articulo/madrid/metro/tendra/2007/museo/estacion/fantasma/Chamberi/elpepiautmad/20060219elpmad_18/Tes.

Ferry, Elizabeth Emma. "Memory as Wealth, History as Commerce: A Changing Economic Landscape in Mexico." *ETHOS* 34.2: 297–324.

Foucault, Michel. *The Archaeology of Knowledge*. 1969. Trans. A. M. Sheridan Smith. London and New York: Routledge, 2002.

Foucault, Michel, and Jay Miskowiec. "Of Other Spaces." *Diacritics* 16.1 (spring 1986): 22–27.

Fraser, Derek, and Anthony Sutcliffe. "The City as a Natural System: Theories of Urban Society in Early Nineteenth-Century Britain." *The Pursuit of Urban History*. Eds. D. Fraser and A. Sutcliffe. London: Edward Arnold, 1983. 349–370.

Gómez-Santos, Marino. *El Metro de Madrid. Medio Siglo al Servicio de la Ciudad 1919–1969*. Madrid: Escelier, 1969.

Goss, Jon. "Once-upon-a-Time in the Commodity World: An Unofficial Guide to Mall of America." *Annals of the Association of American Geographers* 89.1 (1999): 45–75.

"Hallan fósiles de 13 millones de años en obras de Metro de Madrid." *El Universo*. May 26, 2008. www.eluniverso.com/2008/05/26/0001/1064/D8657FC-F114A48E69D897B1B4454C122.html.

Harvey, David. *The Urban Experience*. Baltimore: The John Hopkins University Press, 1989.

———. Heritage Pasts and Heritage Presents: Temporality, Meaning, and the Scope of Heritage Studies." *International Journal of Heritage Studies* 7.4 (2001): 319–338.

Hewison Robert. *The Heritage Industry: Britain in a Climate of Decline*. London: Methuen, 1987.

Hutton, Patrick H. *History as an Art of Memory*. Hanover: University Press of New England, 1993.

Huyssen, Andreas. "Present Pasts: Media, Politics, Amnesia." *Public Culture* 12.1 (2000): 21–38.

"Inauguradas la estación de Metro y la plaza de Opera, modernizadas con 22,1 millones de inversión." *Telemadrid*. March 23, 2011. www.telemadrid. es/?q=noticias/madrid/noticia/inauguradas-la-estacion-de-metro-y-la-plaza-de-opera-modernizadas-con-221-mi.

Kirshenblatt-Gimblett, Barbara. *Destination Culture: Touristm, Museums, and Heritage*. Berkeley: University of California Press, 1998.

"La antigua estación de Metro de Chamberí vuelve a abrirse al público como museo de la historia del suburbano." *Diario Siglo XXI*. March 24, 2008. www.diariosigloxxi. com/texto-ep/mostrar/20080324142159.

"La estación fantasma de Chamberí ha recibido más de 30.000 visitas desde su apertura." *El Mundo* June 17, 2008. www.elmundo.es/elmundo/2008/06/17/madrid/1213703899.html.

Lefebvre, Henri. *The Production of Space*. Oxford, MA: Basil Blackwell, Ltd., 1991.

———. Writings on Cities. Oxford, UK: Blackwell Publishers, 1996.

Logan, John R., and Harvey L. Molotch. *Urban Fortunes. The Political Economy of Place*. Berkeley: University of California Press, 1987.

López, Isidro. "Sin los pies en el suelo. Acumulación de capital y ocupación de territorio en la Comunidad de Madrid." *Madrid, ¿la suma de todos? Globalización, territorio, desigualdad*. Ed. Observatorio Metropolitano. Madrid: Traficantes de Sueños, 2007. 171–220.

"Los madrileños podrán conocer las entrañas de Metro de Madrid." *Telemadrid*. November 7, 2010. www.telemadrid.es/?q=noticias/madrid/noticia/los-madrilenos-podran-conocer-partir-las-entranas-de-metro-de-madrid-dentro-.

"Los primeros usuarios 'no-fantasmas' de la estación fantasma." Video. *El Mundo*. March 25, 2008. www.elmundo.es/elmundo/2008/03/25/videos/1206462511.html.

Martín-Cabrera, Luis. "Los lugares de la memoria: maerialidad y justicia radical en las postdictaduras del Cono Sur y de España." *Memoriando.com*. www.memoriando. com/noticias/101–200/114A.html.

Masterson-Algar, Araceli. "Madrid: Migrants' Place in the MetroCity." Connections. *European Studies Annual Review* 4 (2008): 60–80.

"Metro celebrará el domingo el Día de los Museos con una recreación de la inauguración del suburbano en la estación de Chamberí." *Europapress.es.* May 15, 2009. http://www.europapress.es/madrid/noticia-metro-celebrara-domingo-dia-museos-recreacion-inauguracion-suburbano-estacion-chamberi-20090515162240.html.

Mohedas, Cesar, Juan C. Zamorano, Eduardo Gallego, Jaime Touzón, Javier Bernal, Pedro Muñoz, and Pablo López. *90 Años de metro en Madrid. De Cuatro Caminos a Hospital del Henares.* Ediciones La Libreria: Madrid, 2010.

Morley, Richard. "Madrid Metro Museum at Chamberí." *A View of Madrid: A Guiri's View of Madrid with Occasional Excursions Outside.* March 13, 2009. http://aviewofmadrid.blogspot.com/search?q=Madrid+Metro+Museum.

"Museo en el Metro de Chamberí." *Lukor.* October 16, 2009. www.lukor.com/viajes/08032402.htm.

Nora, Pierre. "Between Memory and History. Les Lieux de Memóire." *Representations* 26 (1989): 7–12.

Philo, C., and G. Kearns (Eds.). *Selling Places: The City as Cultural Capital, Past and Present.* Oxford: Pergamon Press, 1993.

"Retiran de Melilla la última estatua ecuestre de Franco expuesta en España." *El Mundo* August 4, 2010. www.elmundo.es/elmundo/2010/08/04/espana/1280942589.html.

Rodríguez Lopez, Emmanuel. "La ciudad global o la nueva centralidad de Madrid." *Madrid, ¿la suma de todos? Globalización, territorio, desigualdad.* Ed. Observatorio Metropolitano. Madrid: Traficantes de Sueños, 2007. 41–81.

Saler, Michael. "The 'Medieval Modern' Underground: Terminus of the Avant Garde." *Modernism/Modernity* 2.1 (1995): 113–144.

Siemiatycki, Matti. "Message in a Metro: Building Urban Rail Infrastructure and Image in Delhi, India." *International Journal of Urban and Regional Research* 30.2 (2006): 277–292.

Shortland, Michael. "Darkness Visible: Underground Culture in the Golden Age of Geology." *Science History* 32 (1994): 1–61.

Soja, Edward W. *Thirdspace: Journeys to Los Angeles and Other Real-and-Imagined Places.* Cambridge, MA: Blackwell, 1996.

Thrift, Nigel. *Spatial Formations.* London: Sage, 1996.

"Tiran abajo la última estatua de Franco en España." *El País* December 19, 2008. www2.elpais.com.uy/081219/pinter-388264/internacional/tiran-abajo-la-ultima-estatua-de-franco-en-espana/.

Trotter, David. *Circulation: Defoe, Dickens and the Economies of the Novel.* London: MacMillan, 1988.

"Una estación fantasma de Metro convertida en museo." *ADN* March 24, 2008.

"Un usuario de metro equivale a plantar 30 árboles en Madrid." *El Mundo* January 23, 2008. http://www.elmundo.es/elmundo/2008/01/23/madrid/1201113250.htm.

Urry, John. *Consuming Places.* London: Routledge, 1995.

———. *Mobilities.* New York: Polity, 2007.

Verne, Jules. *The Underground City.* Hardpress: Lexington, 2011.

Villaba, Enrique. "La estación fantasma abrirá por primavera." *Madridiario. es*. March 6, 2008. www.madridiario.es/2008/Marzo/madrid/madrid/ 64213/la-estacion-fantasma-abrira-por-primavera-las-artes-ayuntamiento-madrid gallardon-alicia-moreno.html.

Williams, Rosalind. *Notes on the Underground*. Cambridge, MA: MIT Press, 2008.

Young, James. "Memory/Monument." *Critical Terms for Art History*. 2nd ed. Eds. Robert S. Nelson and Richard Shiff. Chicago & London: University of Chicago Press, 2003: 234–250.

Zukin, Sharon. *Loft Living: Culture and Capital in Urban Change*. Baltimore: John Hopkins University Press, 1989.

——. *The Cultures of Cities*. Malden, MA: Blackwell, 1995.

——. "The City as a Landscape of Power." *Global Finance and Urban Living*. Eds. S. Lash and J. Friedman. London: Routledge, 1992.

Part V

Shifting States

Chapter 9

Trains, Modernity, and State Formation in Meiji Japan

Tristan R. Grunow

On a clear day too warm to be the middle of December, a crowd of roughly 1,500 thronged to the plaza in front of the south end of Tokyo Station and gazed up at the magnificent "Renaissance Style" building rising before them. Equally impressive was the lineup of officials and politicians on stage. The chief engineer of the Railway Bureau read a report on the construction of the station, followed by a ceremonial address from the president of the Railway Bureau. Prime Minister Ôkuma Shigenobu added a few words as someone who had supported railways from the beginning. Finally, Tokyo Mayor Sakatani Yoshio gave a congratulatory address, and the crowd celebrated the opening of Tokyo Station, "The Gateway to the Imperial Capital," as fireworks exploded in the early winter sky.[1]

The crowd was exuberant. It was December 18, 1914, and World War I had broken out the previous summer. Japan stood poised to assert itself as a dominant world power as Europe was overcome by internecine warfare. Japan had jumped at the opportunity to declare war on Germany and to expand its power into China by occupying German possessions in Shantung and in the Pacific. Now the general of the Shantung occupying force, Kamio Mitsuomi, was returning to Tokyo to report to the Emperor. According to plan, General Kamio arrived on the first train into Tokyo Station at exactly 10:30 a.m., as the climax of the opening ceremony. Fireworks continued overhead as the crowd enthusiastically cheered the return of their "triumphant general" (*gaisen shôgun*), by waving flags and shouting "*Banzai!*" The general made his way through the Japanese version of the *Arc de Triomphe*, the celebratory "Great Green Arch" and adjacent pair of "Green Pyramidal Towers" specially erected in the stationfront plaza, and was paraded to the Imperial Palace down the appropriately named "Triumphal Return Boulevard" (*Gaisen Dôro*). Such pomp and circumstance was befitting of a country that saw itself as, and that was intent on being recognized as, a first-class power.[2]

It was no accident that such a celebration of Japan's empire coincided with the opening ceremony of Tokyo Station. The Japanese nation-state and its international reputation were directly tied to the station, the capstone of Meiji efforts of state formation through railway construction and centralization on the capital. Charged with shaping an agrarian and politically decentralized Japan into an industrialized and united nation capable of withstanding European and American encroachment, the leaders of the new Meiji government looked to railways and a grand capital city as the most powerful vehicles for achieving their political goals.

A railway network focused on Tokyo provided the infrastructure for national unification, reinforcing government efforts to centralize and standardize the nation. Locomotives and western-style buildings, meanwhile, advanced ideological unification by means of modernity, "civilization and enlightenment," and the emperor system. After fostering and guiding a national railway network of government and private railway lines, the Meiji government set about refashioning Tokyo into the capital of Japanese modernity through the introduction of western architecture and urban planning. The centerpiece of this transformation was Tokyo Station. Located at the heart of the capital, Tokyo Station was the junction of parallel tracks of state formation through political integration and ideological unification: it was the intersection of national railway construction and monumental capital city planning; its Western design, and its roles as a grand metropolitan rail depot and the emperor's personal station, meanwhile, cast the station as the epitome of "civilization and enlightenment." The opening of Tokyo Station in 1914, two years after the end of the Meiji era, marked the forging of a Tokyo model of colonialist state formation. As the Japanese empire expanded during the late nineteenth and early twentieth centuries, this Tokyo model was replicated in Taipei and Seoul toward the goal of integrating the newly acquired colonies of Taiwan and Korea into the empire. Thus guided by the ideas and practices of expansionism perfected by the Western nations, and linked to the goals of progress and civilization, government leaders propelled Japan down a track of state formation that led directly to the establishment of the Japanese Empire.

The contribution of railways to the political unification of nation-states has long been acknowledged and discussed. In Europe, railways played a primary role in the national communication and transportation networks that were so important in integrating distant regions into consolidated nations, as well as in developing national identities. The national railway network was given credit for uniting independent states into the nation of Italy during the

Risorgimento.[3] In France, as Eugen Weber has argued, "There could be no national unity before there was national circulation . . . So roads, of stone or steel, welded the several parts into one."[4] Mathew Truesdell adds:

> Moreover, these new links between Paris and the provinces seemed to many to be uniting the country in a way that went beyond more rapid and efficient travel. France seemed to becoming an integrated unit rather than a miscellaneous collection of provinces. Railroad inaugurations took on a particular fascination because every new line seemed to mark another step in these important transformations.[5]

Railways played a similar role in the integration of individual German states into a united Germany, as Abigail Green has argued:

> Railways linked hitherto distant towns, regions, and countries; facilitated the mobility of goods, people and ideas; encouraged the development of regional, national, and international markets; transformed popular perceptions of time and space. More specifically, railways construction played a crucial role in what Hans-Ulrich Wehler has termed the "dual revolution" — the twin processes of industrialization and national unification that changed the face of Germany during the 1850s and 1860s.[6]

Juan Batista Alberdi, an Argentine statesman, amplified the consolidating effect of railways in the South American context when he observed that the railway:

> will unify the Argentine republic better than any congress. A congress can declare a country one and indivisible; but without the iron road, which draws together a nation's far-flung extremes, the country will for ever remain divisible and divided in spite of all legislative mandates. Thus political unity must begin with territorial unity, and only the railroad can make a single area out of two places separated by 500 leagues.[7]

Studies of modern state formation in Japan, however, have often neglected the role of railways. Such studies have focused more on Meiji efforts to modernize the nation politically and industrially, and to unify the Japanese people ideologically. Replacement of the domains with prefectures, standardization of cadastral surveys, the emperor system, "civilization and enlightenment," the education system, the Imperial Constitution, and the establishment of the Japanese literary canon and historical tradition are all often described as components of Japanese state formation.[8] Two factors that should not be overlooked, however, are the construction of the national railway network and the re-creation of Tokyo into the capital of Japanese modernity. By discussing the growth of the national railway network and the transformation of Tokyo, this chapter will argue that trains and tangible manifestations of "modernity" played a vital role in the creation of the modern Japanese nation-state.

THE JAPANESE NATIONAL RAILWAY NETWORK

Railways were already known in Japan in March of 1854, when American Commodore Mathew Perry presented the Tokugawa Shogunate with a miniature model railway. Although the strange machine circling the track laid down by the Americans fascinated the many gathered Japanese spectators and officials, including one "dignified mandarin" who took a joyride atop the carriage, it was not until after the Meiji Restoration of 1868 that Japan's first railway was completed.[9]

While Japan had been increasingly consolidated by three successive "unifiers" in the sixteenth century and ruled by the Tokugawa for over 250 years, the leaders of the new Meiji government perceived a threatening retention of feudalism and a weak national consciousness on the part of the commoners.[10] "Feudalism still remains even after the downfall of the Shogunate, and stands in the way of national unification," lamented railway proponent and two-time Prime Minister Ôkuma Shigenobu in 1902.[11] Chief of the Railway Bureau Inoue Masaru echoed this sentiment in 1910, explaining that the communication and transportation networks of Japan were inadequate for a modern nation. The mountainous terrain of the Japanese islands forced nation-wide land transportation networks to rely mainly on foot power, making travel slow and difficult, and hampering rapid long-distance communication along the national roads.[12] To impede travel further, the previous Tokugawa government required permits to travel, and barriers (*sekisho*) were placed on major highways to regulate and control transit.[13]

To government leaders, the destruction of this persisting feudalism and the formation of national consciousness were necessary to integrate the nation and defend Japan from Western imperialism. After the Meiji Restoration of 1868, the Meiji leaders assembled a toolkit of modernity to reshape Japan into a strong nation-state. In addition to the government institutions, industries, and policies adopted and adapted from the West, this toolkit also included more tangible elements of modernity such as railways, architecture, telegraphs, modern hygiene, and modern urban planning and infrastructure. Anticipating a unified nation, the Meiji leaders, set to work with this toolkit to construct "modernity" in Japan and to "propagate this idea of a new national structure, and thereby to impress the people of its own *raison d'être*."[14] Modern transportation and communications, such as the railway and the telegraph, contributed to national consciousness, Kenneth Pyle writes, "by overcoming local isolation, also contributed to the growth of national consciousness."[15] New state flags, ceremonies, and traditions were invented and embraced; a new school system was created to foster loyal subjects; a conscript military was formed with modern armaments; state Shinto was crafted with the emperor as its center, all as a means to engender nationalism in the people. As Mary Elizabeth Berry acknowledges: "The work of nationalism, and the creation of its essentially new symbols, was the work of Meiji."[16]

Railways were especially useful tools in the endeavor to eliminate feudalism and centralize and standardize the nation on the capital of Tokyo. Because of their speed, and their ability to "dissolv[e] previous barriers of space and time," railways allowed spatial and temporal connections between the core and periphery that were impossible before.[17] As Eric J. Hobsbawm argued, the "agents" of the state, including postal workers, teachers, police and railway engineers, "increasingly reach[ed] down to the humblest inhabitant of the least of its villages."[18] "Revolutions in transport and communication typified by railway and telegraph," Hobsbawm continued, "tightened and routinized the links between central authority and its remotest outposts."[19] With the advent of a national railway network traversing historical boundaries and linking insular regions, even Japanese living in remote villages would only be a short temporal distance from the capital. No longer would they be far removed, spatially and temporally, from central authority.

This political potential of railways was not lost on the Meiji leaders. As Ôkuma recalled in 1902:

> To consolidate the hearts and minds of all the people, it is imperative to first demolish such an inconvenient transportation and shipping system (*unyu kôtsû*). Furthermore, some project to cause a great stir among the people is vital to demolish feudal regionalist thought (*hôkenteki kakkyo no shisô*). Therefore, just as [I was] pondering whether or not there was any effective means to do this, [I] heard about this railway debate. With such things as motivation, it was then decided that railways were the overall best option, and from then on plans were made to initiate railways.[20]

After securing financing from the London-based Oriental Bank, the government set about building a twenty-nine kilometer line between Tokyo and the nearby treaty port of Yokohama in 1870.[21] Identical terminal stations, designed by the American architect R. P. Bridgens in the image of the Gare de l'Est in Paris, were placed on each end of the line in Tokyo and Yokohama.[22] The official opening ceremony of the line was held in the presence of the Meiji Emperor on October 14, 1872, marking the inauguration of the Japanese national railway network. "At this time, we announce the completion our country's initial railway," the emperor proclaimed to the assembled crowd, " . . . we earnestly pray (*koinegau*) that this enterprise [of railways] will expand, and this line will spread like a vine (*manpu*) across the whole country."[23] With this imperial mandate, the Railway Bureau, led by Inoue Masaru, set about extending the national railway network. The trunk line between Kobe and Osaka was completed in 1874, and extended to the old capital of Kyoto in 1876.[24] Planning and surveying commenced for the trunk line connecting the old capital of Kyoto to the new capital of Tokyo. Government railway construction was interrupted, however, by the Satsuma Rebellion of 1877 and the financial crisis that followed.

Facing financial difficulties the Meiji government allowed the establishment of the Nippon Railway Company in 1881, initiating an important new stage of Japanese railway development. Thereafter, until the nationalization of the seventeen top-performing railway companies in 1906–1907, Japanese railway development was dominated by private enterprise. Seeing profits made the Nippon Railway, private railway companies proliferated rapidly in the first of two private railway "manias" in the second half of the 1880s.[25] As many as fifteen charters were awarded for new companies by 1891, and the number of private railway companies peaked at sixty-six in 1897 before mergers and company failures reduced the number to thirty-nine in 1906. As a result of this private railway speculation, the length of private railways increased rapidly. Whereas the 840 kilometers of private tracks were slightly less than the 881 kilometers of government lines in 1889, private lines surpassed the government lines by the next year, extending to 1,357 kilometers. Private railways continued to far outpace the government lines over the following years, more than doubling the government's 2,413 kilometers of track with 5,213 kilometers of private track in 1906.[26]

Yet although the government yielded construction of railways to private companies, it did not relinquish guidance or control of the expanding national network. Through regulations placed on the private companies, and a succession of legislative initiatives, such as the 1887 Private Railway Ordinance, the 1892 Railway Construction Act, and the 1900 Private Railway Law and Railway Operation Law, the government ensured that the privately constructed lines would be compatible with the government lines. Finally, the government nationalized seventeen private railway companies in 1906–1907.

The regulations placed on Nippon Railway, the largest of the private railway companies, are illustrative of government attempts to influence and direct the private companies. "As part of the special charter awarded to Nippon Railway, the government maintained 'strict and comprehensive control . . . over all phases of railway business, including construction accounts, and rate-making.'"[27] After arranging for local governments to purchase the necessary land, the central government also protected the financial stability of the company and even constructed and operated the lines for Nippon Railway. The concession for the lines and rights-of-way was set to expire after ninety-nine years, and the government reserved the right to repurchase the lines after fifty years. The agreement also stipulated that construction of the lines should begin within six months of the awarding of the charter, and all lines should be completed within seven years. Nippon Railways itself was only responsible for providing funds and purchasing materials, further guaranteeing that the tracks, facilities, and rolling stock of the company would be compatible with those of the government lines.[28]

In addition to attempts to directly influence the private railway companies, the government responded to the private railway "manias" with legislation to ensure that future lines would be built to the same technical standards as the state railways. With strong support from the military, special regulations were issued in the Private Railway Ordinance (*Shisetsu Tetsudô Jôrei*) in May 1887 codifying the concessions made to companies "as a first step towards securing uniformity of operation under State control."[29] As Steven J. Ericson observes, "the regulations were actually meant to control more than to assist railway companies."[30] While this ordinance helped private railway companies in acquiring land, it also reduced the amount of financial aid given by the government and lowered the government repurchase option term to only twenty-five years. The regulations also enabled the government to direct the private companies where to build lines, in order to link individual private networks and to avoid redundancies.[31]

Subsequent laws extended government control over the private network and more directly safeguarded compatibility of the government and private networks. The Railway Construction Law (*Tetsudô Fusetsu Hô*) of 1892 allowed the government the right to purchase private lines judged necessary to complete the projected trunk network centered on Tokyo, and also gave the government the ability to determine where new private trunk lines would be constructed and which lines should be built first. Meanwhile, the Private Railway Law (*Shisetsu Tetsudô Hô*) and the Railway Operation Law (*Tetsudô Eigyô Hô*), both enacted in 1900, greatly enhanced the authority of the Railway Minister over both the government and the private railways, and extended government control to passenger and cargo fares.[32]

Economic prosperity following the Sino–Japanese War of 1894–1895 led to the second railway mania, lasting from 1895–1898. Yet a post-boom recession in 1898–1899 saw the dissolution of no fewer than fifteen companies because of lack of funds. Mergers and absorption of competitors became common, and the number of private railways reduced from sixty-six in 1897 to thirty-nine in 1906. Calls for nationalization, which generally ebbed and flowed corresponding to the strength or weakness of the economy, gained strength.[33]

Sentiment for nationalization increased further during the Russo–Japanese War of 1904–1905. According to a government report on nationalization, two determining factors in the nationalization process were "the national spirit of expansion engendered by the successful war with Russia, and the need of the times for the speedy development of national industry."[34] Indeed, by the time of the Russo–Japanese War, the Japanese economy had turned toward heavy industry, causing an increase in domestic freight volumes. With this shift, even staunch capitalists began to favor nationalization, as it would strengthen distribution networks. Prominent businessman Shibusawa Eiichi, for example, heavily involved in private railways as an investor in the Nippon Railway Company, had argued strongly against calls for nationalization. Realizing the potential for nationalization to improve distribution, however, he became a promoter of nationalization. The military also strongly supported nationalization. Anticipating that future wars on the continent would require efficient lines of logistics, the military advocated consolidating the Japanese, Manchurian, and Korean railways into an integrated imperial railway network.[35]

With the support of prominent businessmen and the military, the Railway Nationalization Law was forced through the Diet in March 1906 after all opposing lawmakers walked out of the voting. This law cleared the way for the purchase and nationalization of seventeen private railways, in addition to the Keifu Railway Company in Korea, the first step in the military's envisioned imperial railway network.[36] As a result of the nationalization, government-owned lines, which had previously only accounted for 30% of the national total, increased to almost 90% of all Japanese railways.[37] After nationalization, tracks owned solely by the government stretched from northern Honshû all the way to Kyûshû in the southwest, and were located on all four of the main islands of the Japanese archipelago. Tokyo, moreover, was located at the physical and conceptual center of an integrated railway network that conveyed central authority to all corners of the nation.

FROM TOKYO TO *TEITO*, THE IMPERIAL CAPITAL

Tokyo's location at the heart of the emerging railway network reinforced its role as the center and the standard for the rest of the nation. Following the Meiji Restoration, the Meiji leaders had sough to re-create Tokyo as *Teito*, the grand "imperial capital" of a unified Japan. Gavin Shatkin has suggested that the first political function of capital cities is to "present an 'argument' for the legitimacy of [the national government's] policies and programmes by presenting the capital as a symbol of progress that represents a template for the rest of the nation to follow."[38] In this way, as the capital of the new Meiji government, Tokyo became a "showcase" for the government to demonstrate to the people of Japan the authority of the central government.[39] As such, Tokyo was the focus of, and the force behind, several methods of what James C. Scott calls "state projects" of "legibility" and "simplification."[40] Similarly, Jeffrey E. Hanes has argued that in the Meiji period "centralization was achieved through standardization."[41] The Tokyo dialect became the standard language of Japan; local Tokyo solar time was made the standard measure of clock-time for the entire country in 1879, and the 1887 Railway Bureau "Service Regulations for Staff Engaged in Operating Railways" declared that "The standard time of each station shall be Tokyo time, and shall be transmitted to station by telegraph every day."[42] Finally, Tokyo was the "standard reference" of the entire national transportation and communication networks, as "all routes were differentiated as either 'going towards Tokyo (*Nobori*)' or 'going away from Tokyo (*Kudari*).'"[43]

Along with expanding bureaucratic control into the periphery, such efforts of centralization and standardization allowed the central government to integrate its population and control its territory, a process that David Nugent has called the "annihilation of regional space by state power."[44] Referring to the similar role of Paris in French modernization and state formation, French historian Eugen Weber has described this centralized process of acculturation on one city as akin to domestic "colonization."[45] Like Paris, Tokyo became the metropole of a colonialist form of state formation through centralization on the national capital.

Yet the intended audience of Tokyo as a showcase was not only internal, but also external, as Japan hoped to renegotiate the unequal treaties it had signed with the Western powers. During the age of imperialism, Anthony D. King points out, national capitals proliferated as one of the "logical outcome[s]" of the nation-state."[46] Internationally, Evelyn Schulz writes, these monumental capital cities were "regarded as symbols of the progress of mankind and as the embodiment of modern civilization," and "physical representations of the power and wealth of the nation-states then competing with each other."[47] For a Meiji government that tied its domestic legitimacy and international reputation to modernity and teleological progress, the national capital, often used to "express a vision of an idealized future," became a space that showcased the modernization and Westernization of Japan.[48] The monumentally refashioned Tokyo thus became the international symbol of the united, modernizing state and "an official sign of Japan's progress and prosperity."[49]

The transformation of Tokyo into a grand national capital culminated in the opening of Tokyo Station as part of a stately and modern urban space. Although not a constant process, this re-creation of the capital started with the construction of the Ginza Bricktown in 1872, and grew stronger in the 1880s with the Yoshikawa Plan and the Tokyo Urban Improvement Ordinance. With these urban planning initiatives, as the Meiji leaders saw the need for and the potential to create a grand capital, Tokyo was recast along lines similar to Napoleon III and Baron Haussmann's Paris and Wilhelmine Berlin to become a symbolic imperial capital on a par with the Western capitals.

The first stage in the re-creation of Tokyo was initiated on February 26, 1872, just four years after the Meiji Restoration, when a great fire broke out in the Ginza district of Tokyo. Raging over ninety-five hectares of land in the center of the city, the burnt area provided the Meiji leaders with a blank canvas on which to paint the model of a modern national capital.[50] Instead of allowing reconstruction of traditional buildings, Meiji leaders Ôkuma Shigenobu and Inoue Kaoru seized the opportunity to rebuild the area in a showcase of "civilization and enlightenment" as a Western-style "impressive and fire-resistance district suitable for the imperial capital."[51] At the hands of the Meiji government, the new Ginza would rise from the smoldering ashes of the traditional Low City as the first step in transforming Tokyo into a beacon of modernity. As Fujimori Terunobu writes, for the Japanese government, "the door to "civilization" (*bunmei*) was in Ginza."[52] Ishizuka Hiromichi has also suggested that the construction of the Ginza Bricktown was the first step of re-creating Tokyo as a grand imperial capital. As Ishizuka argues:

> The new government, at the time the sole external representative of Japan, was in the process of also becoming the sole domestic unified ruler. As such, the first undertaking in the project of establishing an imperial capital suitable for a centrally ruled, unified nation was the construction of the Ginza Bricktown.[53]

The government hired English engineer Thomas Waters to design the building plans in a suitably modern and "civilized" style in the image of Regent Street in London or the Rue de Rivoli in Paris.[54] New Western buildings were constructed of red brick with stuccoed plaster facades, giving the district its popular moniker: the Ginza Bricktown.[55] Roads were widened to 27 m, 18 m, 14.4 m, and 5.4 m, and were paved with brick. When they were completed in 1877, main streets were lined with Japan's first gas lamps, and pine, cherry, and maple trees separated street traffic from pedestrians, marking Japan's first sidewalks.[56]

As the Ginza Bricktown illustrated, the most visually stunning and effective way for Japan to showcase its modernity, and to demonstrate that it was "worthy of being treated as a equal among other developed nations," was through the use of Western architecture in the capital.[57] As William Coaldrake argues, "Architecture was charged with a mission of the highest national significance: proclaiming loudly on every city block and street corner Japan's assurance and authority as a modern state."[58]

In addition to introducing Western architecture into Tokyo, from the 1880s, the Meiji government began attempting to re-create the urban space of Tokyo in the model of the Western capitals, particularly Paris—a process that Schulz has called the "Paris-ization of Tokyo."[59] For Japanese leaders and planners during the Meiji Period, the level of a city's modernity could be measured not only by its buildings, but also by its urban infrastructure, particularly its streets, parks, and sewers. In addition to the famous boulevards carved out of the slums of Paris, for example, Napoleon III and Haussmann's improvements included twenty-two new parks, collector sewers under the streets, and a new system to provide Paris with fresh spring water.[60] Similarly, the transformation of Tokyo into a grand national capital would require more than a superficial facelift of a limited area of the central district, as seen in the Ginza Bricktown. Rather, it would entail a more comprehensive renovation of the city through modernization of its architecture and urban infrastructure.

This endeavor of modeling Tokyo on the European capitals was initiated with the city's first venture into large-scale city planning, the 1880 "Tokyo Central District Demarcation Issues" (*Tôkyô Chûô Shiku Kakutei no Mondai*) submitted by Tokyo Governor Matsuda Michiyuki. Matsuda's plan concentrated redevelopment efforts in the central areas of Tokyo in order to create a high-density central business district, while clearing slums to clearly demarcate the rich and poor areas of the city in the process. Improvements included plans for public buildings, roads, canals, bridges, gas and water lines, and port facilities to make Tokyo into a major international commercial city. This focus on slum clearing, infrastructural improvements, and development of commerce display what André Sorensen calls a "revealing lack of concern for the symbolic project of creating a great imperial capital."[61] Yet they do indicate that Tokyo city planners had begun to incorporate Western urban planning initiatives and advances into plans for the Japanese capital.

Matsuda's "Central District Demarcation Issues" was revised and expanded by Tokyo Governor Yoshikawa Akimasa in 1884. Yoshikawa's new proposal, called the Urban Improvement Statement (*Shiku Kaisei Ikensho*), improved on Matsuda's plan by extending its focus beyond the central areas of the city and envisioning Tokyo as both a commercial and political metropolis.[62] Calling for the modernization of the city transportation network, the plan proposed to widen roads and dig canals, but most importantly, included provisions to build railways and a new "central station" to link the northern and southern Tokyo rail termini.[63] Spurred by Yoshikawa's plan, Home Minister Yamagata Aritomo established the Urban Improvement Investigation Committee (*Shiku Kaisei Shinsakai*) within the Home Ministry with Yoshikawa as chairman. According to one member of the Home Ministry, the goal of the Investigation Committee was to "reconstruct Tokyo into a political city appropriate to the Imperial Capital of the State after the model of the large reconstruction work in Paris conducted by G. E. Haussmann."[64]

Yoshikawa's urban improvement plans were temporarily derailed, however, as they were overshadowed by a competing vision of Tokyo's future as the national capital of Japan. This more opulent plan, sponsored by Foreign Minister Inoue Kaoru, sought to dramatically and instantly transform the central part of Tokyo into a grand political space. Like the earlier Ginza Bricktown project, Inoue proposed a hasty revamping of central Tokyo through the wholesale destruction of the area around Hibiya and the construction of a Baroque-style layout of grand boulevards and monumental buildings. Inoue hoped that a stately political center would aide his efforts to revise Japan's "unequal treaties" with the Western powers, and he hired Wilhelm Böckmann and Hermann Ende of the leading German architectural firm, Böckmann and Ende, to draw up a series of such plans. Yet the amount of destruction necessary, the presence of unstable land in the proposed construction sites, and the prohibitive costs of the proposed buildings, guaranteed that Inoue's "Project for Concentrating Government Offices in Hibiya" (*Hibiya Kanchô Shûchû Keikaku*) never fully materialized.[65] When Inoue's plan was abandoned upon his resignation as Foreign Minister in 1887, only two of Ende and Böckmann's buildings had been constructed.

The vision of Tokyo as a grand national capital, however, did not end with Inoue's resignation. In fact, one contribution of Inoue's expensive plans was that they caused funds for port development in Tokyo to be diverted to Yokohama, eliminating the need for port construction in the Home Ministry's Yoshikawa plan. As Ishizuka Hiromichi and Ishida Yorifusa argue, once port development was eliminated from plans for Tokyo, the city "began to step forwards towards a purely political city, or the Imperial Capital of the State."[66] Although Inoue's grand Hibiya plans would have immediately transformed the superficial appearance of the central part of Tokyo into a monumental political space, the more practical and comprehensive Yoshikawa plan aimed at making Tokyo the capital of Japanese modernity by outfitting the city with modern urban infrastructure and modern amenities as seen in the great capitals of the West.

With the elimination of the Foreign Ministry's Hibiya plans, the Home Ministry was able to refocus on implementing the planning initiatives called for in the Yoshikawa plan. With the legal backing of the Tokyo Urban Improvement Ordinance (*Tôkyô Shiku Kaisei Jôrei*) passed into law by an imperial edict in 1888, a second planning committee, called the Tokyo Urban Improvement Committee (*Tôkyô Shiku Kaisei Iinkai*) was organized to revisit and enact the earlier plans.[67] The Committee approved the building or widening of 315 streets, digging of canals, connection of the northern and southern rail termini and the construction of a monumental "central station" for the capital.[68] The Committee then produced the 1889 Tokyo Improvement Blueprint (*Tôkyô Shiku Kaisei Sekkeizu*) to direct the projects. Financial difficulties forced the Urban Improvement Committee to dramatically scale back the provisions of Tokyo Urban Improvement Ordinance with the New Tokyo Urban Improvement Blueprint (*Tôkyô Shiku Kaisei Shin-sekkeizu*) in 1903.[69]

Yet despite its reduced scale and limited financial resources, this refined New Blueprint contributed much to the monumental transformation of the capital. Greatly reducing the number of street improvement projects delineated in the original Ordinance, the New Blueprint concentrated improvement projects to those deemed most important: notably the rail link between Tokyo's two rail termini and the "central station." A line connecting the two terminals was considered necessary as traffic increased in Tokyo. More significantly, the line had political implications, leading it to be included in urban plans since the Yoshikawa plan. As Fujimori Terunobu notes, "the one railway line laid from north to south in the Yoshikawa plan was a connection between the networks of national territory and cities."[70] As early as 1889, Home Minister Yamagata Aritomo had ordered the Railway Bureau to begin a survey for the construction of this connector line, along with a central station.[71]

Following an 1896 proposal from Prussian engineer Herman Rumshöttel, the Railway Bureau decided that the line should be elevated.[72] As it would pass through dense commercial districts, elevation of the line would allow uninterrupted rail traffic and would also permit the renting-out of commercial space under the tracks, thereby helping to offset costs of acquiring land for the line.[73] The Railway Bureau looked to Europe for an example of a similar urban railway and found an ideal model in Berlin's Stadt und Ringbahn, or City and Circle Line. Resolved to construct a similar system in Tokyo, the Bureau hired the German architect of the Berlin line, Franz Balzer,[74] in 1898, to draw up engineering plans and supervise the construction of Tokyo's own elevated line.[75] In addition to plans for the elevated line, Balzer also drew up the first plans for Tokyo Station.

TOKYO STATION: THE GATEWAY
TO THE IMPERIAL CAPITAL

Hired to design and construct the rail viaduct leading to the proposed "central station," Balzer also sketched architectural elevations for the new station. Basing his designs on extant Edo-period architecture, Balzer designed a station that was, as William Coaldrake argues, "entirely in keeping with Japanese traditions of architecture and authority, but it was entirely out of step with the intention of the Meiji imperial state to represent its new authority as a modern, Westernised [sic] nation."[76] The government rejected Balzer's station plans as not modern enough and dismissed his services in 1903. Although Balzer's Japanese-influenced designs were discarded, Balzer's elevation scheme and location for the station, directly facing the imperial palace, were retained.[77]

Having dismissed Balzer, the government sought a Japanese architect who could design a more suitably Western-style building. In 1903, the government turned to Tatsuno Kingo, the leading Japanese architect of the Meiji Period. Tatsuno had designed many Western-styled buildings, including the Bank of Japan in Osaka, along with its branch offices. He also had designed the Western-style Pusan Station in Korea and Manseibashi Station in Tokyo. Tatsuno understood the symbolic importance of Tokyo's central station, and realized that it would be compared with the stations of the great capitals of Europe. Throughout Europe and the United States in the late nineteenth and early twentieth centuries, similar monumental central railway stations "became an opportunity for propaganda in fierce international competition."[78] According to Richard A. Etlin, railway stations had assumed the role of the traditional triumphal arch gateway to display the city's magnificence.[79] Ever since the construction of the world's first grand metropolitan terminus—London's old Euston Station, with its own triumphal Doric propylaea—stations such as Berlin Station, Amsterdam Central, the Gare du Nord in Paris, and Victoria Terminal in Bombay had become the symbols of their respective cities.[80] Tokyo Station was built, as Coaldrake observes, "in the international context of railway and capital-city stations as the expression of national confidence and authority."[81] "All of the great cities of Europe," Tatsuno wrote in the first line of a report on the construction of Tokyo Station, "even London, even Berlin; they all have central stations."[82]

Directly facing the Imperial Palace across the inner moat, Tatsuno's design for the station building suitably acknowledged its dual role as a symbol of the nation and as the personal station of the emperor. The station design evolved over three generations before its characteristic final "Renaissance" form was determined: a rectilinear central pavilion topped by a hipped roof with cresting, and octagonal pavilions capped by massive octagonal lanterns and ribbed domes anchoring each wing. Lunette-shaped curved open pediments highlighted each pavilion, while domed turrets accentuated the corners of the pavilions and ox-eye dormers windows peaked out from the bay roofs and domes. A pillared porte-cochère/portico in front of the central pavilion denoted the emperor's personal entrance to the station, while the taller domes demarcated waiting rooms and lobbies for passengers—arrivals in the north, departures from the south.

Construction of the station was postponed as a result of financial difficulties and two wars—the Sino–Japanese War in 1894–1895, and the Russo–Japanese War in 1904–1905—but victory over Russia in 1905 revitalized the project, and an even more "heroic" station building was planned once work commenced in March 1908.[83] Serving at the time as a cabinet member and Railway Bureau President, Gotô Shimpei famously urged the building of "a station that befits a Japan that defeated the great power Russia; one that will shock the world."[84] With this connection between Tokyo Station and international prestige in mind, Gotô ordered the plans for the station to be expanded from two floors to three.[85]

As construction of the station neared completion, Tokyo Mayor Sakatani Yoshio moved the opening ceremony forward several months to coincide with the return of General Kamio. Workers hurried to complete the station in time, causing frantic railway officials to wonder if the new electric trains—which had hardly been tested—would even run; or if the train tickets—which had not even been printed yet—would arrive before the station opened. Preparations continued for the joint opening ceremony and "welcoming of the triumphant general" (*gaisen kangei kai*) until the day before the station opened. The station platforms were draped in red and blue lace braids, and flags of all the nations of the world, except those of the Central Powers—Germany, Austria, and the Ottoman Empire—hung from the ceiling. A "Great Green Arch" (*Dairokumon*) was erected in the station front plaza, with two thirty-six-foot "Green Towers" (*Hôsui sôryokutô*) on either side. "Celebrate the opening of the Station," declared one inscription, while the other proclaimed, "Welcome the Triumphant General." More towers lined the avenue between the station and the imperial palace, and tremendous light towers were constructed to illuminate the station until the early hours of the morning. Finally, the Railway Agency had sent out 2,345 special invitations to the ceremony.[86]

As the *Tokyo Asahi Newspaper* reported the next day:

> The grand spectacle of the opening; the brilliance of a triumphant return! On this day, the eighteenth, Commanding Officer Kamio and his general staff were joyously welcome back to the Imperial Capital after their grand and triumphant

military expedition, and marked the first step in the opening for business of the grand Tokyo Station, the largest station in Asia.[87]

Thus after nearly two decades of planning and six years of construction, Tokyo Station was finally opened to great fanfare and celebration in the plaza in front of the station. Popularly known as the "Gateway to the Imperial Capital" (*Teito no Genkan*), Tokyo Station was the junction of efforts to unite the nation both politically and ideologically. In its practical role as a railway station, Tokyo Station was the capstone of the national railway network. When opened, the station replaced Shimbashi Station as the "zero kilometer" point from where distances were measured for all national lines. As Prime Minister Ôkuma proclaimed at the opening ceremony of Tokyo Station: "the heart (*chûshin*) of our country's railways, in other words, is nothing other than this station opening here today."[88]

Yet Tokyo Station had more than a practical role as a rail depot. Symbolically, Tokyo Station was the most powerful beacon of government attempts to ideologically unite the Japanese people through modernity, "civilization and enlightenment," and the emperor system. In *Meiji Revisited: The Sites of Victorian Japan*, Dallas Finn argues that Western-style buildings, such as schools, police stations, clinics, and town halls, were "shining beacons of another government objective, *bunmei kaika*, or civilization and enlightenment, the catch phrase for westernization."[89] Certainly, the same can be said of railway stations, such as Tokyo Station. Built in the Western style typical of Meiji-era construction projects, Tokyo Station was a vivid portrayal of Japanese attempts to adopt and adapt western modernity. As Watanabe Hiroshi writes, Tokyo Station, along with the Akasaka Detached Palace, were "the two buildings that, more than any other, demonstrated the successful assimilation of Western architectural skills and building methods by the Japanese in the Meiji Era."[90] Indeed, the station was a mixture of Western and Japanese designs and materials: the 2,700 tons of steel for the infrastructure were imported from the United States and Great Britain, while the 8 million bricks, 900,000 decorative façade tiles, and 10,800 pine underpinning logs were produced domestically.[91] Moreover, Tatsuno designed the station in what he called his "Renaissance Style," an idiosyncratic version of the Queen Anne Revival architecture popular in Victorian London. The building was constructed in red brick, which had become a symbol of "civilization and enlightenment" after the Ginza Bricktown. The curved pediments, ribbed domes, pilasters, pedimented windows, and front porte-cochère/portico gave the station an Italianate or Neo-Renaissance form, while its domed turrets and red brick accented by white ornamental quoins and stringcourses produced a Queen Anne Revival appearance. Built in this trademark "Tatsuno Style" of red brick and white ornamentation, Tokyo Station fit in perfectly with the Western buildings of the nearby Marunouchi "One-Block London" district, or perhaps London itself, where Tatsuno studied before designing the station.

As with the earlier Ginza Bricktown, the government hoped that Western-style buildings, as beacons of modernity, would literally enlighten the people of Japan and make them "civilized." The celebratory address given by Prime Minister Ôkuma Shigenobu during the opening ceremony of Tokyo Station reflected this expectation. In the "luminatory rhetoric" of the time, Ôkuma described the station as the sun, noting, "its rays would brighten every side of Japanese life."[92] "Just as the sun at the center emits rays in all directions," Ôkuma proclaimed, "we must extend the traffic network in all directions as if railroads were also beams of light."[93] Ôkuma then declared that Tokyo Station "represented *shakai bunmei*—civilized life, itself."[94]

Aside from its Western design, Tokyo Station epitomized "civilization and enlightenment" as a railway depot and as the personal station of the Japanese emperor. As Carol Gluck explains in *Japan's Modern Myths: Ideology in the Late Meiji Period*, "two ubiquitous images gradually emerged as symbols of 'civilization': the monarch, and the locomotive."[95] According to Gluck, both railways and the emperor were "associated with progress" and contributed to the "national and social integration that characterized the modern state," while railways, in particular, were "engines of civilization."[96] Hara Takeshi, meanwhile, has similarly argued that railways were a symbol for the two focal points of government authority: "civilization" and "progress."[97] "Railroads and the monarch together as symbols of 'civilization' and 'progress,'" Hara notes, "fulfilled their important role of spreading forth from Tokyo to every corner of the Japanese archipelago to eliminate regional differences, integrating the national and the social, characteristically of the modern state."[98] From the outset of railway development in Japan, the Meiji leaders had seen the potential of railways, not only for industrial development but also for encouraging the advancement of civilization. For this reason, the earliest government routes had been planned to pass through areas highest in population, in order to promote "civilization and enlightenment."[99]

Tokyo Station also symbolized "civilization and enlightenment" as the station from where the emperor embarked on state visits around the country. The central entrance to the station was reserved for the imperial family, and the gate through which they passed to enter the station was adorned with a symbolic rising sun. Befitting the imperial family, the central entrance rotunda was decorated exquisitely with wood parquet and marble floors, stained glass ceilings, and murals on the walls. At the heart of the station were individual reception rooms for the members of the imperial family, each also lavishly decorated, Finn describes, with "parquet floors, *hinoki* cypress paneling, and Nishijin [silk] hangings: the Plum Room at the right for the Crown Prince, the Bamboo Room at the left for lesser royals, and the Pine Room at the back for the emperor."[100] Besides being far more ornately decorated than the other areas of the station, the central entrance and special rooms reserved for the imperial family were even raised a meter above areas for other passengers.[101]

Tokyo Station's function as the emperor's personal station unified the two symbols of "civilization" in Meiji Japan: "the monarch, and the locomotive."[102] Locomotives, as modern industrial machines, symbolized progress. Railways, meanwhile, embodied the emperor system as they carried the emperor around the country on imperial progressions. As the Imperial Train, or *omeshi ressha*, toured the nation, these two symbols of civilization were physically conjoined as commoners lining the tracks showed their respect to the emperor in the Imperial Carriage (*Goryôsha*). By combining the emperor and the railway, Tokyo Station was cast as the epitome of "civilization and enlightenment." Just as the Meiji Emperor had been re-dressed in the new robes of modernity as an ideological symbol for the nation, Tokyo Station was also constructed as the prime symbol of modernity and "civilization and enlightenment": simultaneously as a grand Western-style building and railway depot, and the emperor's personal station.

The link between Tokyo Station and "civilization and enlightenment" was clearly reflected in Japanese popular media after the station was opened. One 1918 lithograph popularized as a postal stamp in the 1920s portrays Tokyo Station surrounded by other symbols of modernity and "tools of culture" (*bunmei no riki*). Male and female commuters stroll through the electric lamp-lit station-front plaza: the men clad in fancy western dress complete with top hats, the women in a mixture of Japanese and western-influenced kimono. A foreign-looking couple with a child examines the fascinating scene escorted by their Japanese hosts. Rickshaws and taxis line up in front of the station waiting for patrons. Large clocks on the front of each passenger pavilion display the time for all to see. Finally, a dirigible balloon and two early biplanes soar in the sky above the station.[103]

CONCLUSION: THE TOKYO MODEL OF COLONIALISM

When Tokyo Station opened in 1914, it marked the completion of a long process of shaping Japan into a modern nation-state, and of refashioning Tokyo into the imperial capital. Spanning two imperial reigns, the process had started with the first railway line between Tokyo and Yokohama. For the new Meiji government, the locomotive functioned as an engine of state formation and empire building, as the state built railways around the country in order to centralize the nation and spread central influence and authority. Focused on the capital, the national railway system cast a network of central power over the Japanese islands. Traversing historical boundaries and linking insular regions, railways conveyed the authority of the Meiji government to even the smallest, most isolated Japanese villages. With their ability to carry ideas quickly over long distances, government officials and other "agents of the state" used railways to reduce the distance between the capital and countryside, extending central control over the periphery. In this way, trains integrated Japan into a politically unified nation centered on the national capital.

As the national railway network developed with Tokyo at the center, the Meiji leaders re-fashioned the city into a monumental capital city. Modeled on the grand capitals of the West and realized with Western-style architecture and modern urban planning, Tokyo became an imperial capital suitably dressed in symbols of civilization and progress. This re-creation of Tokyo was envisioned most significantly in the planning and construction of Tokyo Station. As Finn points out, although not completed until 1914, two years after the death of the Meiji Emperor, Tokyo Station was the apex of Meiji-era Western style architecture: it was the work of a leading Meiji architect, Tatsuno Kingo, and its planning and construction took place for the most part during the Meiji period.[104] Linking the national railway network to the imperial capital, Tokyo Station was the pinnacle of government efforts of political integration. As a western-style station building and the personal station of the emperor, Tokyo Station, meanwhile, was the epitome of ideological unification through modernity and "civilization and enlightenment."

Yet as the focal point of a colonialist form of state formation, Tokyo Station was also a prime symbol of Japanese colonialism. Indeed, the opening of Tokyo Station marked the completion of the Tokyo model of colonialism: political integration and ideological unification of the colonial periphery through centralization on a primate metropolitan center, specifically by means of railways, western architecture, and modern urban planning. Following the expansion of the Japanese empire into Taiwan and Korea, this Tokyo model of colonialism was enacted in Seoul and Taiwan in an attempt to secure Japanese authority and control. Under the pretense of "the civilizing mission," Taipei and Seoul were re-created as modern colonial capitals through the construction of railways, Western-style public buildings, and modern urban infrastructure. Following the Tokyo model, Japanese leaders in the colonies sought to use urban redevelopment projects to impress the unifying ideas of "progress" and "civilization" upon the colonized, thus compelling submission and subservience to Japan. As with Tokyo Station, the centerpieces of these colonial transformations were monumental western-style structures, such as the Taiwan Bank and Government-General Headquarters in Taiwan, and Seoul Station and the Government-General Headquarters in Korea. As the Japanese empire continued to expand in Manchuria, Tokyo Station became the focal point of a imperial railway network that united the nation, and spread via rail-ferry all the way from Tokyo to Seoul, Changchun, and beyond to the grand capitals of Europe. With the completion of Tokyo Station as the cornerstone of the imperial railway network and at the center of the Imperial Capital, the Japanese government eagerly anticipated international recognition as a united nation and a modern imperial power.

NOTES

1. Harada, *Nihon no Kokutetsu*, 59, and Tokyo Minami Tetsudô Kanrikyoku (Ed.), *Tôkyô-Eki Eki-shi*, 30–31, 34; Tôkyô Hyakunenshi Henshû Iinkai, ed. *Tôkyô Hyakunenshi* 4, 738–739.

2. Harada, *Nihon no Kokutetsu*, 59–61; Tôkyô Minami Tetsudô, *Tôkyô-Eki Eki-shi*, 31; The most detailed description of the opening ceremony is Nakagawa et. al., *Tôkyô-Eki Tanken*, 96–103.

3. This argument was most prominent in the early decades after Italian unification, but has since been contested (Schram, *Railways and the Formation of the Italian Nation State in the Nineteenth Century*, 3).

4. Weber, *Peasants into Frenchmen*, 218.

5. Truesdell, *Spectacular Politics*, 85–86.

6. Green, *Fatherlands*, 223.

7. Quoted in Faith, *The World the Railways Made*, 65.

8. A good example of the wide range of factors said to contribute to Japanese state formation can be found in Umesao et al. (Eds.), *Japanese Civilization in the Modern World XVI: Nation-State and Empire*. See also Gluck, *Japan's Modern Myths*, and Fujitani, *Splendid Monarchy*.

9. Ericson, *The Sound of the Whistle*, 4.

10. The three unifiers, in order, were Oda Nobunaga, Toyotomi Hideyoshi, and Tokugawa Ieyasu. Scholars have argued that early modern Japan was more politically integrated than earlier thought. See, for example, Hall, Nagahara Keiji, and Kozo Yamamura (Eds.), *Japan before Tokugawa*, and Philip C. Brown, *Central Authority and Local Autonomy in the Formation of Early Modern Japan* (Stanford: Stanford University Press, 1993), and Berry, "Was Early Modern Japan Culturally Integrated?", 547–581.

11. Tanaka, "Meiji Government and the Introduction of Railways 2," 752.

12. Inouyé, "Japanese Communications: Railroads," 427–429; Mitsui, "The System of Communications," 90. Constantine Nomikos Vaporis has challenged the assertion of Tokugawa communications' lagging as a result of a poor road network

and lack of bridges. See Constantine Nomikos Vaporis, *Breaking Barriers: Travel and the State in Early Modern Japan* (Cambridge, MA: Harvard University Press, 1994), 11–12.

13. Inouyé, "Japanese Communications: Railroads," 427–429; Vaporis, *Breaking Barriers*, 133.

14. Tanaka, "Meiji Government and the Introduction of Railways 2," 751.

15. Pyle, *The New Generation in Meiji Japan*, 81.

16. Berry, "Was Early Modern Japan Culturally Integrated?", 555. See Gluck, *Japan's Modern Myths*, and Fujitani, *Splendid Monarchy*, on the invention of nationalism.

17. Schivelbusch, *The Railway Journey: The Industrialization of Space and Time in the Nineteenth Century* 36–42; quoted in Hanes, "Contesting Centralization," 491.

18. Hobsbawm, *Nations and Nationalism*, 80.

19. Hobsbawm, *Nations and Nationalism*, 81.

20. Quoted in Harada, *Nihon no Kokutetsu*, 8. Tanaka translates this quote more liberally in "Meiji Government and the Introduction of Railways 2," 752.

21. Free, *Early Japanese Railways*, 62.

22. Finn, *Meiji Revisited*, 46.

23. Hara, *"Minto" tai "Teito,"* 20.

24. Aoki, "The Dawn of Japanese Railroads," 29.

25. Aoki, "Expansion of Railway Network," 34–35. Aoki calls these the "First Railway Mania" of 1885–1890, and the "Second Railway Mania" of 1893–1897.

26. Aoki, "Expansion of Railway Network," 34–35; Imperial Government Railways of Japan, *Railway Nationalization in Japan*, 2, 4–5; Harada, *Technological Independence*, 11.

27. Imperial Government Railways of Japan, *Railway Nationalization in Japan*, 2.

28. Harada, *Technological Independence*, 10; Imperial Government Railways of Japan, *Railway Nationalization in Japan*, 2.

29. Imperial Government Railways of Japan, *Railway Nationalization in Japan*, 3.

30. Ericson, *The Sound of the Whistle*, 116.

31. Ericson, *The Sound of the Whistle*, 116, 121; Imperial Government Railways of Japan, *Railway Nationalization in Japan*, 3.

32. Harada, "Policy, Ch. 3," 47; Kinzley, "Merging Lines," 43; Aoki et. al., *A History of Japanese Railways*, 45; Imperial Government Railways of Japan, *Railway Nationalization in Japan*, 4–5.

33. Aoki et al., *A History of Japanese Railways*, 39; Imperial Government Railways of Japan, *Railway Nationalization in Japan*, 4–5; Kinzley, "Merging Lines," 41.

34. Imperial Government Railways of Japan, *Railway Nationalization in Japan*, 6.

35. Aoki, et al. *A History of Japanese Railways*, 39–40; Harada, "Railroads, Ch. 3," 56.

36. Aoki, et al. *A History of Japanese Railways*, 40–43; Imashiro, "Nationalisation of Railroads," 43; Watarai, *Nationalization of Railways in Japan*, 54. A complete list of all seventeen railways nationalized in 1906–1907 can be found in Dan Free, *Early Japanese Railways*, 272.

37. Kinzley, "Merging Lines," 41–42.

38. Shatkin, "Colonial Capital," 579.

39. Tokyo is often described as a "showcase" or "window." Although the term has since been used by many scholars, Henry Smith is most often credited with first describing Tokyo as "showcase" in English (Smith, "Tokyo as an Idea," 53).

40. Scott, *Seeing Like a State*, Ch. 1–2.

41. Hanes, "Contesting Centralization?", 488.

42. Nakamura, "Railway System and Time Consciousness," 20; The first standard time in Japan was set in reference to Tokyo solar time in 1879, which remained the standard until Imperial Edict number 51 in 1886 set the country on Greenwich Mean time at 135 degrees east longitude (Nakamura, "Railway Systems and Time Consciousness," 20).

43. Hara, *"Minto" tai "Teito,"* 28.

44. Nugent, "Building the State, Making the Nation," 338.

45. Weber, *Peasants into Frenchmen*, 485–496, esp. 486; Scott, *Seeing Like a State*, 72.

46. King, "Cultural Hegemony and Capital Cities," 253.

47. Schulz, "The Past in Tokyo's Future: Kôda Rohan's Thoughts on Urban Reform and the New Citizen in Ikkoku no Shuto (One Nation's Capital)," 286.

48. Shatkin, "Colonial Capital," 579; Smith, "Tokyo as an Idea," 53.

49. Machimura, "Building a Capital for Emperor and Enterprise," 151; Fujitani, "Inventing, Forgetting, Remembering: Toward a Historical Ethnography of the Nation-State," 98.

50. Sorensen, *The Making of Urban Japan*, 61.

51. Sorensen, *The Making of Urban Japan*, 61.

52. Fujimori, *Meiji, no Tôkyô Keikaku*, 3.

53. Ishizuka, "Meiji-ki ni okeru Toshi-keikaku: Tôkyô ni tsuite," 486.

54. Ishizuka and Ishida, "Tokyo, the Metropolis of Japan," 8.

55. The name is also translated as Ginza Brick Quarter.

56. Tôkyô-to Toshi Keikaku-kyoku Sômu-bu Sôdanjôhô-ka, *Tôkyô no Toshi Keikaku Hyakunen* 7; Suzuki and Yamaguchi, *Shin Kenchikugaku Taikei 5: Kindai Gendai kenchikushi* 251.

57. Watanabe, "Josiah Conder's Rokumeikan," 22.

58. Coaldrake, *Architecture and Authority in Japan*, 209–210.

59. Schulz, "The Past in Tokyo's Future," 286.

60. Pinkney, *Napoleon III and the Rebuilding of Paris*, 44, 94.

61. Sorensen, *The Making of Urban Japan*, 64–65.

62. Ishizuka and Ishida, "Tokyo, the Metropolis of Japan," 11.

63. Sorensen, *The Making of Urban Japan*, 65–66; Fujimori, *Meiji no Tôkyô Keikaku*, 115.

64. Quoted in Ishizuka, and Ishida, "Tokyo, the Metropolis of Japan," 11.

65. The most thorough treatment of Ende and Böckmann's work in Japan is Horiuchi Masaaki. *Meiji no Oyatoi Kenchikuka: Ende & Bekkuman* (Tokyo: Inoue Shoin, 1989). Fujimori Terunobu also published a series of five articles on Ende and

Böckmann entitled "Ende Bekkuman ni yoru Kanchô Shûchû Keikaku no Kenkyû," parts 1–5, in the *Nihon Kenchiku Gakkai Ronbun Hôkokushû*, vols. 271, 272, 273, 280, 281.

66. Ishizuka and Ishida, "Tokyo, the Metropolis of Japan," 12.

67. The bill is alternately translated "Tokyo City Improvement Ordinance" in Sorensen, *The Making of Urban Japan*, 67.

68. Sorensen, *The Making of Urban Japan*, 71; Ishizuka and Ishida, "Tokyo, the Metropolis of Japan," 13.

69. Tôkyô-to Toshi Keikaku-kyoku Sômu-bu Sôdanjôhô-ka, *Tôkyô no Toshi Keikaku Hyakunen*, 12.

70. Fujimori Terunobu, *Meiji no Tôkyô Keikaku*, 136.

71. Nihon Kokuyû Tetsudô, *Nihon Kokuyû Tetsudô Hyakunen Shashin-shi*, 157; Tokyo Minami Tetsudô Kanrikyoku (Ed.), *Tôkyô-Eki Eki-shi*, 25.

72. Coaldrake, *Architecture and Authority*, 231; Aoki, et al. *A History of Japanese Railways*, 81.

73. Thanks to Dan Free for providing this insight on reasons for the elevated railway.

74. Balzer's name is often Anglicized as "Baltzer" in English-language sources.

75. Coaldrake, *Architecture and Authorit*, 231; Finn, *Meiji Revisited*, 247; Aoki et al., *A History of Japanese Railways*, 82.

76. Coaldrake, *Architecture and Authority*, 232.

77. Balzer's massive reinforced-brick viaduct between Tokyo Station and Shimbashi Station is still in use today (Finn, *Meiji Revisited*, 247).

78. Coaldrake, *Architecture and Authority*, 229.

79. Etlin, *Symbolic Space*, 3–4.

80. Thanks again to Dan Free for information on London's old Euston Station.

81. Coaldrake, *Architecture and Authority*, 225.

82. Tatsuno, "Chûô Teishajô no Kenchiku," 218.

83. Tôkyô Hyakunenshi Henshû Iinkai (Ed.), *Tôkyô Hyakunenshi*, 4, 736; Finn, *Meiji Revisited*, 248.

84. Tôkyô Minami Tetsudô, *Tôkyô-Eki Eki-shi*, 27.

85. Ôishi, *Ekimei de Yomu Edo Tôkyô*, 24.

86. Nakagawa et al., *Tôkyô-Eki Tanken*, 96; Uchikawa and Matsushima, *Taishô Nyu-su Jiten* I, 563 for missing flags. A picture of the archies and their inscriptions can be found in Nakagawa et al., *Tôkyô-Eki Tanken*, 97.

87. Uchikawa Yoshimi, Matsushima Eiichi, *Taishô Nyu-su Jiten* I, 563; translated in Coaldrake, *Architecture and Authority*, 230.

88. Nakagawa, et al., *Tôkyô-Eki Tanken*, 102.

89. Finn, *Meiji Revisited*, 24.

90. Watanabe, *The Architecture of Tokyo*, 61.

91. Tôkyô Minami Tetsudô, *Tôkyô-Eki Eki-shi*, 27; Ôishi, *Ekimei de Yomu*, 25; Finn, *Meiji Revisited*, 248.

92. Finn, *Meiji Revisited*, 249.

93. Nakagawa, et al., *Tôkyô-Eki Tanken*, 101–102.

94. Finn, *Meiji Revisited*, 249.
95. Gluck, *Japan's Modern Myths*, 101.
96. Gluck, *Japan's Modern Myths*, 101, 261.
97. Hara, *"Minto" tai "Teito,"* 23.
98. Hara, *"Minto" tai "Teito,"* 22–23.
99. Harada, "Railroads, Ch. 2," 16.
100. Finn, *Meiji Revisited* 248–249; Tôkyô Minami Tetsudô, *Tôkyô-Eki Eki-shi* 28, 38–39.
101. Finn, *Meiji Revisited*, 248.
102. Gluck, *Japan's Modern Myths*, 101.
103. The 1918 lithograph, "Drawing of Tokyo Station" (*Tôkyô teishajô no Zu*) by the artists Amijima Kamekichi, is located on the back leaf of Nakagawa, et al., *Tôkyô-Eki Tanken.*
104. Finn, *Meiji Revisited*, 246.

BIBLIOGRAPHY

Aoki Eiichi. "The Dawn of Japanese Railways." *Japan Railway & Transport Review* 1 (1994): 28–30.

Aoki, Eiichi. "Expansion of Railway Network," *Japan Railway & Transport Review* 2 (1994): 34–37.

Aoki Eiichi, Mitsuhide Imashiro, et al. *A History of Japanese Railways: 1872–1999.* Tokyo: East Japan Railway Culture Foundation, 2000.

Berry, Marry Elizabeth. "Was Early Modern Japan Culturally Integrated?" *Modern Asian Studies* 31.3 (1997): 547–581.

Coaldrake, William H. *Architecture and Authority in Japan.* London: Routledge, 1996.

Ericson, Stephen J. *The Sound of the Whistle: Railroads and the State in Meiji Japan.* Cambridge, MA: Harvard University Press, 1996.

Etlin, Richard A. *Symbolic Space: French Enlightenment Architecture and Its Legacy.* Chicago: University of Chicago Press, 1994.

Faith, Nicholas. *The World the Railways Made.* New York: Carroll and Graff, 1990.

Finn, Dallas. *Meiji Revisited: The Sites of Victorian Japan.* New York: Weatherhill, 1995.

Dan Free. *Early Japanese Railways, 1853–1914: Engineering Triumphs that Transformed Meiji-era Japan.* North Clarendon, VT: Tuttle Publishing, 2008.

Fujimori Terunobu. *Meiji no Tôkyô Keikaku.* Tokyo: Iwanami Shoten, 1982.

Fujitani, Takashi. "Inventing, Forgetting, Remembering: Toward a Historical Ethnography of the Nation-State." *Cultural Nationalism in East Asia: Representation and Identity.* Ed. Harumi Befu. Berkeley: University of California Press, 1993. 77–106.

Gluck, Carol. *Japan's Modern Myths: Ideology in the Late Meiji Period.* Princeton, NJ: Princeton University Press, 1985.

Green, Abigail. *Fatherlands: State-building and Nationhood in Nineteenth-Century Germany*. Cambridge, UK: Cambridge University Press, 2001.

Hanes, Jeffrey E. "Contesting Centralization? Space, Time, and Hegemony in Meiji Japan." *New Directions in the Study of Meiji Japan*. Ed. Helen Hardacre with Adam L. Kern. Leiden, New York: Brill, 1997. 485–495.

Hara Takeshi. *"Minto" Osaka tai "Teito" Tôkyô: Shisô toshite Kansai Shitetsu*. Tokyo: Kôdansha, 1998.

Harada Katsumasa, *Nihon no Kokutetsu*. Tokyo: Iwanami Shoten, 1984.

Harada Katsumasa, *Nihon no Tetsudô*. Tokyo: Yoshikawa Kôbunkan, 1991.

Harada Katsumasa. *Technological Independence and Progress of Standardization in the Japanese Railways*. Tokyo: The United Nations University Press, 1981.

Harada, "Policy" in Chapter 3, "Transportation in the Period of Railroad Priority (1892–1909)." *Technological Innovation and the Development of Transportation in Japan*. Ed. Hirofumi Yamamoto. Tokyo: The United Nations University Press, 1993. 45–49.

Harada Katsumasa. "Railroads" in Chapter 2, "Transportation in Transition (1868–1891)." *Technological Innovation and the Development of Transportation in Japan*. Ed. Hirofumi Yamamoto. Tokyo: The United Nations University Press, 1993. 15–21.

Hobsbawm, E. J. *Nations and Nationalism since 1780: Programme, Myth, Reality*. 2nd ed. Cambridge, UK: Cambridge University Press, 1992.

Imashiro Mitsuhide. "Nationalisation of Railroads and Dispute over Reconstruction to Standard Gauge." *Japan Railway & Transport Review* 4 (1995): 42–45.

Imperial Government Railways of Japan. *Railway Nationalization in Japan: Ten Years Progress Under State Management, 1907–1908 to 1916–1917*. Tokyo: Tsukiji Type Foundry, 1919.

Inouyé Masaru. "Japanese Communications: Railroads." *Fifty Years of New Japan*. Ed. Ôkuma Shigenobu. Reprint. New York: Kraus, 1970. 424–446.

Ishizuka Hiromichi. "Meiji-ki ni okeru Toshi-keikaku: Tôkyô ni tsuite." *Toshi-kôzô to Toshi-keikaku*. Ed. Tôkyô-toritsu Daigaku Toshi Kenkyûkai-hen. Tokyo: Tôkyô Daigaku Shuppankai, 1968. 481–497.

Ishizuka Hiromichi and Ishida Yorifusa. "Tokyo, the Metropolis of Japan and Its Urban Development." *Tokyo: Urban Growth and Planning, 1868–1988*. Ed. Center for Urban Studies. Tokyo: Center for Urban Studies, 1988. 3–35.

King, Anthony D. "Cultural Hegemony and Capital Cities." *Capital Cities: International Perspectives*. Eds. Taylor, John, Jean G. Lengellé, and Caroline Andrew. Ottawa: Carleton University Press, 1993. 251–270.

Kinzley, W. Dean. "Merging Lines: Organising Japan's National Railroad, 1906–1914." *The Journal of Transport History* 27 (2006): 39–97.

Machimura, Takashi. "Building a Capital for Emperor and Enterprise: The Changing Urban Meaning of Central Tokyo." *Culture and the City in East Asia*. Eds. Kim, Won Bae, Mike Douglass, Sang-Chuel Choe, and Kong Chong Ho. Oxford: Clarendon Press, 1997. 151–166.

Mitsui, Baron Takaharu. "The System of Communications at the Time of the Meiji Restoration." *Monumenta Nipponica* 4.1 (1941): 88–101.

Nakagawa Ichirô, Yamaguchi Fuminori, and Matsuyama Iwao. *Tôkyô-Eki Tanken*. Tokyo: Shinchosha, 1987.

Nakamura Naofumi. "Railway Systems and Time Consciousness in Modern Japan." *Japan Review* 14 (2002): 13–38.

Nihon Kokuyû Tetsudô. *Nihon Kokuyû Tetsudô Hyakunen Shashin-shi*. Tokyo: Nihon Kokuyû Tetsudô, 1972.

Nugent, David. "Building the State, Making the Nation: The Bases and Limits of State Centralization in 'Modern' Peru." *American Anthropologist*, New Series. 96.2 (1994): 333–369.

Ôishi Manabu, *Ekimei de Yomu Edo Tokyo*. Tokyo: PHP Shinsho, 2003.

Pinkney, David. *Napoleon III and the Rebuilding of Paris*. Princeton: Princeton University Press, 1958.

Pyle, Kenneth B. *The New Generation in Meiji Japan: Problems of Cultural Identity, 1885–1895*. Stanford: Stanford University Press, 1969.

Schivelbusch, Wolfegang. *The Railway Journey: The Industrialization of Space and Time in the Nineteenth Century*. Berkeley: University of California Press, 1986.

Schram, Albert. *Railways and the Formation of the Italian Nation State in the Nineteenth Century*. Cambridge: Cambridge University Press, 1997.

Schulz, Evelyn. "The Past in Tokyo's Future: Kôda Rohan's Thoughts on Urban Reform and the New Citizen in Ikkoku no Shuto (One Nation's Capital)." *Japanese Capitals in Historical Perspective: Place, Power, and Memory in Kyoto, Edo and Tokyo*. Eds. Fiévé, Nicolas, and Paul Waley. London: Routledge, 2003. 283–308.

Scott, James C. *Seeing Like a State: How Certain Schemes to Improve the Human Condition Have Failed*. New Haven: Yale University Press, 1998.

Shatkin, Gavin. "Colonial Capital, Modernist Capital, Global Capital: The Changing Political Symbolism of Urban Space in Metro Manila, the Philippines." *Pacific Affairs* 78 (2005–2006): 577–600.

Smith, Henry D. "Tokyo as an Idea: An Exploration of Japanese Urban Thought until 1945." *Journal of Japanese Studies*. 4.1 (1978): 45–80.

Sorensen, André. *The Making of Urban Japan: Cities and Planning from Edo to the Twenty-First Century*. London and New York: Routledge, 2002.

Suzuki Hiroyuki and Yamaguchi Hiroshi. *Shin Kenchikugaku Taikei 5: Kindai Gendai kenchikushi*. Tokyo: Shôkokusha, 1993.

Tanaka, Tokihiko. "Meiji Government and the Introduction of Railways 2." *Contemporary Japan* 28.4 (1967): 750–788.

Tatsuno Kingo. "Chûô Teishajô no Kenchiku." *Tôkyô-Eki no Sekai*. Ed. Kanô Shobô, 218–231. Tokyo: Kanô Shobô, 1987.

Tôkyô-to Toshi Keikaku-kyoku Sômu-bu Sôdanjôhô-ka. *Tôkyô no Toshi Keikaku Hyakunen*. Tokyo: Tôkyô-to Toshi Keikaku-kyoku, 1989.

Tôkyô Minami Tetsudô Kanrikyoku, ed. *Tôkyô Eki Eki-shi*. Tokyo: Tokyo Minami Tetsudo Kanrikyoku, 1973.

Tôkyô Hyakunenshi Henshû Iinkai (Ed.). *Tôkyô Hyakunenshi 4*. Tokyo: Gyôsei, 1979.

Truesdell, Mathew. *Spectacular Politics: Louis-Napoleon Bonaparte and the Fête Impériale, 1849–1870*. Oxford: Oxford University Press, 1997.

Vaporis, Constantine Nomikos. *Breaking Barriers: Travel and the State in Early Modern Japan*. Cambridge, MA: Harvard University Press, 1994.

Watanabe, Toshio. "Josiah Conder's Rokumeikan: Architecture and National Representation in Meiji Japan." *Art Journal* 55.3 (1996): 21–27.

Watanabe, Hiroshi. *The Architecture of Tokyo: An Architectural History in 571 Individual Presentations*. Stuttgart: Edition Axel Menges, 2001.

Watarai, Toshiharu. *Nationalization of Railways in Japan*. New York: Columbia University Press, 1915.

Weber, Eugen. *Peasants into Frenchmen: The Modernization of Rural France, 1870–1914*. Stanford: Stanford University Press, 1976.

Chapter 10

"The Super-Express of Our Dreams" and Other Mythologies about Postwar Japan

Hiraku Shimoda

INTRODUCTION: TRAINS AS JAPAN'S MODERN SYNECDOCHE

Japan's present-day technological prowess is often symbolized by automobiles and electronics. Brands such as Toyota and Panasonic, Honda and Sony have become global icons, casting a worldwide image of Japan as a premier source of cutting-edge know-how. Less visible to outsiders, but no less significant to Japan's status as a technical innovator, are its railways.

The fabled "Bullet Train" aside, external observers may not easily conjure Japan's robust and extensive rail network as an obvious example of that country's technological sophistication. Nonetheless, even casual visitors to Japan will quickly come to see just how advanced the train system must be to support daily life there as it does, especially in the dense urban centers. It seems apt that many statistics about Japanese railways come in astronomical scales and global superlatives. In 2009, the system served 227 million riders, who traveled a combined 393 billion kilometers, which is astounding in light of the country's population and size (Japanese Ministry, 4). The *shinkansen* is always among the fastest trains anywhere. The world's busiest station is Shinjuku Station in Tokyo, which averages 3.46 million passengers every day. The idea of Japan as a "Railway Kingdom" (*tetsudō ōkoku*) or a "Railway Superpower" (*tetsudō taikoku*) can certainly be substantiated by most any metric.

Beyond such easy statistics and catchy monikers lies something more remarkable, if harder to measure. The conceit that Japan is a world leader—if not *the* leader—in railway technology turns out to be a significant part of Japan's self-image as a thoroughly modern nation. The advanced state of

Japan's rail system is often proudly held, explicitly and implicitly, as proof of the advanced state of the nation at large. There is no small nationalist satisfaction in the self-congratulatory idea that Japan boasts a world-class railway, especially in its impeccable punctuality and sheer capacity. This point of pride is not limited to the justly renowned *shinkansen*, either. The entire industry that supports the vast, complex rail network has often been understood as a synecdoche—that is to say, Japan's global technological ascendance writ small.

Compared to the extensive functional and cultural significance of trains in Japan, English-language scholarship on the subject has been relatively spotty and uneven. The history of Japanese railways has dealt mostly with their initial establishment from the 1870s to the early twentieth century. The pioneering Meiji era (1868–1912) has received its due, thanks to historians such as Steven Ericson and Dan Free, but it is harder to say the same of the later prewar years (i.e., up to the end of World War II) or even the postwar period (1945 to the present) (Ericson; Free). Scholars interested in Japanese industrial relations, management practices, and organizational analysis have occasionally examined the former Japanese National Railways (JNR; now privatized as JR); Paul Noguchi, Andrzej Straszak, and Robert Tuch have produced case studies about these aspects of Japan's railway industry. As for more cultural approaches, Yohko Tsuji used trains in her brief anthropological study of conceptions of time in contemporary Japan.

Not surprisingly, it is the *shinkansen* that has received the most extensive treatment in English. P. W. B. Semmens gave it an admiring, technical-minded look in *High Speed in Japan*. Others have turned to the local and political aspects of *shinkansen* development. For example, David E. Groth captured the sometimes contentious citizens' movements that shaped *shinkansen* planning, and Christopher Hood ("Shinkansen's") described the system's impact upon local economic development. The most comprehensive among the current body of scholarship is Hood's *Shinkansen: From Bullet Train to Symbol of Modern Japan*. Overall, English-language works have tended to present Japanese railways as examples of economic development, technical achievement, and social ethnography, with an understandable if exaggerated emphasis on the flagship *shinkansen*.

This chapter distinguishes itself by thinking about trains as something more than fixed and self-evident social objects, as the above scholarship has done. Rather, it conceptualizes trains as a dynamic field for "cultural production," to invoke an operative term in this anthology. It asserts that trains, as they are in practical function, are also cultural vessels that can be freighted with just about any content and meaning, which makes them a useful site for producing culture. In that regard, this work shares the spirit of

Marilyn Ivy, the anthropologist who studied how JNR's "Discover Japan" marketing campaign contributed to a manufactured nostalgia for "native places" (*furusato*) in the 1970s (see Ivy, chapter 2). In this instance, I will show how some salient characteristics of Japan's postwar railways have been constructed, represented, and deployed as a metaphor for a national culture of industry and achievement. My broad argument is that a manipulative "emplotment" (to use Hayden White's term) of railway history has been complicit in propagating a dubious mythology about postwar Japanese success. I thus locate trains within a larger cultural movement, often carried forth in mass media, that has rendered postwar Japanese history into a troublingly unexamined tale of national triumph.

Such a heuristic agenda means that this effort necessarily stands against the approach taken by Christopher Hood and others. Hood's work on the *shinkansen*, for example, has produced a useful, expository synthesis of existing secondary literature in both Japanese and English, but does so without problematizing its source base or self-examining the ideology embedded in the resultant knowledge. In contrast, by critiquing the nature of the source materials themselves, I demonstrate how these sources have been an accessory to the production of questionable cultural norms and a presumptuous celebration of industrialized modernity. These sources have intentionally objectified trains so that they articulate something fundamental, even essential, about modern Japanese culture and values, thus indulging in a politicized process of cultural production that critical historians must indict.

Contemporary mass media has busily produced many such sources of historical knowledge in Japan; it looms large as a powerful means of projecting an alluring national self-image. One especially telling example, and the subject of critique in this chapter, is a popular documentary series called *Project X: Challengers*. This television program aired weekly on NHK, Japan's public broadcast channel, from March 2000 to December 2005. Each Tuesday night, *Project X* presented a dramatized remembrance of some remarkable technical feat that was achieved in postwar Japan. It showcases the making of engineering marvels such as the VHS, the auto-focus camera, the hands-free "washlet" toilet, the Toyota Crown, and other testimonies to Japan's postwar industrial success. *Project X* dramatizes and glorifies Japanese technical innovation in the postwar period, especially the so-called "High Speed Growth Era" (1955–1973) when the annual economic growth rate regularly topped 10% and Japan famously became the world's second-largest economy.

It is natural that the vaunted *shinkansen* project—heralded at the time as "the super-express of our dreams"—was among the very first *Project X* episodes. However, it was far from the only train-related achievement that was deemed worthy of the *Project X* treatment. The innovation behind automated turnstiles in the 1960s was dramatized in 2001, as was Hitachi's MARS system, which computerized the national train reservation system in 1960. An episode in 2005 lauded the long and difficult birth of the IC card in 2000, which has now largely obviated the need for paper tickets. These dramatized representations are part of a larger trend in mass media to spread a subtle ideological message. This chapter will show how *Project X* has cast trains in a dramatic trope about a splendid modernity in postwar Japan.

PROJECT X: CHALLENGERS

Project X captured the Japanese public imagination in a way that documentaries may never have. At the height of its popularity, in 2002, it boasted a 20% rating, reaching some 12 to 15 million viewers each week (Japan Computer, 4, *Yomiuri shinbun* [eve. ed. May 15, 2002]: 12). *Project X* quickly became NHK's flagship program, and the subject of considerable public attention. A typical airing prompted comments and feedback from as many as 10,000 viewers who shared their reactions with NHK (Japan Computer, 5, *Manichi shinbun* [eve. ed. July 9, 2001]: 2, *Sankei shinbun* [April 21, 2001]: 16). Books based on the show, written by its creator and producer Imai Akira, regularly topped best-seller lists for nonfiction (*Yomiuri shinbun* [September 23, 2001]: 11). The word "Project X" came to be synonymous with syrupy success stories, an adjective to describe any painfully sincere and overwrought act of dramatization (*Shūkan Asashi*, 44.1 [January 3.10, 2002]: 82–92). The program even earned enough attention to warrant a brief *New York Times* piece in 2003, which called it "an improbable television hit and a cultural phenomenon" (Norimitsu Onishi, "Tokyo Journal: At Long Last, the Salarymen Are Given Their Due," *The New York Times*, August 21, 2003).

In its heyday, this award-winning documentary received extensive media coverage and critical acclaim.[1] There was a sense that *Project X* was admirably edifying and beneficial in a way that television rarely is, and that it was good for whatever ailed Japan at the time. This view emerges best in a 2003 PTA survey. Japanese parents identified *Project X* as the television program they would most like their children to watch, and they did so in a landslide.[2] Such a glowing assessment of *Project X* might be outliving the show itself. In 2010, five years after it went off the air, a Mitsubishi Electric Engineering Corporation survey asked 327 employees which television show they would like to leave behind for posterity. *Project X* came in top among male respondents, and second among all respondents ("Gose ni nokoshitai terebi bangumi," *Business Media Makoto* [April 27, 2010], http://bizmakoto.jp/

makoto/articles/1004/27/news058.html). Its perceived didactic value is also conveyed by reports that the show has been used in Japanese schools and corporate training regimens (*Nikkan sports* [October 29, 2000]: 24; *Nikkan sports* [August 11, 2001]: 22).

NHK's official description of *Project X* suggests both the show's appeal and, ultimately, the problem with its means and message:

> *Project X* tells the untold story of organizations and groups featuring anony-mous Japanese who, with burning passion and fiery sense of mission in their hearts, carried out innovative initiatives in the postwar era.
>
> That social phenomenon still fresh in our memories; the development of new products that dramatically changed our lives; enormous projects that demon-strated the true inner strength of the Japanese: [these are the subjects of *Project X*.] In the postwar, the Japanese people have wielded their wisdom, and let indi-vidual ability flower as teamwork. What kinds of people were behind the scenes in the age-defining events of postwar Japan? What drama lay in the shadows of success, and how were the many obstacles overcome through ingenuity?
>
> The Japanese of the twenty-first century now face yet another challenge. By depicting our predecessors' tales of challenge and innovation, this program seeks to endow the Japanese people with the courage to confront new challenges.[3]

As the blurb breathlessly advertises, one of the program's main attractions is its populist sensibility. It is true that the people who are prominently featured are not famous public figures. The heroes of *Project X* tend to be ordinary engineers, designers, technicians, and other corporate cogs who would have been unfamiliar to their viewing audience. CEOs, tycoons, and captains of industry are beside the point here. This "everyman" positionality is emphasized in the show's opening theme song, which entreats, "Why do we look only up at the sky" while "no one remembers the stars right here on earth?"[4]

Likewise, there is, at least ostensibly, a focus here on individuals instead of large groups. Blue-chip corporations like Matsushita, Toyota, and Canon do make their appearances, but the emphasis is not on the company as such. Rather, the protagonist is usually a small team of just a few visionary employees. Indeed, one recurring narrative setup is that this small team gets shunned by the corporate brass who are skeptical of their bold initiative. These underdog mavericks must then fight the corporate current to prove their dream's worth. It is not big capital *per se* that receives credit for postwar innovation, but the derring-do of its single members, often overlooked and underestimated.

The final complement to this bottom-up, grassroots vision of Japan's post-war success is the absence of the state. Powerful central ministries like MITI (the Ministry of International Trade and Industry; now METI, the Ministry of Economy, Trade, and Industry) and the bureaucratic elite seldom enter the picture. *Project X* thus refutes the institutional explanation of the so-called "Japanese Miracle," which credits adroit state leadership for delivering sustained industrial growth (Johnson, Samuels). Instead, the spotlight here—quite literally, when these folks enter the NHK studio—is on ordinary people whose extraordinary moment is now finally being made known to the public.

What we seem to have here, then, is a widely-received form of public history. As a historically minded documentary, *Project X* is akin to museums, commemorative monuments, and heritage sites. Like many such sources of historical knowledge, *Project X* has transmitted an accessible, visualized, and humanized narrative about the past to a wide audience, which has often been moved to identify with that rosy, populist vision of the past. Certainly this is reflected in the way many enchanted viewers and avid supporters have often praised the documentary. Fans credit it as having "energized" and "brought confidence" upon a country that was limping into a second decade of economic malaise, and inspiring a people who had supposedly lost their will and self-esteem.[5] The producer Imai Akira prescribed *Project X* as an antidote to what he perceived as a decline in the nation's confidence that followed the bursting of the bubble economy in the early 1990s (*Sankei shinbun* [eve. ed. November 16, 2000]: 4).

Such glowing receptivity aside, a deeper historiographical inquiry into *Project X* reveals a message with dangerous implications. What the documentary in fact propagates is an objectionable modernist ideology that is complicit with a strain of neoconservative ethnic nationalism that emerged, not coincidentally, just around the same time. As it turns out, trains have been eagerly mobilized to deliver what I will later explain as the "*Project X* mythology."

Project X is not a documentary about trains *per se*, but trains are featured as much as any other single subject, as an analysis of the show's contents indicates. The subjects of the 177 total episodes can be broken down as follows:

Perhaps not surprisingly, consumer and commercial goods and electronics, for which contemporary Japan may be best known, are the most common subject of *Project X*. And it makes sense that construction is second, because postwar Japan is notorious as a concrete-laden pork barrel construction state. Transportation technology, composed chiefly of trains, planes, and automobiles, comes in a healthy third, with trains accounting for four episodes. Numerically, four episodes may not seem like much, but each one effectively captures the spirit—and the inherent problems—of the overall *Project X* message.

Before we proceed, a summary of the four episodes will help substantiate the subsequent analysis of how trains have been made to reinforce a seductive nationalist myth about postwar Japan.

Table 10.1. *Project X* episodes by subject

Subject by Category	# of Episodes	% of total
Consumer and commercial goods and electronics	37	21%
Construction projects	28	16%
Transport technology	22	12%
Medicine and medical technology	16	9%
Art and culture	16	9%
Crisis management, emergency rescue, and logistics	15	8%
Agriculture and environment	11	6%
Scientific exploration	11	6%
Sports and education	8	5%
Humanitarianism	5	3%
Miscellaneous	5	3%
Legal	3	2%

"Determination Gives Birth to the Bullet Train: 90-Year-Old Friends and an Airplane Transformed"

The first *Project X* episode to feature trains went with the obvious—the Bullet Train. The seventh episode, airing for the first time on May 9, 2000, begins with a shot of a small, unassuming elderly man wobbling his way to a reunion with some old friends. He is Miki Tadanao, now 90 years old. His friends are Matsudaira Tadashi, also 90, and Kawanabe Hajime, 85. The narration introduces them as former engineers for the Japanese Imperial Army and Navy who "decided to apply their knowledge to peace." After the usual introductory montage, the two studio hosts introduce tonight's subject: the project to develop "the Bullet Train—the world's premier super-express and the pride of Japan."

The three elderly men first met each other fifty-five years ago, just after the imperial armed forces were dismantled after World War II. At JNR's Railway Technical Research Institute, a thousand former military engineers were assigned the task of updating Japan's war-torn railway system. Among them were the three men, all in their thirties at the time: Matsudaira, who had worked on the vaunted Zero fighter plane for the Imperial Navy; Kawanabe, an ex-colonel in the Imperial Army specializing in communications technology; and Miki, who had designed Navy bombers.

Each man was facing his share of difficulty. Kawanabe would soon lose his job when the American Occupation purged former military leaders from government positions in 1946. Matsudaira found himself held in contempt by railroad specialists at the institute, who made light of his background in aviation. He was relegated to a cold, drafty warehouse for his lab. It was Miki, however, who had to "bear the heaviest cross," we are told. He could not forgive himself for having helped design the Ōka, an infamous bare-bones flying casket used as a *kamikaze* plane in the late stages of the war. Miki converted to Christianity after the war, and promised to use his technical knowledge for peace.

The three men were brought together in 1956. Miki wanted to apply aviation design principles like aerodynamics and weight-reduction to trains. Matsudaira was confident that a properly suspended car can reach unprecedented speeds, unencumbered by vibration and the risk of derailment. Kawanabe, who had recently been de-purged, thought he could devise an automated speed control system to ensure safety even at high speed. They calculated that a new super-express would cut the seven-and-a-half-hour trip between Tokyo and Osaka to just three hours. The research institute held a public symposium in 1956 to tout the idea of a ground-breaking super-express. Even on this rainy day, a standing-room only crowd showed up to hear Miki outline a future in which a top speed of 200 kph was possible.

In August 1957, Miki was invited to pitch the idea of this super-express to the JNR top brass. In April 1959, JNR and the relevant government ministries green-lighted the project and committed 800 engineers to it, with the three men playing prominent roles. Matsudaira focused on handling vibration, applying the know-how he had gained in the Navy working with Zeros. Meanwhile, Kawanabe worked on an ATC (Automatic Train Control) system, field-testing in the snowy north to ensure reliability even in extreme conditions. Miki, working feverishly on form and aerodynamics, "had turned into a demon" as the narration dramatically declares. Refusing to compromise, he destroyed one clay model after another. As his subordinate Tanaka Shin'ichi marveled, "Miki possessed an amazing determination when it came to pursuing high performance." As it turns out, the obstinate Miki was chasing the functional beauty of the Navy dive bomber Ginga (Galaxy), which he had helped design. By the end of 1961, the necessary research was complete. Matsudaira designed a revolutionary air-sprung chassis. Kawanabe made the ATC a reality. The first test train, with its signature bullet silhouette, soon took shape.

The train was now ready for its first test run. Then, just before the experiment, Miki suddenly resigned from the research institute. In a dramatic morale-booster, he explained, "I have done everything I possibly can. I have absolute confidence in our technology." On the appointed date, March 30, 1963, Kawanabe and Matsudaira climbed on board as test leaders. At 9:40 a.m., the train started off and began to accelerate, with a team of researchers on board keeping a close eye on the various measurements. Kirimura Hiroyuki was the co-driver, and Ōtsuka Shigeru the chief driver. Kirimura began to sweat as they topped 200 kph, but

Ōtsuka was confident. "If we succeed, then the Bullet Train succeeds," Ōtsuka recalls in an interview, "There was no room for failure." Just as the train hit 240 kph, however, Matsudaira's team detected abnormal vibration. The monitor showed the wheels begin to wobble, an early sign of derailment. Everyone nervously looked to Matsudaira, expecting him to press the emergency button and halt the experiment. But he did not budge, confident that his design could absorb the vibration. The train soon hit 250 kph, its planned target speed. Kirimura, the driver, moved to decelerate. But Ōtsuka grabbed his hand, telling him to go faster. The train kept going until it finally hit 256 kph at 9:46 a.m., the fastest train on record. A year and a half later, on October 1, 1964, the first Bullet Train went into service. The narration summarizes, "Former engineers of the imperial armed forces had pledged to devote their expertise to peace. Their nineteen years of determination and research gave birth to the world's fastest train."

Back in the studio, Tanaka recalls the nervous tension during the experiment. He is then asked by a studio host whether the Bullet Train's development might have been slowed had it not been for the three former military men. Tanaka answers that if they had not joined JNR after the war, "the Bullet Train may have never been realized." A host asks him what he had learned through his experience. "When it comes to research, I learned something like perseverance, or determination," Tanaka answers, "What I learned, first and foremost, is determination, or the proper posture [toward a technical pursuit]."

His words fade into the closing music, and the conclusion takes us back to the three elderly men, now reminiscing about the old days. Miki comments, "I never thought that the Bullet Train would end up running every four or five minutes." The men agree, "It's like a commuter train now." As the three sit on a riverbed, looking back on their lifework, a Bullet Train speeds by in the background. The narration concludes, "Thirty-five years have passed since the birth of the Bullet Train. Kawanabe's ATC; Matsudaira's air suspension; Miki's aerodynamic form: their know-how still lives on in the Bullet Train today."

"Eradicate Rush Hour: The Birth of the World's First Automated Turnstile"

The automated turnstile, based on magnetic field technology, was featured in the fifty-eighth episode, aired on June 26, 2001. Opening images show Japan's urban workers suffering (literally) crushing commutes. "In the past, congestion at train stations was beyond imagination," the narration tells us. "The problem was the fare gate, where ticket handlers were overwhelmed...."

Just then, a revolutionary machine appeared—the automated turnstile." It could read a ticket in just 0.5 second. What made it possible was a new magnetic technology developed by twelve young men in an obscure electronics parts supplier. "This is the drama of young men who confronted human waves and pioneered the field of magnetism," the narration announces.

The studio hosts explain that, in the past, station personnel rapidly punched tickets by hand at the fare gate, using *shokunin waza* ("masterly technique"), but they became hopelessly outnumbered by passengers. They then demonstrate the latest automated turnstile, which reads magnetically charged tickets, a technology now commonly used in ATM cards and credit cards.

We are taken back to 1963, in the midst of the "High Speed Growth Era" when suburbanization skyrocketed and commuter trains became overloaded. One man making a typical hour-and-a-half commute into the city of Osaka was the 24-year-old Asada Takeo. He was a fan of rock music whose trademark was his flamboyant pompadour. He was an engineer in a small electronics outfit called Tateishi Electronics (now Omron). Tateishi kept producing failures, like an electric acupuncture machine of which only one was ever sold. A fed-up Asada had resolved to quit soon.

Meanwhile, Kintetsu, a major private railway operator in the Osaka region, was discussing the ever-escalating problem of station congestion. Kintetsu approached electronics companies to see if an automated turnstile system was possible. Leading corporations like Matsushita, Sony, and NEC all begged off, declaring it either technically impossible or financially unfeasible. It was then that Tateishi entered the picture, although no one at Kintetsu had heard of that small company. Nonetheless, Tateishi Kazuma, the company president, pleaded passionately with Kintetsu and won a contract in 1964 to develop automated turnstiles.

Tanaka Toshio, 27, was put in charge of the project. His first product at Tateishi was the disastrous acupuncture machine, and he had lost his confidence as an engineer. Asada, who worked on conveyor belts, was also assigned to the turnstile project. "Why do I have to make such a thing?" he fumed. The next day, Tanaka and Asada counted commuters at Umeda Station. They were shocked to learn that eighty customers passed through a fare gate every minute. Asada suddenly felt inspired. "This torturous daily commute—I'll put an end to it," he promised.

In January 1965, the team began to prepare a mock-up. Because their contract with Kintetsu stipulated that Tateishi bear all the R&D costs, the fortune of the entire company rested on the turnstiles. Tanaka and Asada concluded that dedicated turnstiles for passengers with a commuter pass should reduce congestion. Asada adopted the technology in telex machines, and punched holes in commuter passes to store information about the pass. The problem, however, was speed. Each pass needed to be processed through the turnstile in 0.5 second. Asada applied his experience with conveyor belts, but the belts could not withstand the speed. Having broken a thousand belts, even the usually brash Asada began to worry. It is then that we are told Asada had married a former colleague a year earlier. One day, he learns that she is pregnant. The father-to-be decides to grow up and forgo his pompadour, showing up for work the next day with a short, serious haircut. Two months later, Asada was able to produce a reinforced belt that could withstand the rigor.

Tanaka, in charge of electronics, was developing a sensor that would block out passengers without a pass. To test the sensor, thirty children and housewives carrying bags and boxes quickly cycled through the turnstile. They could pass through sixty times in one minute. But there was a problem: passengers carrying a large box would get shut out, because the sensor mistook the baggage for a passenger without a pass. Tanaka was at a loss.

Just then, another problem came up. The powerful JNR, which shared a commuter pass system with Kintetsu, complained of Kintetsu's plan to punch holes in the shared pass because JNR had no plans to implement automated turnstiles. That was enough to make Kintetsu withdraw from the project. Still, Tateishi's president vowed to carry on even without a client. A reinvigorated Tanaka turned in all-nighters and managed to improve his sensor.

Tateishi approached railway operators around the country and tried to sell the turnstiles, but no one would bite. A month later, Hankyū, a private rail operator in Osaka, offered to let Tateishi install its turnstiles at the new Kita Senri Station as an experiment. The field test began in March 1967. An hour into the experiment, one turnstile jammed. A young Tateishi engineer on duty ran over and opened the turnstile. Out came a bunch of crumpled tickets, deposited by passengers who were unaware that this turnstile was for commuter passes only. Soon, all the turnstiles jammed, and the sound of alarms filled the station.

Asada and Tanaka then enter the studio. The studio hosts ask them about the various difficulties they encountered, and Asada, in his subtle Osaka accent, notes that "technology does not advance overnight." The hosts then take us back to the story with the segue, "The project was backed into a corner. But this is where the dramatic, determined comeback begins."

Tanaka worked to redesign the turnstiles to accommodate tickets as well as passes. Because a ticket, unlike a pass, was too small to be punched, Tanaka now needed a completely new way to store information on a ticket. Frustrated, he went home and tried to relax by listening to the Glenn Miller Orchestra. He suddenly realized that the music was recorded on tape, a thin strip of plastic with a magnetic field. He immediately drove over to the

Mitsubishi Paper Company, and asked them to coat paper with a magnetic field. Mitsubishi initially thought this was impossible, but Tanaka implored them, pleading that he was betting his life that his work would change the landscape of train stations everywhere. Mitsubishi relented and, a week later, delivered magnetic paper.

As they tested the new tickets, they soon discovered another problem. When the ticket was inserted into the turnstile widthwise, the turnstile would jam because the ticket had to be oriented lengthwise for the turnstile to process it. Asada worked late every night in vain to devise a solution. One day, after he trudged home well past 2 a.m., his wife told him that their son missed his father. The next Sunday, Asada took his son to a river in Kyoto to fish. He happened to notice a bamboo leaf floating downstream widthwise. The leaf then hit a rock, turned lengthwise, and floated on. Inspired, Asada went straight to his lab that very night and designed a special wheel that would reorient the ticket just like that rock.

In January 1971, the new turnstiles were installed at Kita Senri Station. Tanaka and Asada watched on as commuters passed safely without a single problem. "The automated turnstile was finally introduced to the world," the narration declares, "The employees of a small parts supplier puffed their chests."

In the studio, close-ups of Tanaka and Asada show them smiling with satisfaction. Tanaka explains that they could have simply told the passengers to put their tickets in lengthwise, but this would have been unacceptable to the engineers. "We promised each other that we wouldn't make the customers have to compromise."

The closing music begins. "It's been thirty years since automated turnstiles were born. There are now 20,000 of them installed throughout Japan," the narration announces. "Tanaka had given birth to a technology that is now the foundation of a card-based society. The small parts supplier grew into a major corporation with 25,000 employees. Tanaka, who had first lost his confidence, was able to restore his pride as an engineer. . . . Asada retired three years ago, ultimately staying for forty years at a company he had intended to quit. . . . Every time he passes through an automated turnstile that he had created, he still feels a tinge of pride."

"The Battle for 1 Million Seats: The 'Green Counter' and the World's First Rail Reservation System"

The 140th episode, aired on April 6, 2004, celebrated MARS, a revolutionary online rail reservation system. A shot of the 700 series Bullet Train introduces Japan as "a Railway Superpower, with 70,000 trains running every day." This system is supported by 8,000 reservation centers nationwide called the "Green Counter," which takes just three seconds to issue a ticket. Forty years ago, however, ticket counters were beset by long lines. Everything was done by hand and paper, and impatient crowds grew furious. That was when JNR engineers and a private manufacturer decided to collaborate on the world's first online train reservation system. The usual introductory montage and music begin.

In the studio, the two hosts roleplay train passengers in a hurry. They dash over to a mockup of a reservation counter and make a complicated ticket request. An operator quickly jabs at the touch screen and issues two tickets in no time. The older host remembers his youth, when this might have taken half a day.

The story begins in 1958, when passengers at JNR ticket counters throughout Japan were growing angry because making a reservation for an express train took much too long. The problem was in the central reservation room at Tokyo Station. A black-and-white video shows a bank of giant Lazy Susans spinning madly, loaded with a file for every express train in Japan. Workers sitting around the Lazy Susan quickly fetched the necessary file, manually entered the reservation, and deftly tossed the file back where it came from. Two men were alarmed by this sight of intense manual labor: Hosaka Mamoru of the JNR Railway Technical Research Institute, and Tani Yasuhiko, an engineer at Hitachi. They envisioned a ground-breaking computer network that would connect reservation centers nationwide and print tickets instantaneously. This would be the world's first such system.

Tani named his giant new computer system MARS, after the ancient Roman god of war. In 1960, a test computer was installed next to the Lazy Susans in Tokyo Station. It could process a reservation in just thirty seconds. In 1965, JNR decided to implement the system nationwide, linking reservation counters at 150 stations now renamed the "Green Counter."

During the New Year's holiday, Tani returned to his provincial hometown with his family as most Japanese do. He bought tickets in Tokyo for a sleeper car. His wife pointed at the computer and proudly said to their young daughter, "Daddy made that machine." Just as they settled into their compartment, however, another couple showed up and insisted that this was their seat. It was a case of double-booking. Then came another passenger with the same ticket—it was triple-booking. Tani's daughter said to her father accusingly, "Didn't you make that machine?" The same problem occurred throughout Japan. JNR's head of reservations Iwakiri Chiyuki, who had run the old reservation center and opposed computerization, felt vindicated by the news; how could machines possibly match our "masterly technique" (*shokunin waza*)?

Another problem occurred at Kushiro Station in Hokkaido. At 9 a.m., when the local system connects with the central Tokyo server, Ōkubo Susumu of the Kushiro Green Counter input the reservation data and uploaded it to Tokyo. But no tickets would print. At 9 a.m., all the reservation data from around Japan rushed into the central server in Tokyo. The system got overloaded and crashed, and Ōkubo was berated by angry customers. A few days later, the server crashed yet again at 9 a.m. Hitachi engineers scrambled for a solution, but they could barely keep up with the sharp increase in bookings, which had doubled in six years.

In 1968, JNR greatly expanded its national service, which resulted in 100,000 additional reserved seats. Tani thought MARS was not yet ready for this. Nonetheless, JNR gave Hitachi its expanded timetable and the system update began. One Hitachi engineer soon realized that the system could not load all the new data in time. "We couldn't issue the next day's tickets," he says, "We were in a terrible bind." To compound matters, radical student activists broke into Shinjuku Station that night and destroyed two computers. One project member worked so hard that he got a nosebleed. "Japan's first online system had turned into a bloodbath," the narration says. Tani then enters the studio and remembers that evening. "Towards the end, we passed our physical limits," he says. "We couldn't go home. Some of us slept on scraps of paper on the computer room floor."

The next morning, with the computers still not ready, they were forced to revert to the old manual system. The Hitachi engineers began to bristle at JNR's bossy demands. Then came another problem, this time involving the ticket printer, which was inefficient because it used a unique stamp for each of the thousand stations nationwide. Young engineers at Hitachi, hounded by JNR to improve the printers, finally lost their temper and got into a shouting match. Ozeki Masanori, the new project leader dispatched by JNR, concluded, "This is no project." He remembers in an interview, "The way they were going, they will never function as a team. We've got to 'eat from the same rice pot.'" Ozeki decided to overhaul the project. He offered to put thirty of his JNR men in Tani's charge so they could learn about computers. It was extraordinary for the client's personnel to be subordinate to the vendor like this.

In November 1970, the men from Hitachi and JNR began to write a new program together. But programmers at Hitachi figured that JNR people would never understand computers. Conversely, railroad men from JNR thought that Hitachi people knew nothing about trains. The two sides rarely spoke to another. To break the ice, Ozeki organized a birthday party. The 180 men gathered reluctantly, thinking this was childish. At the party, Ozeki spoke passionately about how he began his railroad career amidst the devastation of war, and conveyed his deep love of trains. He then unfurled a poster with the lyrics to a song he had written about MARS. 180 men slowly began to sing in

unison, "The service at the Green Counter and the speed of the Bullet Train /
Will be travel companions to everyone in the world." After this emotional
climax, Ozeki joins Tani in the studio, and Tani affirms that Ozeki's song
"brought their hearts together as one."

Hitachi programmers began to teach their JNR partners about coding.
The JNR men taught the Hitachi programmers about the peculiarities of
passenger behavior and train logistics. Eventually, they wrote 400,000
lines of code together. Ozeki intentionally assigned Iwakiri, who had been
opposed to digitization, to fix the ticket printer problem. Iwakiri devised
an efficient new butterfly-style terminal that did away with clumsy
stamps.

At last, the new system was ready for final testing in March 1972. "All
this became possible because we finally started working together," Tani says.
Just moments into the final testing, however, the system suddenly shut down.
The project members panicked and soon found that someone had flipped off
the main power switch. After restarting the system safely, they found the
culprit—Ozeki. He told the stunned members, "Conscientious engineers had
better test for the very worst scenario."

The new system was to go online at 9 a.m. on September 7, 1972. At
Kushiro Station, people were already lined up at the Green Counter at 8 a.m.
9 a.m. came, and Ōkubo nervously uploaded fourteen reservations. Back in
Tokyo, everyone held their breath as 300 stations across Japan uploaded their
data at once. The system held up. Ōkubo could print out his tickets in Kushiro
just six seconds later, and customers were thrilled. The narration concludes,
"The Green Counter became indispensable for train travel. The government
and the private sector worked together for fourteen long years, and gave birth
to a train system that is the pride of the world."

Back in the studio, Ozeki recalls that the team leaders were beaming with
confidence on the morning MARS went live. "Everyone came together, and
that made the team possible," he explains. Tani agrees, "People have to get
along in a group. Reason alone won't do. We need tears, because they bring
hearts and minds together."

The ending montage begins. "The Green Counter now issues 1.5 million
tickets every day. It can issue a ticket in less than three seconds," the narration tells us. "Tani's daughter Miki, who had castigated her father on the
day of the triple-booking incident, now realizes the magnitude of her father's
work. 'Back then, I don't think I ever understood how difficult my father's
job was,' she says. 'Now I know.'" After JNR was privatized in 1987, JNR
project members took their newly acquired computer expertise to other fields,
such as subways, aviation, and cellular phone networks. The project leader
Ozeki still hosts a team reunion every year. It always ends with a sing-along

of Ozeki's MARS song—"the theme song of the project that helped these men open their hearts."

"The IC Card of Determination and the Sixteen-year Comeback"

The 181st episode, aired on November 1, 2005, heralds the IC card Suica, which has now largely replaced paper tickets. 200 million IC cards of all kinds, embedded with a tiny computer called an IC chip, have been issued in Japan since 2000; Suica was first among them. Twenty years ago, engineers at JNR took on the challenge of developing IC cards to alleviate bottlenecks at fare gates. However, they were met by one technical problem after another. Then came the privatization of JNR, which was replaced by a new company saddled with enormous debt. Its beleaguered leaders were accused of fooling around with cards. Just then, a new business opportunity from Hong Kong came their way. The intro montage begins.

In the studio, the latest IC card-enabled turnstile has been set up. The studio hosts present it as "cutting-edge technology" now found in 800 stations nationwide. They demonstrate by using a Suica card to pass the turnstile instantaneously. They introduce tonight's story as "a drama about determination."

In the late 1970s, JNR was under fire. 20,000 kilometers of local lines lost 5 billion yen every day. Strikes left passengers stranded and frustrated. One researcher at the JNR Railway Technical Research Institute named Miki Shigeo was especially worried. "We had to embark on a new technology to alter the very foundation of railways," Miki recalls. He turned to a revolutionary theory introduced fifteen years earlier—the IC chip. An IC card could store fare information and transmit it wirelessly to automated turnstiles, helping to relieve congestion.

In 1987, JNR, with its 37 trillion yen debt, was broken up. 39,000 employees lost their jobs, and those who remained were reassigned to the new JR. Even technical specialists were sent off to menial service jobs in stations. Shiibashi Akio, age 33, was one of them. Captivated by trains ever since he first saw a Bullet Train, he eventually became a manager in a JNR train maintenance facility. After privatization, however, he was reassigned to Ueno Station to fix leaky toilets and air conditioning. "I was shocked. I felt like I had been sent off to the back stage of a back stage," he recalls.

At the Research Institute, Miki was struggling to get a turnstile to process an IC card in 0.2 second, his target time. Just then, powerful allies appeared. Engineers at Sony had previously developed a tiny IC chip for a shipping company, but it was too costly to implement. Kusakabe Susumu, one of the Sony engineers, inquired about applying the technology to turnstiles. Sony's

IC technology was fast and accurate, and early experiments were a resounding success. However, in 1990, JR East decided to install 30,000 new automated turnstiles based on the more proven magnetic-field technology. This made Sony demand that JR pledge to implement Sony's IC technology in the future. Miki was in no position to make such a business decision; Sony withdrew from the project.

Now working alone, Miki could not make much progress. His colleagues in marketing accused him of wasting company money to play with cards. Then, in 1992, Miki learned about a solicitation for a contract to update the fare system in Hong Kong. Miki convinced Sony to submit a bid, promising to see the project through to the very end. Kusakabe says, "We felt compelled to answer Miki's passion in kind." Sony was back in the IC game.

Miki now needed to field test his system. Shiibashi, who had come to take station maintenance seriously and had risen to the head of passenger facilities for JR East, was intrigued and offered to coordinate the testing. In April 1995, 700 JR employees, including some top managers, began testing IC cards at thirteen stations. However, the experiment ran into immediate problems. Users were fickle; each held the card at different heights and moved at different speeds, and the reader could not accommodate the variety. JR brass castigated Miki because their experimental cards worked only half the time. Five months later, the team discovered that the electrolyte solution that powered the IC chip evaporated in the cool autumn air. It had to be replenished with a hypodermic needle.

Just then, Kusakabe and the Sony men showed up with a new card they designed for the Hong Kong bid. Amazingly, it did not need its own power source, because it used internal coils to receive power from the reader. "I had no idea how far we could go, but we decided to do everything we possibly can and make it as good as we can," says a confident Kusakabe. "It was pretty astonishing technology," Miki admits.

In March 1999, Shiibashi gave a decisive presentation before JR East's top management, selling them on a 30% reduction in maintenance cost over the existing automated turnstiles, plus monetization from turning IC cards into a virtual wallet. Management unanimously approved full implementation, even though they had just invested in magnetic-field technology. 3,000 IC turnstiles were to be installed in 424 stations, making it the largest such system in the world. The card was named Suica, a riff on a Japanese onomatopoeia for "quick."

Shiibashi became the leader of an 800-person project, and over the course of two years he demanded rigorous testing to ensure system reliability. Just three days before implementation, however, Shiibashi's phone rang. A test station reported that the system overcharged a 1,620 yen fare by 270 yen. Shiibashi's team had just three days to find the error in the vast code and re-test 1,000 possible fare permutations involving that station. On November 18, 2001, Suica began operation to much fanfare. Shiibashi waited all day for his phone to ring with bad news. Seventeen hours later, it rang. Shiibashi was told that the last train completed its run without a hitch. In the next three years, Suica garnered more than ten million users.

Back in the studio, Shiibashi says that when he returned home late at night on the day Suica went live, his wife greeted him with rice and red beans, a traditional celebratory dish. "She must have been pleased, too," he surmises. When asked about the key to success, he replies, "The 820 project members were all really determined to deliver a better customer experience."

The closing segment provides a postscript. Miki retired from JR and took up another job with JR Freight, where he implemented IC technology. Shiibashi, now the head of JR's Suica Department, is working to transform stations into a shopping and dining destination, where Suica can be used to make purchases. He once heard some high school girls in a station exclaim, "This place doesn't feel like a station at all!" Shiibashi says with a satisfied look, "I was really pleased that I could make them feel like they were somewhere other than a station, even though they were right in the middle of one."

PROJECT X AS MYTHOLOGY: THE PROBLEMS OF INTENTIONALITY AND NARRATIVITY

I argue that these tales about trains are best interpreted as a mythology, but not because they are "untrue" or "fictional." Obviously, the Bullet Train, the IC card, and the people who created them are all very real, and to debate the finer points of accuracy and truthfulness in each episode, as some have done, would make for a tedious historiographical exercise.[6] Rather, *Project X* is a mythology because it is a form of selective historical remembrance that is purposeful and predetermined. Two salient features—intentionality and narrativity—are what make it a modern mythology, and an effective one at that.

The prime intent behind *Project X* is highly ideologically charged. The program eagerly promotes an ideology of economism, which has been a pillar of postwar Japanese nationalism. After 1945, militaristic imperial ambitions were thoroughly discredited and replaced by a devotion to economic enterprises, fueled especially by value-added technology. This new national goal has in fact brought affluence and prosperity, of course, but also a systemic single-mindedness that outsiders simultaneously mistrusted as "Japan, Inc." and marveled at as proof of "Japan as Number One" (Vogel).[7] Either way, dogged pursuit of economic growth was long a main engine of a reconfigured postwar nationalism, and it is the fruit of such a national commitment that *Project X* praises whole-heartedly. The show's producer, Imai Akira, has openly flaunted his ethnonationalist sensibilities in discussing his creation. Among his many comments to that effect: "The more I do *Project X*, the more I come to love the Japanese"; "Our boldness upon facing a crisis; then, having done great work, the dignity to return to the quiet of everyday life without fanfare. The Japanese people are really amazing"; and "The Japanese are said to lack individuality, but I think the complete opposite. There is no other ethnicity that is so imbued with individuality, daring, and originality."[8] He unapologetically narrated *Project X* as a heroic nationalist parable, written on the premise that societal devotion to capitalist technological mercantilism was unquestionably good.

To that ideological end, *Project X* celebrates the cult of sheer determination, which makes that devotion possible. "Determined" is a virtue that is repeated *ad nauseum* in *Project X*, including the four episodes related to trains. The word *shūnen* ("determination" or "obsession") is featured in the title of two of the episodes, and the word came easily to the lips of many, including Miki referring to the shape of the Bullet Train, Tanaka in explaining the "proper posture" toward technical pursuit, and Shiibashi in describing his Suica team. This burning spirit of "determination"—"triumph of the will," as it were—leads to a relentless pursuit of perfection and the refusal to compromise. Miki would accept nothing less than a truly revolutionary form for the Bullet Train. Tanaka insisted on engineering a technical solution to overcome human behavioral quirks. Kusakabe wanted to push IC technology to its very limit. They are all praised as true examples of *shokunin*, the uncompromising master craftsman who is obsessed with technical perfection. This ideal of artisanal mastery is often said to be a defining characteristic of Japanese manufacturing, personified by extraordinarily skilled laborers like the ticket punchers and the Lazy Susan operators with their mesmerizing "masterly technique" (*shokunin waza*), as well as the post-industrial heroes of a technological age.[9]

Also trumpeted here are the aesthetics of self-sacrifice. Dream chasers such as Tanaka and Tani routinely burn the midnight oil, foregoing sleep and rest. Husbands and fathers like Asada come home late, if at all. The silent heroics that sustain a desperate struggle, and the alacrity to unthinkingly throw themselves headlong into the task before them, are all applauded enthusiastically. Such praising of selfless devotion and self-erasure is ironic, given the show's claims to honoring the individual. And yet that is precisely what the protagonists of *Project X* always do; they work the grind, neglect their families, and throw themselves in harm's way with no regard for their own well-being, sometimes even paying with their lives. All this sounds suspiciously like an ode to self-sacrifice and self-denial, which is an eerily familiar call from a darker chapter in modern Japanese history. "Extinguish the self in service to the state," intoned a wartime slogan from the 1930s (McCormack and Sugimoto, 10). "Until we win, we shall not want," promised the steadfast subjects of Imperial Japan at war (*Asahi shinbun* [November 27, 1942]: 3). The postwar heroes of *Project X* may not be giving themselves to the state, but they are still lauded for willingly obliterating the self for a higher cause. No wonder cynical commentators chided the show as "promotional programming for 'overworking oneself to death' (*karōshi*)."[10] In short, *Project X* pushes a glorified ethos of industry as a national ideology and a cultural normative, without bothering to consider its human cost or historical baggage.

The other troubling feature of the *Project X* mythology is its narrative determinism. As the four summaries suggest, every episode abides by the same dramatic formula. The story always begins with a problem, be it congestion, the need to improve passenger service, or the desire for a faster train. A select few inspired technical innovators commit themselves to solving this problem. They inevitably run into a series of technical difficulties, skeptics, self-doubt, and other roadblocks and setbacks. They overcome these challenges through the help of understanding partners, serendipitous inspiration, and sheer determination. Ultimately, they succeed, and their hard work not only solves the initial problem itself, but often ends up benefiting Japanese society at large; the knowledge gained through MARS lays the infrastructural foundation of mass society, and Suica enables a card-based digital society. Moreover, the protagonists themselves somehow become better people for having taken on this challenge and end up redeeming themselves; Miki makes up for his war guilt, Tanaka regains his pride as an engineer, and Tani's daughter comes to respect her father's work. This is the sort of dramatic determinism that prompted the Japanese screenwriter Yamada Taichi to critique *Project X* as "story fascism" (*Mainichi shinbun* [eve. ed. [July 9, 2001]: 2). Historians familiar with Hayden White's work might also recognize this narrative strategy as an "emplotment" of history as a romance, in which facts are sequenced so as to yield inevitable triumph and redemption.

This dramatist narration is fortified by emotion and the visceral. Time and again, the *Project X* storyline emphasizes the power of passion for technology. Episodes are peppered with dramatic declarations of a protagonist's burning desire to complete his mission no matter what. Tanaka exclaims that he was "betting his life" on the magnetic-field tickets. Tani insists that projects "need tears" to pull members together and "bring their hearts as one." The sheer force of Miki's will convinces Sony to collaborate on the IC card. These dramatic touches elevate the show above and beyond reason to push the audience toward visceral, emotional empathy. Thus *Project X* asserts that the heroes of the High Speed Growth Era were not mere corporate automatons but rather "real men" who cared deeply about their work, and whose culture recognized and rewarded their labors of love.

Such storytelling techniques, which are par for the course in popular media and the entertainment industry, would not be so objectionable if not for the fact that they have also been used toward more flagrantly politicized ends. At the turn of the twenty-first century, Japan has witnessed a resurgence of neonationalism. This development earned its greatest notoriety from the promotion of a so-called revisionist history textbook in the late 1990s, and its agenda has been publicized through other historical controversies about World War II such as the "comfort women," the Nanjing Massacre, and Yasukuni Shrine.[11] Conservative scholars and public intellectuals opposed what they regarded as the "masochistic view of Japanese history" that pervaded the liberal postwar educational and intellectual milieu. Convinced that their country was being forced to endure excessive guilt for its imperial past, they agitated in the name of ethnic pride, national sovereignty, and spiritual revitalization. This cultural movement, which began just before *Project X* aired in 2000, featured the same purpose and strategy as *Project X*. They both sought to reinvigorate a languid, defeatist post-bubble society by renarrating Japanese history in a new, positive light. This is not to say that *Project X* and neonationalists are one and the same, but rather that they do occupy a similar position in the overall political milieu.

The real danger in this form of popular neonationalism is not necessarily its politics, chauvinism, or even revisionism, but its historiographical method. Just as Kobayashi Yoshinori, a leading neonationalist, gave the Pacific War a rousing makeover through his emotion-laden comics, *Project X* emphasized the positive legacies of the war by turning the postwar period into a golden age of technical achievement like the Bullet Train that was enabled, in no small part, by wartime discoveries (see especially Kobayashi, 1998–2003, 2005). It is no coincidence that the two cultural phenomena rose to prominence at about the same time. Both effectively leveraged easily accessible media—comics and television, respectively—to advertise the pathos of the past and extract sympathy from a wide audience. Neonationalists interpreted the production of history not as a social science but as a *monogatari* (a "tale") in order to appeal to a mass-market audience (Nagahara, 128). Thus they excused themselves from the constraints of academic discipline so as to freely dramatize the past and induce their intended political effect. *Project X* employed the same narrative strategy in order to make millions of viewers feel good about being Japanese, a people who are congratulated for being uniquely ingenious, industrious, and passionate about technology.

When history is compelled to obey the imperatives of genre in this way, the importance of historical multiplicity, conflict, and possibility is erased. Narrative simplification and formulization may facilitate mass consumption, but it also recklessly singularizes what had, in fact, been a much more varied and contested historical experience (Gordon; George & Gerteis). It lets *Project X* run roughshod over historical inconveniences that do not conform to its sunny message. For example, postwar Japan looks very different when viewed through the eyes of women, who in *Project X* are mostly left to twiddle their thumbs as neglected housewives, waiting deep into the night for their busy absentee husbands to finally come home. Likewise, postwar Japan looks very different through the eyes of the 39,000 people who lost their jobs as JR "rationalized" in the 1980s. The *Project X* mythology cannot accommodate such multiplicity because it is avowedly a battle hymn of the technocracy, a paean to the winners and their shiny technical trophies. It is a tale of victory that could not be theirs in wartime. The Zero fighter and the Ginga bombers were all shot down, but their spirit lives on, we are told, in the Bullet Train. Imperial Japan could not win the war, but if Japan's railway advancement is any indication, postwar Japan surely won the peace. *Project X* delivered this satisfying remembrance of recent triumph to a crestfallen society that seemed to yearn for such reminders.

CONCLUSION: MADE IN JAPAN, MADE IN A DREAM

In January 2011, passengers on JR East trains saw a remarkable in-car advertisement by JR.

MADE IN [A] DREAM
Back in the day, when Japan changed, the entire world would change. When the super-express of our dreams ran, our age accelerated along with it.
'Made in Japan' has the power to make dreams a reality. Surely, that power has not been lost today.
The only thing we seem to have lost is our confidence. If anything, Japan as a country has grown up a bit.

There are new things to work on, like the environment and culture. Nothing can begin if we stand still.

Let's walk again with our heads held high. Let's start running toward a distant goal.

Japan is about to gain a new sense of speed and comfort.

We will make yet another dream into reality.

On March 5, 2011, the Tōhoku *shinkansen* E5 "Hayabusa" debuts.

Our Dreams Begin to Run—JR East[12]

Below the copy are the side profiles of the C61 steam locomotive (1947), the Ki-Ha 81 express (1960), the first Tōhoku *shinkansen* (200 series; 1982), the E2 *shinkansen* (1997), and the latest E5 "Hayabusa," running staggered alongside one another. They speed along before a sequence of famous Japanese landmarks: Mount Fuji, the Tokyo Tower (1958), the Yoyogi Olympic Gymnasium (1968), Roppongi Hills (2003), and the Tokyo Sky Tree (2012). The earlier portion of this visual "timeline" is lit warmly by a rising sun, and it gradually leads to a bright blue sky in the present and the future. The supersaturated coloration conveys a vivid sense of both nostalgia and vitality. It is not much of an exaggeration to say that this poster is a veritable genealogy of infrastructural technology in postwar Japan, all in a single striking image.

The spirit, the iconography, and the assertions of this dramatic advertise-ment echo much of what has been argued in this chapter. This image sends Japan speeding along—recent slowdowns aside—on a rail toward a brighter future. Trains here are made to express a powerful faith in technology, the persistent pursuit of material progress, the state of Japan's national self-esteem across the postwar continuum, and the urge to keep pushing Japan toward its historical destiny, all wrapped up in a visually arresting and inspi-rational package that could be consumed quickly. These are also the defining themes of *Project X*, which trains helped to deliver into living rooms across Japan in the early twenty-first century.

The invocation of a "dream" in this ad also happens to be useful to the analysis here. Back in the early postwar, when the Bullet Train was touted as "the super-express of our dreams," that dream was assumed to be shared by all, and it served as a compelling societal motivator. As inspirational as the "dream" trope can be, however, we must not forget—as *Project X* does—that it is also fraught with danger. After all, the "Great Japanese Empire" and "Greater East Asian Co-Prosperity Sphere" were once dreams, too, until they turned into veritable nightmares. The dream theme is also relevant in thinking about *Project X* as a mythology, because a myth is essentially a presentist dream about the past, a wishful imagination of what once was, and what it might continue to be. Indeed, by looking back on the postwar past in its distinctly hopeful way, *Project X* also anticipates a future that is equally inspirational and triumphant. Every episode ends on this uplifting note as it looks both backward and forward in time. The ending theme song, "Headlight/Taillight," illuminates both the path Japan has trod and will tread in the future, and promises that "our journey has not yet ended" (Nakajima).

If *Project X* is a worship of technical progress, trains provided a perfect altar. Japan's trains embody the modern imperative "bigger, faster, better." 250 kph is not fast enough; we must push to 256. 0.5 second is not quick enough; it must be 0.2 second. Even the heroic effort that gave us magnetically charged tickets is inevitably topped by the subsequent IC card, which will itself be supplanted sooner, rather than later, by something no doubt even better. *Project X* confirmed trains as proof positive that the march of progress continues, even now, when the chips are down in Japan. Everything seems to be made in China nowadays, the Nikkei Index may never recover the heights of the 1980s, and prime ministers still come and go, but as long as we stoke the fire that birthed the Bullet Train, Japan will be all right. Such a soothing thought also reaffirmed a foundational conceit in modernity: the faith that technical knowledge, when pushed along by individual agency and determination—for even "technology does not advance overnight," as Asada said—will bring a better tomorrow. In that sense, *Project X* is a model trope of a hopeful modernity, easily enjoyed in forty-five fleeting minutes in front of a television. And what better way to carry that message than by rail, where even a "super-express of our dreams" can end up seeming as ordinary as a commuter train.

ACKNOWLEDGMENTS

The author thanks the generous support of the Elinor Nims Brink Fund at Vassar College and a Grant-in-Aid for Scientific Research from the Japan Society for the Promotion of Science for underwriting this project. Japanese names are rendered in the original order: surname first, then personal name.

NOTES

1. It won four awards in 2001: the 49th Kikuchi Kan Award from Bungeishunshū; the 9th Hashida Award from the Hashida Cultural Foundation; the Television Journalists Award from the Association of All Japan TV Program Production Companies; and the 27th Hōsō Bunka Foundation Award for Cultural Broadcasting. *Yomiuiri*

shinbun (Oct. 24, 2001), 31; *Sankei shinbun* (April 21, 2001), 16; *Sports Nippon* (August 13, 2001), 23.

2. Nihon PTA, "Katei kyōiku ni okeru terebi media chōsa chōsakekka hōkokusho" (March 2004), 18. *Project X* received 27.4% of the vote, while the two second-place shows received just 9.7%.

3. www.nhk.or.jp/projectx/index.htm; now inaccessible.

4. Nakajima Miyuki, "Chijō no Hoshi" (Yamaha Music Communications, 2000). The song ("Stars on Earth") spent an unprecedented 174 consecutive weeks on Japan's Top 100 singles chart, thanks in large part *Project X*'s popularity. *Yomiuri shinbun*, evening ed. (August 6, 2004), 7.

5. E.g., *Yomiuri shinbun* (October 24, 2001), 31; *Sankei shinbun* (September 21, 2001), 16; *Mainichi shinbun*, Osaka ed. (November 11, 2000), 1; *Sankei shinbun*, evening ed. (November 16, 2001), 4.

6. Critical viewers questioned some of the show's depictions over the years, accusing them of hyperbole, factual errors, and outright falsification. One especially public controversy in 2005 contributed to the show's cancellation at the end of that year.

7. Ezra Vogel, *Japan as Number One: Lessons for America* (Harvard, 1979). Foreign contempt for the Japan's postwar economism is perhaps best expressed by Charles de Gaulle's famous dismissal of Prime Minister Ikeda Hayato as "that transistor salesman" in 1962. It seems just that a *Project X* episode in 2000 heralded actual Japanese transistor salesman who introduced Sony to American consumers in the 1960s.

8. *Zaikai* 50, no. 19 (August 2002): 96; *Mainichi shinbun*, evening ed. (July 9, 2001), 2; *Sankei shinbun*, evening ed. (November 16, 2000), 4.

9. It is no coincidence that Toyota used "the relentless pursuit of perfection" as the promotional slogan for Lexus in the United States. It is one succinct articulation of the ideal Japanese "master craftsman" mentality.

10. *Shūkan Asahi* 108, no. 57 (December 12, 2003): 25. As a fatal form of work-induced stress, *karōshi* is often considered a phenomenon that is distinct to post-industrial Japan. The Ministry of Health, Labor, and Welfare recognizes *karōshi* as a formal cause of death.

11. The "comfort women" controversy involved the coercion of mostly Asian women into providing sexual service for the Japanese imperial military. The "Nanjing Massacre" is the debate over Japanese atrocities committed in Nanjing in 1937, which some extreme Japanese rightists have denied or discounted. Yasukuni Shrine is a controversial Shinto shrine in Tokyo that deifies the souls of Japanese war dead, including 14 Class-A war criminals of World War II.

12. The copy features some interesting textual subtleties. The words "Japan," "Made in Japan," and "culture" are rendered in the *katakana* phonetic, which suggest a feeling of globality because *katakana* is usually used to express foreign words in Japanese. The phrase "let's walk with our heads held high" echoes Sakamoto Kyū's classic song "Ue o muite arukou," better known in English as "Sukiyaki." Incidentally, "Hayabusa" (peregrine falcon), aside from being the name of a now-retired sleeper car, was also the name of a WWII fighter plane.

BIBLIOGRAPHY

Business Media Makoto (Tokyo, Japan).

Ericson, Steven J. *The Sound of the Whistle: Railroads and the State in Meiji Japan.* Cambridge, MA: Harvard University Press, 1996.

Free, Dan. *Early Japanese Railways, 1853–1914.* North Clarendon, VT: Tuttle, 2008.

George, Timothy and Gerteis, Christopher (Eds.). *Mirror of an Uncertain Age: Japan at the Dawn of a Post-Industrial Era* (forthcoming).

Gordon, Andrew (Ed.). *Postwar Japan as History.* Berkeley: University of California Press, 1993.

Groth, David E. "Media and Political Protest: The Bullet Train Movements." Eds. Susan Pharr and Ellis Krauss. *Media and Politics in Japan. Honolulu:* University of Hawaii Press, 1996.

Hood, Christopher P. "Shinkansen's Local Impact," *Social Science Japan Journal* 13.2 (2010): 211–225.

——. *Shinkansen: From Bullet Train to Symbol of Modern Japan.* London; New York: Routledge, 2006.

Ivy, Marilyn. *Discourses of the Vanishing: Modernity, Phantasm, Japan.* Chicago: University of Chicago Press, 1995.

Japan Computer System Sellers Association. *JCSSA News* 43 (summer 2007): 3–5.

The Japanese Ministry of Land, Infrastructure, Transport and Tourism (Kokudo kōtsū shō). *2009 Tetsudō yusō tōkei chōsa.* Tokyo, Japan: Kokudo kōtsū shō, 2010.

Johnson, Chalmers. *MITI and the Japanese Miracle.* Stanford, CA: Stanford University Press, 1982.

Kobayashi Yoshinori. *Shin Gōmanizumu sengen Special Yasukuniron.* Tokyo: Gentōsha, 2005.

——. *Shin Gōmanizumu sengen Special Sensōron*, 3 vols. Tokyo: Gentōsha, 1998–2003.

Mainichi shinbun (Tokyo, Japan).

McCormack, Gavan, and Yoshio Sugimoto. *Democracy in Contemporary Japan.* New York: M.E. Sharpe, 1986.

Nagahara Keiji. *Rekishikyōkasho o dōtsukuruka.* Tokyo: Iwanami, 2001.

Nakajima Miyuki, "Heddoraito-tēruraito." Yamaha Music Communications, 2000.

The New York Times (New York).

NHK, *Purojekuto X: Chōsenshatachi* (NHK Enterprise, 2000–2005)

Nihon PTA. "Katei kyōiku ni okeru terebi media chōsa chōsakekka hōkokusho" (March 2004).

Nikkan sports (Tokyo, Japan).

Noguchi, Paul H. *Delayed Departures, Overdue Arrivals: Industrial Familialism and the Japanese National Railways.* Honolulu: The University of Hawaii, 1990.

Samuels, Richard J. *The Business of the Japanese State.* Ithaca, NY: Cornell University Press, 1987.

Sankei shinbun (Tokyo, Japan).

Semmens, P. W. B. *High Speed in Japan: Shinkansen—The World's Busiest High Speed Railway.* Sheffield, UK: Platform 5, 2000.

Shūkan Asashi (Tokyo, Japan).

Sports Nippon (Tokyo, Japan).

Straszak, Andrzej, and Robert Tuch (Eds.). *The Shinkansen High-Speed Rail Network of Japan: Proceedings of a IIASA Conference, June 27–30, 1977.* Oxford; New York: Pergamon, 1980.

Tsuji, Yohko. "Railway Time and Rubber Time: The Paradox in the Japanese Conception of Time." *Time & Society* 15.2/3 (2006): 177–195.

Vogel, Ezra. *Japan as Number One: Lessons for America.* Cambridge, MA: Harvard University Press, 1979.

White, Hayden. *Metahistory.* Stanford, CA: Stanford University Press, 1973.

Yomiuri shinbun (Tokyo, Japan).

Zaikai (Tokyo, Japan).

Index

Notes on Contributors

Samuel Gerald Collins is professor and chair of the Department of Sociology, Anthropology, and Criminal Justice at Towson University. He researches information society and information and communication technologies in the United States and South Korea, and in particular the formation of multi-agent socialities composed of human and nonhuman agents. He has published on multi-agent systems in regard to cybernetics, social networks, and actor–network theory. Dr. Collins is the author of two books (*Library of Walls: the Library of Congress and the Contradictions of Information Society* [2009] and *All Tomorrow's Cultures: Anthropological Engagements with the Future* [2008]) and has co-edited a third (*Handbook of Research on Agent-Based Societies* [2009]). He has been at Towson University since 1999, and teaches on social theory, qualitative methods, and science and technology studies.

Colin Divall heads the Institute of Railway Studies and Transport History, run jointly by the University of York and the National Railway Museum. His books include *Making Histories in Transport Museums* (with Andrew Scott, Leicester University Press, 2001) and *Suburbanizing the Masses: Public Transport and Urban Development in Historical Perspective* (edited with Winstan Bond, Ashgate, 2003).

Benjamin Fraser is assistant professor of Spanish at the College of Charleston (South Carolina, United States). Currently the managing editor of the *Arizona Journal of Hispanic Cultural Studies*, he is the author of the monographs *Disability Studies and Spanish Culture* (Liverpool UP, forthcoming), *Henri Lefebvre and the Spanish Urban Experience* (Bucknell UP, 2011) and *Encounters with Bergson(ism) in Spain* (U of North Carolina P, 2010) as well as the editor and translator of *Deaf History and Culture in Spain* (Gallaudet UP, 2009). Fraser is also the author of over thirty peer-reviewed essays in journals from the field of Hispanic studies (e.g., *Journal of Spanish Cultural Studies, Hispania, Studies in Hispanic Cinemas,* and *Catalan Review*) and beyond (*Cultural Studies, Social & Cultural Geography, The Journal of Gaming and Virtual Worlds,* and *Emotion, Space and Society*).

Tristan R. Grunow is a Ph.D. candidate in modern Japanese history at the University of Oregon. He is currently on a Fulbright Fellowship in Tokyo, Japan, conducting research for his dissertation, which will examine the integrative roles of railways, architecture, and urban planning in the Japanese colonization of Taiwan and Korea.

Araceli Masterson-Algar is assistant professor at Augustana College in Rock Island (Illinois). She obtained a Ph.D. from the University of Arizona with a concentration in border studies. Her research is largely on Ecuador–Spain migration dynamics, and specifically on the ties between transnational social dynamics, cultural production, and urban planning in both Quito and Madrid. Regarding Madrid's subway, she has addressed immigrants' use and representations of the Metro and has analyzed some of its most successful advertising campaigns.

Alexander Medcalf is a Ph.D. candidate at the Institute of Railway Studies and Transport History based at the University of York. His research examines the commercial cultures of the Great Western Railway as part of his thesis "Picturing the Railway Passenger as Customer in Britain: The Great Western Railway 1903–1939." This research is supported by the Arts and Humanities Research Council and the National Railway Museum, York.

Agata Morka received her Ph.D. in architectural history at the Art History Department of the University of Washington in June 2011. Her dissertation explored the questions of place and placelessness in postwar French rail architecture and its relation to theories of modernity and postmodernity. Her research and publications focus on contemporary transportation and museum architecture, with an emphasis on the relation of postmodern urban architectural interventions and the question of local and global identities. She is also interested in the practice of museum curatorship and architectural history pedagogy.

Hiraku Shimoda is an associate professor at Waseda University School of Law in Tokyo, Japan. He received his B.A. from Vassar College and Ph.D. in Japanese history from Harvard University. His works include *Lost and Found:*

Recovering Regional Identity in Imperial Japan (Harvard University Asia Center, forthcoming in 2012) and "Tongues-Tied: National Language and the Discovery of Dialects" in the *American Historical Review* 115: 3 (2010).

Hiroki Shin is AHRC postdoctoral research associate of the Institute of Railway Studies & Transport History, University of York/National Railway Museum. He is currently working on the AHRC-funded project "The Commercial Cultures of Britain's Railways, 1872–1977." His most recent publication on railway history is "Business Strategy and Corporate Image: Britain's Railways, 1872–1977," in *Railways as an Innovative Regional Factor*, edited by Heli Mäki and Jenni Korjus (University of Helsinki, 2009).

Peter Soppelsa received his Ph.D. in history from the University of Michigan in 2009. He was awarded the Western Society for French History's Millstone Prize in 2010 for his paper "Finding Fragility in Paris: The Politics of Infrastructure after Haussmann." He is currently an assistant professor in the history of science, and the managing editor of *Technology and Culture* at the University of Oklahoma.

Steven D. Spalding is assistant professor of French at Christopher Newport University (Newport News, Virginia). His research interests include French cultural studies, film, literature, and publishing history. He has published a number of articles on topics ranging from translation to French theory and sociology of literature. He is currently completing a history of French publisher Editions de Minuit.

Rowan Wilken is lecturer in media and communication, Swinburne University of Technology, Melbourne, Australia. He is author of a number of articles that examine the relationship between place and media. His present research interests include digital technologies and culture, mobile and locative media, old and new media, and theories and practices of everyday life. He is author of *Teletechnologies, Place, and Community* (Routledge, 2011) and is co-editor (with Gerard Goggin) of *Mobile Technology and Place* (Routledge, 2012).